LITERATURE
for Life and Work
BOOK 2

Elaine Bowe Johnson, Ph.D.
Associate Dean
Language and Literature Division
Mt. Hood Community College
Gresham, Oregon

Christine Bideganeta LaRocco
Integrated and Applied Curriculum Consultant
English Instructor
Arlington, Virginia

National Textbook Company
a division of NTC/CONTEMPORARY PUBLISHING GROUP
Lincolnwood, Illinois USA

Cover Design:	Photonics Graphics
Series Design:	Learning Design Associates, Inc., Columbus, Ohio

Cover Photography Credits: Holland windmill—Photograph by Jack K. Blonk, Laval, Quebec, Canada; all other photos royalty free.

ACKNOWLEDGEMENT

"Abuela" by Rosa Elena Yzquierdo. Reprinted with permission from the publisher of *The American Review* Vol. 14 Nos. 3-4 (Houston: Art Publico Press–University of Houston, 1986).

"After You, My Dear Alphonse" from *The Lottery and Other Stories* by Shirley Jackson.
Copyright © 1948, 1949 by Shirley Jackson, and copyright renewed ©1976, 1977 by Laurence Hyman, Barry Hyman, Mrs. Sarah Webster and Mrs. Joanne Schnurer. Reprinted by permission of Farrar, Straus & Giroux, Inc.

Excerpt from "Antigone" by Sophocles. From *Sophocles: The Oedipus Cycle,* An English version by Dudley Fitts and Robert Fitzgerald, copyright 1939 by Harcourt Brace & Company and renewed 1967 by Dudley Fitts and Robert Fitzgerald, reprinted and recorded by permission of the publisher. CAUTION: All rights, including professional, amateur, motion picture, recitation, lecturing, performance, public reading, radio broadcasting, and television are strictly reserved. Inquiries on all rights should be addressed to Harcourt Brace & Company, Permission Department, Orlando, FL 32887-6777.

ISBN: 0-538-66714-1

Published by National Textbook Company,
a division of NTC/Contemporary Publishing Group, Inc.
4255 West Touhy Avenue,
Lincolnwood, Illinois 60712-1975 U.S.A.
© 1998 NTC/Contemporary Publishing Group, Inc.

7 8 9 10 11 12 071 08 07 06 05 04 03

For Tom, Thom, and Roussel and in memory of Elaine Larson.

Elaine B. Johnson

The authors and editors of *Literature for Life and Work* gratefully acknowledge the following educators for their insightful reviews of literature selections, sample lessons, and manuscript:

Nancy Barker
Norwood High School
Cincinnati, OH

Ken Brown
Lakeland, FL

Susan Clark
Michel Junior High School
Biloxi, MS

Audie Cline
California High School
Jefferson City, MO

Jerry Collins
Wilson High School
Tacoma, WA

Dr. Willard Daggett
International Center for
    Leadership in Education, Inc.

Stephanie Dew
Santa Monica High School
Santa Monica, CA

Randy Gingrich
Hughes High School
Cincinnati, OH

Donna Helo
Rayne High School
Crowley, LA

Nicole Hochholzer
Kaukauna High School
Kaukauna, WI

Dorothy Hoover
Huntingdon Area High School
Huntingdon, PA

Judy Kayse
Huntsville High School
Huntsville, TX

Marcia Lubell
Yorktown High School
Yorktown Heights, NY

Carter Nicely
Old Mill High School
Arnold, MD

Jan Smith
Upsala Area Schools
Little Falls, MN

Theresa Spangler
Brunswick High School
Brunswick, GA

Alice Jane Stephens
Triton Central High School
Fairland, IN

Ruth Townsend
Yorktown High School
Yorktown Heights, NY

Special Contributor

Frances Caldwell
Educational Consultant
Portland, OR

TABLE OF CONTENTS

UNIT 2 THE INDIVIDUAL AND SOCIETY

v

UNIT 7 COURAGE AND DETERMINATION

WORKSHOPS

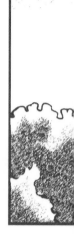

To the Student:

When you first looked at this book, you probably thought, "Oh, sure, I've seen this kind of textbook before. It's just another collection of readings with predictable questions for me to answer."

But this textbook differs from any you have used before because everything in it connects with your own experiences, interests, and ambitions. All the poetry, fiction, and nonfiction, both classical and modern, were chosen because they deal with life experiences shared by people of all times and places.

This book takes you seriously. It asks you to develop the art of thinking. It encourages you to apply what you read in a way that affects your daily life. That's what makes it unique. We hope you enjoy it and discover the excitement of connecting literature to life and work.

The literature is arranged in units under a common theme. Our goal was to allow you to read about experiences and ideas that matter in your lives. Once the literature was chosen, we then set out to challenge you with real world assignments that connect the course with your experience.

The assignments in the "Exploring," "Understanding," and "Connecting" sections invite you to express your own views, to share them with others, to work on teams, and to make a significant difference in your community. You learn best when you connect learning to your own experiences and knowledge. The assignments invite you to learn not only by studying, but also by becoming involved in activities in the real world. You learn to write, read, and think critically by doing work that joins academic material with everyday life.

Expect some changes in your classroom. The lessons emphasize practical writing for the real world, where there is no room for a misspelled word or missing comma. Meeting the high standards of business is not the only new thing. Working in groups with other students to prepare different parts of a document may also be foreign to you. However, collaborative writing is common in the world of work. Workshops in the back of this text will give you practice in moving from school assignments to workplace tasks.

Our approach to writing assignments trains you in skills you'll actually use in your lifetime as an individual, a family member, worker, customer, and consumer. You will practice the reading, writing, listening, and speaking skills expected of you by employers, clients, colleagues, neighbors, businesses, and the person on the other end of the phone. Whether you go on to college, vocational school, the military, special training, or the world of work, the exercises in this book will prepare you for success.

This book will help you discover how much you already know. We challenge you to become involved in your English class this year in a new way and because of one simple fact: you'll be using these communication skills every day of your life.

Elaine B. Johnson

Christine B. LaRocco

Elaine B. Johnson   Christine B. LaRocco

P.S. Be sure to visit the *Literature for Life and Work Home Page* at **www.litlinks.com** for exciting Internet activities related to the units in this text!

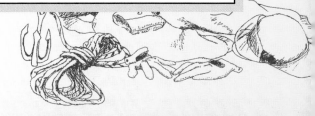

UNIT
①
RELATIONSHIPS

Relationships influence our lives in numerous ways. They help us decide what we do and what we value. They can build our confidence, increase our self-knowledge, and inspire us to do our best. Relationships keep us going when we face challenges. Even when they turn out to be painful, relationships help us figure out what is important to us. Sometimes relationships are long past before we realize how much they influenced our lives.

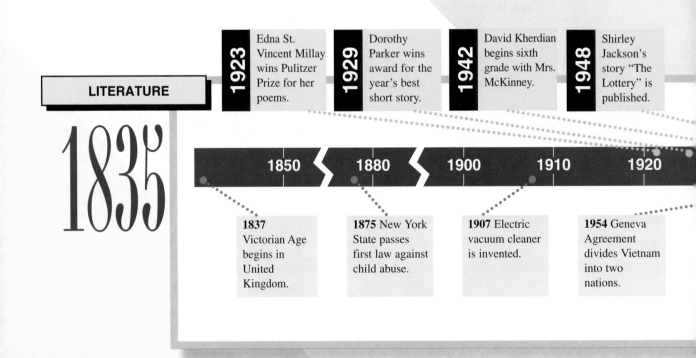

LITERATURE

1923 Edna St. Vincent Millay wins Pulitzer Prize for her poems.

1929 Dorothy Parker wins award for the year's best short story.

1942 David Kherdian begins sixth grade with Mrs. McKinney.

1948 Shirley Jackson's story "The Lottery" is published.

1835

1850   1880   1900   1910   1920

1837 Victorian Age begins in United Kingdom.

1875 New York State passes first law against child abuse.

1907 Electric vacuum cleaner is invented.

1954 Geneva Agreement divides Vietnam into two nations.

from **When Heaven and Earth Changed Places**
—Le Ly Hayslip

The Teenage Bedroom
—Lynda Barry

The Old Man and Woman Who Switched Jobs
—Swedish Folktale

from **In Contempt**
—Christopher A. Darden

Dear Mrs. McKinney of the Sixth Grade
—David Kherdian

After You, My Dear Alphonse
—Shirley Jackson

The Choice
—Dorothy Parker

If I were loved, as I desire to be
—Alfred, Lord Tennyson

Love is not all: it is not meat nor drink
—Edna St. Vincent Millay

Loathe at First Sight
—Ellen Conford

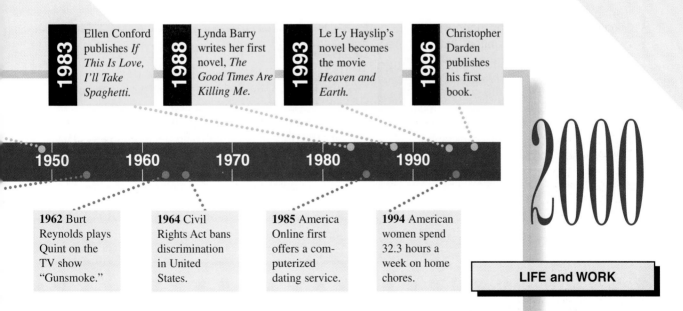

1983 Ellen Conford publishes *If This Is Love, I'll Take Spaghetti.*

1988 Lynda Barry writes her first novel, *The Good Times Are Killing Me.*

1993 Le Ly Hayslip's novel becomes the movie *Heaven and Earth.*

1996 Christopher Darden publishes his first book.

2000

1950   1960   1970   1980   1990

1962 Burt Reynolds plays Quint on the TV show "Gunsmoke."

1964 Civil Rights Act bans discrimination in United States.

1985 America Online first offers a computerized dating service.

1994 American women spend 32.3 hours a week on home chores.

LIFE and WORK

from *When Heaven and Earth Changed Places*

EXPLORING

●●●●●●●●●●●●●●●●●●●●●●

Do you think that someone must experience a narrow escape to appreciate life? To appreciate peace, must one see war? Having grown up in a country continually ravaged by war, Le Ly's father has come to treasure life and peace. Naturally, he wishes to pass these values on to his daughter. Psychologists tell us a person's values are ingrained by the age of 10. Do you think children live by their parents' teachings even after they are no longer under the parents' influence? Will you carry on the values of your parents?

THEME CONNECTION...
PARENTAL VALUES

Part of a parent's job is to instill values in his or her children. Often this is done unintentionally simply by being a role model; sometimes it is accomplished by purposeful teaching. Regardless of the method, a parent's influence on a child is critically important and amazingly long lasting. A parent's model may scar a child's future or enhance it.

TIME & PLACE

In the 1970s and 1980s, thousands of Vietnamese of Chinese ancestry fled their war-torn country to come to America and begin new lives. As many as 500,000 of the 1.8 million Vietnamese Chinese were believed to have escaped, traveling by land or sea to China, Thailand, Malaysia, Indonesia, and Hong Kong, and many ended up in the United States. Years of fighting—from the French takeover in the mid-19th century, through Japan's occupation in 1940, to the civil war in the 1960s in which the United States became involved—add up to a lifetime of war and strife for more than one generation of Vietnamese people.

THE WRITER'S CRAFT
POINT OF VIEW IN BIOGRAPHY

An autobiography is a form of nonfiction in which a person tells his or her own life story. It is told from the first person point of view, using the pronoun *I,* so the reader sees the story through the narrator's eyes. This excerpt from *When Heaven and Earth Changed Places* is an example of an autobiography.

In a biography, however, the writer tells the life story of another person. It is told from the third person point of view, using pronouns such as *he, she,* and *they,* and the narrator is not a character in the story.

from *When Heaven and Earth Changed Places*
Fathers and Daughters

Le Ly Hayslip

fter my brother Bon went North, I began to pay more attention to my father.

He was built solidly—big-boned—for a Vietnamese man, which meant he probably had well-fed, noble ancestors. People said he had the body of a natural-born warrior. He was a year younger and an inch shorter than my mother, but just as good-looking. His face was round, like a **Khmer** or **Thai**, and his complexion was brown as soy from working all his life in the sun. He was very easygoing about everything and seldom in a hurry. Seldom, too, did he say no to a request—from his children or his neighbors. Although he took everything in stride, he was a hard and diligent worker. Even on holidays, he was always mending things or tending to our house and animals. He would not wait to be asked for help if he saw someone in trouble. Similarly, he always said what he thought, although he knew, like most honest men, when to keep silent. Because of his honesty, his empathy, and his openness to people, he understood life deeply. Perhaps that is why he was so easygoing. Only a half-trained mechanic thinks everything needs fixing.

He loved to smoke cigars and grew a little tobacco in our yard. My mother always wanted him to sell it, but there was hardly ever enough to take to market. I think for her it was the principle of the thing: smoking cigars was like burning money. Naturally, she had a song for such gentle vices—her own habit of chewing **betel** nuts included:

> Get rid of your tobacco,
> And you will get a water buffalo.
> Give away your betel,
> And you will get more paddy land.

Despite her own good advice, she never **abstained** from chewing betel, nor my father from smoking cigars. They were rare luxuries that life and the war allowed them.

My father also liked rice wine, which we made, and enjoyed an occasional beer, which he purchased when there was nothing else we needed. After he'd had a few sips, he would tell jokes and happy stories and the village kids would flock around. Because I was his youngest daughter, I was entitled to listen from his knee—the place of honor. Sometimes he would sing funny songs about whoever threatened the village and we would feel better. For example, when the French or Moroccan soldiers were near, he would sing:

> There are many kinds of vegetables,
> Why do you like spinach?

About the Author

Le Ly Hayslip (b. 1949) was the youngest child in a close-knit Buddhist farming family in Central Vietnam. The Vietnam War broke out when she was 12 years old. *When Heaven and Earth Changed Places* is her haunting memoir about her emotional and physical survival. Hayslip now lives in Southern California with her three sons. She is the founder of East Meets West, a nonprofit relief and peace organization.

Khmer—one of the native races of Cambodia

Thai—natives of Thailand

betel nuts—nuts from a climbing pepper plant

abstained— stopped, resisted

Minh—Ho Chih Minh led the struggle to release Vietnam from French colonial rule; his North Vietnamese followers were called Viet Minh

Viet Cong—South Vietnamese who supported Ho Chih Minh

cadres—people trained by the North Vietnamese to win South Vietnamese citizens over to their side

lenient—mild and tolerant

There are many kinds of wealth,
Why do you use **Minh** money?
There are many kinds of people,
Why do you love terrorists?

We laughed because these were all the things the French told us about the Viet Minh fighters, whom we favored in the war. Years later, when the **Viet Cong** were near, he would sing:

There are many kinds of vegetables,
Why do you like spinach?
There are many kinds of money,
Why do you use Yankee dollars,
There are many kinds of people,
Why do you disobey your ancestors?

This was funny because the words were taken from the speeches the North Vietnamese **cadres** delivered to shame us for helping the Republic. He used to have a song for when the Viet Minh were near too, which asked in the same way, "Why do you use francs?" and "Why do you love French traitors?" Because he sang these songs with a comical voice, my mother never appreciated them. She couldn't see the absurdity of our situation as clearly as we children. To her, war and real life were different. To us, they were all the same.

Even as a parent, my father was more **lenient** than our mother, and we sometimes ran to him for help when she was angry. Most of the time it didn't work, and he would lovingly rub our heads as we were dragged off to be spanked. The village saying went: "A naughty child

● ● ● ● ● ● ● ● ● ●
"To her, war and real life were different. To us, they were all the same."
● ● ● ● ● ● ● ● ● ●

learns more from a whipping stick than a sweet stick." We children were never quite sure about that but agreed the stick was an eloquent teacher. When he absolutely had to punish us himself, he didn't waste time. Wordlessly, he would find a long, supple bamboo stick and let us have it behind our thighs. It stung, but he could have whipped us harder. I think seeing the pain in his face hurt more than receiving his half-hearted blows. Because of that, we seldom did anything to merit a father's spanking—the highest penalty in our family. Violence in any form offended him. For this reason, I think, he grew old before his time.

One of the few times my father ever touched my mother in a way not consistent with love was during one of the yearly floods, when people came to our village for safety from the lower ground. We sheltered many in our house, which was nothing more than a two-room hut with woven mats for a floor. I came home one day in winter rain to see refugees and Republican soldiers milling around outside. They did not know I lived there, so I had to elbow my way inside. It was nearly supper time, and I knew my mother would be fixing as much food as we could spare.

In the part of the house we used as our kitchen, I discovered my mother crying. She and my father had gotten into an argument outside a few minutes before. He had assured the refugees he would find something to eat for everyone, and she insisted there would not be

FOCUS ON... HISTORY

Le Ly Hayslip was 12 years old when U.S. helicopters landed in her village of Ky La in Central Vietnam. Find out when the first U.S. troops arrived in Vietnam. What events led to our government's decision to send troops into combat there? Which side did the United States support? Why were antiwar feelings so strong at home? Research the many controversial issues surrounding the Vietnam War. You may also wish to prepare a map that illustrates boundaries and key locations in North and South Vietnam.

enough for her children if everyone was fed. He repeated his order to her, this time loud enough for all to hear. Naturally, he thought this would end the argument. She persisted in contradicting him, so he had slapped her.

This show of male power—we called it *do danh vo*—was usual behavior for Vietnamese husbands but unusual for my father. My mother could be as strict as she wished with his children, and he would seldom interfere. Now, I discovered there were limits even to his great patience. I saw the glowing red mark on her cheek and asked if she was crying because it hurt. She said no. She said she was crying because her action had caused my father to lose face in front of strangers. She promised that if I ever did what she had done to a husband, I would have both cheeks glowing: one from his blow and one from hers.

Once, when I was the only child at home, my mother went to **Da Nang** to visit Uncle Nhu, and my father had to take care of me. I woke up from my nap in the empty house and cried for my mother. My father came in from the yard and reassured me, but I was still cranky and continued crying. Finally, he gave me a rice cookie to shut me up. Needless to say, this was a tactic my mother never used.

The next afternoon I woke up, and although I was not feeling cranky, I thought a rice cookie might be nice. I cried a fake cry, and my father came running in.

"What's this?" he asked, making a worried face. "Little Bay Ly doesn't want a cookie?"

I was confused again.

"Look under your pillow," he said with a smile.

I twisted around and saw that, while I was sleeping, he had placed a rice cookie under my pillow. We both laughed, and he picked me up like a sack of rice and carried me outside while I gobbled the cookie.

Da Nang— seaport in Central Vietnam

SPOTLIGHT ON...
GRAPHIC ORGANIZERS

Chart the similarities and differences between Le Ly's father in the story and traditional Vietnamese fathers on a *Venn Diagram.* On a piece of paper, draw two large intersecting circles. In one circle, make a list of Hayslip's father's unique characteristics. In the other circle, make a list of the unique characteristics of traditional Vietnamese fathers. Where the circles intersect, or overlap, write the characteristics that they have in common.

◆ ◆

Han—rulers of a Chinese dynasty in the third century B.C.

In the yard, he plunked me down under a tree and told me some stories. After that, he got some scraps of wood and showed me how to make things: a doorstop for my mother and a toy duck for me. This was unheard of—a father doing these things with a child that was not a son! Where my mother would instruct me on cooking and cleaning and tell stories about brides, my father showed me the mystery of hammers and explained the customs of our people.

His knowledge of the Vietnamese went back to the Chinese Wars in ancient times. I learned how one of my distant ancestors, a woman named Phung Thi Chinh, led Vietnamese fighters against the **Han**. In one battle, even though she was pregnant and surrounded by Chinese, she delivered the baby, tied it to her back, and cut her way to safety wielding a sword in each hand. I was amazed at this warrior's bravery and impressed that I was her descendant. Even more, I was amazed and impressed by my father's pride in her accomplishments (she was,

after all, a humble female) and his belief that I was worthy of her example. *"Con phai theo got chan co ta"* (follow in her footsteps), he said. Only later would I learn what he truly meant.

Never again did I cry after my nap. Phung Thi women were too strong for that. Besides, I was my father's daughter, and we had many things to do together.

On the eve of my mother's return, my father cooked a feast of roast duck. When we sat down to eat it, I felt guilty and my feelings showed on my face. He asked why I acted so sad.

"You've killed one of mother's ducks," I said. "One of the fat kind she sells at the market. She says the money buys gold, which she saves for her daughters' weddings. Without gold for a dowry—*con o gia*—I will be an old maid!"

My father looked suitably concerned, then brightened and said, "Well, Bay Ly, if you can't get married, you will just have to live at home forever with me!"

I clapped my hands at the happy prospect.

My father cut into the rich, juicy bird and said, "Even so, we won't tell your mother about the duck, okay?"

I giggled and swore myself to secrecy.

The next day, I took some water out to him in the fields. My mother was due home any time, and I used every opportunity to step outside and watch for her. My father stopped working, drank gratefully, then took my hand and led me to the top of a nearby hill. It had a good view of the village and the land beyond it, almost to the ocean. I thought he was going to show me my mother coming back, but he had something else in mind.

He said, "Bay Ly, you see all this here? This is the Vietnam we have been talking about. You understand that a country is more than a lot of dirt, rivers, and forests, don't you?"

I said, "Yes, I understand." After all, we had learned in school that one's country is as sacred as a father's grave.

"Good. You know, some of these lands are battlefields where your brothers and cousins are fighting. They may never come back. Even your sisters have all left home in search of a better life. You are the only one left in my house. If the enemy comes back, you must be both a daughter and a son. I told you how the Chinese used to rule our land. People in this village had to risk their lives diving in the ocean just to find pearls for the Chinese emperor's gown. They had to risk tigers and snakes in the jungle just to find herbs for his table. Their payment for this hardship was a bowl of rice and another day of life. That is why Le Loi, Gia Long, the Trung Sisters, and Phung Thi Chinh fought so hard to expel the Chinese. When the French came, it was the same old story. Your mother and I were taken to Da Nang to build a runway for their airplanes. We labored from sunup to sundown and well after dark. If we stopped to rest or have a smoke, a Moroccan would come up and whip our behinds. Our reward was a bowl of rice and another day of life. Freedom is never a gift, Bay Ly. It must be won and won again. Do you understand?"

I said that I did.

"Good." He moved his finger from the patchwork of brown dikes, silver water, and rippling stalks to our house at the edge of the village. "This land here belongs to me. Do you know how I got it?"

I thought a moment, trying to remember mother's stories, then said honestly, "I can't remember."

He squeezed me lovingly. "I got it from your mother."

"What? That can't be true!" I said. Everyone in the family knew my mother was poor and my father's family was wealthy. Her parents were dead, and she had to work like a slave for her mother-in-law to prove herself worthy. Such women don't have land to give away!

"It's true." My father's smile widened. "When I was a young man, my parents needed someone to look after their lands. They had to be very careful about whom they chose as wives for their three sons. In the village, your mother had a reputation as the hardest worker of all. She raised herself and her brothers without parents. At the same time, I noticed a beautiful woman working in the fields. When my mother said she was going to talk to the matchmaker about this hard-working village girl she'd heard about, my heart sank. I was too attracted to this mysterious tall woman I had seen in the rice paddies. You can imagine my surprise when I found out the girl my mother heard about and the woman I admired were the same.

"Well, we were married and my mother tested your mother severely. She not only had to cook and clean and know everything about children, but she had to be able to manage several farms and know when and how to take the extra produce to the market. Of course, she was testing her other daughters-in-law as well. When my parents died, they divided their several farms among their sons, but you know what? They gave your mother and me the biggest share because they knew we would take care of it best. That's why I say the land came from her, because it did."

I suddenly missed my mother very much and looked down the road to the south, hoping to see her. My father noticed my sad expression.

"Hey." He poked me in the ribs. "Are you getting hungry for lunch?"

"No. I want to learn how to take care of the farm. What happens if the soldiers come back? What did you and Mother do when the soldiers came?"

My father squatted on the dusty hilltop and wiped the sweat from his forehead. "The first thing I did was to tell myself that it was my duty to survive—to take care of my family and my farm. That is a tricky job in wartime. It's as hard as being a soldier. The Moroccans were very savage. One day the rumor passed that they were coming to destroy the village. You may remember the night I sent you and your brothers and sisters away with your mother to Da Nang."

"You didn't go with us!" My voice still held the horror of the night I thought I had lost my father.

"Right! I stayed near the village— right on this hill—to keep an eye on the enemy and on our house. If they really wanted to destroy the village, I would save some of our things so that we could start over. Sure enough, that was their plan.

"The real problem was to keep things safe and avoid being captured. Their patrols were everywhere. Sometimes I went so deep in the forest that I worried

● ● ● ● ● ● ●
"What happens if the soldiers come back?"
● ● ● ● ● ● ●

ACCENT ON...
PHOTOGRAPHY
● ● ● ● ● ● ● ● ● ● ● ● ● ● ● ● ● ● ● ●

Photographs can have a great power to inform and even persuade audiences. During the Vietnam War, thousands of photographs of soldiers and civilians appeared in magazines and newspapers, having a profound impact on people's opinions about the conflict. Locate some Vietnam War photographs that you think must have strongly affected their viewers. What makes the images so powerful? What stories do the images tell? Select one photograph and write an essay explaining its impact from a photographic point of view. If possible, work with students from an art or photography class to study photographic elements. Consider lighting, the position of the images, and the images themselves.

about getting lost, but all I had to do was follow the smoke from the burning huts and I could find my way back.

"Once, I was trapped between two patrols that had camped on both sides of a river. I had to wait in the water for two days before one of them moved on. When I got out, my skin was shriveled like an old melon's. I was so cold I could hardly move. From the waist down, my body was black with leeches. But it was worth all the pain. When your mother came back, we still had some furniture and tools to cultivate the earth. Many people lost everything. Yes, we were very lucky."

My father put his arms around me. "My brother Huong—your uncle Huong—had three sons and four daughters. Of his four daughters, only one is still alive. Of his three sons, two went north to **Hanoi** and one went south to **Saigon**. Huong's house is very empty. My other brother, your uncle Luc, had only two sons. One went north to Hanoi, the other was killed in the field. His daughter is deaf and dumb. No wonder he has taken to drink, eh? Who does he have to sing in his house and tend his shrine when he is gone? My sister Lien had three daughters and four sons. Three of the four sons went to Hanoi and the fourth went to Saigon to find his fortune. The girls all tend their in-laws and mourn **slain** husbands. Who will care for Lien when she is too feeble to care for herself? Finally, my baby sister Nhien lost her husband to French bombers. Of her two sons, one went to Hanoi and the other joined the Republic, then defected, then was murdered in his house. Nobody knows which side killed him. It doesn't really matter."

My father drew me out to arm's length and looked me squarely in the eye. "Now, Bay Ly, do you understand what your job is?"

I squared my shoulders and put on a soldier's face. "My job is to avenge my family. To protect my farm by killing the enemy. I must become a woman warrior like Phung Thi Chinh!"

My father laughed and pulled me close. "No, little peach blossom. Your job is to stay alive—to keep an eye on things and keep the village safe. To find a husband and have babies and tell the story of what you've seen to your children and anyone else who'll listen. Most of all, it is to live in peace and tend the shrine of our ancestors. Do these things well, Bay Ly, and you will be worth more than any soldier who ever took up a sword." ❖

Hanoi—formerly the capital of North Vietnam, now capital of the unified country of Vietnam

Saigon—capital of South Vietnam from 1954 to 1976, now called Ho Chi Minh City

slain—murdered

UNDERSTANDING

1. This is a daughter's memory of a beloved father. Do you think love for her father has colored this memory or does she see his faults as well as his merits? Cite examples from the story to support your answer.

    Write a character sketch of Le Ly's father. Include his physical characteristics, but also consider carefully his words and behavior, primary clues to his character. ***Workshop 10***

2. Can you determine the status of women in Vietnamese culture from this story? Cite passages to prove your point. Is Le Ly's father following cultural tradition?

     With a group devise a chart listing ten activities of women in the United States. Activities might include working, going to school, housekeeping, doing volunteer work, participating in sports, and raising a family. Opposite each activity on your chart, note whether each activity is driven by individual choice, by society's attitudes, or both. Be ready to discuss your reasons.

3. In spite of hardship, Le Ly's father maintains a sense of humor. Give examples of his actions that lightened his family members' moods as well as his own.

    Research the effects of humor. How is it used to maintain good spirits in the workplace, to help patients in hospitals get well, and to liven up a classroom? Write a one-page report on your findings. ***Workshop 7***

A LAST WORD

The author Le Ly Hayslip is taught by her father to love and respect her ancestors. What can our ancestors, who lived and died long ago, teach us about living today? How can we show our love and respect for them?

CONNECTING

1. This story is filled with memorable quotations that are suitable for motivational posters and bumper stickers. One is: "A country is more than a lot of dirt, rivers, and forests." Locate and write down at least three more. On computer or by hand, create several posters or bumper stickers using these quotations.

2. A movie entitled *Heaven and Earth* has been made of Le Ly's story. It is available on video. With your parents' and teacher's permission, watch it and write a movie review. Take notes on questions such as these as you watch: Is the scenery realistic and effective? Is the movie camera used to give interesting views or angles of events? Is the pace fast or slow? Does the movie depict the characters as the story does? In what ways, if any, does it differ from the story? Answer these questions in a movie review for your school paper. ***Workshop 17***

The Teenage
Bedroom

EXPLORING

Privacy is a privilege that people come to value as they grow out of childhood. Although teenagers may have a strong need for privacy, their parents may be reluctant to give it to them. Do you have a bedroom or other space for your own special belongings and your own decorations? Can you invite people to visit you in this special place? How do you feel about your own privacy?

THEME CONNECTION...
PRIVATE SPACE

All people have a need for private time in a place of their own. When a home does not have room for each individual to have a special room or place, relationships sometimes suffer. Even the closest of family members—young and old—need individual private space. It helps them appreciate other family members when they are together.

TIME & PLACE

Teenagers in the 1990s are perhaps more assertive about their rights than were teens of earlier decades. The teenager in this story is both assertive and defensive. Note the way he defends ruining his dresser and marring the walls. Note how he talks back to his mother.

This story reflects the insensitivity of one young person who is, understandably, striving to be independent. His concern with his own wishes prevents him from thinking about others and the effects of his actions.

THE WRITER'S CRAFT

HYPERBOLE

The narrator in this story uses a technique called hyperbole, a literary term meaning exaggeration. Everyday speech often contains hyperbole when the speaker wants to emphasize a point. (Example—"I haven't seen you for ages.") Think of the times you and your friends use hyperbole. Do you ever exaggerate to make something seem bigger, smaller, or better than it actually is? Give your own examples of hyperbole.

The Teenage Bedroom
(Except It's About a Boy's Room)

Lynda Barry

About the Author

Linda Barry is not only an accomplished short-story writer but also the creator of the nationally syndicated cartoon strip "Ernie Pook." Barry began drawing comics, she says, while attending Evergreen State College. She has also been a speaker on National Public Radio and is an award-winning playwright. She grew up in Seattle, Washington, and now lives in Evanston, Illinois.

Keep Out. Keep OUT. THIS MEANS YOU. Keep! Out! But Mom always comes in with the bogus excuse of "Here are some clean socks and underwear, I'll put them in your drawer." As if I can't get my own socks and underwear from the laundry room, as if I need to get them at all, why can't I just keep them by the dryer but no, she just needs any excuse to come into my room and yell "This room looks like a tornado hit it!" as if she has ever seen anything hit by a tornado, and then she's coming back dragging the vacuum cleaner, as if she has the right to vacuum my room! I go, "MOM, NEVER VACUUM IN HERE!" I got too many important things of life on that floor. Stuff that dropped that I'll need later. And my tarantula who I swear . . . hates my mom so much that the hairs fall off its abdomen which is what happens to tarantulas when they get freaked and Mom is always freaking my tarantula with the vacuum. She said I could have a gerbil so I got a tarantula, tell me what is the basic difference? I use the same fish tank that leaked all over the dresser and wrecked it which I had to hear about for five thousand years because that was her dresser when she was a kid, SO WHY GIVE IT TO ME IF SHE DOESN'T WANT ME TO WRECK IT! LIKE IT'S MY FAULT THE FISH TANK LEAKED AND I DIDN'T NOTICE UNTIL ALL THE WATER WAS OUT! WHAT ABOUT MY FISH, MOM, HUH? WHAT ABOUT THEM DYING, MOM, HUH? So that's why the dresser is all warped. It took a while for the water to leak out. I just thought it was evaporating super fast. I thought it was like a freak of the environment of my bedroom. CAN I HELP IT IF IT WAS LEAKING DOWN THE SIDE OF THE DRESSER I NEVER LOOK AT, MOM? And then you'd think that if it was already wrecked she wouldn't care if I put my eyeball stickers on the mirror and the wood, right? A normal person would normally think it's Already Wrecked So What's The Dif? But she has a total attack and she has another total attack that I put eyeball stickers on my bed, IT IS MY BED BUT SHE HAS A TOTAL ATTACK, because it was her brother's bed or her cousin's bed or someone of her family's bed WHO IS OBVIOUSLY MORE IMPORTANT THAN THE HAPPINESS OF HER SON WHO JUST WANTS TO PUT HIS EYEBALL STICKERS WHERE HE WANTS EXCEPT HE CAN'T BECAUSE HE LIVES IN A CONCENTRATION CAMP. Same goes for tape and nail holes in the wall. I go, "Mom, how am I supposed to put up my posters then?"

SPOTLIGHT ON...
WORKING
TOWARD COMPROMISE

In "The Teenage Bedroom," the narrator and his mother disagree about the appearance of the teenager's bedroom. How could they resolve their conflict? You, too, will need to negotiate changes and resolve conflicts in the workplace, in school, and in your personal life. As you work to solve problems through compromise, keep these questions in mind:
1. What is the problem or area of conflict?
2. What are some probable causes for the problem?
3. What are some possible solutions to the problem? Is a compromise possible?
4. Who can best put the solutions into practice? How?
5. How will the solutions affect those involved?
6. Will a compromise serve as a long-term solution?

and she goes, "Oh, I'll buy you a bulletin board." THAT BULLETIN BOARD RIGHT THERE WHICH I FILLED UP IN THREE SECONDS WAS HER IDEA OF HOW I SHOULD PUT UP MY POSTERS! I said forget it, man, this is **boag,** forget it. I'm using tape and then she has another attack and makes me sign a Family Contract that when I leave for college I will personally paint my own room and sand down the tape marks or whatever it is you do with tape marks, which I will have to figure out because as you have noticed there is hardly no wall showing. That is my goal. Total posters. Including the ceiling. Oh, that's another thing. You notice the green light bulbs, right? At first when I bought them WITH MY OWN MONEY, MOM she totally freaked because "Green light

bulbs? Green light bulbs? The neighbors will think you are growing drugs!" I go, Mom. What kind of drugs do you grow with green light bulbs? I mean SERIOUSLY! And she freaked and we had to have a family meeting where my dad was even there which is totally weird because I think the total times my dad has even been in this room is like around zero AND NOW HE GETS A VOTE ON MY LIFE? Mom was freaking because she said it brought the value of the house down because my bedroom used to be in the front where the world could see it so that is how I scored this room which used to be my sister's. It smelled like a girl for around a month during which I couldn't have no one over but it was worth it for the green light bulbs don't they make you feel peaceful? Wait.

boag—bogus (slang); unbelievable

The Teenage Bedroom

Listen to this song. Isn't it the perfect combination? So I said can I get a gerbil, Mom? Because I wanted a tarantula but I knew she would totally freak if I said Can I Get A Tarantula Mom EVEN THOUGH IT WAS MY OWN MONEY and she goes, "Let me think about it." Which means I have to do something like vacuum my room or change my sheets which I HATE because the laundry soap she uses smells like actual perfume, smell, smell here, doesn't it? Doesn't it smell exactly like perfume? Like I should go around smelling like that. But I go, OK Mom, I'll change the sheets, I'll vacuum if you'll let me have a gerbil and she goes, "I'll think about it." Which means I do something else for her like put new strings on the clothesline which I did, you can see them from this window, see there, pretty good job, right? So "OK," she says, "you can get the gerbil." And she says she'll take me

ACCENT ON...
INTERIOR DESIGN
· ·

The narrator of "The Teenage Bedroom" has definite opinions about how his bedroom should look. In fact, one of his goals is "Total posters." Needless to say, the teenager and his mother are in conflict over the appearance of his room. Create a floor plan of the teenager's bedroom, including the placement of accent details such as the tarantula tank and dresser, that shows a compromise between the mother's and son's wishes for the room. Write a one-paragraph explanation that states why the plan is an effective compromise.

down to Mitchell's Pets and I say No Mom That's OK I Want To Walk which if she was thinking about it she would have known right there because normally I don't want to walk anywhere. Normally I want to just listen to my station and lay in the peaceful green light and let my tarantula free its name is Dana for this girl Dana Speers at my school who I swear . . . looks just like a tarantula but in a cool way. No one knows I named it Dana. They think I named it Boris. It would be embarrassing if people knew I named it after Dana Speers. My mom would get all happy. "Oh, a girl in my son's life!" So if she comes in, call it Boris. Actually I snuck the actual Dana Speers up here to meet Dana Speers the tarantula. Actually it is very easy to sneak people up here and to sneak out of here you can see how you can just go out that window and go down the roof to right there, then you just go onto the garage and down that tree. Cinchy. Dana Speers is a more interesting girl than normal. You wouldn't even think she's a girl from the way she is. She doesn't make no one nervous. I have sat right here and the actual Dana Speers has sat right where you are and we let the tarantula Dana Speers walk from my hand onto her hand then from her hand onto my hand, you know, that thing of letting a tarantula walk on you? And it was a trip because no hairs fell off the tarantula Dana Speers' abdomen when we did that which means that the tarantula wasn't nervous at all. Which shows you what I said about the actual Dana Speers. And she, the actual Dana, has these super-long eyelashes and eyebrows which some people think is freaky because it does look slightly monstery because there's hair all around her eyes, even right here in the corner part which I think looks insanely cool and you know that thing where if you get an eyelash from someone you can wish on it? And maybe even an eyebrow hair counts too, I don't know. I just know for sure that one eyelash fell off of the actual Dana Speers when she was last over but it would have been too weird of me to go for it while she was sitting there so I waited until after she left and I was looking for it and I am still looking for it because I got a really good wish I want to make and that's why I don't want mom to vacuum in here. That and also she might suck up my tarantula. Shhh! Here she comes! WHAT, MOM?! WHAT?! If she comes in just Act Normal. Just sit there and act like you're normal. What?! OK! OK! I'M COMING! ❖

UNDERSTANDING

1. Look at the appearance of this story on the page. Do you notice anything unusual? The story has no paragraphs. Everything flows in one long piece. Why do you think the author does this? Find other specific aspects of format and punctuation that are unconventional or out of the ordinary. What is the effect of these unconventional features?

2.  The boy in the story refers to a number of conflicts with his mother that are typical between parents and teens. Make a list of these conflicts. How do you recommend such conflicts be resolved?

   Discuss conflict resolution in a small group. Write a process paper presenting a conflict resolution method you think might work for the teenager and the mother in this story. *Workshop 12*

3. Teenage bedrooms carry a bad reputation. Signs reading "Enter At Your Own Risk" and "Hazardous Area" may be posted outside. What elements of the narrator's room might merit this kind of sign?

   Think of a teenager's room you have seen, perhaps your own, that could be labeled "Dangerous" or at least "Use Caution When Entering." Describe this room using sensory details, hyperbole, and strong nouns and verbs.
   Workshop 10

A LAST WORD

Conflicts between parents and children can arise from their having different expectations and goals. How might they respect each other's point of view? How can humor help parents and children better understand each other?

CONNECTING

1. Inventory in the business world is the annual counting and recording of every item that a company owns, from office furniture to merchandise. The inventory form often has blanks for item, quantity, value (price), color, serial number, and year purchased. Conduct an inventory of your bedroom, closet, or locker. Create an appropriate inventory form or use a sample provided by your teacher. How do companies benefit from conducting annual inventories? How might you benefit from yours?

2. The boy's language is filled with slang and other nonstandard English. Give examples.

   Teens of every decade have created their own slang. You may hear a parent use slang that was popular when he or she was young, and you may think it's crazy or strange. Compile a glossary of present-day slang words and phrases collected from friends and family. Provide the word or phrase and a definition for each one.

The Old Man and Woman Who Switched Jobs

EXPLORING

Sometime in history, jobs became categorized as "women's work" and "men's work." Though today it may be hard to see the reasoning behind such classification, many men and women still limit themselves to jobs they identify as appropriate to their gender. In reality, most of the work we do has no connection with gender. Describe work you have observed that suggests work is not dependent on gender.

TIME & PLACE

The settings of most folktales are timeless and placeless. This story is effective without any particular setting. Small details, such as the description of the stove, indicate that the story took place "a long time ago."

THEME CONNECTION... MEN'S AND WOMEN'S WORK

Viewed as requiring little or no skill, housework is often undervalued in today's society. Even between members of a compatible married couple, household tasks tend to be divided along traditional lines. A successful couple understands that they are co-workers. They should appreciate each other's work and be willing to do any task around the house.

THE WRITER'S CRAFT

FOLKTALE

A folktale is a traditional story handed down through the generations, usually by word of mouth. Every culture has a set of such stories. They preserve the culture's ideas, customs, and wisdom gathered over time. Today, anthropologists study folktales to gain insight into issues that concern all human beings.

The Old Man and Woman Who Switched Jobs

About the Author

The Swedish folktale "The Old Man and Woman Who Switched Jobs" had no single author. Like all folktales, this story was passed down from one generation to another. In some cases, folktales may be based on actual events. As is characteristic of many folktales, this one teaches a lesson in a humorous way.

Once there was an old man, just like any other old man. This old man worked in the forest, chopping wood, and burning charcoal, while his old woman stayed at home spinning, cooking, and taking care of the house. In this way their days passed one after another. But the old man always complained that he had to labor and toil all day long to support both of them while the old woman merely sat at home cooking porridge, eating, and enjoying herself. Even though the old woman told him that there was plenty to do at home as well and that the old man would be badly fed and clothed if she did not look after the house, the old man turned a deaf ear; he was convinced that he alone was pulling their entire load.

One day, after they'd bickered longer than usual, the old woman said, "Have it your way! Tomorrow we'll switch jobs. I'll go to the forest and cut wood for the fire, and you'll stay home and do my chores."

This suited the old man just fine. "I'll take good care of the house," he said. "But how you'll fare in the woods is another story."

Early the next morning the old woman said, "Don't forget to bake the bread, churn the butter, watch the cow, and cook the greens for dinner."

These were all mere trifles, thought the old man, and so they parted. The old woman took the old man's axe and went off to the forest while the old man began to build a fire under the oven and make the dough. When he thought it was ready, he began to bake it. But what sort of bread it was going to be was hard to say, for he forgot the yeast and put the loaves into the oven without first sweeping away the ashes.

The old man thought he'd managed the baking very well, and the thought of fresh bread awakened his appetite.

"Fresh bread is fine," he said to himself, "but if you have some bacon to go along with it, it tastes even better!"

So the next moment he went to the storehouse to fetch their last piece of bacon. But since the bacon was salty, he wanted something to drink with it. He put the bacon on the cellar steps and went downstairs.

Just as he was taking the plug out of the beer barrel, a dog came by and grabbed the bacon. The old man certainly didn't want to lose it, so he jumped up and ran off after the dog. But

> ● ● ● ● ● ● ●
> **"Tomorrow we'll switch jobs."**
> ● ● ● ● ● ● ●

FOCUS ON...
ART

The old man's experience performing his wife's job is filled with humorous disasters. Create a visual "snapshot" that catches him in the midst of one of his attempts to do the household chores. Use details from the story to make your "snapshot" as realistic and humorous as possible. You may choose to create an ink drawing, a watercolor or acrylic painting, or an image using computer graphics or any other medium.

as he was running he discovered that he still had the plug in his hand, and he abandoned the bacon and ran back so that he could at least save the beer.

But it was too late. The barrel was empty and all the good beer had run out. This made him very unhappy, but he comforted himself with the thought that the old woman probably wasn't doing any better in the forest. Even if he had to do without bacon and beer, at least he still had the nice fresh-baked bread. With bread to eat, life is complete! as the saying goes.

But his comfort was short-lived. When he got inside the hut he found the bread burned to a crisp. Not a single bite was left for him to taste. It was a terrible state of affairs.

"This is no good at all," he moaned. "If only I'd let mother stay at home! If I'm doing this badly, how might she be doing in the forest? By now she may have chopped off both arms and legs!"

But there was no time for thinking. The sun was already high in the sky, and he had to cook greens for dinner. For greens one must have something green, the old man said to himself, and as he couldn't find anything else green, he took the old woman's new homespun jacket, chopped it into little bits, and put the pieces in the pot.

He realized that he couldn't cook greens without water, but the spring was so far away. And besides, he also had to churn butter! How on earth was he going to manage it all?

"If I put the churn on my back and shake it while I'm running to the spring, it'll probably turn to butter by the time I get back," he thought.

And that is what he did. But in his haste he forgot to put the lid on, and when he bent to haul up the water bucket, the cream poured over his shoulders and head and down into the spring.

Disheartened, he returned with the soupy, creamy water.

Now he had to tend to the cow, and since he couldn't be both inside and outside at the same time, how was he going to manage? On top of the house's sod roof, the grass shone a bright green in the sunshine; *there* was a juicy pasture! He tied a long rope around the cow's neck and pulled her up onto the roof, then threw the other end of the rope down the chimney.

Feeling a little happier, he went back inside the cottage and tied the tether hanging down through the chimney around his own waist so that the cow wouldn't get away from him. Then he started blowing on the fire under the pot. But while he was occupied blowing, the cow fell off the roof and pulled him up into the chimney!

At that very moment the old woman came home with a big bundle of firewood on her back. When she saw the cow hanging alongside the cottage wall, she hurried as fast as she could and cut the rope. Then she went inside. There on the floor lay the old man, smoked, burned, and half suffocated.

"God preserve us!" she exclaimed. "Is this how you've been managing at home?"

The poor old man couldn't utter a word; he just moaned and groaned. But it didn't take the old woman long to see how he'd managed: the bacon was gone, the beer run out, the bread burned to coal. The cream was in the spring and her jacket chopped up in the pot. The cow was hanged and the old man himself badly bruised and burned.

What happened later is not hard to guess. The old woman was allowed to care for her house in peace and quiet while the old man went off to the forest. Never again was he heard to complain of his lot. ❖

ON THE JOB
FORESTRY TECHNICIAN

Forestry technicians help professional foresters manage forest reserves. They work for federal and state agencies that manage public forest lands and for private logging companies that harvest timber. They also build roads through forest lands designated for harvest. Many technicians are involved in reforestation, planting trees on land that has been logged or destroyed by fire. Forestry technicians need strong math skills and at least one-to-two years of training in forest technology from a community college.

UNDERSTANDING

1. Compare the old man's daily work with the old woman's daily work. Which job requires more skill? More strength? Realistically, could both jobs be done by either a male or female?

   Create a six-column chart. In the first column, list the tasks mentioned in the story. Across the top, list the criteria of skill, strength, intelligence, height, and manual dexterity. Now determine the criteria necessary for performing each task. What conclusions can you draw?

2.  Look closely at each of the old man's mistakes. What was the cause of each mistake? Could the mistakes have been avoided?

   Working with a partner, write an analysis of the old man's careless mistakes. Identify the cause of each accident and then estimate how much the accident cost; for example, how much do the ingredients for another loaf of bread cost? Write a plan to help him avoid future mistakes. ***Workshop 14***

3. Is there any indication of how the old woman did with the old man's chores? How do you think she did?

   Investigate the kinds of nontraditional work women are now involved in: plumbing, construction, and so on. How many women do these kinds of jobs? How do the pay and working conditions compare to jobs that are traditionally women's work? Share your findings in an oral report. ***Workshop 23***

A LAST WORD

The old man in the folktale learns through a disastrous experience to respect his wife's work. How can we learn to respect one another's work at home, at school, or on the job? Is first-hand experience needed to learn such a lesson?

CONNECTING

1. List all the tasks that must be done around your home, from making beds to doing laundry, vacuuming, and cooking meals. Opposite each task, list who in the family does that chore. Are the tasks evenly distributed? If not, who does the most work around the house? Who does the least? Why do you think the household tasks are divided this way? Establish a plan for redistributing the household tasks fairly.

2. Choose two jobs outside the home that you know well. Write job descriptions for each one, including the kinds of skills required and a list of tasks the worker must perform. Do research to find all the information you need. If any kind of licensing or certification is required, be sure to add that information to the job description. ***Workshop 10***

Mentors

- *from* In Contempt
- *Dear Mrs. McKinney of the 6th Grade*

EXPLORING

Almost everyone who has become successful owes a debt of gratitude to at least one person who pushed, prodded, and encouraged. It may take only one person who believes in us to help us believe in ourselves. Parents and teachers supply advice and encouragement, but another person may also do so. Who in your life is your mentor, the one who encourages you and helps you believe in yourself?

THEME CONNECTION... MENTORSHIP

Young people often seek and benefit from the guidance and support of those who have experienced a great deal. Mature advice and encouragement go a long way to help students understand and value their own talents and abilities.

TIME & PLACE

Both Darden and Kherdian write about growing up in the United States. Both grew up during a time when mild corporal punishment from teachers and parents was acceptable and expected. At home and at school, young people were likely to experience a slap, a cheek twist, a spanking, or a whipping if they broke the rules. Such punishment is strictly forbidden in schools today, and most parents have learned other ways to discipline their children.

THE WRITER'S CRAFT
ACTIVE VOICE

Good writers use active sentences. An active sentence is strong and clear because it begins with the subject, and its verbs describe the subject *doing* something. Notice how much more effective the active "He kicked the ball" is than the passive "The ball was kicked by him." Both Darden and Kherdian also use active sentences to convey their meanings with strength.

from *In Contempt*

Christopher A. Darden

hat Nanny's house meant to me was space, quiet, a place to think and talk. And so she would invite me over sometimes by myself and I would stretch out there and talk to her about things no one else seemed to understand. Like becoming a lawyer.

I couldn't talk to my parents then; they were overwhelmed with the business of raising a family, and so I talked to Nanny, especially when I started my teenage years. I felt as if my parents and siblings didn't understand me at all, as if I spoke a different language than they did, a language only Nanny understood.

Sometimes Nanny would let one of us kids spend the night on a Saturday, then get us up for church the next morning. Grandpop was a steward at Davis Chapel, a **CME** church, where women would start shouting and trembling, shaking and chanting: "O Jesus! O Lord! Hallelujah!" One time I burst into laughter and Nanny reached over and slapped me right across the face. Of all the beatings I'd gotten or seen, that was the worst. I was so embarrassed. That was the only time Nanny ever hit me.

I think Nanny knew that I needed to get out of my house. Sometimes she would call over to my house and say she needed some weeds pulled, and I'd race over there and she'd pay me a dollar and a half. Later she gave me money to buy myself cologne and we'd talk a lot about girls, Nanny and I. When I was in high school and college, I'd bring the girls by to meet Nanny and she would tell me if this girl was going to hurt me or if that girl was playing games. I still miss her judgment and I miss the pride she showed in me.

"This is my grandson Chris," she'd say to her friends. "He's gonna be a lawyer someday." ❖

About the Author

Christopher A. Darden is a 15-year veteran of the Los Angeles County District Attorney's office. He was one of the prosecutors in the highly publicized case against O. J. Simpson. Since the trial, Darden, on a leave of absence from the District Attorney's office, has been an Associate Professor of Law at Southwestern University School of Law in Los Angeles.

CME—Christian Methodist Episcopal

austere—
serious

regard—respect

Dear Mrs. McKinney of the Sixth Grade

David Kherdian

About the Author

David Kherdian was born in Racine, Wisconsin, in 1931. Before becoming a writer, Kherdian worked at a variety of jobs, including door-to-door magazine salesperson, bartender, factory worker, and bookstore owner. His poems have been included in many collections. The poem "Dear Mrs. McKinney of the Sixth Grade" appears in Kherdian's book of poetry, *I Remember Root River.* The poet now lives in Oregon with his wife Nonny Hogrogian, an artist who illustrates many of Kherdian's books.

ON THE JOB
TEACHER

Elementary school teachers instruct children from kindergarten through the sixth grade. Generally, they have the same class for the whole school day. They teach students the basic skills they will need throughout their lives: reading, writing, arithmetic, and basic science concepts. Because teachers work closely with students, they must have strong interpersonal skills, good communication skills, patience, and creativity. A bachelor's degree and a teaching credential are required.

Hands down, you were my favorite
teacher at Garfield elementary,
or at any school since:
your stern, **austere** face, that
held an objective judgment of
everything in charge;
the patient way you taught,
out of a deep belief and respect
for learning,
and the good books you chose
to read aloud—
in particular, Mark Twain;
and the punishment you handed
out (a twin cheek twist, just
once, with forefingers and thumbs)
embarrassed us only because
we had failed ourselves,
for we had wisely learned from you
the need for discipline and **regard**.

Long after I left that place
I saw you once waiting for a bus,
and though I returned your warm
smile, I hurried on.
Why didn't I stop, as I could
see you wanted me to? I deeply
regretted it for weeks, and there
are moments when I remember it still.
And nothing, not poem, not time,
not anything for which I might
stand proud, can erase that seeming
failure of feeling and regard on
my part.
I loved you, I really did, and I
wish now that in stopping and chatting
with you for a moment I could have
shown it to you then,
instead of now, in this poem,
in which only time and loss, not
you and I, are the subject to be held. ❖

UNDERSTANDING

1. Most of what Nanny gives Christopher is acceptance and encouragement. What kind of lesson did she teach him when she slapped him in church for laughing? How do you think this might have affected his character?

   Can you think of a lesson you learned through embarrassment? Write a narrative telling the story. Use the active voice as much as possible. ***Workshop 9***

2. What kinds of things did Nanny do for Chris that helped him during the tough growing-up years?

   What important lessons have you learned about how to get along in life successfully? Make a list of them, each followed by the person or event that taught you. Then indicate how you think each lesson will help you throughout life.

3. Kherdian, directly and indirectly, cites a number of characteristics of a good teacher. What are they?

   Think of your ideal teacher. Write a description of him or her, specifically stating the qualities this person has. What attitudes and ideas does he or she possess? How does this ideal teacher treat students? ***Workshop 10***

CONNECTING

1. With a partner, find out about the mentor programs in your school district. You may need to consult a counselor or someone in the superintendent's office. Together, write a feature article for the school newspaper that describes the benefits of the mentor program and how to get involved in it. If your school does not have such a program, investigate a program at a nearby school, or talk with a counselor to find out how mentoring works. Write an article that explains why your school would benefit from a mentor program. ***Workshop 17***

2. Do a research report on a legal occupation other than lawyer. How much schooling is necessary? What are the job prospects for legal secretaries, court reporters, and so on? Also include information on salary, hours, and working conditions. ***Workshop 21***

3. The O. J. Simpson trial was probably the most sensational in recent history. Research the role Christopher Darden played in this trial. Locate a transcript of his closing arguments, which have received high praise. Write a report on why his role as an African American prosecuting another African American was especially demanding. ***Workshop 8***

A LAST WORD

Nanny and Mrs. McKinney made a difference in the lives of two young men. Who has made a difference in your life? How can you express your appreciation?

After You, My Dear Alphonse

EXPLORING

A stereotype is like a box inside our heads. People often place other people in stereotype boxes and refuse to let them out even when confronted with facts that contradict the stereotype. For example, if you place a male who wears glasses and likes math and computers in a "computer nerd" box, you may fail to see the intelligent, creative person he really is. What kind of stereotype is operating in this story, and how does it affect the situation? Do you ever think in stereotypes?

THEME CONNECTION... STEREOTYPES

The mother in this story is blind to the real Boyd. She sees him only within the stereotype she carries in her head. The boys, however, have an innocent, pure friendship that is not affected by grown-up attitudes. Unless people see others as individuals, they will never really know them.

TIME & PLACE

The title of this story, "After You, My Dear Alphonse," is taken from a popular cartoon strip of the 1920s and 1930s called "Happy Hooligan." It was about two Frenchmen, Alphonse and Gaston, who were excruciatingly polite and continually said, "After you, my dear Gaston" and "After you, my dear Alphonse." The boys in the story are having fun with the phrase. Their war game of running over "dead Japanese" is based on World War II in the 1940s. At that time, the United States was engaged in war with Japan and Germany.

THE WRITER'S CRAFT

DIALOGUE

Dialogue in a story is conversation. What characters say to one another is often critical to delivering the story line, as in this story. Authors work hard to give characters words that make their personalities unique, understandable, and believable.

After You, My Dear Alphonse

Shirley Jackson

rs. Wilson was just taking the gingerbread out of the oven when she heard Johnny outside talking to someone.

"Johnny," she called, "you're late. Come in and get your lunch."

"Just a minute, Mother," Johnny said. "After you, my dear Alphonse."

"After *you,* my dear Alphonse," another voice said.

"No, after *you,* my dear Alphonse," Johnny said.

Mrs. Wilson opened the door. "Johnny," she said, "you come in this minute and get your lunch. You can play after you've eaten."

Johnny came in after her, slowly. "Mother," he said, "I brought Boyd home for lunch with me."

"Boyd?" Mrs. Wilson thought for a moment. "I don't believe I've met Boyd. Bring him in, dear, since you've invited him. Lunch is ready."

"Boyd!" Johnny yelled. "Hey, Boyd, come on in!"

"I'm coming. Just got to unload this stuff."

"Well, hurry, or my mother'll be sore."

"Johnny, that's not very polite to either your friend or your mother," Mrs. Wilson said. "Come sit down, Boyd."

As she turned to show Boyd where to sit, she saw he was a Negro boy, smaller than Johnny but about the same age. His arms were loaded with split kindling wood. "Where'll I put this stuff, Johnny?" he asked.

Mrs. Wilson turned to Johnny. "Johnny," she said, "what did you make Boyd do? What is that wood?"

"Dead Japanese," Johnny said mildly. "We stand them in the ground and run over them with tanks."

"How do you do, Mrs. Wilson?" Boyd said.

"How do you do, Boyd? You shouldn't let Johnny make you carry all that wood. Sit down now and eat lunch, both of you."

"Why shouldn't he carry the wood, Mother? It's his wood. We got it at his place."

"Johnny," Mrs. Wilson said, "go on and eat your lunch."

"Sure," Johnny said. He held out the dish of scrambled eggs to Boyd. "After you, my dear Alphonse."

"After *you,* my dear Alphonse," Boyd said.

"After *you,* my dear Alphonse," Johnny said. They began to giggle.

"Are you hungry, Boyd?" Mrs. Wilson asked.

"Yes, Mrs. Wilson."

"Well, don't you let Johnny stop you. He always fusses about eating, so you just see that you get a good lunch. There's plenty of food here for you to have all you want."

"Thank you, Mrs. Wilson."

"Come on, Alphonse," Johnny said. He pushed half the scrambled eggs on to

About the Author

SPOTLIGHT ON...
RECOGNIZING BIASES

How can you recognize cultural and racial biases and avoid them? Here are some ideas:

1. To recognize bias, you have to distinguish objective thinking from subjective thinking.
2. An objective statement or reaction is based on fact or direct observation. When you react objectively, you do not let your personal feelings or opinions bias your observations or understanding.
3. Cultural or racial biases are caused by opinions and fears that can be inherited from living in a particular place (culture) at a particular time.
4. As you make conclusions about people, be objective. Rely on facts and observations, not personal feelings.

◆ ◆

Boyd's plate. Boyd watched while Mrs. Wilson put a dish of stewed tomatoes beside his plate.

"Boyd don't eat tomatoes, do you, Boyd?" Johnny said.

"*Doesn't* eat tomatoes, Johnny. And just because you don't like them, don't say that about Boyd. Boyd will eat *anything.*"

"Bet he won't," Johnny said, attacking his scrambled eggs.

"Boyd wants to grow up and be a big strong man so he can work hard," Mrs. Wilson said. "I'll bet Boyd's father eats stewed tomatoes."

"My father eats anything he wants to," Boyd said.

"So does mine," Johnny said. "Sometimes he doesn't eat hardly anything. He's a little guy, though. Wouldn't hurt a flea."

"Mine's a little guy, too," Boyd said.

"I'll bet he's strong, though," Mrs. Wilson said. She hesitated. "Does he . . . work?"

"Sure," Johnny said. "Boyd's father works in a factory."

"There, you see?" Mrs. Wilson said. "And he certainly has to be strong to do that—all that lifting and carrying at a factory."

"Boyd's father doesn't have to," Johnny said. "He's a foreman."

Mrs. Wilson felt defeated. "What does your mother do, Boyd?"

"My mother?" Boyd was surprised. "She takes care of us kids."

"Oh. She doesn't work, then?"

"Why should she?" Johnny said through a mouthful of eggs. "You don't work."

"You really don't want any stewed tomatoes, Boyd?"

"No, thank you, Mrs. Wilson," Boyd said.

"No, thank you, Mrs. Wilson, no, thank you, Mrs. Wilson, no thank you, Mrs. Wilson," Johnny said. "Boyd's sister's going to work, though. She's going to be a teacher."

"That's a very fine attitude for her to have, Boyd." Mrs. Wilson restrained an impulse to pat Boyd on the head. "I imagine you're all very proud of her?"

"I guess so," Boyd said.

"What about all your other brothers and sisters? I guess all of you want to make just as much of yourselves as you can."

"There's only me and Jean," Boyd said. "I don't know yet what I want to be when I grow up."

"We're going to be tank drivers, Boyd and me," Johnny said. "Zoom." Mrs. Wilson caught Boyd's glass of milk as Johnny's napkin ring, suddenly transformed into a tank, plowed heavily across the table.

"Look, Johnny," Boyd said. "Here's a foxhole. I'm shooting at you."

Mrs. Wilson, with the speed born of long experience, took the gingerbread off the shelf and placed it carefully between the tank and the foxhole.

"Now eat as much as you want to, Boyd," she said. "I want to see you get filled up."

"Boyd eats a lot, but not as much as I do," Johnny said. "I'm bigger than he is."

"You're not much bigger," Boyd said. "I can beat you running."

Mrs. Wilson took a deep breath. "Boyd," she said. Both boys turned to her. "Boyd, Johnny has some suits that are a little too small for him, and a winter coat. It's not new, of course, but there's lots of wear in it still. And I have a few dresses that your mother or sister could probably use. Your mother can make them over into lots of things for all of you, and I'd be very happy to give them to you. Suppose before you leave I make up a big bundle and then you and Johnny can take it over to your mother right away . . ." Her voice trailed off as she saw Boyd's puzzled expression.

"But I have plenty of clothes, thank you," he said. "And I don't think my mother knows how to sew very well, and anyway I guess we buy about everything we need. Thank you very much, though."

"We don't have time to carry that old stuff around, Mother," Johnny said. "We got to play tanks with the kids today."

Mrs. Wilson lifted the plate of gingerbread off the table as Boyd was about to take another piece. "There are many little boys like you, Boyd, who would be very grateful for the clothes someone was kind enough to give them."

"Boyd will take them if you want him to, Mother," Johnny said.

"I didn't mean to make you mad, Mrs. Wilson," Boyd said.

"Don't think I'm angry, Boyd. I'm just disappointed in you, that's all. Now let's not say anything more about it."

She began clearing the plates off the table, and Johnny took Boyd's hand and pulled him to the door. "Bye, Mother," Johnny said. Boyd stood for a minute, staring at Mrs. Wilson's back.

"After you, my dear Alphonse," Johnny said, holding the door open.

"Is your mother still mad?" Mrs. Wilson heard Boyd ask in a low voice.

"I don't know," Johnny said. "She's screwy sometimes."

"So's mine," Boyd said. He hesitated, "After *you*, my dear Alphonse." ❖

UNDERSTANDING

1. Some people may think the mother is being kind and generous to Boyd. Why are her attitude and behavior more offensive than kind?

   Consider how society often stereotypes teenagers. Write a descriptive essay on the teenage stereotype. Give specific examples. ***Workshop 10***

2. Look closely at the details of this story. If no one had told you the time and place of the story, what details would have given these facts away?

   Write a scene from a short story that includes dialogue. Inject details into the dialogue that give away the time and place of the story without stating it directly. Share the scene with another student or a group. Can your audience determine the time and place by reading the scene? ***Workshop 7***

3.  This story is almost entirely dialogue—conversation among characters. What is the effect of this writing technique? Consider what the story might be like if the writer had used straight description to tell the story.

   Radio plays were extremely popular at the time this story was written. Working with several classmates, turn the story into a radio play. Include sound effects and background information in your taped "broadcast."

CONNECTING

1. Can you remember the imaginative games you played as a child? Discuss childhood games with several classmates. Working together, produce a book of games for young children. Include clear, simple instructions for several games that explain each game's goal, what the players *should* do, are *allowed* to do, and are *not* allowed to do. ***Workshop 12***

2. The children seem to be puzzled at the mother's prejudiced remarks and attitude, shrugging her off as being "screwy." Does this mean that children are not racially prejudiced? Conduct a poll of adults asking the question: Is racial prejudice something one is born with, or is it learned behavior? Summarize the poll's results and report to the class.

ACCENT ON...
THEATER ARTS

Most of the action in the story "After You, My Dear Alphonse" takes place in the dialogue. In small groups of three students each, write a dramatic adaptation of the story in the form of a play script. Students should play the roles of the mother, Johnny, and Boyd. Rehearse the script, and perform it for the class. Each group may want to find and use props to re-create the kitchen setting.

We Choose to Love

- *The Choice*
- *If I were loved as I desire to be*
- *Love is not all: it is not meat nor drink*

EXPLORING

Love is a great mystery. Thinkers throughout the ages have tried to describe its patterns and nature, and to tell us how to, why to, and when to love. But love cannot be tracked. As Shakespeare wrote, "The course of true love never did run smooth." Have you found love to be mysterious, sometimes wonderful, sometimes miserable?

What do you view as the behavior and characteristics of those in love? Discuss which you think is more difficult—establishing a relationship or making it last.

THEME CONNECTION...
RELATIONSHIP DECISIONS

Decisions regarding relationships are important enough to take seriously because they could affect your life forever after. Few decisions are as critical as choosing a mate. In this age of painful divorce, relationship decisions are more important than ever before.

TIME & PLACE

The 1920s was a period of liberation for women. Cutting their hair, shortening their skirts, and dancing the Charleston were daring new things for women to do. These women, called *flappers,* broke the unwritten rules for females, thus preparing the way for more important issues, such as the right to vote, to gain acceptance later. Poets Dorothy Parker and Edna St. Vincent Millay lived during this time.

Alfred, Lord Tennyson was a Victorian poet of immense popularity during the reign of Queen Victoria of England in the nineteenth century.

THE WRITER'S CRAFT
IMAGERY

All three poets use images to paint pictures in our minds. An image consists of words that appeal to our senses in a vivid way. It is real and solid and clearly visible in our minds. Images help us imagine how a thing looks, sounds, or tastes, for example. Find examples of imagery in the three poems in this lesson.

The Choice

Dorothy Parker

He'd have given me rolling lands,
　　Houses of marble, and billowing farms,
Pearls, to trickle between my hands,
　　Smoldering rubies, to circle my arms.
You—you'd only a lilting song.
　　Only a melody, happy and high.
You were sudden and swift and strong,—
　　Never a thought for another had I.

He'd have given me laces rare,
　　Dresses that glimmered with frosty sheen,
Shining ribbons to wrap my hair,
　　Horses to draw me, as fine as a queen.
You—you'd only to whistle low,
　　Gaily I followed wherever you led.
I took you, and I let him go,—
　　Somebody ought to examine my head! ❖

If I were loved, as I desire to be

Alfred, Lord Tennyson

If I were loved, as I desire to be,
What is there in the great sphere of the earth,
And range of evil between death and birth,
That I should fear,—if I were loved by thee?
All the inner, all the outer world of pain
Clear Love would pierce and **cleave**, if thou **wert** mine,
As I have heard that, somewhere in the main,
Fresh-water springs come up through bitter brine.
'T were joy, not fear, claspt hand-in-hand with thee,
To wait for death—mute—careless of all ills,
Apart upon a mountain, tho' the surge
Of some new **deluge** from a thousand hills
Flung leagues of roaring foam into the gorge
Below us, as far on as eye could see. ❖

About the Author

Alfred, Lord Tennyson (1809–1892) is regarded as one of the greatest poets of the Victorian Age in England. Early in his career, Tennyson was influenced by the English Romantic poets, particularly John Keats. Immensely popular and successful throughout his later career, Tennyson was appointed poet laureate in 1850. The range of Tennyson's work is wide, including lyric songs, elegies, and epics. The elegy "In Memoriam" is often considered his greatest poem.

cleave—cut open

wert—archaic form for *were*

deluge—flood

Love is not all: it is not meat nor drink

Edna St. Vincent Millay

Love is not all: it is not meat nor drink
Nor slumber nor a roof against the rain;
Nor yet a floating **spar** to men that sink
And rise and sink and rise and sink again;
Love can not fill the thickened lung with breath,
Nor clean the blood, nor set the fractured bone;
Yet many a man is making friends with death
Even as I speak, for lack of love alone.
It well may be that in a difficult hour,
Pinned down by pain and moaning for release,
Or nagged by want past resolution's power,
I might be driven to sell your love for peace,
Or trade the memory of this night for food.
It well may be. I do not think I would. ❖

spar—a stout pole, such as a mast, used to support the rigging on a sailing vessel

SPOTLIGHT ON... IN-DEPTH READING

Sometimes stories or poems, such as Millay's sonnet, are written in a complex style that requires careful reading. For greater understanding when reading more complex materials, follow these guidelines:

1. Before you read, scan the poem, story, or article to see if and how the piece is divided or organized.
2. Read each section (chapter, couplet, line) slowly and carefully.
3. As you read, make notes, an outline, or summary to help you understand the meaning of each section.
4. Reread any sections you did not thoroughly understand and note confusing passages.

◆ ◆

UNDERSTANDING

1. Both Edna St. Vincent Millay and Alfred, Lord Tennyson have written sonnets. Look closely at the form of these works. What seem to be the defining characteristics of a sonnet?

   Write a sonnet of your own. Though sonnets are often love poems, they can be on any subject. ***Workshop 2***

2. People choose partners in relationships for many reasons—sometimes the wrong ones. In the poem "The Choice," compare the narrator's two alternatives. She regrets her choice, yet do you think she based her decision on the wrong criteria?

   Make a list of the qualities you value in a person whom you might marry or with whom you might share a close relationship. Now number the qualities in order of importance. Are your top five based on heart, mind, or both? Discuss things to consider in selecting a person for a close relationship.

3. All three poets use images to paint pictures in our minds. List the words from each poem that cause us to see, hear, smell, touch, or taste actual things such as "pearls" and "rubies."

   Practice using images in your own writing. Describe a person or place by comparing it to someone or something else. Use words in your comparison that appeal to the five senses. Exchange papers with a classmate and have him or her underline the words that make a strong impression.

A LAST WORD

Poets have been writing about the power of love for many centuries. How do love and compassion make the world a better place in which to live? What happens when we have the ability to express love and compassion toward others?

CONNECTING

1. Collect magazine advertisements that show couples. In a small group, discuss the following: Do advertisements emphasize some personal qualities more than others? Do you think advertisements and other media have an effect on how people choose relationships? Make a collage of these advertisements and write a summary of your group's conclusions.

2. Conduct research to discover how people in love benefit the business world. Survey florists, candy sellers, balloon sellers, and others who sell services and products to express love. What percentage of sales are made specifically to people who are part of a couple? What time of year does this business peak? How does each advertise? Write a report with statistical charts and graphs on your findings. ***Workshop 22***

Loathe at First Sight

EXPLORING

● ●

Strangers at a party, in a classroom, at the beach, in a library—how do they meet? Who takes the initiative? Who risks rejection? Talking to a stranger, particularly one you'd really like to know, can be awkward, even embarrassing. Words may not come easily, and when they do, they may not be what you had in mind. Some people are good at opening lines; others are at a loss. How do you approach a stranger you'd like to know better?

THEME CONNECTION...
FIRST IMPRESSIONS

Relationships have to start somewhere. Someone must take the risk of reaching out to another. Rejection is therefore a distinct possibility. Sometimes the key to acceptance is in the approach—it pays to polish the first impression you leave with others.

TIME & PLACE

When the time of a piece of literature is described as "modern time" or "present day," it could mean anything from the 1950s to the 1990s. This story takes place in the 1970s or 1980s, a time when Burt Reynolds, an actor, was at the peak.

THE WRITER'S CRAFT
METAPHOR

A metaphor is an image that makes a comparison between two unlike things. "Loathe at First Sight" ends with the clever use of metaphor. Starting a relationship or a friendship is compared to jumping into the ocean: "It's very cold when you first go in, but it warms up after a while." Sometimes the best way to describe what something is like is to compare it to something else. Think of other metaphors you've heard or read, or make up some of your own.

● ●

Loathe at First Sight

Ellen Conford

"You are dripping on my toes."

"I'm sorry. I was admiring you from afar, and I wanted to admire you from a near. From afar you looked terrific."

"Oh, thanks a lot. Meaning, up close I look like a toad."

"That's not what I meant at all! You look good up close, too. I love your bathing suit."

"Then why do you keep staring at my toes?"

"It's that stuff you've got on them. What do you call that?"

"Nail polish."

"I know, I know. I meant, what color is it?"

"Rosy Dawn. Look, what is this with my toes?"

"Rosy Dawn. That's kind of romantic. I would have thought it was just pink."

"Will you stop talking about my toes? What are you, weird or something?"

"No! Oh, boy, this whole conversation has gotten off on the wrong foot. Wrong foot—ha! Get it? Foot, toes?"

"Ha ha."

"Just a little humor to lighten up a tense situation. I thought you'd appreciate a good joke."

"I do appreciate a *good* joke."

"I just thought it was too early in our relationship to make personal comments about how great you look in a bathing suit."

"Our relationship? *What* relationship?"

"The one we're going to have."

"Oh, really? Have you always been this unsure of yourself?"

"Have you always been this sarcastic? Look, I just wanted—"

"And besides, toes are personal. Personal comments about toes are just as— as personal as comments about how I look in a bathing suit."

"Well, all right, do you want me to tell you how I think you look in your bathing suit?"

"No. I'm really not interested in your opinion of how I look in my bathing suit."

"Okay, then. How do I look in mine?"

"Wet."

"Picture me dry."

"Please. I already had a nightmare last night."

"That's not very nice."

"Look, I'm sorry, but you just walk up to me, drip on my feet, and start raving about my toes and have the gall to make this incredible assumption that I'm going to be so devastated by your wit and charm—"

"And my good looks."

"—and your *modesty,* that I'll fall madly in love with you."

"Well, actually, I didn't expect you to fall madly in love with me in the first five minutes of our relationship."

"See, that's just what I mean! We don't have a relationship."

"I'm working on it. How'm I doing so far? Say, on a scale of one to ten."

About the Author

Ellen Conford (b. 1942) has been successfully writing and publishing books for children and teens since the 1960s, when she began writing books for her own child. Because one of her goals is to show young people that books can be read strictly for entertainment, she creates plots and characters that have high appeal. This story is from a book of short stories for teens called *If This Is Love, I'll Take Spaghetti.* Conford lives in New York with her husband, who is an English professor.

SPOTLIGHT ON...
ACTIVE LISTENING

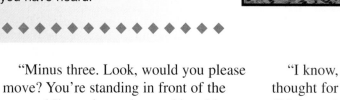

Being an active listener is important in conversations, in interviews, and on the job. Here are some guidelines for being an active listener:

1. Direct your attention to the speaker.
2. Listen courteously.
3. Pay attention to details.
4. Take notes if appropriate.
5. Ask questions.
6. Analyze what you have heard.

◆ ◆ ◆ ◆ ◆ ◆ ◆ ◆ ◆ ◆ ◆ ◆ ◆ ◆ ◆ ◆ ◆ ◆

"Minus three. Look, would you please move? You're standing in front of the sun and I'm going to have a big white stripe right in the middle of my back."

"Okay."

"I didn't mean for you to sit down. I meant for you to go away."

"But you didn't get a good look at me yet. All you could see when I was standing up was my knees. They're not necessarily my best feature. This way, you can look straight at me."

"Goody."

"Now, come on. I'm really pretty nice-looking."

"You're really pretty conceited."

"I'm just repeating what other people have told me. Some people think I look a lot like Burt Reynolds."

"Some people think the Earth is flat."

"I'm getting this definite impression that you're not being dazzled by my wit and charm."

"How very observant of you."

"That's the first nice thing you've said to me."

"I was being sarcastic."

"I know, but I'm grasping at straws. I thought for sure if the wit and charm didn't work, I could always fall back on my good looks."

"You can fall back on your head, for all I care."

"This isn't going exactly as I planned it. Could we start all over again? Hi, there, my name's Alan. What's yours?"

"Hepzibah."

" . . . Hepzibah? . . . I see. And what do your friends call you?"

"Hepzibah."

"Uh, I don't want to insult you or anything, just in case your name really is Hepzibah, but I have this funny suspicion you're putting me on."

"Flurge."

"I beg your pardon?"

"My last name. Flurge."

"Hepzibah Flurge?"

"Right."

"You're going to burst out laughing any minute, I can tell. Come on, look me straight in the eye and tell me your name is Hepzibah Flurge."

"My name is Hep—Hep—"

"I knew it! You can't even keep a straight face. You can't even say it . . . You know, you have beautiful eyes. What color are they, exactly?"

"Brown."

"I know, but there are little specks of something in them that—"

"Probably sand."

"Now, come on, don't go all cold and sarcastic on me again. We were doing so well a minute ago."

"I hadn't noticed."

"Sure, you were laughing and everything. Really sort of loosening up, know what I mean? You were right here; you wouldn't have missed it. What's your name, really?"

"Anne."

"There, that's better. Mine's Alan."

"You told me."

"I know, but I'm running out of ideas. I did all my best stuff already."

"That was your best stuff? You're in trouble."

"Well, help me out. What kind of a person are you to leave me floundering around for something to say like this? I mean this is really embarrassing. The least you could do is hold up your end of the discussion."

"I didn't start this ridiculous conversation—if you can even call it a conversation. I don't see why I have to take any responsibility for keeping it up."

"What kind of an attitude is that? What if everybody felt that way? What kind of a world would this be?"

"Quiet."

"Boring."

"Peaceful."

"Not necessarily. If nobody communicated with anybody else there'd be wars all the time."

"There *are* wars all the time."

" . . . Uh, yeah. Well. Good point. Would you—um—like me to rub some suntan oil on your shoulders?"

"No, thank you."

"Would you like to rub some on mine?"

"Not particularly."

"Look, Anne, I'm getting desperate here. Where did I go wrong? Did I come on too strong?"

"Yes."

"A little heavy on the wit and charm?"

"Hey, I like wit and charm as much as the next person, but—"

"I overdid it."

"Yes."

"It was the toes, wasn't it? I really turned you off with that stuff about your toes."

"Yes."

"It was just what you call a conversational gambit. You know, an ice-breaker. I mean, not that I don't think your toes are extremely attractive—"

"Alan—"

All right, all right, I swear I'll never mention your toes again. From this minute on, as far as I'm concerned, your toes don't exist. It's just—well, what *should* I have said?"

"What's wrong with hello?"

"Hello? Just hello? But what about after that? What happens after I say hello?"

"Who knows? If you don't try it you'll never find out."

"All right. Here goes. But I don't think this is going to work . . . Hello, Anne."

"Hello, Alan. How's the water?"

"Uh, it's very cold when you first go in, but it warms up after a while."

"A lot of things are like that, don't you think so, Alan?"

"I . . . I think I see what you mean."

"I felt certain you would . . . " ❖

UNDERSTANDING

1. Did the young man in the story really start off "on the wrong foot"? Was he too personal too soon? What might have been a better opening?

   Rewrite the opening lines of the characters' conversation, revising their words to fit your idea of a better, or at least different, approach and response. Compare your version to those of others in the class. Discuss what you changed in the text and why. **Workshop 7**

2. The word sarcasm comes from the Greek verb *sarcazo,* which means "to tear flesh." The girl uses sarcasm repeatedly in her comments. Cite some examples. What is the effect?

   From your own experience, does sarcasm injure, cause humor, or both? How do you feel when someone is sarcastic toward you? Should teachers use sarcasm on students? When is sarcasm safe and appropriate to use? Write a paper defining and discussing "sarcasm." **Workshop 8**

3. A fine line exists between flirting and sexual harassment. The key characteristic of sexual harassment is unwanted attention. Flirting feels good to the respondent; harassment does not. Would you classify the interchange between the boy and girl as harassment or flirting? Give good reasons for your answer.

4. The end of the story leaves the reader wondering if this really is the end. Will the couple begin a friendship, or is this relationship doomed after a bad beginning? What do you think?

   Write a dialogue of a phone conversation between Alan and Anne taking place a few days after this first encounter. Will they be enemies or friends?

A LAST WORD

First impressions aren't always lasting impressions. However, good speaking and listening skills can put a bright shine on a first impression. How do we all benefit from becoming better listeners?

CONNECTING

1. First impressions are important in the development of a relationship. They are also critical in job interviews. Working in a small group, read articles on job interviews, compare notes with others in the group, and discuss the steps to making a good impression in a job interview. With several classmates, develop a job interview skit in which the person being interviewed does something "wrong," based on the articles you read. It may be something very subtle. The rest of the class will then evaluate the interviewee to identify the strengths and weaknesses of the person seeking a job.

2. Federal law prohibits sexual harassment in the workplace and in public schools. Work with a partner to carry out the following activity. Contact the human services departments of several large companies or organizations and ask for a copy of their sexual harassment policies. Even your school will have one. Compare the policies you receive. What are their similarities? Are some more stringent than others?

Interview a school counselor or company human service representative on the topic. Prepare an informative pamphlet in which you define sexual harassment according to federal law, discuss appropriate policies, give examples of harassment at work and school, and tell how to respond to harassment if it happens. ***Workshops 20 and 24***

3. Adapt the story into a one-act play. Use context clues from the story to make up any unavailable information needed for characters, setting, scenes, and stage directions. Find a partner and present your play to an audience. ***Workshop 4***

WRAP IT UP

1. In the excerpt from *When Heaven and Earth Changed Places,* Le Ly Hayslip admires her parents' strength, patience, and endurance. In the excerpt from *In Contempt,* Christopher Darden describes his grandmother, Nanny, who had a great influence on his life. The poet David Kherdian regrets not telling a special teacher what she meant to him in "Dear Mrs. McKinney of the 6th Grade." How are the authors' views toward these people similar? Use details from the selections to support your opinions.

2. "The Teenage Bedroom" and "Loathe at First Sight" both feature a character struggling with one of the problems of growing up—love. In the poems written by Millay, Tennyson, and Parker, the adult speakers also struggle with love. Is there a difference between teenage and adult attitudes toward love? Write an essay comparing and contrasting attitudes on the subject of love in these selections. Include examples to illustrate your main points.

UNIT
◇2
THE INDIVIDUAL AND SOCIETY

Americans pride themselves on their individuality and carefully protect their individual rights. Each person cherishes his or her right to satisfy personal goals and desires. However, each person also lives among others in society. As members of society, furthermore, people belong to various communities. A community is any group—such as a family, club, or team.

When should we focus on our individual wishes and when should we put the community's well-being ahead of our own? Everyone must balance the rights and private desires of the individual against the needs and expectations of a community. When does a person owe a community service and aid? When do we choose the communities, or groups, we support? These are some of the issues explored in the selections that follow.

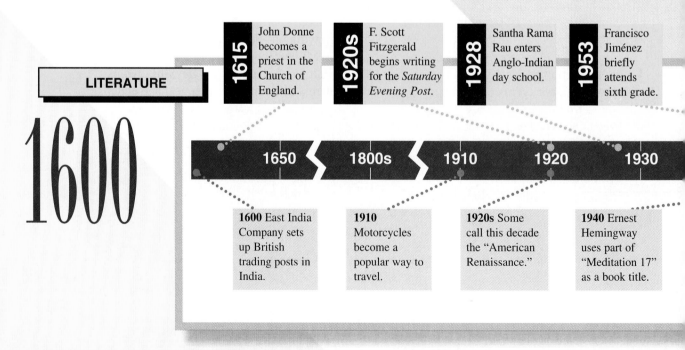

LITERATURE

1600

1615 John Donne becomes a priest in the Church of England.

1920s F. Scott Fitzgerald begins writing for the *Saturday Evening Post*.

1928 Santha Rama Rau enters Anglo-Indian day school.

1953 Francisco Jiménez briefly attends sixth grade.

1650 1800s 1910 1920 1930

1600 East India Company sets up British trading posts in India.

1910 Motorcycles become a popular way to travel.

1920s Some call this decade the "American Renaissance."

1940 Ernest Hemingway uses part of "Meditation 17" as a book title.

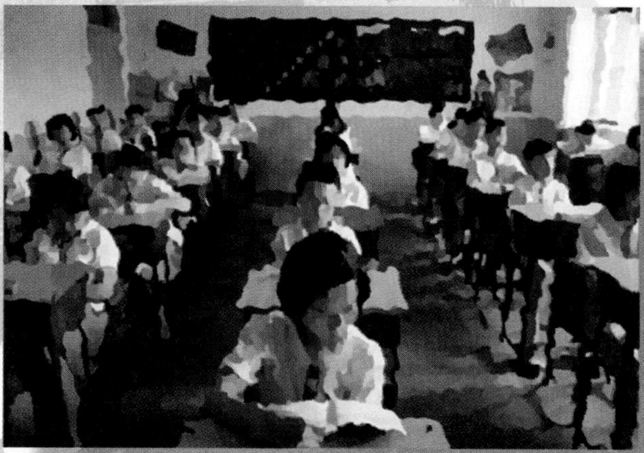

1958 Chinua Achebe writes his first novel, *Things Fall Apart.*

1960s Maya Angelou works with Dr. Martin Luther King, Jr.

1962 Bob Green turns 15.

1963 Lalita Gandbhir emigrates from India to Boston.

1940   1950   1960

1970

1953 Asia begins to produce world champions in table tennis.

1960 Lagos becomes the capital of the free nation of Nigeria.

1964 Businesses receiving federal funds must have affirmative action programs.

1964 The first enclosed mall on the West Coast opens.

LIFE and WORK

Virtues in Society

- *from Wouldn't Take Nothing for My Journey Now*
- *from Letters to His Daughter*
- *from Tao te Ching*

EXPLORING

● ● ● ● ● ● ● ● ● ● ● ● ● ● ● ● ● ● ●

A virtue is a commendable trait or behavior. We all have virtues—honesty, generosity, courage, kindness, and more. Their virtues make it possible for people to live together in harmony and peace. Virtues cause us to help others and to move beyond thinking only of our own interests. Why do you think virtues are important? What virtuous qualities do you especially admire?

THEME CONNECTION...
INDIVIDUAL VIRTUES INFLUENCE SOCIETY

Three writers from three distinct eras agree that individuals should practice virtue. They agree that virtuous individuals benefit themselves and society. The idea that virtuous conduct enriches personal life and strengthens society is ancient. This call to virtue will persist as long as human beings live in communities.

TIME & PLACE

Writing in 1993, American writer Maya Angelou shares her concern for virtue in an essay.

F. Scott Fitzgerald's letter was written to his daughter, Frances Scott Fitzgerald, in 1933. She was 12 years old and attending a summer camp.

Tao Te Ching, translated as *The Book of the Way*, was composed in China in the sixth century B.C. It contains 81 brief chapters.

THE WRITER'S CRAFT

PERSONAL ESSAY

An essay is a brief nonfiction discussion of a single topic. Fitzgerald's letter to his daughter conforms to this definition. A personal, rather than a formal, essay, it expresses the writer's feelings and ideas about how his daughter should think and behave. Maya Angelou's "When Virtue Becomes Redundant" is also a personal essay. Angelou's tone is that of a friend urging us to care about virtue.

● ●

from *Wouldn't Take Nothing for My Journey Now*
When Virtue Becomes Redundant

Maya Angelou

 urious, but we have come to a place, a time, when virtue is no longer considered a virtue. The mention of virtue is ridiculed, and even the word itself has fallen out of favor. Contemporary writers rarely employ such words as *purity,* **temperance**, *goodness, worth,* or even *moderation.* Students, save those enrolled in philosophy courses or studying in seminaries, seldom encounter questions on morality and piety.

We need to examine what the absence of those qualities has done to our communal spirit, and we must learn how to retrieve them from the dust heap of nonuse and return them to a vigorous role in our lives.

Nature will not abide a vacuum, and because we have let the positive particulars go, they have been replaced with **degeneracy**, indifference, and vice. Our streets explode with cruelty and criminality, and our homes are rife with violence and abuse. Too many of our leaders shun the higher moral road and take the path to satisfy greed while they voice **hollow rhetoric**.

Everything costs and costs the earth. In order to win, we pay with energy and effort and discipline. If we lose, we pay in disappointment, discontent, and lack of fulfillment.

So, since a price will be exacted from us for everything we do or leave undone, we should pluck up the courage to win, to win back our finer and kinder and healthier selves.

I would like to see us go calling on the good example and upon virtue itself with the purpose of inviting them back into our conversations, our businesses, homes, and our lives, to reside in those places as favored friends.

❖

About the Author

Maya Angelou was born Marguerite Johnson in 1928 in St. Louis, Missouri. After going to school in Arkansas and California, Angelou eventually moved to New York, where she studied dance and performed in *Porgy and Bess* and in off-Broadway shows. Angelou spent four years in Ghana, Africa, where she worked as an editor and teacher. When she returned to the United States, she began writing—poetry, songs, screenplays, and a television series.

temperance—
moderation

degeneracy—
having sunk to corruption

hollow rhetoric—
insincere language

SPOTLIGHT ON... BUSINESS ETHICS

In her essay, Angelou claims we live in a time when virtue is scarce and sometimes ridiculed. However, people do perform effectively *and* virtuously on the job and at school. Just keep in mind the following:
1. Work honestly and be just.
2. Perform each task, whether small or large responsibly. Always do your best.
3. Treat others with kindness, patience, and respect.

◆ ◆ ◆ ◆ ◆ ◆ ◆ ◆ ◆ ◆ ◆ ◆ ◆ ◆ ◆ ◆ ◆ ◆ ◆ ◆

from *Letters to His Daughter*

F. Scott Fitzgerald

La Paix, Rodgers' Forge
Towson, Maryland

AUGUST 8, 1933

About the Author

Born in St. Paul, Minnesota, in 1896, F. Scott Fitzgerald came of age during World War I. During his brief life he was known for his glamorous, perhaps extravagant, lifestyle. He left Princeton University before graduating to enlist in the U.S. Army. While waiting to be shipped overseas, Fitzgerald worked on his first novel, *This Side of Paradise*. It became an instant and immense success on its publication in 1920. He died at age 44 having written more than 180 short stories and many novels.

Dear Pie:

I feel very strongly about you doing [your] duty. Would you give Me a little more documentation about your reading in French? I am glad you are happy—but I never believe much in happiness. I never believe in misery either. Those are things you see on the stage or the screen or the printed page, they never really happen to you in life.

All I believe in in life is the rewards for virtue (according to your talents) and the *punishments* for not fulfilling your duties, which are double costly. If there is such a volume in the camp library, will you ask Mrs. Tyson to let you look up a sonnet of Shakespeare's in which the line occurs *"Lilies that fester smell far worse than weeds."*

Have had no thoughts today, life seems composed of getting up a *Saturday Evening Post* story. I think of you, and always pleasantly; but if you call me "Pappy" again I am going to take the White Cat out and beat his bottom *hard, six times for every time you are* **impertinent**. Do you react to that?

I will arrange the camp bill.
Halfwit, I will conclude.
Things to worry about:
Worry about courage
Worry about cleanliness
Worry about efficiency
Worry about horsemanship
Worry about . . .
Things not to worry about:
Don't worry about popular opinion
Don't worry about dolls
Don't worry about the past
Don't worry about the future
Don't worry about growing up
Don't worry about anybody getting ahead of you
Don't worry about triumph
Don't worry about failure unless it comes through your
own fault
Don't worry about mosquitoes
Don't worry about flies
Don't worry about insects in general
Don't worry about parents
Don't worry about boys
Don't worry about disappointments
Don't worry about pleasures
Don't worry about satisfactions
Things to think about:
What am I really aiming at?
How good am I really in comparison to my contemporaries in regard to:
(a) Scholarship
(b) Do I really understand about people and am I able to get along
with them?
(c) Am I trying to make my body a useful instrument or am I neglecting it?

With dearest love,
[*Daddy*] ❖

Tao te Ching

Lao-Tzu

About the Author

Lao-Tzu was a Chinese philosopher of the sixth century B.C. He is credited with writing *Tao te Ching,* a brief text consisting of 81 paragraphs in both verse and prose. Lao-Tzu is revered as one of the founders of Taoism, a Chinese philosophical system that advocates following the *Tao,* or Way, which is the natural order of things. *Tao te Ching* has been translated into more languages than any work except the Bible.

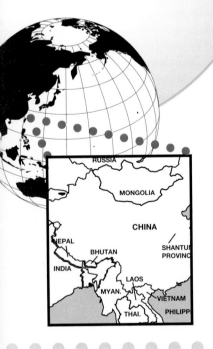

8

The supreme good is like water,
which nourishes all things without trying to.
It is content with the low places that people disdain.
Thus it is like the Tao.

In dwelling, live close to the ground.
In thinking, keep to the simple.
In conflict, be fair and generous.
In governing, don't try to control.
In work, do what you enjoy.
In family life, be completely present.

When you are content to be simply yourself
and don't compare or compete,
everybody will respect you.

9

Fill your bowl to the brim
and it will spill.
Keep sharpening your knife
and it will blunt.
Chase after money and security
and your heart will never unclench.
Care about people's approval
and you will be their prisoner.

Do your work, then step back.
The only path to serenity. ❖

UNDERSTANDING

1. In the excerpts from *Letters to His Daughter* and *Wouldn't Take Nothing for My Journey Now,* find evidence of the idea that virtue is not just an attitude, but a condition that requires action.

   During class discussion, agree on specific virtues that would improve your experience at school if they were practiced by everyone. On your own, develop and write a plan for making students aware of, and willing to practice, a particular virtue. In your plan, state your goal clearly, then lay out the steps of the plan in an orderly way. *Workshop 12*

2. List the qualities and ideas in the excerpt from *Tao te Ching.* Imagine that you know someone with many of the qualities on this list. Also imagine that this person is seeking a specific job. Write a letter of recommendation explaining why your friend's qualities make him or her exactly right for this particular job. Use examples from your friend's past actions to support the points you make. *Workshop 18*

3. *Tao te Ching* claims: "When you are content to be simply yourself and don't compare or compete, everybody will respect you." It is possible to argue both for and against this statement. In a group, list arguments first to support the statement, and then to refute—to disprove—the claim. Present both sides of the argument in a classroom debate. A panel of students will decide which case is more persuasive.

CONNECTING

1. *Tao te Ching* is a set of recommendations for behavior. Working with a partner, write your own *Tao*—in prose or poetry—to serve as a guide on conduct for students in your grade. This guide should consist of short "chapters" on specific topics. In a preface, explain the book's purpose and the audience for whom it is intended. Use computer software to publish your book. *Workshop 7*

2. Fitzgerald tells his daughter Scottie not to worry about popular opinion. Most people, however, *do* worry about it. Research the impact of public opinion on behavior. Your research might include interviewing students or studying how politicians respond to polls. In a brief speech, present your discoveries to the class. Be sure that your findings are arranged to express a central idea, or thesis. *Workshop 23*

> **A LAST WORD**
> What virtues are important to you? What steps might you take to keep your aims high and live a virtuous life?

Marriage Is a Private Affair

EXPLORING

Arguments—we all have them, at least occasionally. Have you ever "won" an argument? Did the other person "lose"? Is winning what arguing is all about?

Maybe you have had to settle a disagreement between *other* people. What issues were they arguing about? What did you do to help bring about harmony?

THEME CONNECTION...
TRADITIONS vs. NEW IDEAS

Every culture in the world has traditions. It is not uncommon for family members to come into conflict over those traditions and to dispute whether they are binding on young and old alike. In "Marriage Is a Private Affair," Achebe examines the conflict between a father, who adheres to his culture's marriage tradition, and his son, who chooses not to honor the tradition.

TIME & PLACE

"Marriage Is a Private Affair," written in 1972, portrays the clash of cultures in Nigeria. The Ibo (or Igbo) live in Eastern Nigeria and have their own distinctive language and customs. The Yoruba live in Western Nigeria and are the dominant population in Lagos, capital of Nigeria.

THE WRITER'S CRAFT

DIALOGUE

Dialogue is the conversation that takes place among characters. Writers reveal a character's attitude, personality, and background through his or her remarks. In "Marriage Is a Private Affair," readers learn about the father's attitudes from his own words and from the words of the villagers, who share his views.

Marriage Is a Private Affair

Chinua Achebe

"Have you written to your dad yet?" asked Nene one afternoon as she sat with Nnaemeka in her room at 16 Kasanga Street, Lagos.

"No. I've been thinking about it. I think it's better to tell him when I get home on leave!"

"But why? Your leave is such a long way off yet—six whole weeks. He should be let into our happiness now."

Nnaemeka was silent for a while, and then began very slowly as if he groped for his words: "I wish I were sure it would be happiness to him."

"Of course it must," replied Nene, a little surprised. "Why shouldn't it?"

"You have lived in Lagos all your life, and you know very little about people in remote parts of the country."

"That's what you always say. But I don't believe anybody will be so unlike other people that they will be unhappy when their sons are engaged to marry."

"Yes. They are most unhappy if the engagement is not arranged by them. In our case it's worse—you are not even an Ibo."

This was said so seriously and so bluntly that Nene could not find speech immediately. In the cosmopolitan atmosphere of the city it had always seemed to her something of a joke that a person's tribe could determine whom he married.

At last she said, "You don't really mean that he will object to your marrying me simply on that account? I had always thought you Ibos were kindly disposed to other people."

"So we are. But when it comes to marriage, well, it's not quite so simple. And this," he added, "is not peculiar to the Ibos. If your father were alive and lived in the heart of Ibibio-land he would be exactly like my father."

"I don't know. But anyway, as your father is so fond of you, I'm sure he will forgive you soon enough. Come on then, be a good boy and send him a nice lovely letter . . . "

"It would not be wise to break the news to him by writing. A letter will bring it upon him with a shock. I'm quite sure about that."

"All right, honey, suit yourself. You know your father."

As Nnaemeka walked home that evening he turned over in his mind the different ways of overcoming his father's opposition, especially now that he had gone and found a girl for him. He had thought of showing his letter to Nene but decided on second thoughts not to, at least for the moment. He read it again when he got home and couldn't help smiling to himself. He remembered Ugoye quite well, an Amazon of a girl who used to beat up all the boys, himself included, on the way to the stream, a complete dunce at school.

About the Author

Chinua Achebe (b. 1930) was born in Ogidi in Eastern Nigeria. He entered University College, Ibadan, as a medical student, but turned to the study of English literature. Although Achebe's native language is the African language of Ibo, he writes in English, which he began to learn when he was eight years old. He published his first short stories while still a student. In 1958, Achebe published his first novel, *Things Fall Apart,* which may well be Africa's best-loved novel.

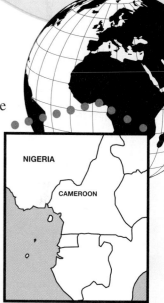

NIGERIA

CAMEROON

I have found a girl who will suit you admirably—Ugoye Nweke, the eldest daughter of our neighbor, Jacob Nweke. She has a proper Christian upbringing. When she stopped schooling some years ago her father (a man of sound judgment) sent her to live in the house of a pastor where she has received all the training a wife could need. Her Sunday School teacher has told me that she reads her Bible very fluently. I hope we shall begin negotiations when you come home in December.

On the second evening of his return from Lagos Nnaemeka sat with his father under a cassia tree. This was the old man's retreat where he went to read his Bible when the parching December sun had set and a fresh, reviving wind blew on the leaves.

"Father," began Nnaemeka suddenly, "I have come to ask forgiveness."

"Forgiveness? For what, my son?" he asked in amazement.

"It's about this marriage question."

"Which marriage question?"

"I can't—we must—I mean it is impossible for me to marry Nweke's daughter."

"Impossible? Why?" asked his father.

"I don't love her."

"Nobody said you did. Why should you?" he asked.

"Marriage today is different . . . "

"Look here, my son," interrupted his father, "nothing is different. What one looks for in a wife are a good character and a Christian background."

● ● ● ● ● ● ●
"Marriage today is different . . . "
● ● ● ● ● ● ●

Nnaemeka saw there was no hope along the present line of argument.

"Moreover," he said, "I am engaged to marry another girl who has all of Ugoye's good qualities, and who . . . "

His father did not believe his ears. "What did you say?" he asked slowly and **disconcertingly**.

"She is a good Christian," his son went on, "and a teacher in a Girls' School in Lagos."

"Teacher, did you say? If you consider that a qualification for a good wife I should like to point out to you, Emeka, that no Christian woman should teach. St. Paul in his letter to the Corinthians says that women should keep silence." He rose slowly from his seat and paced forwards and backwards. This was his pet subject, and he condemned vehemently those church leaders who encouraged women to teach in their schools. After he had spent his emotion on a long **homily** he at last came back to his son's engagement, in a seemingly milder tone.

"Whose daughter is she, anyway?"

"She is Nene Atang."

"What!" All the mildness was gone again. "Did you say Neneataga, what does that mean?"

"Nene Atang from Calabar. She is the only girl I can marry." This was a very rash reply and Nnaemeka expected the storm to burst. But it did not. His father merely walked away into his room. This was most unexpected and perplexed Nnaemeka. His father's silence was infinitely more menacing than a flood of threatening speech. That night the old man did not eat.

FOCUS ON...
SOCIAL STUDIES

In the Ibo culture described in "Marriage Is a Private Affair," it is traditional for a marriage to be arranged by the couple's fathers. Marital customs and laws are found in all human societies, but they are as varied as the great number of cultures practicing them. What marital customs and laws are universal? What varieties exist? Research the customs and laws of marriage in at least three different cultures and present your findings to the class.

◆ ◆ ◆ ◆ ◆ ◆ ◆ ◆ ◆ ◆ ◆ ◆ ◆ ◆ ◆ ◆ ◆ ◆

When he sent for Nnaemeka a day later he applied all possible ways of dissuasion. But the young man's heart was hardened, and his father eventually gave him up as lost.

"I owe it to you, my son, as a duty to show you what is right and what is wrong. Whoever put this idea into your head might as well have cut your throat. It is Satan's work." He waved his son away.

"You will change your mind, Father, when you know Nene."

"I shall never see her," was the reply. From that night the father scarcely spoke to his son. He did not, however, cease hoping that he would realize how serious was the danger he was heading for. Day and night he put him in his prayers.

Nnaemeka, for his own part, was very deeply affected by his father's grief. But he kept hoping that it would pass away. If it had occurred to him that never in the history of his people had a man married a woman who spoke a different tongue, he might have been less optimistic. "It

has never been heard," was the verdict of an old man speaking a few weeks later. In that short sentence he spoke for all of his people. This man had come with others to **commiserate** with Okeke when news went round about his son's behavior. By that time the son had gone back to Lagos.

"It has never been heard," said the old man again with a sad shake of his head.

"What did Our Lord say?" asked another gentleman. "Sons shall rise against their Fathers; it is there in the Holy Book."

"It is the beginning of the end," said another.

The discussion thus tending to become theological, Madubogwu, a highly practical man, brought it down once more to the ordinary level.

"Have you thought of consulting a native doctor about your son?" he asked Nnaemeka's father.

"He isn't sick," was the reply.

"What is he then? The boy's mind is diseased and only a good herbalist can

commiserate—sympathize with

bring him back to his right senses. The medicine he requires is *Amalile,* the same that women apply with success to recapture their husbands' straying affection."

"Madubogwu is right," said another gentleman. "This thing calls for medicine."

"I shall not call in a native doctor." Nnaemeka's father was known to be obstinately ahead of his more superstitious neighbors in these matters. "I will not be another Mrs. Ochuba. If my son wants to kill himself let him do it with his own hands. It is not for me to help him."

"But it was her fault," said Madubogwu. "She ought to have gone to an honest herbalist. She was a clever woman, nevertheless."

"She was a wicked murderess," said Jonathan who rarely argued with his neighbors because, he often said, they were incapable of reasoning. "The medicine was prepared for her husband, it was his name they called in its preparation and I am sure it would have been perfectly beneficial to him. It was wicked to put it into the herbalist's food, and say you were only trying it out."

Six months later, Nnaemeka was showing his young wife a short letter from his father:

> It amazes me that you could be so unfeeling as to send me your wedding picture. I would have sent it back. But on further thought I decided just to cut off your wife and send it back to you because I have nothing to do with her. How I wish that I had nothing to do with you either.

When Nene read through this letter and looked at the mutilated picture her eyes filled with tears, and she began to sob.

"Don't cry, my darling," said her husband. "He is essentially good-natured and will one day look more kindly on our marriage." But years passed and that one day did not come.

For eight years, Okeke would have nothing to do with his son, Nnaemeka. Only three times (when Nnaemeka asked to come home and spend his leave) did he write to him.

"I can't have you in my house," he replied on one occasion. "It can be of no interest to me where or how you spend your leave—or your life, for that matter."

The prejudice against Nnaemeka's marriage was not confined to his little village. In Lagos, especially among his people who worked there, it showed itself in a different way. Their women, when they met at their village meeting, were not hostile to Nene. Rather, they paid her such excessive **deference** as to make her feel she was not one of them. But as time went on, Nene gradually broke through some of this prejudice and even began to make friends among them. Slowly and grudgingly they began to admit that she kept her home much better than most of them.

The story eventually got to the little village in the heart of the Ibo country that Nnaemeka and his young wife were a most happy couple. But his father was one of the few people who knew nothing about this. He always displayed so much temper whenever his son's name was mentioned that everyone avoided it in his presence. By a tremendous effort of will he had succeeded in pushing his son to the back of his mind. The strain had nearly killed him but he had persevered, and won.

Then one day he received a letter from Nene, and in spite of himself he began to glance through it **perfunctorily** until all of a sudden the expression on his face changed and he began to read more carefully.

> . . . Our two sons, from the day they learned that they have a grandfather, have insisted on being taken to him. I find it impossible to tell them that you will not see them. I implore you to allow Nnaemeka to bring them home for a short time during his leave next month. I shall remain here in Lagos . . .

The old man at once felt the resolution he had built up over so many years falling in. He was telling himself that he must not give in. He tried to steel his heart against all emotional appeals. It was a reenactment of that other struggle. He leaned against a window and looked out. The sky was overcast with heavy black clouds and a high wind began to blow filling the air with dust and dry leaves. It was one of those rare occasions when even Nature takes a hand in a human fight. Very soon it began to rain, the first rain in the year. It came down in large sharp drops and was accompanied by the lightning and thunder which mark a change of season. Okeke was trying hard not to think of his two grandsons. But he knew he was now fighting a losing battle. He tried to hum a favorite hymn but the pattering of large rain drops on the roof broke up the tune. His mind immediately returned to the children. How could he shut his door against them? By a curious mental process he imagined them standing, sad and forsaken, under the harsh angry weather—shut out from his house.

That night he hardly slept, from remorse—and a vague fear that he might die without making it up to them. ❖

perfunctorily—
without interest
or enthusiasm

ON THE JOB

MARRIAGE AND FAMILY COUNSELOR

Marriage counselors and family counselors help people understand themselves and their relationships with others and then help them use their new understanding to develop better relationships. Counselors must have excellent listening and communication skills. High school courses in psychology are helpful preparation and may offer field work opportunities at local social service agencies or hospitals. Sociology and psychology are essential college courses.

UNDERSTANDING

1.  To show that Okeke is not a whimsical tyrant, but instead is acting as any Ibo might act under the circumstances, Achebe presents the villagers conversing. Find evidence in their conversation that they share Okeke's attitude about Nnaemeka's proposed marriage.

   When two people disagree about an issue, the best solution is one that satisfies both of them. In groups, brainstorm and write down steps to problem solving that will likely lead to a good conclusion for both parties in a dispute. Create a poster that shows the steps. Then share your results with the class.

2. Achebe makes the weather fit Okeke's mood when Okeke receives Nene's letter. Find and reread that passage in the story.

   In a paragraph, describe a familiar room in such a way that you influence the reader's feelings about the place. Be sure to include vivid details and present them in a logical order. *Workshop 10*

3. Although we do not learn much about Nene, we learn enough to form an opinion about her. Find evidence in the text to show the kind of person she is. What is your opinion about Nene?

   Suppose that Nnaemeka does take his children to the village. You are a reporter, and you see Okeke meet his grandchildren for the first time. Write an eyewitness account of the reconciliation of Nnaemeke and his two children with Okeke. *Workshop 17*

CONNECTING

1.  Nigeria is the most populous country in Africa. From 1967 to 1970, the Nigerian civil war took place. The eastern territory, home of the Ibo people, declared independence from the rest of Nigeria, called itself Biafra, and fought to be separate. The attempt failed.

   Working cooperatively, find additional information about Nigeria's history, political leaders, cities, tribes, and customs. Present the information in a travel pamphlet that contains illustrations and graphs as well as written text. *Workshops 20 and 22*

2. Invite a panel of experts to visit your classroom to discuss various cultures in America. Take notes on their presentations. After their visit, write a paper explaining how your newly acquired knowledge and understanding of another culture influences your thoughts about and attitude toward that culture's people and customs. *Workshop 8*

By Any Other Name

EXPLORING

If you saw or heard about students being treated unjustly at your school for any reason, how would you respond? What if you were the one being treated unjustly? Develop strategies for resisting injustice. Since prejudice is a source of injustice, your strategies should include ways to deal with prejudice.

THEME CONNECTION...
TAKING A STAND

In "By Any Other Name," two sisters attend a British-run day school and in so doing enter a world of British teachers and students. Although the older sister is willing to adjust to some British customs, she refuses to yield to one particular demand. Her refusal shows the importance of standing up for yourself.

TIME & PLACE

Set in India around 1928, this story describes the experiences of two young Indian sisters, Santha, five and a half, and Premila, eight, during their first week at a British-run school in their hometown. Britain had actually ruled India since 1857, and had brought British schools and a system of education there. This story takes place just as British rule was being challenged and coming to an end.

THE WRITER'S CRAFT
AUTOBIOGRAPHY

Autobiography is nonfiction narrative. Like all narrative writing, it tells what happens. Because it is autobiography, it tells about a real person's life. An autobiography is usually told in the first person, using the pronoun *I*, and since truth is often stranger than fiction, it can be very entertaining. Autobiographies express ideas drawn from personal experience, describe events, and explain the impact of these events on the author.

By Any Other Name

Santha Rama Rau

At the Anglo-Indian day school in Zorinabad to which my sister and I were sent when she was eight and I was five and a half, they changed our names. On the first day of school, a hot, windless morning of a north Indian September, we stood in the headmistress's study and she said, "Now you're the *new* girls. What are your names?"

My sister answered for us. "I am Premila, and she"—nodding in my direction—"is Santha."

The headmistress had been in India, I suppose, fifteen years or so, but she still smiled her helpless inability to cope with Indian names. Her rimless half-glasses glittered, and the **precarious** bun on the top of her head trembled as she shook her head. "Oh, my dears, those are much too hard for me. Suppose we give you pretty English names. Wouldn't that be more jolly? Let's see, now—Pamela for you, I think." She shrugged in a baffled way at my sister. "That's as close as I can get. And for *you*," she said to me, "how about Cynthia? Isn't that nice?"

About the Author

Born in Madras, India, in 1923, Santha Rama Rau studied at home, except for her brief time at the British-run school described in "By Any Other Name." She went with her family to England when she was six, attended English boarding schools, and earned a bachelor's degree in 1944 at Wellesley College in Massachusetts. A world traveler, Rau writes about peoples in India, Africa, China, Spain, Russia, Japan, England, and the U.S.

My sister was always less easily intimidated than I was, and while she kept a stubborn silence, I said, "Thank you," in a very tiny voice.

We had been sent to that school because my father, among his responsibilities as an officer of the civil service, had a tour of duty to perform in the villages around that steamy little provincial town, where he had his headquarters at that time. He used to make his shorter inspection tours on horseback, and a week before, in the stale heat of a typically **postmonsoon** day, we had waved good-bye to him and a little procession—an assistant, a secretary, two bearers, and the man to look after the bedding rolls and luggage. They rode away through our large garden, still bright green from the rains, and we turned back into the twilight of the house and the sound of fans whispering in every room.

Up to then, my mother had refused to send Premila to school in the British-run establishments of that time, because, she used to say, "you can bury a dog's tail for seven years and it still comes out curly, and you can take a Britisher away from his home for a lifetime and he still remains **insular**." The examinations and degrees from entirely Indian schools were not, in those days, considered valid. In my case, the question had never come up, and probably never would have come up if Mother's extraordinary good health had not broken down. For the first time in my life, she was not able to continue the lessons she had been giving us every morning. So our **Hindi** books were put away, the stories of the **Lord Krishna** as a little boy were left in midair, and we were sent to the Anglo-Indian school.

That first day at school is still, when I think of it, a remarkable one. At that age, if one's name is changed, one develops a curious form of dual personality. I remember having a certain detached and disbelieving concern in the actions of "Cynthia," but certainly no responsibility. Accordingly, I followed the thin, erect back of the headmistress down the veranda to my classroom feeling, at most, a passing interest in what was going to happen to me in this strange, new atmosphere of School.

The building was Indian in design, with wide verandas opening onto a central courtyard, but Indian verandas are usually whitewashed, with stone floors. These, in the tradition of British schools, were painted dark brown and had matting on the floors. It gave a feeling of extra intensity to the heat.

I suppose there were about a dozen Indian children in the school—which contained perhaps forty children in all—and four of them were in my class. They were all sitting at the back of the room, and I went to join them. I sat next to a small, solemn girl who didn't smile at me. She had long, glossy-black braids and wore a cotton dress, but she still kept on her Indian jewelry—a gold chain around her neck, thin gold bracelets, and tiny ruby studs in her ears. Like most Indian children, she had a rim of black **kohl** around her eyes. The cotton dress should have looked strange, but all I could think of was that I should ask my mother if I couldn't wear a dress to school, too, instead of my Indian clothes.

I can't remember too much about the proceedings in class that day, except for the beginning. The teacher pointed to me and asked me to stand up. "Now, dear, tell the class your name."

I said nothing.

"Come along," she said, frowning slightly. "What's your name, dear?"

"I don't know," I said, finally.

The English children in the front of the class—there were about eight or ten of them—giggled and twisted around in their chairs to look at me. I sat down quickly and opened my eyes very wide, hoping in that way to dry them off. The little girl with the braids put out her hand and very lightly touched my arm. She still didn't smile.

Most of that morning I was rather bored. I looked briefly at the children's drawings pinned to the wall and then concentrated on a lizard clinging to the ledge of the high, barred window behind the teacher's head. Occasionally, it would shoot out its long yellow tongue for a fly, and then it would rest, with its eyes closed and its belly **palpitating**, as though it were swallowing several times quickly. The lessons were mostly concerned with reading and writing and simple numbers—things that my mother had already taught me—and I paid very little attention. The teacher wrote on the easel blackboard words like *bat* and *cat,* which seemed babyish to me; only *apple* was new and **incomprehensible**.

When it was time for the lunch recess, I followed the girl with braids out onto the veranda. There the children from the other classes were assembled. I saw Premila at once and ran over to her, as she had charge of our lunch box. The children were all opening packages and sitting down to eat sandwiches. Premila and I were the only ones who had Indian

FOCUS ON... HISTORY

For 90 years the British ruled India. When did India win independence from British rule? With a small group, research the history of India's independence movement and the people who led it. What strategies were used? What key events intensified the struggle for independence? Present your findings in the form of an outline.

◆ ◆ ◆ ◆ ◆ ◆ ◆ ◆ ◆ ◆ ◆ ◆ ◆

chapatties—thin pieces of bread baked in a hot, dry skillet

curry—a dish made with curry powder, which is a combination of strong ground spices

ayah—an Indian "nurse"; the equivalent of a nanny

wizened—dried, wrinkled

sari—a garment worn by Hindu women consisting of yards of cloth that are wrapped or draped to form a skirt and a shoulder covering

sedately—quietly and calmly

food—thin wheat **chapatties**, some vegetable **curry**, and a bottle of buttermilk. Premila thrust half of it into my hand and whispered fiercely that I should go and sit with my class, because that was what the others seemed to be doing.

The enormous black eyes of the little Indian girl from my class looked at my food longingly, so I offered her some. But she only shook her head and plowed her way solemnly through her sandwiches.

I was very sleepy after lunch, because at home we always took a siesta. It was usually a pleasant time of day, with the bedroom darkened against the harsh afternoon sun, then drifting off into sleep with the sound of Mother's voice reading a story in one's mind and, finally, the shrill, fussy voice of the **ayah** waking one for tea.

At school, we rested for a short time on low, folding cots on the veranda, and then we were expected to play games. During the hot part of the afternoon, we played indoors, and after the shadows

had begun to lengthen and the light breeze of the evening had come up, we moved outside to the wide courtyard.

I had never really grasped the system of competitive games. At home, whenever we played tag or guessing games, I was always allowed to "win"—"because," Mother used to tell Premila, "she is the youngest, and we have to allow for that." I had often heard her say it, and it seemed quite reasonable to me, but the result was that I had no clear idea of what "winning" meant.

When we played twos-and-threes that afternoon at school, in accordance with my training, I let one of the small English boys catch me, but was naturally rather puzzled when the other children did not return the courtesy. I ran about for what seemed like hours without ever catching anyone, until it was time for school to close. Much later I learned that my attitude was called "not being a good sport," and I stopped allowing myself to be caught, but it was not for years that I really learned the spirit of the thing.

When I saw our car come up to the school gate, I broke away from my classmates and rushed toward it yelling, "Ayah! Ayah!" It seemed like an eternity since I had seen her that morning—a **wizened**, affectionate figure in her white cotton **sari**, giving me dozens of urgent and useless instructions on how to be a good girl at school. Premila followed more **sedately**, and she told me on the way home never to do that again in front of the other children.

When we got home we went straight to Mother's high white room to have tea with her, and I immediately climbed onto the bed and bounced gently up and down on the springs. Mother asked how we had liked our first day in school. I was so pleased to be home and to have left that peculiar Cynthia behind that I had nothing whatever to say about school, except to ask what *apple* meant. But Premila told Mother about the classes, and added that in her class they had weekly tests to see if they had learned their lessons well.

I asked, "What's a test?"

Premila said, "You're too small to have them. You won't have them in your class for donkey's years." She had learned the expression that day and was using it for the first time. We all laughed enormously at her wit. She also told Mother, in an aside, that we should take sandwiches to school the next day. Not, she said, that *she* minded. But they would be simpler for me to handle.

That whole lovely evening I didn't think about school at all. I sprinted barefoot across the lawns with my favorite playmate, the cook's son, to the stream at the end of the garden. We quarreled in our usual way, waded in the **tepid** water under the lime trees, and waited for the night to bring out the smell of the jasmine. I listened with fascination to his stories of ghosts and demons, until I was too frightened to cross the garden alone in the semidarkness. The ayah found me, shouted at the cook's son, scolded me, hurried me in to supper—it was an entirely usual, wonderful evening.

It was a week later, the day of Premila's first test, that our lives changed rather abruptly. I was sitting at the back of my class, in my usual inattentive way, only half listening to the teacher. I had started a rather guarded friendship with the girl with the braids, whose name turned out to be Nalini (Nancy, in school). The three other Indian children were already fast friends. Even at that age it was apparent to all of us that friendship with the English or Anglo-Indian children was out of the question. Occasionally, during the class, my new friend and I would draw pictures and show them to each other secretly.

The door opened sharply and Premila marched in. At first, the teacher smiled at her in a kindly and encouraging way and said, "Now, you're little Cynthia's sister?"

Premila didn't even look at her. She stood with her feet planted firmly apart and her shoulders rigid, and addressed herself directly to me. "Get up," she said. "We're going home."

I didn't know what had happened, but I was aware that it was a crisis of some sort. I rose obediently and started to walk toward my sister.

"Bring your pencils and your notebook," she said.

I went back for them, and together we left the room. The teacher started to say something

tepid—medium warm

just as Premila closed the door, but we didn't wait to hear what it was.

In complete silence we left the school grounds and started to walk home. Then I asked Premila what the matter was. All she would say was "We're going home for good."

It was a very tiring walk for a child of five and a half, and I dragged along behind Premila with my pencils growing sticky in my hand. I can still remember looking at the dusty hedges and the tangles of thorns in the ditches by the side of the road, smelling the faint fragrance from the eucalyptus trees and wondering whether we would ever reach home. Occasionally, a horse-drawn **tonga** passed us, and the women, in their pink or green silks, stared at Premila and me trudging along on the side of the road. A few **coolies** and a line of women carrying baskets of vegetables on their heads smiled at us. But it was nearing the hottest time of day, and the road was almost deserted. I walked more and more slowly and shouted to Premila from time to time, "Wait for me!" with increasing **peevishness**. She spoke to me only once, and that was to tell me to carry my notebook on my head, because of the sun.

When we got to our house, the ayah was just taking a tray of lunch into Mother's room. She immediately started a long, worried questioning, about what are you children doing back here at this hour of the day.

Mother looked very startled and very concerned, and asked Premila what had happened.

Premila said, "We had our test today, and she made me and the other Indians

sit at the back of the room, with a desk between each one."

Mother said, "Why was that, darling?"

"She said it was because Indians cheat," Premila added. "So I don't think we should go back to that school."

Mother looked very distant and was silent a long time. At last she said, "Of course not, darling." She sounded displeased.

We all shared the curry she was having for lunch and afterward I was sent off to the beautifully familiar bedroom for my siesta. I could hear Mother and Premila talking through the open door.

Mother said, "Do you suppose she understood all that?"

Premila said, "I shouldn't think so. She's a baby."

Mother said, "Well, I hope it won't bother her."

Of course, they were both wrong. I understood it perfectly, and I remember it all very clearly. But I put it happily away because it had all happened to a girl called Cynthia, and I never was really particularly interested in her. ❖

ACCENT ON...
ARCHITECTURE

• •

In the story, young Santha notes that the design of the school building had been modified to resemble British schools. Find out what a traditional Indian building design would be. Then create a 3-D model of it, complete with its unique features. To accompany your model, write a brief report explaining the elements in the Indian design of the building.

UNDERSTANDING

1. The title "By Any Other Name" refers to Shakespeare's *Romeo and Juliet*. In the play, Juliet regrets Romeo's name; it identifies him as a member of a family hated by her relatives. She says: "What's in a name? That which we call a rose/By any other name would smell as sweet." Locate passages in the story that refer to the impact of names. Then write a paragraph explaining what Rau says about the importance of names. Does she agree with Shakespeare?

2. Santha's mother had a specific reason for not sending her daughters to a British-run school. Find the reason given in the story. Then find evidence that the mother's fears were justified.

    Write a brief narrative about an encounter between someone who tries, successfully or unsuccessfully, to resist the influence of a narrow-minded person. Write in first person—using the pronoun *I*. Treat the incident as if it actually happened to you. *Workshop 9*

3. Find evidence that Premila was willing to adjust to *some* British ways. When and why does she refuse to adjust?

    Consider a time when you stood up for what you felt was right. In a memo to an adult you respect, discuss the situation and explain why you refused to go along with it. *Workshop 19*

CONNECTING

1.   Working as a class, research and prepare an informative report on India. Individuals may cover India's struggle for self-government, influential writers, social problems, or religions. Features of daily life such as dress, food, and celebrations are also interesting topics. Each person's part of the final written report should contain both text and some kind of visual aid. As a class, agree on overall organization and final format. *Workshop 21*

2. Work with several classmates to write a description of the ideal school. Consider such issues as building design, size, and location; class size; the behavior of teachers and students; instructional methods; and extracurricular activities. Once you have considered these and any other issues you feel are important, prepare a written report accompanied by illustrations. Describe your ideal school in detail, giving reasons for the decisions you have made about facilities, size, and so on. Use persuasive language to convince your readers that your school plan has merit. *Workshop 13*

The Circuit

EXPLORING

Every child has the right to develop his or her talents and abilities. Laws requiring children to attend school exist to guarantee people the chance to make the most of their potential. Sometimes, however, young people cannot attend school, or if they do attend, they find it hard to learn. Discuss conditions both in school and out that might interfere with getting an education. How important is school to you?

THEME CONNECTION...
BELONGING TO A COMMUNITY

As the child of migrant laborers, Francisco Jiménez never gets to stay in one place very long. When strawberry season ends and his family must set out to find new work, Francisco is sorry to move on, even though the work has been hard. When the harvest ends in Fresno, he again regrets moving. The only stable community in Francisco's life is that of his family.

TIME & PLACE

This autobiographical incident describes the demands of itinerant—traveling—life on a migrant laborer's family. Being on "the circuit" meant moving to wherever there were crops that needed picking. The story takes place from late August to late November in the 1950s. During that period, the family in the story moves twice.

THE WRITER'S CRAFT
DECLARATIVE SENTENCE

"The Circuit" is told by a migrant worker who briefly attends the sixth grade. Because the story is told by a young person, it should sound like a young person. To achieve this effect, the author uses simple declarative sentences. In other words, many of the sentences contain one subject and one verb. "He had a right to be proud of it. He spent a lot of time looking at other cars. . . . He examined every inch of the car. He listened to the motor. . . ."

The Circuit

Francisco Jiménez

t was that time of year again. Ito, the strawberry sharecropper, did not smile. It was natural. The peak of the strawberry season was over and the last few days the workers, most of them **braceros,** were not picking as many boxes as they had during the months of June and July.

As the last days of August disappeared, so did the number of braceros. Sunday, only one—the best picker—came to work. I liked him. Sometimes we talked during our half-hour lunch break. That is how I found out he was from **Jalisco,** the same state in Mexico my family was from. That Sunday was the last time I saw him.

When the sun had tired and sunk behind the mountains, Ito signaled us that it was time to go home. "Ya esora," he yelled in his broken Spanish. Those were the words I waited for twelve hours a day, every day, seven days a week, week after week. And the thought of not hearing them again saddened me.

As we drove home Papá did not say a word. With both hands on the wheel, he stared at the dirt road. My older brother, Roberto, was also silent. He leaned his head back and closed his eyes. Once in a while he cleared from his throat the dust that blew in from outside.

Yes, it was that time of year. When I opened the front door to the shack, I stopped. Everything we owned was neatly packed in cardboard boxes. Suddenly I felt even more the weight of hours, days, weeks, and months of work. I sat down on a box. The thought of having to move to Fresno and knowing what was in store for me there brought tears to my eyes.

That night I could not sleep. I lay in bed thinking about how much I hated this move.

A little before five o'clock in the morning, Papá woke everyone up. A few minutes later, the yelling and screaming of my little brothers and sisters, for whom the move was a great adventure, broke the silence of dawn. Shortly, the barking of the dogs accompanied them.

While we packed the breakfast dishes, Papá went outside to start the "Carcanchita." That was the name Papá gave his '38 black Plymouth. He bought it in a used-car lot in Santa Rosa in the winter of 1949. Papá was very proud of his little **jalopy.** He had a right to be proud of it. He spent a lot of time looking at other cars before buying this one. When he finally chose the "Carcanchita," he checked it thoroughly before driving it out of the car lot. He examined every inch of the car. He listened to the motor, tilting his head from side to side like a parrot, trying to detect any noises that spelled car trouble. After being satisfied with the looks and sounds of the car, Papá then insisted

About the Author

Francisco Jiménez was born in 1943 in San Pedro, Tlaquepaque, Mexico. At age four, he moved to the United States with his father, who came as a migrant worker. In 1965, Jiménez became a United States citizen and later earned master's and doctorate degrees at Columbia University. In addition to writing stories about his own childhood, he contributes to textbooks on Spanish and literature. Jiménez is a professor of modern languages and literature at the University of Santa Clara, California.

UNITED STATES

MEXICO

The Circuit

FOCUS ON...
LANGUAGE

In "The Circuit," the narrator and his family speak many Spanish words. Locate the English definitions for each word or phrase listed below, writing a sample sentence in English for each.

braceros   Tienen que tener cuidado
listo   vámonos
mi carcanchita   quince
mi olla   corridos
es todo

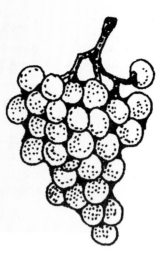

♦ ♦ ♦ ♦ ♦ ♦ ♦ ♦ ♦ ♦ ♦ ♦ ♦ ♦ ♦ ♦

braceros—See Focus On... Language (above) regarding this word and other Spanish words and phrases in the story.

Jalisco—a state in West Central Mexico

jalopy—a run-down automobile

on knowing who the original owner was. He never did find out from the car salesman, but he bought the car anyway. Papá figured the original owner must have been an important man because behind the rear seat of the car he found a blue necktie.

Papá parked the car out in front and left the motor running. "Listo," he yelled. Without saying a word, Roberto and I began to carry the boxes out to the car. Roberto carried the two big boxes and I carried the two smaller ones. Papá then threw the mattress on top of the car roof and tied it with ropes to the front and rear bumpers.

Everything was packed except Mamá's pot. It was an old large galvanized pot she had picked up at an army surplus store in Santa María the year I was born. The pot had many dents and nicks, and the more dents and nicks it acquired the more Mamá liked it. "Mi olla," she used to say proudly.

I held the front door open as Mamá carefully carried out her pot by both handles, making sure not to spill the cooked beans. When she got to the car, Papá reached out to help her with it. Roberto opened the rear car door and Papá gently placed it on the floor behind the front seat. All of us then climbed in. Papá sighed, wiped the sweat off his forehead with his sleeve, and said wearily: "Es todo."

As we drove away, I felt a lump in my throat. I turned around and looked at our little shack for the last time.

At sunset we drove into a labor camp near Fresno. Since Papá did not speak English, Mamá asked the camp foreman if he needed any more workers. "We don't need no more," said the foreman, scratching his head. "Check with Sullivan down the road. Can't miss him. He lives in a big white house with a fence around it."

When we got there, Mamá walked up to the house. She went through a white gate, past a row of rose bushes, up the stairs to the front door. She rang the doorbell. The porch light went on and a tall husky man came out. They exchanged a few words. After the man went in, Mamá clasped her hands and hurried back to the car. "We have work! Mr. Sullivan said we can stay there the whole season," she said, gasping and pointing to an old garage near the stables.

The garage was worn out by the years. It had no windows. The walls, eaten by termites, strained to support the roof full of holes. The dirt floor, populated by earth worms, looked like a gray road map.

That night, by the light of a kerosene lamp, we unpacked and cleaned our new home. Roberto swept away the loose dirt, leaving the hard ground. Papá plugged the holes in the walls with old newspapers and tin can tops. Mamá fed my little brothers and sisters. Papá and Roberto then brought in the mattress and placed it in the far corner of the garage. "Mamá, you and the little ones sleep on the mattress. Roberto, Panchito, and I will sleep outside under the trees," Papá said.

Early next morning Mr. Sullivan showed us where his crop was, and after breakfast, Papá, Roberto, and I headed for the vineyard to pick.

Around nine o'clock the temperature had risen to almost one hundred degrees. I was completely soaked in sweat and my mouth felt as if I had been chewing on a handkerchief. I walked over to the end of the row, picked up the jug of water we had brought, and began drinking. "Don't drink too much; you'll get sick," Roberto shouted. No sooner had he said that than I felt sick to my stomach. I dropped to my knees and let the jug roll off my hands. I remained motionless with my eyes glued on the hot sandy ground. All I could hear was the drone of insects. Slowly I began to recover. I poured water over my face and neck and watched the dirty water run down my arms to the ground.

I still felt a little dizzy when we took a break to eat lunch. It was past two o'clock and we sat underneath a large walnut tree that was on the side of the road. While we ate, Papá jotted down the number of boxes we had picked. Roberto drew designs on the ground with a stick. Suddenly I noticed Papá's face turn pale as he looked down the road. "Here comes the school bus," he whispered loudly in alarm. Instinctively, Roberto and I ran and hid in the vineyards. We did not want to get in trouble for not going to school. The neatly dressed boys about my age got off. They carried books under their arms. After they crossed the street, the bus drove away. Roberto and I came out from hiding and joined Papá. "Tienen que tener cuidado," he warned us.

After lunch we went back to work. The sun kept beating down. The buzzing insects, the wet sweat, and the hot dry dust made the afternoon seem to last forever. Finally the mountains around the valley reached out and swallowed the sun. Within an hour it was too dark to continue picking. The vines blanketed the grapes, making it difficult to see the bunches. "Vámonos," said Papá, signaling to us that it was time to quit work. Papá then took out a pencil and began to

● ● ● ● ● ● ●
"The grape season was over and I could now go to school."
● ● ● ● ● ● ●

SPOTLIGHT ON...
DRAWING CONCLUSIONS

"The Circuit" invites you to draw conclusions about the narrator's character. In your personal and professional life, repeatedly you will have to draw conclusions about situations and people you meet. Use these guidelines to draw your conclusions:

1. Collect relevant facts and information. Observe details.
2. Compare this evidence with what you already know, and have heard. Look for similarities or inconsistencies.
3. Ask yourself if you have enough evidence to draw a conclusion. If you don't, remain open-minded.

◆◆◆◆◆◆◆◆◆◆◆◆◆◆◆◆◆◆◆◆◆◆

figure out how much we had earned our first day. He wrote down numbers, crossed some out, wrote down some more. "Quince," he murmured.

When we arrived home, we took a cold shower underneath a waterhose. We then sat down to eat dinner around some wooden crates that served as a table. Mamá had cooked a special meal for us. We had rice and tortillas with "carne con chile," my favorite dish.

The next morning I could hardly move. My body ached all over. I felt little control over my arms and legs. This feeling went on every morning for days until my muscles finally got used to the work.

It was Monday, the first week of November. The grape season was over and I could now go to school. I woke up early that morning and lay in bed, looking at the stars and savoring the thought of not going to work and of starting sixth grade for the first time that year. Since I could not sleep, I decided to get up and join Papá and Roberto at breakfast. I sat at the table across from Roberto, but I

kept my head down. I did not want to look up and face him. I knew he was sad. He was not going to school today. He was not going tomorrow, or next week, or next month. He would not go until the cotton season was over, and that was sometime in February. I rubbed my hands together and watched the dry, acid-stained skin fall to the floor in little rolls.

When Papá and Roberto left for work, I felt relief. I walked to the top of a small grade next to the shack and watched the "Carcanchita" disappear in the distance in a cloud of dust.

Two hours later, around eight o'clock, I stood by the side of the road waiting for school bus number twenty. When it arrived I climbed in. Everyone was busy either talking or yelling. I sat in an empty seat in the back.

When the bus stopped in front of the school, I felt very nervous. I looked out the bus window and saw boys and girls carrying books under their arms. I put my hands in my pant pockets and walked to the principal's office. When I entered I heard a woman's voice say: "May I help you?" I was startled. I had not heard English for months. For a few seconds I remained speechless. I looked at the lady who waited for an answer. My first instinct was to answer her in Spanish, but I held back. Finally, after struggling for English words, I managed to tell her that I wanted to enroll in the sixth grade. After answering many questions, I was led to the classroom.

Mr. Lema, the sixth grade teacher, greeted me and assigned me a desk. He then introduced me to the class. I was so nervous and scared at that moment when everyone's eyes were on me that I wished I were with Papá and Roberto picking cotton. After taking roll, Mr. Lema gave the class the assignment for the first hour. "The first thing we have to do this morning is finish reading the story we began yesterday," he said enthusiastically. He walked up to me, handed me an English book, and asked me to read. "We are on page 125," he said politely. When I heard this, I felt my blood rush to my head; I felt dizzy. "Would you like to read?" he asked hesitantly. I opened the book to page 125. My mouth was dry. My eyes began to water. I could not begin. "You can read later," Mr. Lema said understandingly.

For the rest of the reading period I kept getting angrier and angrier with myself. I should have read, I thought to myself.

During recess I went into the restroom and opened my English book to page 125. I began to read in a low voice, pretending I was in class. There were

ACCENT ON...
CULINARY ARTS

In the story, the narrator's mother prepares his favorite dish, *carne con chile*. Find recipes for various Mexican dishes in cookbooks or from family and friends. As a class, plan a Mexican food fiesta, featuring a variety of Mexican dishes, recipes, and descriptions of meals or foods eaten on special occasions or holidays.

ON THE JOB
FARM LABORER

Farm laborers work on all kinds of farms in all regions of the country. They perform seasonal tasks that involve the care of animals and crop cultivation. Migrant laborers travel from job to job, picking crops that are too delicate to be harvested by machine. The work is physically demanding. Nearly all laborers learn their skills on the job. High school and vocational school courses on farming methods, carpentry, and equipment repair can help workers prepare for their job.

many words I did not know. I closed the book and headed back to the classroom.

Mr. Lema was sitting at his desk correcting papers. When I entered he looked up at me and smiled. I felt better. I walked up to him and asked if he could help me with the new words.

"Gladly," he said.

The rest of the month I spent my lunch hours working on English with Mr. Lema, my best friend at school.

One Friday during lunch hour Mr. Lema asked me to take a walk with him to the music room. "Do you like music?" he asked me as we entered the building.

"Yes, I like corridos," I answered. He then picked up a trumpet, blew on it and handed it to me. The sound gave me goose bumps. I knew that sound. I had heard it in many corridos. "How would you like to learn how to play it?" he asked. He must have read my face because before I could answer, he added; "I'll teach you how to play it during our lunch hours."

That day I could hardly wait to get home to tell Papá and Mamá the great news. As I got off the bus, my little brothers and sisters ran up to meet me. They were yelling and screaming. I thought they were happy to see me, but when I opened the door to our shack, I saw that everything we owned was neatly packed in cardboard boxes. ❖

UNDERSTANDING

1.  Using information in the story, list Francisco Jiménez's qualities and abilities. In a group, decide if each of these traits and abilities would help or hinder a modern student's efforts to succeed in an actual school situation, such as belonging to a team or club.

2. Mr. Lema gives time and attention to Francisco. In what passages do we discover the kind of teacher he is?

    Interview and write a feature article about a person you admire who deserves recognition. The purpose of this article is to make the audience understand and share your feelings about this person. *Workshops 17 and 24*

3. The only community—group—that Francisco belongs to is that of his family. With several classmates, discuss the kind of community his family provides. Base your comments on evidence from the text.

    A community is a group of people with common interests. In your group, list communities—other than those at school—that teenagers seem to join. Give reasons for their interest in these groups.

4. Although he does not complain, the narrator has a harsh life. List details in the text that reveal the hardship and poverty Francisco and his family experience.

    Prepare a chart comparing Francisco's average workday and living conditions with your own. To the chart, add a written statement of the conclusions you draw from this comparison. *Workshop 15*

A LAST WORD

To the narrator in "The Circuit," an education is a valuable and cherished opportunity. What does an education mean to you? What other opportunities might be opened to you because of a good education?

CONNECTING

1. The condition of migrant workers has long demanded, and continues to demand, serious attention. With a partner, gather information about the history and treatment of migrant workers from the Great Depression in the 1930s until today. Present your findings in a report to be sent to your representative in the state legislature or in Congress. *Workshop 21*

2. Jiménez says that he wrote about his experience as a field-worker because "it is what motivated me to work hard in acquiring my education." Do you think his attitude toward education is shared by those in your school? Conduct a survey of students in your school to find out what they think about education. Your survey should include at least five questions. Two of them might be, "Do you think school is preparing you for life after school?" and "If so, how?" Publish the survey results in the student paper. *Workshop 17*

Free and Equal

EXPLORING

• • • • • • • • • • • • • • • • • • • •

Partners and co-workers—and even spouses—sometimes compete for success. Success can take many forms. How do *you* measure it? When two friends are competing, does the competition weaken or otherwise damage their relationship, or do such competitors give each other support and help? Give examples to illustrate your ideas.

THEME CONNECTION... STRIVING TO BELONG

Ramesh, a native of India, is striving to find work in America. He fears that his individual merits will not be sufficient to earn acceptance in the workplace. Though he has the skills and knowledge for the job he seeks, he lacks the self-confidence to see himself as a qualified candidate.

TIME & PLACE

Written in 1988, "Free and Equal" takes place in a modern American city. References to action and setting are few as the author explains the thoughts of a member of a minority culture searching for work in a competitive job market.

THE WRITER'S CRAFT
INTERIOR MONOLOGUE

An interior monologue reveals a character's thoughts and feelings directly, as if the reader had entered the character's mind. In this interior monologue, Gandbhir presents only the *main* character's internal reflections, not those of other characters. We are in the main character's mind, reading his thoughts as he looks for work and considers people and circumstances.

Free and Equal
Lalita Gandbhir

 amesh carefully studied his reflection in the mirror hung in the hallway. His hair, shirt, tie, suit, nothing escaped his **scrutiny**. His tie seemed a little crooked, so he undid it and fixed it with slow deliberate movements. Then he reexamined the tie. A conservative shade of maroon, not too wide, not too narrow, just right for the occasion, for the image he wanted to project.

All of a sudden he was aware of two eyes staring at him. He turned to Jay, his little son. Jay sat on the steps leading to the second floor, his eyes focused on his father.

"Why are you staring at me?" Ramesh inquired.

"Going to work now?" Jay **intimated** the reason for the surprised stare.

Ramesh understood the reason behind Jay's confusion. He used to go to work dressed like this in the mornings. Jay had not seen him dressed in a suit in the evening.

For a moment Ramesh was proud of his son. "What a keen observer Jay is!" Ramesh thought to himself. "For six months I have not worked, yet he noticed a change in my old routine."

However, the implications behind the question bothered Ramesh.

"I am going to a job fair," he answered irritably and again attempted to focus on his tie.

"Can I come?" Jay promptly hurled a question in Ramesh's direction. To him a fair was a fun event. He had been to fairs with his mother before and did not wish to miss this one.

"Jay, this is not the kind of fair you are thinking of. This is a job fair."

"Do they sell jobs at job fairs?"

"Yes." Jay's question struck a sensitive spot. "No, they don't sell jobs. They are buyers. They shop for skills. It's me who is selling my skills. Unfortunately, it's a buyer's market."

The question stimulated Ramesh's chain of thought. "Is my skill for sale?" Ramesh wondered. "If that is true, then why did I dress so carefully? Why did I rehearse answers to imaginary questions from interviewers?"

"No, this job hunting is no longer a simple straightforward business transaction like it used to be when engineers were in demand. I am desperate. I am selling my soul. The job market is no longer a two-way street, I have no negotiating power. I just have to accept what I can get."

Ramesh pulled on his socks mechanically and longingly thought of the good old days like a sick old man thinking of his healthful youth.

Just ten years ago he had hopped from job to job at will. Money, interesting work, more responsibility, benefits, a whim for any reason that appealed to

About the Author
Lalita Gandbhir (b. 1938) has lived in Boston since 1963, when she arrived from India. Although she is a practicing physician, Gandbhir's avocation is writing. She has published short stories in Canadian and American journals and reviews.

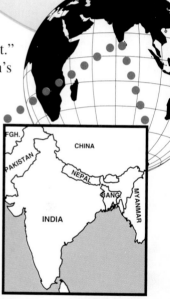

scrutiny—close inspection

intimated—hinted at

him, and he had switched jobs. Responding to advertisements was his hobby. Head hunters called him offering better and better situations. He went to job fairs casually dressed and never gave a second thought to his attire.

He had job offers, not one or two, but six or seven. The industry needed him then. It was so nice to be **coveted**!

Ramesh wiped his polished, spotless shoes with a soft cloth.

How carefree he used to be! He dressed like this every morning in five minutes and, yes, Jay remembers.

He never polished his shoes then. His hand moving the cloth on his shoes stood still for a minute. Yes, Rani, his wife, did it for him. Nowadays she seemed to do less and less for him. Why? He asked himself.

Rani had found a part-time job on her own when companies in the area had started to lay off engineers. She had not bothered to discuss the matter with him, just informed him of her decision. In a year she accepted a full-time slot. "How did she manage to receive promotions so soon?" Ramesh wondered.

Rani still ran the home and cared for their young children. Ramesh had seen her busy at all kinds of tasks from early morning until late at night.

Over the last three months she did less and less for Ramesh. She no longer did his laundry or ironing. She had stopped polishing his shoes and did not wait up for him when he returned late from job fairs.

"She is often tired," Ramesh tried to understand, but he felt that she had let him down, wronged him just when his spirit was sinking and he needed her most.

"She should have made an effort for the sake of appearance. It was her duty toward a jobless, incomeless husband."

He pushed all thoughts out of his mind.

He tied his polished shoes, dragged his heavy winter coat out of the closet, and picked up his keys.

"Tell your Ma that I have left," he ordered Jay, and closed the door without saying good-bye to Rani.

In the car, thoughts flooded his mind again.

Perhaps he made a mistake in coming to study abroad for his master's in engineering. No! That was not the error. He should not have stayed on after he received his master's. He should have returned home as he originally planned.

He intended to return, but unfortunately he attended a job fair after graduation just for fun and ended up accepting a job offer. A high salary in dollars converted into a small fortune in rupees, proved impossible to resist. He always converted dollars into rupees then, before buying or selling. He offered himself an excuse of short-term American experience and stayed on. The company that hired him sponsored him for a green card.

He still wanted to return home, but he postponed it, went for a visit instead and picked Rani from several prospective brides, married her and returned to the United States.

The trip left bitter memories, especially for Rani. He could not talk his mother out of accepting a dowry.

"Mother, Rani will earn the entire sum of a dowry in a month in the United States. A dowry is a hardship for her

FOCUS ON...
ECONOMICS

Ramesh, the husband in the story, was the wage earner for his family until he became unemployed. To cover the family's expenses, his wife finds part-time, then full-time work. Explore economic ways in which a family might survive unemployment. Interview people who have been laid off or unemployed. What steps did they take to meet their essential expenses? What items did they consider to be essential? On what things did they cut back?

middle-class family. Let us not insist on it. Just accept what her family offers."

But Mother, with Father's **tacit** support, insisted. "You are my only son. I have waited for this occasion all my life. I want a proper wedding, the kind of wedding our friends and relatives will remember forever."

Ramesh gave in to her wishes and had a wedding with pomp and special traditional honors for his family. His mother was only partially gratified because she felt that their family did not get what was due them with her foreign returned son! The dowry, however, succeeded in upsetting Rani, who looked miserable throughout the ceremony.

"We will refund all the money once you come to the United States," Ramesh promised her. "It's a minor sum when dollars are converted to rupees."

Instead of talking in his **conciliatory** tone, Rani demanded, too harshly for a bride, "If it's a minor sum, why did you let your family insist on a dowry? You know my parents' savings are wiped out."

Over a few years they refunded the money, but Rani's wounds never healed and during fights she referred to the dowry spitefully.

Her caustic remarks did not bother Ramesh before, but now with her income supporting the family, they were beginning to hurt. "Write your mother that your wife works and makes up for part of the dowry her father failed to provide!" she had remarked once.

"Don't women ever forgive?" he had wondered.

"I am extra sensitive." He brushed off the pain that Rani's words caused.

The job fair was at a big hotel. He followed the directions and turned into a full parking lot. As he pulled into the tight space close to the exit, he glanced at the hotel lobby. Through the glass exterior wall, underneath a brightly lit chandelier, he could see a huge crowd milling in the lobby.

Panic struck him. He was late. So many people had made it there ahead of him. All applicants with his experience and background might be turned away.

Another car approached and pulled into the last parking space in the lot.

tacit—silent

conciliatory— trying to please or gain goodwill

SPOTLIGHT ON...
BUILDING
SELF-ESTEEM

In the story, Ramesh's self-esteem has diminished during his six-month period of unemployment. When Ramesh does find work, Rani reminds him that he was hired because of his qualifications and experience. It is important for people to feel good about their abilities. You, too, can take satisfaction in the work you do. Keep in mind the following:

- Working hard and doing your best build self-esteem.
- All jobs are important, because each is part of a larger whole.
- Working responsibly and honestly helps you feel good about yourself and your work and earns the respect of others.

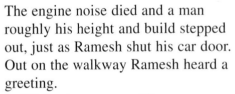

The engine noise died and a man roughly his height and build stepped out, just as Ramesh shut his car door. Out on the walkway Ramesh heard a greeting.

"Hello, how are you?"

Ramesh looked up.

In the fluorescent lights his eyes met friendly blue eyes. He noticed a slightly wrinkled forehead and receding hairline, like his own.

"Hello," Ramesh responded.

The stranger smiled. "Sometimes I wonder why I come to these fairs. In the last six months I must have been to at least ten."

"Really? So have I!" He must have been laid off at the same time, Ramesh thought.

"We must have attended the same ones. I don't remember seeing you," the newcomer said.

"Too many engineers looking for a job—you know," Ramesh offered as explanation.

The pair had approached the revolving lobby doors. Ramesh had a strong urge to turn back and return home.

"Come on, we must try." The newcomer apparently had sensed the urge. "My name is Bruce. Would you like to meet me at the door in an hour? We will have a drink before we go home. It will—kind of lift my spirits."

"All right," Ramesh agreed without thinking and added, "I am Ramesh."

Bruce waited for Ramesh to step into the revolving door.

Ramesh mechanically pushed into the lobby. His heart sagged even further. "With persons like Bruce looking for a job, who will hire a foreigner like me?" he wondered. He looked around. Bruce had vanished into the crowd.

Ramesh looked at a row of booths set up by the side wall. He approached one looking for engineers with his qualifications. A few Americans had already lined up to talk to the woman screening the applicants.

She looked at him and repeated the same questions she had asked applicants before him. "Your name, sir?"

He had to spell it. She made a mistake in noting it down. He had to correct her.

"Please fill out this application." He sensed a slight irritation in her voice.

"Thank you," he said. His accent seemed to have intensified. He took the application and retreated to a long table.

He visited six or seven booths of companies who might need—directly, indirectly, or remotely—someone of his experience and education; challenge, benefit package, location, salary, nothing mattered to him any more. He had to find a job.

An hour and a half later, as he approached the revolving door, he noticed Bruce waiting for him.

During the discussion over drinks, he discovered that Bruce had the same qualifications as himself. However, Bruce had spent several years wandering around the world, so he had only four years of experience. Ramesh had guessed right. Bruce had been laid off the same time as himself.

"It's been very hard," Bruce said. "What little savings we had are wiped out and my wife is fed up with me. She thinks I don't try hard. This role reversal is not good for a man's ego."

"Yes," Ramesh agreed.

"I may have to move but my wife doesn't want to. Her family is here."

"I understand."

"I figure you don't have that problem."

"No. You must have guessed I'm from India."

After a couple of drinks they walked out into an empty lobby and empty parking lot.

Two days later Bruce called. "Want to go to a job fair? It's in Woodland, two hundred miles from here. I hate to drive out alone." Ramesh agreed.

"Who will hire me when Americans are available?" he complained to Rani afterward.

"You must not think like that. You are as good as any of them," Rani snapped. "Remember what Alexander said."

Ramesh remembered. Alexander was a crazy history student with whom he had shared an apartment. Rani always referred to Alexander's message.

Ramesh had responded to an advertisement on his university's bulletin board and Alexander had answered the phone.

"You have to be crazy to share an apartment with me. My last roommate left because he could not live with me."

"What did you do? I mean, why did he leave?" Ramesh asked.

"I like to talk. You see, I wake up people and tell them about my ideas at night. They call me crazy Alexander."

"I will get back to you." Ramesh put the receiver down and talked to the student who had moved out.

"You see, Alexander's a nut. He sleeps during the day and studies at night. He's a history buff. He studies revolutions. He wakes up people just to talk to them, about theories, others and his own! He will offer to discount the rent if you put up with him."

Short of funds, Ramesh moved in with Alexander.

Much of Alexander's oratory bounced off Ramesh's half-asleep brain, but off and on a few sentences made an impression and stuck in his memory.

"You must first view yourself as free and equal," Alexander had said.

"Equal to whom?"

"To those around you who consider you less than equal . . . "

"Me? Less than equal?"

"No! Not you, stupid. The oppressed person. Oppression could be social, religious, foreign, traditional."

"Who oppressed me?"

"No! No! Not you! An imaginary oppressed person who must first see himself as the equal of his oppressors. The idea of equality will ultimately sow seeds of freedom and revolution in his mind. That idea is the first step. You see . . . stop snoring . . . That's the first step toward liberation."

Soon Ramesh walked like a zombie.

In another month, he too moved out.

After his marriage he told Rani some of his conversations with Alexander.

"Makes sense," she said, looking very earnest.

"Really! You mean you understand?" Rani's reaction amazed Ramesh.

"Yes, I do. I am an oppressed person, socially and traditionally. That's why my parents had to come up with a dowry."

A month went by and Ramesh was called for an interview.

● ● ● ● ● ● ●
"You must first view yourself as free and equal."
● ● ● ● ● ● ●

Bruce telephoned the same night. He and some other engineers he knew had also been called. Had Ramesh received a call, too?

Ramesh swallowed hard. "No, I didn't." He felt guilty and ashamed. He had lied to Bruce, who was so open, friendly, and supportive, despite his own difficulties.

Ramesh's ego had already suffered a major trauma. He was convinced that he would not get a job if Americans were available and he did not wish to admit to Bruce later on, "I had an interview, but they didn't hire me." It was easier to lie now.

The interview over, Ramesh decided to put the job out of his mind. His confidence at a low ebb, he dared not hope.

Three weeks went by and he received a phone call from the company that interviewed him. He had the job.

"They must have hired several engineers," Ramesh thought, elated.

Bruce called again. "I didn't get the job. The other guys I know have also received negative replies."

The news stunned Ramesh. He could not believe that he had the job and the others did not. As he pondered this, he realized he owed an embarrassing explanation to Bruce. How was he going to tell him that he had the job?

As Bruce jabbered about something, Ramesh collected his courage.

"I have an offer from them," he stated in a flat tone and strained his ear for a response.

Unit 2: The Individual and Society

After a few unbearable seconds of silence, Bruce exclaimed, "Congratulations! At least one of us made it. Now we can all hope. I know you have better qualifications."

Ramesh knew that the voice was sincere, without a touch of the envy he had anticipated.

They agreed to meet Saturday for a drink, a small celebration, Bruce suggested.

"Rani, I got the job. The others didn't." Ramesh hung up the receiver and bounded up to Rani.

"I told you you are as good as any of them," Rani responded nonchalantly and continued to fold laundry.

"Maybe . . . possibly . . . they needed a minority candidate," Ramesh muttered.

Rani stopped folding. "Ramesh," she said as her eyes scanned Ramesh's face, "You may have the job and the knowledge and the qualifications, but you are not free and equal."

"What do you mean?" Ramesh asked. ❖

ON THE JOB
CABLE TELEVISION ENGINEER

Cable television engineers design and develop cable television systems. They are skilled in electronics and work with all forms of cable and telecommunications equipment that receive satellite and microwave signals. In this rapidly changing field, engineers need to continually upgrade their knowledge. Helpful high school courses include math, computer science, and electronics. To enter the field, a bachelor's degree in electronics engineering is generally needed.

UNDERSTANDING

1. Ramesh's wife says, "I am an oppressed person, socially and traditionally." Locate in the text passages that support her claim. Consider whether she oppresses Ramesh; look for evidence.

   Governments can be guilty of oppression, but so can individuals. Brainstorm with several classmates about situations in which one person oppresses another. Suggest ways to deal with such behavior. Report your group's recommendations in an oral presentation. *Workshop 23*

2. Gandbhir describes the thoughts and feelings of a native of India seeking a job in America. Find passages that indicate Ramesh's feelings and attitudes.

   Probably you or someone you know has tried to find a job. In your journal, write a paragraph that describes your hopes, uncertainties, and other feelings about getting a job. Then, working with a partner, develop a 10-point list of ways to *prepare* for the job-hunting process and to overcome anxieties.

3. Bruce does not allow competition to make him behave badly. Find passages in the text that reveal Bruce's good nature.

   Competition often brings out people's bad traits. Interview adults to ask them about their experiences competing with others. List the qualities these adults assign to competitors. Compare this list with a list of Bruce's traits. Do the two lists agree? Share your conclusions with several classmates. Discuss the attitudes people *should* adopt in competitive situations.

A LAST WORD

In what way is equality a frame of mind? How might a clear understanding of your abilities and qualities lead you to believe in your individual freedom and equality? How will such a belief help you when looking for a job?

CONNECTING

1. According to crazy Alexander's philosophy, freedom is largely a state of mind. Gather information about the idea of freedom. Often individuals want to have their own way. How do we balance private, individual desires with those of the larger group? When is it appropriate, if ever, for an individual to give up personal freedom for the good of the community? Write a composition answering these questions. *Workshop 8*

2. In a group, design a one-day job fair for students at your school. Make a list of businesses you would like to invite. Write a standard letter of invitation to the businesses. In the letter, be sure to include date, location, and a schedule for the day. *Workshop 18*

Connections with Each Other

- *from Meditation 17*
- *A Break in the Rain*

EXPLORING

How do you balance being an individual with being a member of a community, whether the community is your family, school, athletic team, town, or some other group to which you belong? Does the need to belong come in conflict at times with the need to be independent? How deep is our longing to connect with others? Are we inevitably linked with other people?

THEME CONNECTION...
CONNECTING WITH OTHERS

Different though they are in form and style, both the 17th-century "Meditation 17" by John Donne and Marilyn Chin's modern poem "A Break in the Rain" explore the issue of our connection with others. Both writers remind us that we live among other human beings. Both imply that we need to care about each other.

TIME & PLACE

John Donne wrote "Meditation 17" in 1624 when he was recovering from a serious fever that had killed a great many of London's citizens. Gravely ill and likely to die, Donne heard church bells tolling around London. The Church of England required the priest in every parish church to ring the church bells when a person lay dying, and again when the person died, and once again to mark the funeral.

Marilyn Chin writes a modern-day poem about feeling left out by others. The speaker's desire to belong could happen anywhere, among any group of people.

THE WRITER'S CRAFT

REPETITION

Donne repeats ideas, saying the same thing in different ways to dramatize his point. "Every man is a piece of the continent" is the same as saying that every man is "a part of the main[land]." Repeating the word "tolls" underlines Donne's view that the funeral bell tolls not just for the dead man, but for all other human beings, too.

Marilyn Chin repeats words for effect. For instance, "better," "play," and "wait" are repeated as the speaker advises "you" to play, yet to wait for a chance to be accepted. Notice that Chin uses familiar words and the word order of daily conversation.

from Meditation 17
John Donne

 o man is an island, entire of itself; every man is a piece of the continent, a part of the main. If a clod be washed away by the sea, Europe is the less, as well as if a promontory were, as well as if a manor of thy friend's or of thine own were. Any man's death diminishes me because I am involved in mankind, and therefore never **send to know** for whom the bell tolls; it tolls for thee. ❖

send to know— meaning "send someone to find out"

About the Author

John Donne (1572–1631) is among the greatest of England's poets. As a young man, he studied at Oxford, traveled abroad, served as a soldier, and wrote love poems. In 1615, Donne—who had converted from Catholicism to the Anglican Church—finally became an Anglican priest and was made dean of St. Paul's Cathedral in London. He was a popular preacher, and many of his sermons and meditations were published during his lifetime.

SCOTLAND

IRELAND

ENGLAND

LONDON

FRANCE

FOCUS ON... LITERATURE

John Donne created vividly striking metaphors in his writing. The 17th century was an age of intellectual turbulence and great discovery. In his images and metaphors, Donne draws on new discoveries and material in astronomy, natural science, medicine, metallurgy, law, philosophy, and theology. Read a number of other songs, sonnets, and elegies written by Donne. Identify their metaphors. Then analyze the comparisons Donne is making with them.

◆ ◆ ◆ ◆ ◆ ◆ ◆ ◆ ◆ ◆ ◆ ◆

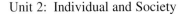

A Break in the Rain
Marilyn Chin

Better squat
Better squat than sit—
   sitting is too comfortable.
Better squat than stand—
   standing is too expectant.
Better squat and wait—
   as many have done before you,
head bent, knees hugged, body curled.

Better play
And after all,
it is only Ping-Pong,
a game,
one to a side,
fixed points & boundaries,
a net that divides.
You needn't talent
or money,
only a green table
& white balls.
At first you play at the Y,
perhaps later
at Julie's or Mary's
in a freshly paneled room,
should you be invited.

Better dance
With the one named Rochester
who likes your kind.
Let us dub him
"the point of entry."
Suddenly, he noticed
your latticed hair.

Better wait
The queues are long
& the amenities spare.

But *do* play.
Play,
dance, sing,
wait for a break in the rain. ❖

About the Author
Marilyn Chin, born in Hong Kong in 1955, grew up in Portland, Oregon. She earned a bachelor's degree in ancient Chinese literature at the University of Massachusetts and received a master of fine arts degree in poetry from Iowa State University. She is the recipient of numerous awards for her poetry.

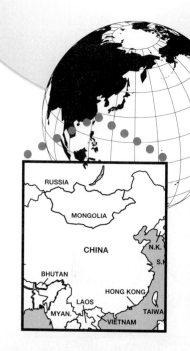

Connections with Each Other

UNDERSTANDING

1. "A Break in the Rain" refers to waiting. Where is waiting mentioned in the poem and what is it that "you" are waiting for?

   Write an essay explaining a time when you had to wait. Maybe you were waiting for someone, or to hear some news. Your essay should contain a central point you wish to make, as well as an introduction, conclusion, and vivid details. *Workshop 8*

2. Marilyn Chin pays close attention to crafting sentences. Write out the complete sentences in her poem. Are the sentences easy to understand? If so, why? Are the sentences of similar length? Do they include adjectives and nouns?

   Write a letter giving a new student advice on how to make friends at school, using the poem as a guide. In your letter, use sentences that vary in length, that follow the basic subject-verb pattern, and that use few adjectives and adverbs.

3. Chin's poem suggests a longing to be accepted. However, it also acknowledges the need to wait. What experiences does Chin compare with waiting?

   Donne and Chin both use comparisons, or analogies, to convey their ideas. Analogies can involve familiar, concrete things or abstract, unusual things. Write about a time when you faced a serious, perhaps dangerous, challenge. Use an analogy in this essay to help the reader grasp what you went through. *Workshop 9*

A LAST WORD

Some people seem to have a gift for making every moment of life count. How might you embrace life? How does the fact of your mortality affect the way you choose to live ?

CONNECTING

1. Have you ever been disappointed or frustrated because you wanted to do something or go somewhere but couldn't? With two classmates, discuss and agree on one such activity or project that you think your class would enjoy and benefit from—and that must be worked toward as a goal.

   Collaborate with group members to develop a feasibility report explaining this goal and exactly how it might be achieved. Present your report to your classmates.

2. During the 17th century, social principles about marriage and death were very clear. Gather information about today's customs and practices concerning either marriage or death. Research extensively, consulting, for example, the library's On-line Public Access Catalogue System and *Reader's Guide to Periodical Literature*. Present your findings in a written research report accompanied by appropriate visual aids. *Workshop 21*

Teenage Roles

- *Fifteen*
- *Fifteen*

EXPLORING

● ● ● ● ● ● ● ● ● ● ● ● ● ● ● ● ● ●

Longing is an emotion common to all human beings. We may fantasize and long for something unattainable—something impossible. Or we may long for something we *can* achieve, such as getting a driver's license. Brainstorm with several classmates about things teenagers long for. List these things under either "Attainable Longings" or "Impossible Dreams." After each entry, note whether the longing is for something that satisfies a basic human need or a personal desire.

THEME CONNECTION...
LONGING TO FIND A PLACE

According to Stafford and Greene, fifteen-year-olds live in a state of longing. Greene's teenagers—Dan and Dave—long especially for things that will help them connect with other teenagers: a driver's license, girlfriends, and athletic skill. Stafford's teenager longs for adventure and freedom.

TIME & PLACE

Greene's essay "Fifteen" was published in 1983. Stafford's poem "Fifteen" was written two decades earlier. In spite of changing times, the themes are similar. The settings differ, from a city mall to a country road, but the portraits of teenagers have a good deal in common.

THE WRITER'S CRAFT
DESCRIPTION

Description consists of vivid details that show the reader how things feel, sound, taste, look, and smell. These details etch a story or poem on the reader's mind. Stafford and Greene both use description for various, specific purposes.

Fifteen

Bob Greene

"This would be excellent, to go in the ocean with this thing," says Dave Gembutis, fifteen.

He's looking at a $170 Sea Cruiser raft. "Great," says his companion, Dan Holmes, also fifteen.

This is at Herman's World of Sporting Goods, in the middle of the Woodfield Mall in Schaumburg, Illinois.

The two of them keep staring at the raft. It is unlikely that they will purchase it. For one thing, Dan has only twenty dollars in his pocket, Dave five dollars. For another thing—ocean voyages aside—neither of them is even old enough to drive. Dave's older sister, Kim, has dropped them off at the mall. They will be taking the bus home.

Fifteen. What a weird age to be male. Most of us have forgotten about it, or have idealized it. But when you are fifteen . . . well, things tend to be less than perfect.

You can't drive. You are only in Grade 10 in high school. The girls your age look older than you and go out with older guys who have cars. You probably don't shave. You have nothing to do on the weekends.

So how do you spend your time? In the 1990s, most likely at a mall. Woodfield is an enclosed shopping center sprawling over 686,507 square feet in northern Illinois. There are 230 stores at Woodfield, and on any given Saturday those stores are cruised in and out by thousands of teenagers killing time. Today two of these teenagers are Dave Gembutis and Dan Holmes.

Dave is wearing a purple Rolling Meadows High School Mustangs windbreaker over a gray "M*A*S*H" T-shirt, jeans, and Nike running shoes. He has a red plastic spoon in his mouth and will keep it there for most of the afternoon. Dan is wearing a white Ohio State Buckeyes T-shirt, jeans, and Nike running shoes.

We are in the Video Forum store. Paul Simon and Art Garfunkel are singing "Wake Up Little Susie" from their Central Park concert on four television screens. Dave and Dan have already been wandering around Woodfield for an hour.

"There's not too much to do at my house," Dan says to me.

"Here we can at least look around," Dave says. "At home I don't know what we'd do."

"Play catch or something," Dan says. "Here there's lots of things to see."

"See some girls or something, start talking," Dave says.

I ask them how they would start a conversation with girls they had never met.

"Ask them what school they're from," Dan says. "Then if they say Arlington Heights High School or something, you can say, 'Oh, I know somebody from there.'"

About the Author

Newspaper and magazine columnist Bob Greene presents the human side of news stories. As Greene says, "I like to think of my stories as snapshots of life in America . . . snapshots taken as I wander around the country seeing what turns up." Greene is a syndicated columnist for the *Chicago Tribune;* his column appears in more than 200 newspapers in the United States. Greene is also a contributing editor of *Esquire* magazine, where his "American Beat" column appears each month.

I ask them how important meeting girls is to their lives.

"About forty-five percent," Dan says.

"About half your life," Dave says.

"Half is girls," Dan says. "Half is going out for sports."

An hour later, Dave and Dan have yet to meet any girls. They have seen a girl from their own class at Rolling Meadows High, but she is walking with an older boy, holding his hand. Now we are in the Woodfield McDonald's. Dave is eating a McRib sandwich, a small fries, and a small Coke. Dan is eating a cheeseburger, a small fries, and a medium root beer.

In here, the dilemma is obvious. The McDonald's is filled with girls who are precisely as old as Dave and Dan. The girls are wearing eye shadow, are fully developed, and generally look as if they could be dating the Green Bay Packers. Dave and Dan, on the other hand . . . well, when you're a fifteen-year-old boy, you look like a fifteen-year-old boy.

"They go with the older guys who have the cars," Dan says.

"It makes them more popular," Dave says.

"My ex-girlfriend is seeing a junior," Dan says.

I ask him what happened.

"Well, I was in Florida over spring vacation," he says. "And when I got back I heard that she was at Cinderella Rockefella one night, and she was dancing with this guy, and she liked him, and he drove her home and stuff."

"She two-timed him," Dave says.

"The guy's on the basketball team," Dan says.

I ask Dan what he did about it.

"I broke up with her," he says, as if I had asked the stupidest question in the world.

I ask him how he did it.

"Well, she was at her locker," he says. "She was working the combination. And I said, 'Hey, Linda, I want to break up.' And she was opening her locker door and she just nodded her head yes. And I said, 'I hear you had a good time while I was gone, but I had a better time in Florida.'"

I ask him if he feels bad about it.

"Well, I feel bad," he says. "But a lot of guys told me, 'I heard you broke up with her. Way to be.'"

"It's too bad the Puppy Palace isn't open," Dan says.

"They're remodeling," Dave says.

We are walking around the upper level of Woodfield. I ask them why they would want to go to the Puppy Palace.

"The dogs are real cute and you feel sorry for them," Dan says.

We are in a fast-food restaurant called the Orange Bowl. Dave is eating a frozen concoction called an O-Joy. They still have not met any girls.

"I feel like I'd be wasting my time if I sat at home," Dan says. "If it's Friday or Saturday and you sit home, it's considered . . . low."

"Coming to the mall is about all there is," Dave says. "Until we can drive."

"Then I'll cruise," Dan says. "Look for action a little farther away from my house, instead of just riding my bike around."

"When you're sixteen, you can do anything," Dave says. "You can go all the way across town."

SPOTLIGHT ON...
USING
NONVERBAL CUES

In Greene's article, Dan and Dave understand the nonverbal snub communicated to them by a couple of girls. Nonverbal communication, however, can be used for other, more positive purposes. As you talk with friends or family members, give oral presentations in school, or communicate with co-workers on the job, you probably use some of the following nonverbal cues:

- **Body language**—Hand or arm motions can emphasize key points or show concern, whereas shrugging shoulders can communicate lack of knowledge or interest.
- **Facial expression**—Smiles, scowls, raising eyebrows, and rolling the eyes are just a few expressions that can communicate happiness, anger, surprise, disgust, or other emotions.
- **Tone of voice**—Sadness, sarcasm, seriousness, and so on, can be conveyed through tone of voice.

◆ ◆ ◆ ◆ ◆ ◆ ◆ ◆ ◆ ◆ ◆ ◆ ◆ ◆ ◆ ◆ ◆ ◆ ◆

"When you have to ride your bike . . ." Dan says. "When it rains, it ruins everything."

In the J. C. Penney store, the Penney Fashion Carnival is under way. Wally the Clown is handing out favors to children, but Dave and Dan are watching the young female models parade onto a stage in bathing suits.

"Just looking is enough for me," Dan says.

Dave suggests that they head out back into the mall and pick out some girls to wave to. I ask why.

"Well, see, even if they don't wave back, you might see them later in the day," Dan says. "And then they might remember that you waved at them, and you can meet them."

We are at the Cookie Factory. These guys eat approximately every twenty minutes.

It is clear that Dan is attracted to the girl behind the counter. He walks up, and his voice is slower and about half an octave lower than before.

The tone of voice is going to have to carry the day, because the words are not all that romantic:

"Can I have a chocolate-chip cookie?"

The girl does not even look up as she wraps the cookie in tissue paper.

Dan persists. The voice might be Clark Gable's:

"What do they cost?"

The girl is still looking down.

"Forty-seven," she says and takes his money, still looking away, and we move on.

Dave and Dan tell me that there are lots of girls at Woodfield's indoor ice-skating rink. It costs money to get inside, but they lead me to an exit door, and when a woman walks out we slip into the rink. It is chilly in here, but only three people are on the ice.

"It's not time for open skating yet," Dan says. "This is all private lessons."

"Not much in here," Dave says.

We sit on benches. I ask them if they wish they were older.

"Well," Dan says, "when you get there, you look back and you remember. Like I'm glad that I'm not in the fourth or fifth grade now. But I'm glad I'm not twenty-five, either."

"Once in a while I'm sorry I'm not twenty-one," Dave says. "There's not much you can do when you're fifteen. This summer I'm going to caddy and try to save some money."

"Yeah," Dan says. "I want to save up for a dirt bike."

"Right now, being fifteen is starting to bother me a little bit." Dave says. "Like when you have to get your parents to drive you to Homecoming with a girl."

I ask him how that works.

"Well, your mom is in the front seat driving," he says. "And you're in the back seat with your date."

I ask him how he feels about that.

"It's embarrassing," he says. "Your date understands that there's nothing you can do about it, but it's still embarrassing."

Dave says he wants to go to Pet World.

"I think they closed it down," Dan says, but we head in that direction anyway.

I ask them what the difference is between Pet World and the Puppy Palace.

"They've got snakes and fish and another assortment of dogs," Dan says. "But not as much as the Puppy Palace."

When we arrive, Pet World is, indeed, boarded up.

We are on the upper level of the mall. Dave and Dan have spotted two girls sitting on a bench directly below them, on the mall's main level.

"Whistle," Dan says. Dave whistles, but the girls keep talking.

"Dave, wave to them and see if they look," Dan says.

"They aren't looking," Dave says.

"There's another one over there," Dan says.

"Where?" Dave says.

"Oh, that's a mother," Dan says. "She's got her kid with her."

They return their attention to the two downstairs.

Dan calls to them: "Would you girls get the dollar I just dropped?"

The girls look up.

"Just kidding," Dan says.

The girls resume their conversation.

"I think they're laughing," Dan says.

"What are you going to do when the dumb girls won't respond," Dave says.

"At least we tried," Dan says.

I ask him what response would have satisfied him.

"The way we would have known that we succeeded," he says, "they'd have looked up here and started laughing."

The boys keep staring at the two girls.

"Ask her to look up," Dan says. "Ask her what school they go to."

"I did," Dave says. "I did."

The two boys lean over the railing.

"Bye, girls," Dave yells.

"See you later," Dan yells.

The girls do not look up.

"Too hard," Dan says. "Some girls are stuck on themselves, if you know what I mean by that."

We go to a store called the Foot Locker, where all the salespeople are dressed in striped referee's shirts.

"Dave!" Dan says. "Look at this! Seventy bucks!" He holds up a pair of New Balance running shoes. Both boys shake their heads.

We move on to a store called Passage to China. A huge stuffed tiger is placed by the doorway. There is a PLEASE DO NOT TOUCH sign attached to it. Dan rubs his hand over the tiger's back. "This would look so great in my room," he says.

We head over to Alan's TV and Stereo. Two salesmen ask the boys if they are interested in buying anything, so they go back outside and look at the store's window. A color television set is tuned to a baseball game.

They watch for five minutes. The sound is muted, so they cannot hear the announcers.

"I wish they'd show the score," Dave says.

They watch for five minutes more.

"Hey, Dave," Dan says. "You want to go home?"

"I guess so," Dave says.

They do. We wave good-bye. I watch them walk out of the mall toward the bus stop. I wish them girls, dirt bikes, puppies, and happiness. ❖

ON THE JOB
JOURNALIST

Journalists gather the news in order to keep the public informed about important events. They obtain the information they need from a variety of sources: personal interviews, news briefings, and reports from wire services. Some reporters specialize in covering the news in a certain field, such as sports, science, or crime. Journalists must have excellent writing and communication skills. Helpful high school courses include English, journalism, social studies, and typing.

Fifteen

William Stafford

South of the Bridge on Seventeenth
I found back of the willows one summer
day a motorcycle with engine running
as it lay on its side, ticking over
slowly in the high grass. I was fifteen.

I admired all that pulsing gleam, the
shiny flanks, the **demure** headlights
fringed where it lay; I led it gently
to the road and stood with that
companion, ready and friendly. I was fifteen.

We could find the end of a road, meet
the sky on out Seventeenth. I thought about
hills, and patting the handle got back a
confident opinion. On the bridge we indulged
a forward feeling, a tremble. I was fifteen.

Thinking, back farther in the grass I found
the owner, just coming to, where he had flipped
over the rail. He had blood on his hand, was pale—
I helped him walk to his machine. He ran his hand
over it, called me good man, roared away.

I stood there, fifteen. ❖

About the Author

William Stafford (1914–1993) grew
up in Kansas and received a bachelor's degree from the University of
Kansas, where he supported himself
in part by waiting tables. As World
War II broke out, he declared himself
a conscientious objector and was
forced to serve in a government
camp from 1940 to 1946. In 1948
Stafford was hired to teach at
Lewis and Clark College in
Portland, Oregon. His books of
poetry have earned him
recognition as an accom-
plished American
poet.

demure—
modest

UNDERSTANDING

1.  Bob Greene's "Fifteen" was originally published in an *Esquire* magazine column titled "American Beat." Though the column is not written in interview form, Greene does ask Dan and Dave several questions. List these questions.

   With a partner, prepare 12 interview questions you think should be asked by anyone trying to understand what students in your grade are like.

2. In Stafford's poem, the speaker faces and passes a test of character. Confronted with a choice, he chooses well. His decision earns him praise: "good man." Identify the lines in the poem that support these claims.

   Write a narrative essay that tells about some test of character you faced and handled well. Use concrete details to make your narrative clear and memorable. *Workshop 9*

3. Both Stafford and Greene depict the unsatisfied longings of teenagers. List these longings. In an essay, compare and contrast the things you think teenagers want with the things Greene and Stafford say they long for. *Workshop 15*

A LAST WORD

Do you think each age has certain characteristics or types of experiences? How might you let yourself enjoy each age to the fullest?

CONNECTING

1.  In a volume titled *You Must Revise Your Life,* Stafford states that in the 1960s—during the Vietnam War—poetry brought people together. Audiences came to hear poets express everyone's thoughts and emotions. With your class, identify an issue that people feel strongly about. Schedule a time and place to hold a Community Reading on that issue. Seek volunteers to read their own writing or selections from writing they admire. Prepare and read your own material. Plan to follow the readings with audience participation in discussion.

2. Dan Holmes and Dave Gembutis in "Fifteen" spend the day at Woodfield Mall in Schaumburg, Illinois. Work with several classmates to examine a local mall and propose changes that would improve the way it serves young people. If no mall exists nearby, write to the manager of a well-known mall such as the Mall of America in Bloomington, Minnesota, asking for a complete description of the mall's features. Write a proposal, accompanied by graphics, setting forth your ideas for how the mall could best serve teenagers. Send it to the manager of the mall you study. *Workshops 13 and 22*

3. Dave and Dan in Greene's article go to the mall because they don't know what else to do with themselves. They can't drive, they haven't much money, and there's not much to do at home. In a group, research entertainment for teenagers living in your area. List and describe available entertainment on a colorful poster to display in the school.

UNIT 2

WRAP IT UP

1. Angelou's essay urges us to pluck up the courage "to win back our finer and kinder and healthier selves." In his letter, Fitzgerald advises his daughter not to worry about popular opinion, but instead to worry about courage. The selections from *Tao te Ching* teach that the paths toward respect and serenity come from being yourself and doing your work. Donne's meditation reminds us that we are not alone, we are connected to all humanity. In Chin's poem, "A Break in the Rain," the narrator urges, "But *do* play." Select two authors from this unit and compare and contrast each author's philosophy about how an individual should live his or her life. Consider, for instance, how an individual should interact with society.

2. Each of the characters in "Marriage Is a Private Affair," "By Any Other Name," "The Circuit," and "Free and Equal" struggles to be an equal and free individual in society. How are the characters' struggles similar? How are they different? What do each of the characters believe will make a difference in their lives—will make them equal? Use details from the selections to support your conclusions.

Teenage Roles

95

UNIT

③

IMAGINATION AND REALITY

Imagination is the creative power that enables us to make things we have never seen and to picture things that do not exist. "What if . . . ?" is a question that drives the imagination to change society, make discoveries, and write books. The imagination reveals that learning to cook, studying music, or following some other path will improve our own lives. It helps scientists think up cures for diseases. In addition to showing us how to improve the realities of ordinary life, the imagination gives us wings. It lets us picture non-existent worlds exactly to our liking, to paint pictures and write novels. Human beings have flourished because of the power of imagination.

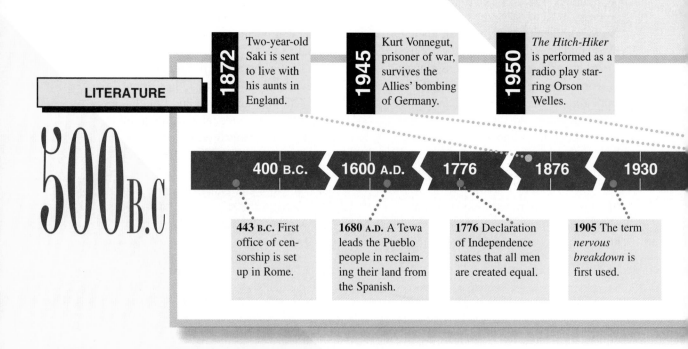

LITERATURE

500 B.C

1872 Two-year-old Saki is sent to live with his aunts in England.

1945 Kurt Vonnegut, prisoner of war, survives the Allies' bombing of Germany.

1950 *The Hitch-Hiker* is performed as a radio play starring Orson Welles.

400 B.C. — 1600 A.D. — 1776 — 1876 — 1930

443 B.C. First office of censorship is set up in Rome.

1680 A.D. A Tewa leads the Pueblo people in reclaiming their land from the Spanish.

1776 Declaration of Independence states that all men are created equal.

1905 The term *nervous breakdown* is first used.

The Hitch-Hiker
—Lucille Fletcher

The Open Window
—Saki

I'm Making You Up
—Chrystos

Future Tense
—Robert Lipsyte

Beware: Do Not Read This Poem
—Ishmael Reed

The Snow Woman
—Norah Burke

Deer Hunter and White Corn Maiden
—American Indian (Tewa) Folktale

from *An American Childhood*
—Annie Dillard

Harrison Bergeron
—Kurt Vonnegut

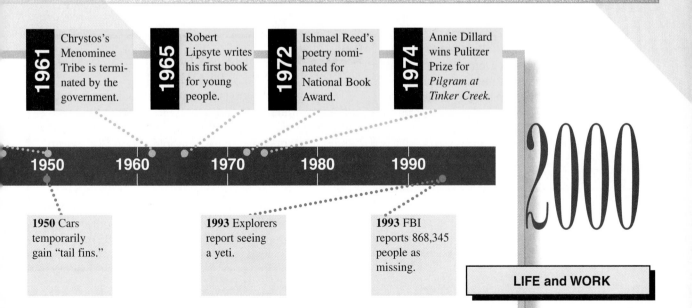

1961 Chrystos's Menominee Tribe is terminated by the government.

1965 Robert Lipsyte writes his first book for young people.

1972 Ishmael Reed's poetry nominated for National Book Award.

1974 Annie Dillard wins Pulitzer Prize for *Pilgram at Tinker Creek.*

1950 1960 1970 1980 1990

2000

1950 Cars temporarily gain "tail fins."

1993 Explorers report seeing a yeti.

1993 FBI reports 868,345 people as missing.

LIFE and WORK

The Hitch-Hiker

EXPLORING

Every culture has beliefs concerning what happens to people when they die. For example, some believe that the spirit of a person who has died lingers on Earth until rituals release it. Others believe that a spirit is sent immediately to accompany the dying person's soul to the next world. With your class, consider whether you want spirits to reside on Earth. What problems or benefits might result from their presence?

THEME CONNECTION...
APPEARANCES DECEIVE

Sometimes things are not what they seem. For instance, the well-dressed hitch-hiker may be dangerous, and the unkempt hitch-hiker may be kind. In "The Hitch-Hiker," things appear to Ronald Adams to be normal. Furthermore, when others first meet him, he looks as ordinary as any other person. We discover that reality is quite different than Adams or others might imagine it to be. When our imaginations accept appearances at face value, we are likely to be deceived.

TIME & PLACE

This play occurs in the 1950s when freeways were being constructed and cross-country driving was becoming a possibility. Under President Dwight D. Eisenhower's administration in the 1950s, building a system of roads linking one coast with the other was a major priority. Before that time, highway construction had come almost to a halt because of the Great Depression and World War II. Mrs. Adams' concern about her son's safety when he embarks on his trip reflects the hesitancy of someone unaccustomed to the idea of a cross-country drive.

THE WRITER'S CRAFT
ESTABLISHING CREDIBILITY

The playwright's job is to make the audience accept and enjoy characters and events, even when they are fantastic. Lucille Fletcher does so in several ways. She has characters speak as real people might. She is true to the logic of her tale. For instance, Ronald Adams begins telling his story by saying he is struggling to keep sane. Events in the story show why his sanity would be threatened. By keeping details consistent with one another and by using effective dialogue, dramatists can persuade people to accept their plays, no matter how unrealistic they might be.

The Hitch-Hiker
Lucille Fletcher

Cast
Ronald Adams
Mrs. Adams
The Hitch-Hiker
Filling Station Man
Road Stand Proprietor
Road Stand Proprietor's Wife
Girl Hitch-Hiker
Local Gallup Operator
Long Distance Operator
New York Operator
Albuquerque Operator
Mrs. Whitney

Technical Crew
Director
Music
Sound Recordings
Manual Recordings One
Manual Recordings Two

Music: *Opening chords, dark and ominous. A piano may be used, or a brief passage from some orchestral record. The selection will depend on the* **Director's** *individual taste, but its major effect should consist of a strong, terrifying opening, followed by a kind of monotonous eeriness. The eerie part of the music continues throughout the following speech, but faded down so that the words are audible.*

[**Scene:** *As curtains part, we see a stage set up for a radio broadcast. Central microphone, at which* **Ronald Adams** *is standing. A semicircle of chairs, rear, on which entire cast is seated. Sound effects and music grouped wherever their level will complement and bolster the voice, but not overbalance it. Relative sound levels are vitally important in this production, and should be carefully studied for maximum effectiveness.*]

RONALD ADAMS. I am in an auto camp on Route Sixty-six just west of Gallup, New Mexico. If I tell it, perhaps it will help me. It will keep me from going mad. But I must tell this quickly. I am not mad now. I feel perfectly well, except that I am running a slight temperature. My name is Ronald Adams. I am thirty-six years of age, unmarried, tall, dark, with a black moustache. I drive a Buick, license number 6Y-175-189. I was born in Brooklyn. All this I know. I know that I am at this moment perfectly sane. That it is not me who has gone mad—but something else—something utterly beyond my control. But I must speak quickly. At any moment the link may break. This may be the last thing I ever tell on earth . . . the last night I ever see the stars . . . (*Pause. Music fades out.*) [**Scene: Mrs. Adams** *rises from chair, rear, and comes forward to microphone.*] Six days ago I left Brooklyn, to drive to California.

MRS. ADAMS. Good-bye, son. Good luck to you, my boy.

ADAMS. Good-bye, Mother. Here— give me a kiss, and then I'll go.

MRS. A. I'll come out with you to the car.

ADAMS. No. It's raining. Stay here at the door. Hey—what's this? Tears? I thought you promised me you wouldn't cry.

MRS. A. I know, dear. I'm sorry. But I— do hate to see you go.

ADAMS. I'll be back. I'll only be on the Coast three months.

MRS. A. Oh—it isn't that. It's just—the trip. Ronald—I wish you weren't driving.

ADAMS. Oh, Mother. There you go again. People do it every day.

MRS. A. I know. But you'll be careful, won't you? Promise me you'll be extra careful. Don't fall asleep—or drive fast—or pick up any strangers on the road.

ADAMS. Gosh—no. You'd think I was still seventeen to hear you talk.

MRS. A. And wire me as soon as you get to Hollywood, won't you, son?

ADAMS. Of course I will. Now, don't you worry. There isn't anything going to happen. It's just eight days of perfectly simple driving on smooth civilized roads. (**Manual Sound:** *Slam of car door.* **Sound Recording:** *Car starts. Sound of car motor running.*) With a hot dog or a hamburger stand every ten miles . . . (*He chuckles slightly.*) (**Sound Recording:** *Automobile in motion full.*) (*Calling.*) G'bye, Mom— [**Scene: Mrs. Adams** *leaves microphone, returning to row of chairs at rear stage.*] (*Sound recording of automobile continues behind following.*) I was in excellent spirits. The drive ahead of me, even the loneliness, seemed like a lark. But I reckoned— without—*him.* (**Music:** *Dark opening chords, followed by theme of eerie quality. Continue faded down as before, mingling with sound of car motor running.*) Crossing Brooklyn Bridge that morning in the rain, I saw a man leaning against the cables. He seemed to be waiting for a lift. There were spots of fresh rain on his shoulders. He was carrying a cheap overnight bag in one hand. He was thin, **nondescript,** with a cap pulled down over his eyes . . . (*Music fades out. Sound of auto continues.*) I would have forgotten him completely, except that just an hour later, while crossing the Pulaski Skyway over the Jersey flats, I saw him again. At least he looked like the same person. He was standing now, with one thumb pointing west. I couldn't figure out how he'd got there, but I thought probably one of those fast trucks had picked him up, beaten me to the Skyway, and let him off. I didn't stop for him. Then—late that night—I saw him again. (**Music:** *Dark ominous chords, followed by eerie theme.*

Continue through following speech.)
It was on the new Pennsylvania
Turnpike between Harrisburg and
Pittsburgh. It's two hundred sixty-five
miles long with a very high speed
limit. I was just slowing down for one
of the tunnels, when I saw him—
standing under an arc light by the side
of the road. I could see him quite distinctly. The bag, the cap, even the
spots of fresh rain spattered over his
shoulders. (*Music stops.*) He hailed
me this time.

HITCH-HIKER. (*Off-stage, through
megaphone, hollowly.*) Halloo . . .
(*Slightly closer.*) Hall . . . llooo . . .
(**Sound Recording:** *Automobile
running faster.*)

ADAMS. I stepped on the gas like a
shot. That's lonely country through
the Alleghenies, and I had no intention of stopping. Besides, the coincidence, or whatever it was, gave me
the willies. (**Sound Recording:**
Automobile out.) I stopped at the next
gas station. (**Manual Sound:** *Nervous
honking of horn.*) [**Scene:** *The filling
station attendant leaves chair and
advances to microphone.*]

FILLING STATION MAN. Yes, sir.

ADAMS. Fill her up.

FILLING STATION MAN. Certainly,
sir. Check your oil, sir?

ADAMS. No, thanks. (**Manual Sound:**
*Clank of hose. Sound of insertion into
gas tank. Tinkle of bell at regular
intervals as though from filling
station pump. This continues behind
following conversation.*)

FILLING STATION MAN. Nice night,
isn't it?

ADAMS. Yes. It hasn't been raining here
recently, has it?

FILLING STATION MAN. Not a drop
of rain all week.

ADAMS. H'm. I suppose that hasn't
done your business any harm?

FILLING STATION MAN. Oh—people
drive through here all kinds of
weather. Mostly business, you know.
There aren't many pleasure cars out on
the Turnpike this season of the year.

ADAMS. I suppose not. (*Casually.*)
What about hitch-hikers?

FILLING STATION MAN. Hitch-
hikers—*here?* (**Manual Sound:**
*Tinkling bell stops. Sound of hose
being detached.*)

ADAMS. What's the matter? Don't you
ever see any?

FILLING STATION MAN. Not much. If
we did, it'd be a sight for sore eyes.
(*Manual sound stops.*)

ADAMS. Why?

FILLING STATION MAN. A guy'd be a
fool who started out to hitch rides on
this road. Look at it.

ADAMS. Then you've never seen
anybody?

FILLING STATION MAN. Nope.
Mebbe they get the lift before the
Turnpike starts—I mean—you
know—just before the tollhouse—but
then it'd be a mighty long ride. Most
cars wouldn't want to pick up a guy
for that long a ride. This is pretty
lonesome country here—mountains
and woods . . . You ain't seen
anybody like that, have you?

ADAMS. No. (*Quickly.*) Oh, no, not at
all. It was—just a technical question.

FOCUS ON... MUSIC

Throughout the script for *The Hitch-Hiker* numerous music and sound-recording cues are given. Using these cues, create the soundtrack for this radio play from a number of different musical pieces and sound effects. Share your soundtrack with the rest of the class. Then, working in small groups, create a "master soundtrack" with at least one selection or effect taken from each team member's original soundtrack. Use this master soundtrack for your group's dramatic presentation of part of the play (see Accent On . . . Dramatic Arts on page 110).

◆ ◆ ◆ ◆ ◆ ◆ ◆ ◆ ◆ ◆ ◆ ◆ ◆ ◆ ◆

FILLING STATION MAN. I see. Well—that'll be just a dollar forty-nine—with the tax . . . . [**Scene: Filling Station Man** *steps back from microphone and returns to seat at rear of stage, as:*] (*Sound recording fades in automobile starting motor hum. Continue through following.*)

ADAMS. The thing gradually passed from my mind, as sheer coincidence. I had a good night's sleep in Pittsburgh. I didn't think about the man all next day—until just outside of Zanesville, Ohio, I saw him again. (**Music:** *Dark chords, followed by eeriness. Continue through following: Sound recording of auto motor fade down behind music and words, but continue quietly.*) It was a bright sunshiny afternoon. The peaceful Ohio fields, brown with the autumn stubble, lay dreaming in the golden light. I was driving slowly, drinking it in, when the road suddenly ended in a detour. In front of the barrier—*he* was standing. (**Sound Recording:** *Motor hum fades out. Music continues.*) Let me explain about his appearance before I go on. I repeat. There was nothing sinister about him. He was as drab as a mud fence. Nor was his attitude menacing. He merely stood there, waiting, almost drooping a little, the cheap overnight bag in his hand. He looked as though he had been waiting there for hours. Then he looked up—(*Music stops.*) He hailed me. He started to walk forward . . .

HITCH-HIKER. (*Off-stage, through megaphone, hollowly.*) Hallooo . . . Hallo . . . ooo. . . . (**Manual Sound:** *Starter button. Sound of gears* jamming. *Through megaphone off-stage, closer.*) Hall-ooo. . . . (*Manual sound continues. Clash of gears. Dead starter.*)

ADAMS. (*Panicky.*) No—not just now. Sorry. . . .

HITCH-HIKER. (*Through megaphone offstage.*) Going to California . . . a . . . ?

ADAMS. (*Panicky.*) No. Not today. The other way. Going to New York. Sorry . . . (**Sound Recording:** *Automobile starts noisily. Wildly.*) Sorry . . . ! (**Sound Recording:** *Automobile hum continuing through following:*) After I got the car back onto the road again, I felt like a fool. Yet the thought of picking him up, of having him sit beside me was somehow unbearable. Yet at the same time, I felt more than ever unspeakably alone. . . . (**Music:** *Just the eerie section fades in above sound of automobile hum. It continues through following:*) Hour after hour went by. The fields, the towns, ticked off one by one. The light changed. I knew now, that I was going to see him again. And though I dreaded the sight, I caught myself searching the side of the road, waiting for him to appear. . . . (*Music and sound recording out.* **Manual Recording:** *Horn honk two or three times. Pause. Nervous honk again.*) [**Scene: Roadside Stand Proprietor,** *elderly rural type, comes forward to microphone.*] (**Manual Sound Two:** *Creak of squeaky door.*)

PROPRIETOR. (**Querulous,** *mountain voice.*) Yep? What is it? What do you want?

ADAMS. (*Breathless.*) You sell sandwiches and pop here, don't you?

PROPRIETOR. (*Cranky.*) Yep. We do. In the daytime. But we're closed up now for the night.

ADAMS. I know. But—I was wondering if you could possibly let me have a cup of coffee—black coffee.

PROPRIETOR. Not at this time of night, mister. My wife's the cook, and she's in bed. Mebbe further down the road, at the Honeysuckle Rest. (**Manual Sound:** *Creak of door closing.*)

ADAMS. No—no—don't shut the door. Listen—just a minute ago, there was a man standing here——right beside this stand—a suspicious-looking man. . . . (**Scene: Proprietor's Wife** *stands up, calling from chair at rear of stage, not moving forward.*)

PROPRIETOR'S WIFE. (*A quavery, whiny voice.*) Hen-ry? Who is it, Hen-ry?

PROPRIETOR. It's nobuddy, Mother. Just a feller thinks he wants a cup of coffee. Go back into bed. [**Scene: Wife** *stands beside chair, listening, then slowly begins creeping forward.*]

ADAMS. I don't mean to disturb you. But you see, I was driving along—when I just happened to look—and there he was. . . .

PROPRIETOR. What was he doing?

ADAMS. Nothing. He ran off—when I stopped the car.

PROPRIETOR. Then what of it? That's nothing to wake a man in the middle of his sleep about. . . .

WIFE. Mebbe he's been drinkin', Henry. . . . (*Calling.*)

querulous— complaining; whining

The Hitch-Hiker

103

PROPRIETOR. (*Sternly.*) Young man, I've got a good mind to turn you over to the sheriff—

ADAMS. But—I—

PROPRIETOR. You've been taking a nip, that's what you've been doing. And you haven't got anything better to do than wake decent folk out of their hard-earned sleep. Get going. Go on.

WIFE. (*Calling.*) Jes' shet the door on him, Henry—

ADAMS. But he looked as though he were going to rob you.

HENRY. I ain't got nothin' in this stand to lose. (**Manual Sound:** *Door creaking closed.*) Now—on your way before I call out Sheriff Oakes. (*Door slams shut. Bolted.*) [**Scene: Proprietor** *and his wife return to their seats at rear of stage.*] (**Sound Recording:** *Auto starting, motor running.*)

ADAMS. I got into the car again, and drove on slowly. I was beginning to hate the car. If I could have found a place to stop . . . to rest a little. But I was in the Ozark Mountains of Missouri now. The few resort places there were closed. Only an occasional log cabin, seemingly deserted, broke the monotony of the wild wooded landscape. I *had* seen him at that roadside stand. I knew I would see him again—perhaps at the next turn of the road. I knew that when I saw him next—I would run him down.

● ● ● ● ● ● ● ●
"I knew I would see him again—perhaps at the next turn of the road."
● ● ● ● ● ● ● ●

(**Music:** *Dark chords, followed by eerie melody.*) But I did not see him again until late next afternoon.

(*Music continues eerily.* **Manual Sound:** *The tinkling of signal bell at railroad crossroads. Continue through following:*) I had stopped the car at a sleepy little junction just across the border into Oklahoma . . . to let a train pass by—when he appeared across the tracks, leaning against a telephone pole. . . . (*Music and manual sound continuing. Very tense.*) It was a perfectly airless, dry day. The red clay of Oklahoma was baking under the south-western sun. Yet there were spots of fresh rain on his shoulders. . . . (*Music stops.*) I couldn't stand that. Without thinking, blindly, I started the car across the tracks. (**Sound Recording:** *Distant, very faint cry of train whistle approaching. Manual sound of bell continuing.*)

He didn't even look up at me. He was staring at the ground. I stepped on the gas hard, veering the wheel sharply toward him. (**Sound Recording:** *Train whistle closer. Chugging of wheels fading in.*) I could hear the train in the distance now. But I didn't care. (**Manual Sound One** *continues signal bell.* **Manual Sound Two:** *Jamming of gears. Clash of metal.*) Then—something went wrong with the car. (**Manual Sound Two:** *Gears jamming. Starter button dead.* **Sound Recording:** *Train chugging up, louder.*) The train was coming closer.

I could hear the cry of its whistle. (**Sound Recording:** *Train chugging. Cry of whistle closer. All this should be a* **cacophony** *of sound blended together, almost overriding* **Adams's** *voice, which tries to rise above it, almost hysterical with panic.*) Still he stood there. And now—I knew that he was beckoning—beckoning me to my death. . . . (**Sound Recording:** *Full train chugging topped by wild cry of train whistle overpowering all other sound, full, then dying away slowly to silence. Music fades in with the eerie part of the theme. We hear this a second or two; then* **Adams** *says breathlessly, quietly:*) Well—I frustrated him that time. The starter worked at last. I managed to back up. But when the train passed, he was gone. I was all alone, in the hot dry afternoon. (*Music continuing.* **Sound Recording:** *Fade in auto hum.*) After that, I knew I had to do something. I didn't know who this man was, or what he wanted of me. I only knew that from now on, I must not let myself be alone on the road for one moment. (*Music and sound recording of auto out.*) [**Scene: Girl Hitch-Hiker** *comes forward to microphone.*] (**Manual Recording:** *Honk of horn.*) Hello, there. Like a ride?

GIRL. What do you think? How far you going?

ADAMS. Where do you want to go?

GIRL. Amarillo, Texas. (**Manual Sound:** *Car door opening.*)

ADAMS. I'll drive you there.

GIRL. Gee! (**Manual Sound:** *Car door slams.* **Sound Recording:** *Auto starting up, hum. It continues through following.*) Mind if I take off my shoes? My dogs are killing me.

ADAMS. Go right ahead.

GIRL. Gee, what a break this is. A swell car, a decent guy, and driving all the way to Amarillo. All I been getting so far is trucks.

ADAMS. Hitch-hike much?

GIRL. Sure. Only it's tough sometimes, in these great open spaces, to get the breaks.

ADAMS. I should think it would be. Though I'll bet if you get a good pickup in a fast car, you can get to places faster than, say, another person in another car.

GIRL. I don't get you.

ADAMS. Well, take me, for instance. Suppose I'm driving across the country, say, at a nice steady clip of about forty-five miles per hour. Couldn't a girl like you, just standing beside the road, waiting for lifts, beat me to town after town—provided she got picked up every time in a car doing from sixty-five to seventy miles per hour?

GIRL. I dunno. What difference does it make?

ADAMS. Oh—no difference. It's just a—crazy idea I had sitting here in the car.

GIRL. (*Laughing.*) Imagine spending your time in a swell car and thinking of things like that.

ADAMS. What would you do instead?

GIRL. (*Admiringly.*) What would I do? If I was a good-looking fellow like yourself? Why—I'd just *enjoy*

cacophony— harsh, jumbled sounds

steer—singular
used for plural
steers; cattle

myself—every minute of the time. I'd sit back and relax, and if I saw a good-looking girl along the side of the road . . . (*Sharply.*) Hey—look out! (**Sound Recording:** *Auto hum continuing.*)

ADAMS. (*Breathlessly.*) Did you see him, too?

GIRL. See who?

ADAMS. That man. Standing beside the barbed-wire fence.

GIRL. I didn't see—nobody. There wasn't nothing but a bunch of **steer**—and the wire fence. What did you think you was doing? Trying to run into the barbed-wire fence? (**Sound Recording:** *Auto motor continuing.*)

ADAMS. There was a man there, I tell you . . . a thin grey man, with an overnight bag in his hand. And I was trying to run him down.

GIRL. Run him down? You mean—kill him?

ADAMS. But—(*Desperately.*) you say you didn't see him back there? You're sure?

GIRL. (*Strangely.*) I didn't see a soul. And as far as I'm concerned, mister . . .

ADAMS. Watch for him the next time then. Keep watching. Keep your eyes peeled on the road. He'll turn up again—maybe any minute now. (*Excitedly.*) There! Look there. . . . (**Manual Recording:** *Car skidding. Screech. A crash of metal as of car going into barbed-wire fence.* **Girl screams. Manual Recording:** *A bump.* **Manual Recording Two:** *Sound of door handle of car turning.*)

GIRL. How does this door work? I—I'm gettin' out of here.

ADAMS. Did you see him that time?

GIRL. (*Sharply, choked.*) No. I didn't see him that time. And personally, mister, I don't expect never to see him. All I want to do is go on living—and I don't see how I will very long, driving with you.

ADAMS. I'm sorry. I—I don't know what came over me. (*Frightened.*) Please . . . don't go. . . .

GIRL. So if you'll excuse me, mister.

ADAMS. You can't go. Listen, how would you like to go to California? I'll drive you to California.

GIRL. Seeing pink elephants all the way? No, thanks. (**Manual Sound:** *Door handle turning.*)

ADAMS. Listen. Please. For just one moment—

GIRL. You know what I think you need, big boy? Not a girlfriend. Just a dose of good sleep. There. I got it now. . . . (**Manual Sound:** *Door opens. Slams. Metallic.*)

ADAMS. No. You can't go.

GIRL. (*Wildly.*) Leave your hands offa me, do you hear? Leave your—(**Manual Sound:** *Sharp slap.* **2nd Manual Sound:** *Footsteps over gravel, running. They die away. A pause.*)

ADAMS. She ran from me, as though I were a monster. A few minutes later, I saw a passing truck pick her up. I knew then that I was utterly alone. (**Manual Sound:** *Imitation of low mooing of steer or sound recording of same.*) I was in the heart of the great

Actors, radio broadcasters, and many other professionals depend on strong verbal skills in order to excel in their fields. You, too, can become more effective in your verbal communication at school, at home, or on the job. Keep these guidelines in mind:

1. *Volume:* Speak loudly enough to be heard.
2. *Tone:* Match your tone to the message. Use variety in your tone or voice pitch.
3. *Emphasis:* Stress important ideas.
4. *Enunciation:* Slightly exaggerate your pronunciation of syllables to make sure they are understood.
5. *Pace:* Do not speak too quickly or too slowly.

Texas prairies. There wasn't a car on the road after the truck went by. I tried to figure out what to do, how to get hold of myself. If I could find a place to rest. Or even if I could sleep right there in the car for a few hours, along the side of the road. (**Music:** *The eerie theme stealing in softly.*) I was getting my winter overcoat out of the back seat to use as a blanket, when I saw him coming toward me, emerging from the herd of moving steer. . . . (**Sound:** *Mooing of steer, low. Out of it emerges voice of:*)

HITCH-HIKER. (*Hollowly offstage through megaphone.*) Hall . . . ooo. . . . Hall . . . oo. . . . (**Sound Recording:** *Auto starting. Auto hum steady up. Music continuing.*)

ADAMS. Perhaps I should have spoken to him then, fought it out then and there. For now he began to be everywhere. Wherever I stopped, even for a moment—for gas, for oil, for a drink of pop, a cup of coffee, a sandwich—he was there. (*Music continuing. Auto sound continuing. More tense and rapid.*) I saw him standing outside the auto camp in Amarillo, that night, when I dared to slow down. He was sitting near the drinking fountain in a little camping spot just inside the border of New Mexico. . . . (*Music steady. Rapid, more breathless.*) He was waiting for me outside the Navajo Reservation where I stopped to check my tires. I saw him in Albuquerque, where I bought twenty gallons of gas. I was afraid now, afraid to stop. I began to drive faster and faster. I was in **lunar** landscape now—the great arid **mesa** country of New Mexico. I drove

lunar—of or related to the moon; the narrator is comparing the desert to what he thinks the moon must look like

mesa—an isolated, relatively flat natural elevation

through it with the indifference of a fly crawling over the face of the moon. . . . (*Auto hum up. Music more and more eerie. More desperately.*) But now he didn't even wait for me to stop. Unless I drove at eight-five miles per hour over those endless roads, he waited for me at every other mile. I would see his figure, shadow-less, flitting before me, still in its same attitude, over the cold lifeless ground, flitting over dried-up rivers, over broken stones cast up by old glacial upheavals, flitting in the pure and cloudless air. . . . (*Music reaches eerie climax. Stops. Sound recording of auto hum stops. A low voice in the silence.*) I was beside myself when I finally reached Gallup, New Mexico, this morning. There is an auto camp here—cold, almost deserted at this time of year. I went inside and asked if there was a telephone. . . . (**Manual Recording:** *Sound of footsteps on wood, heavy, echoing.*) I had the feeling that if only I could speak to someone familiar, someone I loved, I could pull myself together. [**Scene: First Operator** *rises, comes forward to microphone.*] (**Manual Sound:** *Dime put into phone.*)

OPERATOR. Number, please?

ADAMS. Long distance.

OPERATOR. Thank you. [**Scene: Long Distance Operator** *comes forward to microphone.*] (**Manual Sound:** *Return of dime. Buzz.*)

> ● ● ● ● ● ● ●
> "Wherever I stopped, even for a moment— he was there."
> ● ● ● ● ● ● ●

LONG DISTANCE. This is Long Distance.

ADAMS. I'd like to put in a call to my home in Brooklyn, New York. I'm Ronald Adams. The number is 555-0128.

LONG DISTANCE. Thank you. What is your number? [*A mechanical tone.*]

ADAMS. My number . . . 312. [**Scene: Third Operator** *rises from chair, remaining at rear stage.*] (**Manual Sound:** *A buzz.*)

3RD OPERATOR. (*From distance.*) Albuquerque.

LONG DISTANCE OPERATOR. New York for Gallup. [**Scene: Fourth Operator** *rises, stands beside chair at rear stage.*]

4TH OPERATOR. New York.

LONG DISTANCE. Gallup, New Mexico, calling 555-0128. [**Scene: Fourth Operator** *steps back a little distance from microphone during following.*]

ADAMS. I had read somewhere that love could banish demons. It was the middle of the morning. I knew Mother would be home. I pictured her tall, white-haired, in her crisp house dress, going about her tasks. It would be enough, I thought, merely to hear the even calmness of her voice.

LONG DISTANCE. Will you please deposit three dollars and eighty-five cents for the first three minutes? When you have deposited a dollar and a half will you wait until I have collected the money? [**Scene:** *Other three* **Operators** *sit down.*] (**Manual Sound:** *Clunk of three fifty-cent pieces as through telephone.*) All right, deposit another dollar and a half. (**Manual Sound:** *Clunk of three fifty-cent pieces as through telephone.*) Will you please deposit the remaining eighty-five cents? (**Sound:** *Clunk of three quarters and one dime as through telephone.*) Ready with Brooklyn—go ahead, please. [**Scene: Long Distance** *steps back a little farther toward rear, as* **Mrs. Whitney** *comes forward to c. microphone.*]

ADAMS. Hello.

MRS. WHITNEY. Mrs. Adams's residence.

ADAMS. Hello. Hello—Mother?

MRS. WHITNEY. (*Very flat and proper.*) This is Mrs. Adams' residence. Who is it you wished to speak to, please?

ADAMS. Why—who's this?

MRS. WHITNEY. This is Mrs. Whitney.

ADAMS. Mrs. Whitney? I don't know any Mrs. Whitney. Is this 232-0828?

MRS. WHITNEY. Yes.

ADAMS. Where's my mother? Where's Mrs. Adams?

MRS. WHITNEY. Mrs. Adams is not at home. She is still in the hospital.

ADAMS. The hospital?

MRS. WHITNEY. Yes. Who is this calling, please? Is it a member of the family?

ADAMS. What's she in the hospital for?

MRS. WHITNEY. She's been **prostrated** for five days. Nervous breakdown. But who is this calling?

ADAMS. Nervous breakdown? But—my mother was never nervous.

MRS. WHITNEY. It's all taken place since the death of her oldest son, Ronald.

ADAMS. Death of her oldest son, Ronald . . . ? Hey—what is this? What number is this?

MRS. WHITNEY. This is 232-0828. It's all been very sudden. He was killed just six days ago in an automobile accident on the Brooklyn Bridge. [**Scene: Long Distance Operator** *comes forward.*]

LONG DISTANCE. Your three minutes are up, sir. (*Pause.*) Your three minutes are up, sir. . . . [**Scene: Long Distance Operator** *and* **Mrs. Whitney** *sit down.*] Your three minutes are up, sir. . . . (*Softly. A pause.* **Music:** *Fade in eerie theme softly.*)

ADAMS. (*A strange voice.*) And so, I am sitting here in this deserted auto camp in Gallup, New Mexico. I am trying to think. I am trying to get hold of myself. Otherwise I shall go mad. . . . Outside it is night—the vast, soulless night of New Mexico. A million stars are in the sky. Ahead of me stretch a thousand miles of empty mesa, mountains, prairies, desert. Somewhere, among them, he is waiting for me. . . . [**Scene:** *He turns slowly from microphone, looking off-stage, in direction of* **Hitch-Hiker's** *voice.*] Somewhere I shall know who he is—and who . . . I am. . . . (*Music continues to an eerie climax.*) [**Scene: Adams** *walks slowly away from microphone, and off stage, as curtain falls.*] ❖

prostrated—overcome; mentally and/or physically exhausted

The Hitch-Hiker

UNDERSTANDING

1.  Working with a group trace Ronald Adams's route. Where does he begin, what places does he visit, and where does he end up? On a map, chart his journey, placing a marker at each place he spots the hitch-hiker. Keep a travel log from Adams' point of view, noting each time he stops, what he sees, and what he does. With your group, analyze your entries to decide if Adams' behavior makes sense. Given his situation, would you act as he does?

2. What happens to the people Adams meets? How do they react to him? Find evidence to support your conclusions. Working with a group, brainstorm your view of hitch-hiking. Is it legal in your state? Should it be legalized or outlawed? Prepare lists of arguments for both sides of this question. On your own, choose one side and write a persuasive essay to argue your position. ***Workshop 13***

3.  The time of the story is given away by certain details. What clues tell you that events take place in the past? Working with a small group, modernize this play. List the details you would change or add to bring events into the 1990s? Compare your ideas with those of other groups.

CONNECTING

1.  When Ronald calls his mother, he discovers that his death has caused her to have a nervous breakdown. Mrs. Adams' grief has overwhelmed her. Where in your community could a grief-stricken person turn to receive comfort and advice? Working with a group, locate and interview persons and agencies that offer help to those who are experiencing loss and grief. Prepare a brochure to be used by counselors, clergy, and others who might find it useful. ***Workshop 20***

2. Plan an auto trip across the United States. Determine how many miles you will drive each day, what highways you will travel, where you will stay each night, and what sights you will want to see. Use a United States road map to plot your journey. You may want to consult the American Automobile Association for information. Compose a travel agenda, indicating all stops, mileage, and sightseeing tours planned. Include cost estimates for gas, food, and lodging.

ACCENT ON...
DRAMATIC ARTS

Working in small groups, rehearse and then perform the play for the rest of the class. Choose a director and sound engineer, and assign acting roles to other group members. Using props, create the stage set for a radio broadcast. Remember to use the soundtracks you create (see Focus On . . . Music on page 102) to make a master soundtrack for your performance.

The Power of Imagination

- *The Open Window*
- *I'm Making You Up*

EXPLORING

What fun it is to let our imaginations run wild, conjuring up images and stories complete with extraordinary and fascinating details. Imagining is an ability that all humans have. Our imagination can amuse us, and also help us to persuade and motivate other people as well as ourselves. Those with vivid imaginations can create surprise and inspire. How have you used your imagination to inspire, shock, motivate, or delight others? Under what circumstances? What were the results?

TIME & PLACE

Saki's stories usually take place in England because that's where he lived most of his life. He wrote his stories, most of them unsettling and with trick endings, before World War I, a war in which he died fighting for the British.

Chrystos is a member of the Menominee Tribe, which has lived in Wisconsin and upper Michigan for more than 5,000 years. The tribal name means "wild rice people," indicating they were hunters and gatherers. The tribe was terminated by the federal government in 1961 but was reinstated to tribal status in 1971. Today there are only about 7,500 tribal members left.

THEME CONNECTION... IMAGINATION: CREATIVE POWER

Imagination is the power to create. Imagination is also the power to think of original ideas that eventually take form and shape in the real world. For instance, that car you like had to be imagined before it could be built. The imagination can be used to do good things or bad. These selections invite you to see some of the ways that the creative power known as "imagination" shapes life.

THE WRITER'S CRAFT
LITERARY "TWIST"

Writers sometimes surprise readers by giving a sudden turn to a story or poem, one that is unexpected. Both "The Open Window" and "I'm Making You Up" have surprise twists at the end. As you read, notice hints that help readers predict what will happen.

The Open Window

Saki

"My aunt will be down presently, Mr. Nuttel," said a very self-possessed young lady of fifteen. "In the meantime you must try and put up with me."

Framton Nuttel endeavored to say the correct something which should duly flatter the niece of the moment without unduly discounting the aunt that was to come. Privately he doubted more than ever whether these formal visits on a succession of total strangers would do much towards helping the nerve cure which he was supposed to be undergoing.

"I know how it will be," his sister had said when he was preparing to migrate to this rural retreat; "You will bury yourself down there and not speak to a living soul, and your nerves will be worse than ever from moping. I shall just give you letters of introduction to all the people I know there. Some of them, as far as I can remember, were quite nice."

Framton wondered whether Mrs. Sappleton, the lady to whom he was presenting one of the letters of introduction, came into the nice division.

About the Author

Born in Akyab, Burma (Myanmar), Hector Hugh Munro (1870–1916) took the pen name of Saki, which is a Burmese word. He traveled the world widely, though most of his stories take place in England. Fighting in the British armed forces, he died in World War I at the hands of a German sniper.

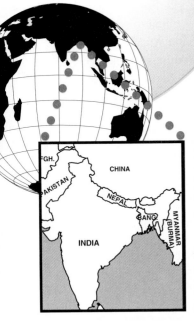

"Do you know many of the people round here?" asked the niece, when she judged that they had had sufficient silent communion.

"Hardly a soul," said Framton. "My sister was staying here, at the **rectory**, you know, some four years ago, and she gave me letters of introduction to some of the people here."

He made the last statement in a tone of distinct regret.

"Then you know practically nothing about my aunt?" pursued the self-possessed young lady.

"Only her name and address," admitted the caller. He was wondering whether Mrs. Sappleton was in the married or widowed state. An undefinable something about the room seemed to suggest masculine habitation.

"Her great tragedy happened just three years ago," said the child; "that would be since your sister's time."

"Her tragedy?" asked Framton. Somehow in this restful country spot tragedies seemed out of place.

"You may wonder why we keep that window wide open on an October afternoon," said the niece, indicating a large French window that opened on to a lawn.

"It is quite warm for the time of the year," said Framton; "but has that window got anything to do with the tragedy?"

"Out through that window, three years ago to a day, her husband and her two young brothers went off for their day's shooting. They never came back. In crossing the **moor** to their favorite **snipe-shooting** ground they were all three engulfed in a treacherous piece of bog. It had been that dreadful wet summer, you know, and places that were safe in other years gave way suddenly without warning. Their bodies were never recovered. That was the dreadful part of it." Here the child's voice lost its self-possessed note and became falteringly human. "Poor aunt always thinks that they will come back some day, they and the little brown spaniel that was lost with them, and walk in at that window just as they used to do. That is why the window is kept open every evening till it is quite dusk. Poor dear aunt, she has often told me how they went out, her husband with his white waterproof coat over his arm, and Ronnie, her youngest brother, singing, 'Bertie, why do you bound?' as he always did to tease her, because she said it got on her nerves. Do you know, sometimes on still, quiet evenings like this, I almost get a creepy feeling that they will all walk in through that window—"

She broke off with a little shudder. It was a relief to Framton when the aunt bustled into the room with a whirl of

apologies for being late in making her appearance.

"I hope Vera has been amusing you?" she said.

"She has been very interesting," said Framton.

"I hope you don't mind the open window," said Mrs. Sappleton briskly. "My husband and brothers will be home directly from shooting, and they always come in this way. They've been out for snipe in the marshes today, so they'll make a fine mess over my poor carpets. So like you menfolk, isn't it?"

She rattled on cheerfully about the shooting and the scarcity of birds, and the prospects for duck in the winter. To Framton it was all purely horrible. He made a desperate but only partially successful effort to turn the talk on to a less ghastly topic. He was conscious that his hostess was giving him only a fragment of her attention, and her eyes were constantly straying past him to the open window and the lawn beyond. It was certainly an unfortunate coincidence that he should have paid his visit on this tragic anniversary.

"The doctors agree in ordering me complete rest, and absence of mental excitement, and avoidance of anything in the nature of violent physical exercise," announced Framton, who labored under the tolerably widespread **delusion** that total strangers and chance acquaintances are hungry for the least detail of one's ailments and infirmities, their cause and cure. "On the matter of diet they are not so much in agreement," he continued.

"No?" said Mrs. Sappleton, in a voice which only replaced a yawn at the last moment. Then she suddenly brightened

rectory—house in which a clergyman lives

moor—open, rolling land, often containing boggy or swampy areas

snipe-shooting—snipe refers to any of several game birds that dwell in marshy areas

delusion—a false belief

mackintosh—
(British) a rain-
coat made of a
lightweight
waterproof
fabric, named
for Charles
Macintosh, the
inventor of the
fabric

Ganges—
pronounced
GAN jeez; river
in northern India

pariah—wild

into alert attention—but not to what Framton was saying.

"Here they are at last!" she cried. "Just in time for tea, and don't they look as if they were muddy up to the eyes!"

Framton shivered slightly and turned towards the niece with a look intended to convey sympathetic comprehension. The child was staring out through the open window with dazed horror in her eyes. In a chill shock of nameless fear Framton swung round in his seat and looked in the same direction.

In the deepening twilight three figures were walking across the lawn towards the window. They all carried guns under their arms, and one of them was additionally burdened with a white coat hung over his shoulders. A tired brown spaniel kept close at their heels. Noiselessly they neared the house, and then a hoarse young voice chanted out of the dusk: "I said, Bertie, why do you bound?"

Framton grabbed wildly at his stick and hat. The hall door, the gravel drive, and the front gate were dimly noted stages in his headlong retreat. A cyclist coming along the road had to run into the hedge to avoid imminent collision.

"Here we are, my dear," said the bearer of the white **mackintosh**, coming in through the window; "fairly muddy, but most of it's dry. Who was that who bolted out as we came up?"

"A most extraordinary man, a Mr. Nuttel," said Mrs. Sappleton; "could only talk about his illness, and dashed off without a word of good-by or apology when you arrived. One would think he had seen a ghost."

"I expect it was the spaniel," said the niece calmly. "He told me he had a

horror of dogs. He was once hunted into a cemetery somewhere on the banks of the **Ganges** by a pack of **pariah** dogs, and had to spend the night in a newly-dug grave with the creatures snarling and grinning and foaming just above him. Enough to make any one lose their nerve."

Romance at short notice was her specialty. ❖

ACCENT ON...
HEALTH CARE
● ●

In "The Open Window," Framton Nuttel is sent by his doctors to the countryside in order to cure his "nerves." "Nerves" was used loosely in the early 1900's to refer to a range of mental disorders from tension caused by stress to manic depression. For fatigue and restlessness, today a doctor might order a series of tests and exercises to reduce stress. Find out how stress is measured today and what the outcome of a "stress test" might indicate about a patient's health. Present your findings to the class.

I'm Making You Up

Chrystos

Grandma we all need
partially deaf & busy with weaving
    listens   through a thick blanket of years & sore feet
nods   while I cry about everything they did to me
how horrible   & can't stand another
while brown wrinkled you smile at me like sun coming up
    I stand next to you   pass wool absently
    you lay aside the wrong colors   without comment
I'm simply   Grandchild
babbling   your sympathy warm & comforting as dust
I sit in your lap   your loom pushed aside
you feed me fry bread with too much maple syrup
I pull your braids   you cradle me deeper in
your legs folded to make a basket for me
Grandma   who died long before I was born
             Come Back
              Come Back ❖

About the Author

Pointing out the hardships suffered by Native Americans is one of the aims of the self-educated poet Chrystos. She was born in San Francisco in 1946 and has written three books about Native Americans. She travels throughout North America reading from her works and speaking out against injustices to Native-American people.

UNDERSTANDING

1. Framton Nuttel has been sent to the country for peace and quiet. The girl sends him off in a panic. Do you feel sympathy for him? What has the author done to help us understand Nuttel? Will the country help his condition?

   In a well-constructed essay, compare and contrast living in the country as opposed to living in the city. Discuss aspects such as noise, conveniences, crime, and other features. Which do you prefer? *Workshop 15*

2.  The girl uses words as well as acting skills to tell her stories. Cite examples in the story where she uses tone and body language to express her message.

   With a partner, prepare an audio- or videotape giving two versions of a story. One version should be told without special effort to add expression; the other should put all of the elements of expression to work. Play the tape for your class. *Workshop 23*

3. The poet Chrystos imagines how her grandmother used to comfort her. Find details in the text that show the picture of the grandmother that emerges. Why would you like, or dislike, this grandmother?

   Write a prose paragraph or a brief poem that explains how someone treated either you, or someone you know. In your writing, you may wish to blend real facts and imaginary details. *Workshops 2 and 9*

A LAST WORD

Have you ever made up a story to tell someone else or to tell yourself? What was the purpose of your story? What did you learn about your imagination while creating the story?

CONNECTING

1.  Vera has a remarkably vivid imagination. Unfortunately she uses her imaginative powers to deceive. What can parents and teachers do to help young people learn to use their imaginations for good results? With your group, prepare a written report on how to train children to develop good manners and a sense of social responsibility. You will need to do research on the imagination, and on what educators and psychologists say about methods for teaching children. Present your final report to parents and teachers. *Workshop 21*

2. Many Americans are saddened to see aspects of traditional Native-American life disappearing. Language, crafts, religions, music, and traditional dress are all fading. Research a Native-American tribe in your area to discover what is being done to preserve its culture and traditions. Consult the Bureau of Indian Affairs for names of organizations and individuals who might have information on this subject. Write a report on your findings.

Future Tense

EXPLORING

● ● ● ● ● ● ● ● ● ● ● ● ● ● ● ● ● ● ●

The fantastic situations presented by science fiction writers usually contain some references to existing science or technology. These details make it seem at least slightly possible that the story could happen. Brainstorm about elements in science fiction stories and movies that made you think they could one day happen. If a movie or story seemed absolutely unbelievable, why was that?

THEME CONNECTION...
IMAGINATION AND VISION

The imagination—the power to think creatively—allows us to have vision. "Vision" is the imaginative power to see in your mind something that is not there. You may have a vision of winning a race, or a vision of what your team could be like under certain conditions. Your parents may have a vision of what they would like you to become. In this story, Gary expresses his vision of a typical day at school assuming a new teacher is an alien.

TIME & PLACE

"Future Tense" takes place in a high school much like yours. The students, like you, are concerned about school assignments, sports, and social relationships. The very common setting helps readers believe the story and assume that the characters are everyday teenagers and teachers. The main character's use of a typewriter is the only clue that the story probably takes place prior to the present-day computer age.

THE WRITER'S CRAFT
AMBIGUITY

"Future Tense" portrays an enthusiastic young writer striving to earn his teacher's approval. To win the teacher's approval on his essay, Gary writes science fiction, unwittingly describing a situation that might actually exist. We do not know for certain whether Gary's claims are true. Thus, the story is ambiguous. *Ambiguity* occurs when a writer intentionally leaves things uncertain and indefinite, so they could be understood in more than one way.

● ●

Future Tense

Robert Lipsyte

Gary couldn't wait for tenth grade to start so he could strut his sentences, parade his paragraphs, renew his reputation as the top creative writer in school. At the opening assembly, he felt on edge, psyched, like a boxer before the first-round bell. He leaned forward as Dr. Proctor, the principal, introduced two new staff members. He wasn't particularly interested in the new vice-principal, Ms. Jones; Gary never had discipline problems, he'd never even had to stay after school. But his head cocked alertly as Dr. Proctor introduced the new Honors English teacher, Mr. Smith. Here was the person he'd have to impress.

He studied Mr. Smith. The man was hard to describe. He looked as though he'd been manufactured to fit his name. Average height, brownish hair, pale white skin, medium build. Middle age. He was the sort of person you began to forget the minute you met him. Even his clothes had no particular style. They merely covered his body.

Mr. Smith was . . . just there.

Gary was studying Mr. Smith so intently that he didn't hear Dr. Proctor call him up to the stage to receive an award from last term. Jim Baggs jabbed an elbow into his ribs and said, "Let's get up there, Dude."

Dr. Proctor shook Gary's hand and gave him the County Medal for Best Composition. While Dr. Proctor was giving Jim Baggs the County Trophy for Best All-Round Athlete, Gary glanced over his shoulder to see if Mr. Smith was so ordinary he was invisible when no one was talking about him.

On the way home, Dani Belzer, the prettiest poet in school, asked Gary, "What did you think of our new Mr. Wordsmith?"

"If he was a color he'd be beige," said Gary. "If he was a taste he'd be water. If he was a sound he'd be a low hum."

"Fancy, empty words," sneered Mike Chung, ace reporter on the school paper. "All you've told me is you've got nothing to tell me."

Dani quickly stepped between them. "What did you think of the first assignment?"

"Describe a Typical Day at School," said Gary, trying unsuccessfully to mimic Mr. Smith's bland voice. "That's about as exciting as tofu."

"A real artist," said Dani, "accepts the commonplace as a challenge."

That night, hunched over his humming electric typewriter, Gary wrote a description of a typical day at school from the viewpoint of a new teacher who was seeing everything for the first time, who took nothing for granted. He described the shredded edges of the limp flag outside the dented front door, the worn flooring where generations of kids had nervously paced outside the principal's office, the nauseatingly sweet pipe-smoke seeping out of the teachers' lounge.

And then, in the last line, he gave the composition that extra twist, the little kicker on which his reputation rested. He wrote:

The new teacher's beady little eyes missed nothing, for they were the optical recorders of an alien creature who had come to earth to gather information.

The next morning, when Mr. Smith asked for a volunteer to read aloud, Gary was on his feet and moving toward the front of the classroom before Mike Chung got his hand out of his pocket.

The class loved Gary's composition. They laughed and stamped their feet. Chung shrugged, which meant he couldn't think of any criticism, and Dani flashed thumbs up. Best of all, Jim Baggs shouldered Gary against the blackboard after class and said, "Awesome tale, Dude."

Gary felt good until he got the composition back. Along the margin, in perfect script, Mr. Smith had written:

You can do better.

"How would he know?" Gary complained on the way home.

"You should be grateful," said Dani. "He's pushing you to the farthest limits of your talent."

"Which may be nearer than you think," snickered Mike.

Gary rewrote his composition, expanded it, complicated it, thickened it. Not only was this new teacher an alien, he was part of an extraterrestrial conspiracy to take over Earth. Gary's final sentence was:

Every iota of information, fragment of fact, morsel of minutiae sucked up by those vacuuming eyes was beamed directly into a computer circling the planet. The data would eventually become a program that would control the mind of every school kid on earth.

Gary showed the new draft to Dani before class. He stood on tiptoes so he could read over her shoulder. Sometimes he wished she were shorter, but mostly he wished he were taller.

"What do you think?"

"The assignment was to describe a typical day," said Dani. "This is off the wall."

He snatched the papers back. "Creative writing means creating." He walked away, hurt and angry. He thought: *If she doesn't like my compositions, how can I ever get her to like me?*

That morning, Mike Chung read his own composition aloud to the class. He described a typical day through the eyes of a student in a wheelchair. Everything most students take for granted was an obstacle: the bathroom door too heavy to open, the gym steps too steep to climb, the light switch too high on the wall. The class applauded and Mr. Smith smiled approvingly. Even Gary had to admit it was really good—if you considered plain-fact journalism as creative writing, that is.

Gary's rewrite came back the next day marked:

Improving. Try again.

Saturday he locked himself in his room after breakfast and rewrote the rewrite. He carefully selected his nouns and verbs and adjectives. He polished and arranged them in sentences like a jeweller strings pearls. He felt good as he wrote, as the electric typewriter hummed and buzzed and sometimes coughed. He thought: *Every champion knows that as hard as it is to get to the top, it's even harder to stay up there.*

His mother knocked on his door around noon. When he let her in, she said, "It's a beautiful day."

"Big project," he mumbled. He wanted to avoid a distracting conversation.

She smiled. "If you spend too much time in your room, you'll turn into a mushroom."

He wasn't listening. "Thanks. Anything's okay. Don't forget the mayonnaise."

Gary wrote:

The alien's probes trembled as he read the student's composition. Could that skinny, bespectacled earthling really suspect its extraterrestrial identity? Or was his composition merely the result of a creative thunderstorm in a brilliant young mind?

Before Gary turned in his composition on Monday morning, he showed it to Mike Chung. He should have known better.

"You're trying too hard," chortled Chung. "Truth is stranger than fiction."

Gary flinched at that. It hurt. It might be true. But he couldn't let his competition know he had scored. "You journalists are stuck in the present and the past," growled Gary. "Imagination prepares us for what's going to happen."

Dani read her composition aloud to the class. It described a typical day from the perspective of a louse choosing a head of hair to nest in. The louse moved from a thicket of a varsity crew cut to the matted jumble of a sagging perm to a straight, sleek blond cascade.

The class cheered and Mr. Smith smiled. Gary felt a twinge of jealousy. Dani and Mike were coming on. There wasn't room for more than one at the top.

In the hallway, he said to Dani, "And you called my composition off the wall?"

Mike jumped in, "There's a big difference between poetical metaphor and hack science fiction."

> • • • • • • •
> ## "Imagination prepares us for what's going to happen."
> • • • • • • •

Gary felt choked by a lump in his throat. He hurried away.

Mr. Smith handed back Gary's composition the next day marked:

See me after school.

Gary was nervous all day. What was there to talk about? Maybe Mr. Smith hated science fiction. One of those traditional English teachers. Didn't understand that science fiction could be literature. *Maybe I can educate him,* thought Gary.

When Gary arrived at the English office, Mr. Smith seemed nervous, too. He kept folding and unfolding Gary's composition. "Where do you get such ideas?" he asked in his monotone voice.

Gary shrugged. "They just come to me."

"Alien teachers. Taking over the minds of schoolchildren." Mr. Smith's empty eyes were blinking. "What made you think of that?"

FOCUS ON... ART

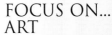

Gary mistakenly suspects that Mr. Smith and Ms. Jones are aliens. What do you think an alien might look like? From which planet would "it" come? Create a portrait of an alien, trying to be as imaginative in your use of materials as you are in creating the alien's features. To accompany the portrait, write a letter of introduction for your alien. Include information such as the alien's name, age, place of birth, favorite food, favorite activity, and so on in the letter.

"I've always had this vivid imagination."

Mr. Smith looked relieved. "I guess everything will work out." He handed back Gary's composition. "No more fantasy, Gary. Reality. That's your assignment. Write only about what you know."

Outside school, Gary ran into Jim Baggs, who looked surprised to see him. "Don't tell me you had to stay after, Dude."

"I had to see Mr. Smith about my composition. He didn't like it. Told me to stick to reality."

"Don't listen." Jim Baggs body-checked Gary into the schoolyard fence. "Dude, you got to be yourself."

Gary ran all the way home and locked himself into his room. He felt feverish with creativity. Dude, you got to be yourself, Dude. It doesn't matter what your so-called friends say, or your English teacher. You've got to play your own kind of game, write your own kind of stories.

The words flowed out of Gary's mind and through his fingers and out of the machine onto sheets of paper. He wrote and rewrote until he felt the words were exactly right:

> With great effort, the alien shut down the electrical panic impulses coursing through its system and turned on Logical Overdrive. There were two possibilities:
>
> 1. This high school boy was exactly what he seemed to be, a brilliant, imaginative, apprentice best-selling author and screen-writer, or,
>
> 2. He had somehow stumbled onto the secret plan and he would have to be either enlisted into the conspiracy or erased off the face of the planet.

First thing in the morning, Gary turned in his new rewrite to Mr. Smith. A half hour later, Mr. Smith called Gary out of Spanish. There was no expression on his regular features. He said, "I'm going to need some help with you."

SPOTLIGHT ON...
CREATIVE THINKING

The story "Future Tense" is a story within a story. The author Robert Lipsyte tells the story of Gary and what happens to him because of the assignment he writes. The "other" story is the assignment Gary writes, which unbeknownst to him reveals the secret alien plot. Looking at problems from unconventional angles is one way to be creative in your own writing and thinking. When you approach a problem:

1. Invert an established order or pattern of events.
2. Use free association to explore options and solutions.
3. Try what seems implausible or impossible.

◆ ◆ ◆ ◆ ◆ ◆ ◆ ◆ ◆ ◆ ◆ ◆ ◆ ◆ ◆ ◆ ◆ ◆

Cold sweat covered Gary's body as Mr. Smith grabbed his arm and led him to the new vice-principal. She read the composition while they waited. Gary got a good look at her for the first time. Ms. Jones was . . . just there. She looked as though she'd been manufactured to fit her name. Average. Standard. Typical. The cold sweat turned into goose pimples.

How could he have missed the clues? Smith and Jones were aliens! He had stumbled on their secret and now they'd have to deal with him.

He blurted, "Are you going to enlist me or erase me?"

Ms. Jones ignored him. "In my opinion, Mr. Smith, you are over-reacting. This sort of nonsense"—she waved Gary's composition—"is the typical response of an overstimulated adolescent to the mixture of reality and fantasy in an environment dominated by manipulative music, television, and films. Nothing for us to worry about."

"If you're sure, Ms. Jones," said Mr. Smith. He didn't sound sure.

The vice-principal looked at Gary for the first time. There was no expression in her eyes. Her voice was flat. "You'd better get off this science-fiction kick," she said. "If you know what's good for you."

"I'll never tell another human being, I swear," he babbled.

"What are you talking about?" asked Ms. Jones.

"Your secret is safe with me," he lied. He thought, *If I can just get away from them. Alert the authorities. Save the planet.*

"You see," said Ms. Jones, "you're writing yourself into a crazed state."

"You're beginning to believe your own fantasies," said Mr. Smith.

"I'm not going to do anything this time," said Ms. Jones, "but you must promise to write only about what you know."

"Or I'll have to fail you," said Mr. Smith.

"For your own good," said Ms. Jones. "Writing can be very dangerous."

"Especially for writers," said Mr. Smith, "who write about things they shouldn't."

"Absolutely," said Gary, "positively no question about it. Only what I know." He backed out of the door, nodding his head, thinking, *Just a few more steps and I'm okay. I hope these aliens can't read minds.*

Jim Baggs was practicing head fakes in the hallway. He slammed Gary into the wall with a hip block. "How's it going, Dude?" he asked, helping Gary up.

"Aliens," gasped Gary. "Told me no more science fiction."

"They can't treat a star writer like that," said Jim. "See what the head honcho's got to say." He grabbed Gary's wrist and dragged him into the principal's office.

"What can I do for you, boys?" boomed Dr. Proctor.

"They're messing with his moves, Doc," said Jim Baggs. "You got to let the aces run their races."

"Thank you, James." Dr. Proctor popped his forefinger at the door. "I'll handle this."

"You're home free, Dude," said Jim, whacking Gary across the shoulder blades as he left.

"From the beginning," ordered Dr. Proctor. He nodded sympathetically as Gary told the entire story, from the opening assembly to the meeting with Mr. Smith and Ms. Jones. When Gary

was finished, Dr. Proctor took the papers from Gary's hand. He shook his head as he read Gary's last rewrite.

"You really have a way with words, Gary. I should have sensed you were on to something."

Gary's stomach flipped. "You really think there could be aliens trying to take over Earth?"

"Certainly," said Dr. Proctor, matter-of-factly. "Earth is the ripest plum in the universe."

Gary wasn't sure if he should feel relieved that he wasn't crazy or be scared out of his mind. He took a deep breath to control the quaver in his voice, and said: "I spotted Smith and Jones right away. They look like they were manufactured to fit their names. Obviously humanoids. Panicked as soon as they knew I was on to them."

Dr. Proctor chuckled and shook his head. "No self-respecting civilization would send those two stiffs to Earth."

ACCENT ON...
SCIENCE AND TECHNOLOGY

• •

Many science-fiction stories make use of developments and inventions in science and technology. Find out about a new invention or technological system and write a brief informative report, explaining its function and purpose. Then describe in the closing of your report how you imagine this invention or technology changing 100 years from now. How might it be used differently? With what kind of technology might it be replaced?

"They're not aliens?" He felt relieved and disappointed at the same time.

"I checked them out myself," said Dr. Proctor. "Just two average, standard, typical human beings, with no imagination, no creativity."

"So why'd you hire them?"

Dr. Proctor laughed. "Because they'd never spot an alien. No creative imagination. That's why I got rid of the last vice-principal and the last Honors English teacher. They were giving me odd little glances when they thought I wasn't looking. After ten years on your planet, I've learned to smell trouble."

Gary's spine turned to ice and dripped down the backs of his legs. "You're an alien!"

"Great composition," said Dr. Proctor, waving Gary's papers. "Grammatical, vividly written, and totally accurate."

"It's just a composition," babbled Gary, "made the whole thing up, imagination, you know."

Dr. Proctor removed the face of his wristwatch and began tapping tiny buttons. "Always liked writers. I majored in your planet's literature. Writers are the keepers of the past and the hope of the future. Too bad they cause so much trouble in the present."

"I won't tell anyone," cried Gary. "Your secret's safe with me." He began to back slowly toward the door.

Dr. Proctor shook his head. "How can writers keep secrets, Gary? It's their nature to share their creations with the world." He tapped three times and froze Gary in place, one foot raised to step out the door.

"But it was only a composition," screamed Gary as his body disappeared before his eyes.

"And I can't wait to hear what the folks back home say when you read it to them," said Dr. Proctor.

"I made it all up." Gary had the sensation of rocketing upward. "I made up the whole . . . " ❖

UNDERSTANDING

1. This story takes several sharp turns. Did you predict any of them? What gave you clues? Where did the story surprise you?

   Predictable is a term used to describe a story or film that fails to surprise readers or viewers. Think about the last book you read or movie you saw. Was it predictable? Did this make the story less or more appealing? Write an essay explaining your opinion. *Workshop 8*

2. Between the lines we can read something about Gary's personality. What are his weaknesses and strengths? What tipped you off to these? Is he a fairly typical teenage boy? Explain.

   An alien from another planet asks you to send a description of the typical American teenage boy or girl. What would you write? Keep in mind that the reader is not familiar with American slang and idioms. Write a description for a reader who has never visited here, and who understands only standard, formal English. *Workshop 10*

3. Examine the characters in this story. Using evidence from the text to support your position, explain in an essay how the teenagers have been portrayed. Are they patterned after stereotypes of teenagers, or do they possess special qualities that make them seem like unique individuals. *Workshop 7*

CONNECTING

1. Science has made great progress in developing robots, machines that work in place of humans. However, rarely are they made to look like humans. Research the field of robotics. How are robots used in industry? What skills are necessary for workers who deal with robots? Include a sketch of an industrial robot with your written report. *Workshop 21*

2.  A continuing debate exists among high school English teachers. One group believes it is important to teach as much classical literature—famous, traditional literature—as possible. Another group of teachers thinks students should read a variety of works, traditional and recent, literature and popular publications. Working with a partner, survey the English teachers in your school and in other schools to find out what they think about teaching literature. What are the reasons for the teachers' differing opinions? Write a report, using charts and graphs, to present your findings. Be sure to draw your own conclusions after listening to the reasoning of both sides. *Workshop 22*

A LAST WORD

Do you agree with Ms. Jones's statement, "Writing can be very dangerous"? What power does writing hold? How can we use that power for a worthwhile purpose?

Beware: Do Not Read This Poem

EXPLORING

● ●

Poets can have fun with their readers. They can puzzle them, trick them, scare them, and make them laugh. Human imagination is powerful. Once a poet, a writer of prose, or a film director has captured the imagination of a reader or viewer, amazing things can happen. Ordinary homes become castles or dungeons; normal air becomes polluted with smoke or sweetened with forest smells; poems on a page become ravenous beasts. Can you recall a story, film, or poem that completely took over your imagination? How did it take you in?

THEME CONNECTION...
DISTINGUISHING BETWEEN IMAGINATION AND REALITY

Scientists tell us that the nervous system sometimes has trouble distinguishing between imagination and reality. Thus, we can understand the power of scary stories to fill us with terror and pleasure. Writers who tap our imaginative power can take us far from reality, creating new worlds inhabited by strange creatures—including poems with the ability to swallow humans whole.

TIME & PLACE

Ishmael Reed began publishing poetry in the early 1970s. Having experienced the 1960s, when African Americans won passage of civil rights laws, he writes from a distinctly African-American perspective. Abandoning traditional literary forms, Reed creates new forms appropriate to his culture. By refusing to follow standard poetic conventions, he has made his poetry a form of protest.

THE WRITER'S CRAFT

PERSONIFICATION

The act of giving nonliving things the characteristics of living things is a literary technique called *personification*. Plastic food containers can burp, cars can cough, flowers can smile, and computers can choke. Giving these items human characteristics enhances our understanding of them and their functions.

Beware: Do Not Read This Poem

Ishmael Reed

tonite, *thriller* was
abt an ol woman, so vain she
surrounded herself w/
   many mirrors

It got so bad that finally she
locked herself indoors & her
whole life became the
   mirrors

one day the villagers broke
into her house, but she was too
swift for them, she disappeared
   into a mirror
each tenant who bought the house
after that, lost a loved one to
   the ol woman in the mirror:
   first a little girl
   then a young woman
   then the young woman/s husband

the hunger of this poem is legendary
it has taken in many victims
back off from this poem
it has drawn in yr feet
back off from this poem
it has drawn in yr legs
back off from this poem
it is a greedy mirror
you are into this poem, from
   the waist down
nobody can hear you can they?
this poem has had you up to here
   belch
this poem aint got no manners
you cant call out frm this poem
relax now & go w/ this poem
move & roll on to this poem

About the Author

Ishmael Reed (b. 1938) has written eight novels, four volumes of poetry, and two collections of essays, and has served as editor and publisher of a number of literature anthologies. As a member of the Umbra Workshop, a black writers group, he is a leader in African-American poetry. One of his collections of poetry, *Conjure* (1972), was nominated for the National Book Award. He rebels against traditional literary conventions. In his own words, "I try to do what has never been done before."

FOCUS ON...
MUSIC

How might "Beware: Do Not Read This Poem" sound if it were set to music? Would it have a classical melody? Would it have a strong beat? Working with a partner, create an audio reading of the poem over a taped music selection. If you wish, create the music yourselves. Share your musical interpretation of the poem with the rest of the class.

◆◆◆◆◆◆◆◆◆◆◆◆◆◆◆◆◆◆

do not resist this poem
this poem has yr eyes
this poem has his head
this poem has his arms
this poem has his fingers
this poem has his fingertips

this poem is the reader & the
  reader this poem

statistic: the us bureau of missing persons reports
  that in 1968 over 100,000 people disappeared
  leaving no solid clues
    nor trace   only
  a space   in the lives of their friends ❖

UNDERSTANDING

1. Two abrupt changes occur in the poem. The first occurs with the switch from the old woman story to you and the poem; the second when "you" and "your" become "he" and "his." What does the second change indicate?

    Extend the poet's idea by imagining what it might be like to be inside a poem. Add a third section to the poem by writing from your viewpoint inside the poem. ***Workshop 2***

2. The poet has turned the poem into a living creature. Identify the words and phrases in the poem that are examples of this personification.

    Using personification, turn your school locker, an article of clothing, or other nonliving item into a living creature. Write about your interactions with and observations of this creature. ***Workshop 10***

3.  The poet places words on the page to achieve an effect. Examine the placement of each line and word. What unusual placements or spacing can you find? What is the poet's purpose behind each?

    Imagine the movement and sound of a specific machine or animal, such as a lawn mower or a rabbit. Write a poem about it, placing lines and words on the page to illustrate movement and sound. Share your creation with a small group. Group members will decide if your poem conveys movement and sound as you desired. ***Workshop 2***

CONNECTING

1. e. e. cummings is another poet who plays with the words and their spacing in a poem. Locate a collection of cummings's poems. What unusual techniques do you see in his poetry? Share your observations orally in a group or write a paper explaining them. ***Workshops 8 and 23***

2. The poet uses phrases that are idioms or slang, language that cannot be translated literally by dictionary definition. Examples from the poem are "back off" and "go with this poem." Listen carefully to the speech of people around you. Compile a list of common American idioms and slang. Write each word or phrase and its accepted definition.

    Working in a group, ask some adults you know if they use special words at work. Technical language used in a certain field or occupation is called jargon. Make a dictionary of the jargon you learn from the adults you talk to. Use some of the jargon with other classmates to see if they can come up with definitions.

A LAST WORD

Does poetry need a warning label? What effect might a poem have on a reader? If you were a poet, what effect would you want your poetry to have on your readers?

The Snow Woman

EXPLORING

Bigfoot, Sasquatch, yeti, Abominable Snowman—all these names apply to the giant, hairy creature reported to roam the world's tallest mountain ranges. Sightings occur from time to time, but no one has ever produced solid evidence that proves the creature's existence. What kind of evidence would it take to convince you? If this creature exists, should efforts be made to capture and study it, or should it be allowed to continue its solitary way of life?

THEME CONNECTION... STILL A MYSTERY

Lha-mo lives in the Himalayas, where more than once she has seen the trail of a yeti. Eager for huge rewards promised by outsiders for evidence of the yeti, Lha-mo successfully subdues the creature. She lets it go, however, when she sees the yeti's real situation, a situation comparable to her own.

TIME & PLACE

Bhutan, where Lha-mo lives, is a small, developing, independent country in the eastern Himalayas between India and Tibet. It is rugged and mountainous and has great extremes in climate. The people are hardy mountaineers who farm and raise stock. Ninety percent of them cannot read or write.

THE WRITER'S CRAFT
THIRD PERSON POINT OF VIEW

The author has chosen to write this story in the third person omniscient point of view. This means that the author uses the pronouns *she* and *her* to tell the story. The narrator is *not* a part of the story; there is no *I* involved in the action. Through third person, the author can reveal things about the main character and about the action in general that are not necessarily noticed by the main or secondary characters.

The Snow Woman

Norah Burke

One morning Lha-mo found the tracks of a snow man and followed them.

Normally she would have been far too frightened to do so, but this time there was a compelling reason.

She stood dumbfounded, staring at that mark of a naked foot in the drift. The prints were large and fresh, but filling up fast with falling snow.

This was not the first time Lha-mo had seen the trail of a yeti, for all her life had been lived here in the high Himalayas, and she had grown up with the knowledge that among these thousands of miles of snow there lived a great creature unknown to the rest of the world. But such prints were rare, and these were nearly as fresh as her own.

Lha-mo was a **Bhutia** woman, always smiling. The piercing climate had made her people squat and sturdy. She too. She stood now, a little dumpy figure in a vast landscape. Alone among giant peaks, in the snow, under the lowering sky, she was a bundle of old but handsome and workmanlike clothes. Snow-roses glowed in her brown cheeks. There was a knife in her belt, and her heart was strong.

She looked up now, after the tracks which continued steadily over the snowfield and up some **scree** and along a ridge and—

She was already far from home, having come to search for some strayed animals. Her husband and all her brothers-in-law were out too. There was no one left behind in the yak-hair tents except her little son and his grandmother.

Lha-mo smiled, thinking of him, her jewel. How he had yelled when he realized that his mother was going out and that he was to be left behind! How he had clung to her, burying his face in her clothing and drawing the cloth over his ears, to shut out unpleasant things.

He, like Lha-mo, had been born into this life of tents and herds, and movement from place to place, as they pastured their animals or traded in salt and **borax**, in musk, wool, yak tails, herbs, and such; and just now they were crossing this high range, on their way to other valleys.

Once a year, the nomads descended from their **steppes** and snows into the little raggle-taggle towns to sell and to buy.

It was there that Lha-mo had heard about the expedition come from **Darjeeling** into these mountains to search for the yeti. It was there that she had seen white faces for the first time in her life, and been told of the huge rewards which were on offer for news of tracks, for descriptions of the animals, bits of skin, anything.

And it was there that she had seen the necklace!

Kokh Bazaar was one of the last villages for climbers on their way to

> ● ● ● ● ● ● ●
> ## "How he had clung to her, burying his face in her clothing and drawing the cloth over his ears."
> ● ● ● ● ● ● ●

Bhutia—the people of Bhutan, a small kingdom in the eastern Himalayan Mountains, on the border between India and China

scree—stones or rocks lying at the base of a hill or cliff

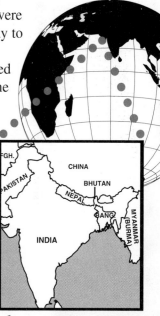

borax—a white crystalline compound that occurs as a mineral; used for an antiseptic and cleansing agent, among other things

Everest and other peaks; and this new scientific expedition was making the place its headquarters, from which mobile units could dart out with camera and rifle after information of any kind.

"These madmen," smiled Lha-mo, "they do not believe the yeti exists, but they have come to look for it! Imagine!"

But the foreigners said: "The tracks could be those of a bear or of a langur monkey. Any marks a day or two old become larger as they melt under strong sun. Such prints may be made sometimes by one creature, sometimes another, which would account for the conflicting descriptions of them. Some four-footed animals place the hind foot in the print of the front one, thus giving the impression of a two-footed upright being."

As Lha-mo and her people had moved about in the stinking bazaar—filth protects from cold—she had heard all the talk.

She saw pomegranates and watermelons laid out for sale, and guns being made. She examined beads and cloth.

The silversmith sat in front of his open shop, making a necklace. Turquoise, amber, and coral were being put into silver, and he was using **prodigious** quantities of all these things.

It was no ordinary necklace. Up till that moment, Lha-mo had been perfectly content—even proud—with her own numerous ornaments, but now she saw that they were only thin silver hoops. This necklace that was being made to some lady's order was broad, new, and splendid, unlike anything she'd ever imagined. In the sun it flashed, not extinguished by the grime of wear. The intricacies of the silver were not filled level with black dirt. The necklace was not for sale, but it could be copied.

She had thought of the thing ever since, and now here were yeti tracks—

Her heart began to pound.

All that she had ever heard about the beast came back to her.

"It is fierce. It eats people. To meet one is to die. It is unlucky even to come upon the tracks. Whenever you see them, Lha-mo, run away!"

But now she made up her mind to follow, and alone. There was no time to fetch anyone else. Snow was covering the tracks fast, and she was already a long way from camp. If this trail was to be followed, to discover the gorge or cave where the creature lived, it must be now, at once. When she had pinpointed the area, she could return with others to kill the beast, or capture it.

After all, the rewards were great. Besides the necklace, there would be splendid clothes for all the family. Much food. She could see already a blue satin

steppes—vast, level, treeless areas

Darjeeling—a town in the lower Himalayas in India

prodigious—plentiful

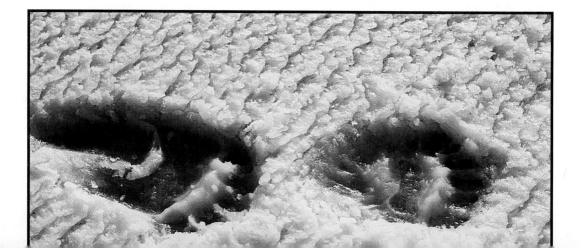

cap, stitched with gold thread, for the boy. Next year when they went down into the warm valleys, they would buy apricots and peaches, and boxes made of poplar or walnut in which to store their wealth. There would be something more to eat than meat and tea and barley. Already she could taste pink apricot juice on her tongue; and her good teeth cracked peach stones to get at the green nut-marrow inside. She saw her whole family warmed by food and good fortune.

There were all these reasons, but the necklace sparkled clearest of all.

She listened.

Wind and snow whispered together. She heard the long singing crack of ice. She heard her own breath and heart. Nothing else.

Her knife was a fine one, kept sharp, to **flay** meat and shape leather. It had a rough turquoise in the hilt, and enamel. Now she whetted it on a stone till the sound quavered on the glassy air.

The footprints had toes, and so she hesitated, wondering which way to go, because it is well known that the yeti's toes are on the back of its feet.

But a glance at the tracks convinced her that this could not be so. The pressure and the drag indicated that the creature was going the other way.

Tibetan women are independent and resolute; Lha-mo was as bold as any, and impulsive too. She decided to rely on her lifelong knowledge of tracks and follow forward as she would have done for any other animal.

She set out, leaning into the driving snow.

It was second nature to her to notice landmarks as she went, and thus remember the way back; so she had no fear of losing herself, however far she might go.

The air was so cold that her breath not only smoked but seemed as if it must drop in ice. Yet she herself, fortified by all the cups of buttered tea which she had already drunk this morning, and for which she carried always the ingredients in the blousing of her clothes, so that no weather would catch her out without it— she herself was so hot, she steamed, and had to open her clothing to let the cruel air cool her skin.

Flakes whirled, the sky was full, and all the world was lit by the dark light of snow.

Although the yeti tracks were disappearing, they were easy to follow.

"It is taller than I am," she thought, "and heavier."

Now and then Lha-mo stopped to see if the wind could tell her anything. Scent of any kind means life, but up here no **resin** or animals altered the thin air. Each lungful was the purest in the world. Although she did see the **lollop** of hare-tracks in the snow, and once a flick of black and red—a **chough** hopping among rocks—she was almost **above life** now.

Several miles of snow-desert lay between her and the smoky smelly tents of home, where her little son waited to burrow his face against her, in shy joy at her return.

She settled into a steady plod that took her across drifts and packed snow, over swept rock and ice, and glacier and **moraine**, up and down steep slopes; and still the tracks chained on and on into unknown country.

Snow squeaked underfoot. There was the brushbrush of her own clothes.

flay—to strip meat off the skin

resin—referring to the sticky substance that oozes from fir and pine trees, which grow at altitudes far below where Lha-mo is

lollop—referring to the bounding motion with which a hare moves in the snow

chough—pronounced CHUFF; a bird related to crows that has red legs and glossy black feathers

above life—at such a high altitude that little or no animal life dwelled there

moraine—an accumulation of dirt and stones deposited by a glacier

FOCUS ON...
GEOGRAPHY

Lha-mo lives in Bhutan, a small kingdom in the eastern Himalayan Mountains on the border between India and China. Find out about Bhutan; its climate, weather, crops, and terrain. If possible, find information about Bhutan's shared borders with India and China and the relationship Bhutan has with each country. Give an oral presentation of your findings, including maps and diagrams of Bhutan and its geographical features.

◆ ◆ ◆ ◆ ◆ ◆ ◆ ◆ ◆ ◆ ◆ ◆ ◆ ◆ ◆ ◆

escarpment—
steep slope

Otherwise only the wind. Once she broke through a snow-crust on to rock and jarred her spine.

But look! Here the creature had stopped by the wayside. And here snow was still melted where it had sat down. Steppe grasses were showing through. Lha-mo knelt and sniffed. There was scent, but nothing she recognized. An unknown animal.

She got up, brushing her knees, and gazed ahead, her heart going. In front rose an **escarpment**, broken by gullies. Was it time to turn back? Was this the place?

Even as she looked, she thought she glimpsed something moving, a tall white figure, sometimes upright and sometimes down like an animal; but next minute she rubbed the snow mirages from her eyes and saw that there was nothing.

She walked on.

The tracks went forward into a narrow ravine and Lha-mo halted.

In the gorge a pebble rattled.

It would be mad to enter such a place.

Instead, she climbed swiftly and silently on to the ridge alongside, then wriggled to the knife-edge to look down into the gulley below.

For a moment there was nothing. Then movement showed up a live thing. Almost directly below her and unaware of her presence was an animal she had never seen before. Was it a bear or ape? She had no idea. She could see only that it was large, and for a moment she took it to be white. Then the wind, blowing from behind, lifted the floppy silver gloss of topcoat, and she saw that underneath the white was cinnamon. If this animal took to living lower down, it would turn brown.

Ah, if only she had got with her one of those beautiful guns from Kokh Bazaar, she could have killed and skinned this treasure, and gone home in triumph, with the pelt folded on her back and edged with red icicles. The chance of a lifetime was here to hand, never to come again.

A weapon?

Beside her lay a big boulder.

Lha-mo got her shoulder against it, and at the third heave she pushed it over the edge.

The boulder whistled down on to the yeti. The animal leaped for safety, but too late. The rock took it on the head, and rock and animal rolled together to the bottom of the defile where the yeti lay motionless. Echoes went ringing everywhere, and setting off avalanches.

Lha-mo, glittering with success, waited for the commotion to be over. Then, as the animal did not move, she drew her knife and scrambled down after it.

There it lay, among snow and pebbles, a mound of heavy silvery hair, much bigger than she had expected from above. She threw one or two stones at it first, to make sure it was dead.

When it still did not move, she approached, but as she got nearer, she saw that it was breathing.

Stunned perhaps?

She sprinted to finish it off with her knife before it regained consciousness.

But it was not a snow man. It was a snow woman with a baby.

The baby was unhurt. He was about the size of a human baby. Her own, for instance. And as she raced up to them, he gave a cry and buried his face against his mother, drawing her long fur over his ears.

Lha-mo **recoiled** as if shot.

She gasped a horrified breath into her.

Then she backed out, and turned and ran.

That rich mad expedition would now go home and tell the world that there

> ●●●●●●●●
> "He gave a cry and buried his face against his mother, drawing her long fur over his ears."
> ●●●●●●●●

was no such thing as a yeti, and that all the hill people were ignorant and superstitious, but she did not care.

Before she was out of sight, she looked back. The yeti was rising and shaking her head. She picked up her child and bounded away.

Lha-mo made for home as fast as ever she could. As she approached it, she saw that the strayed animals were back, rounded up by one of the others, no doubt. She went in and sat down by the fire, and began to shake.

She was late, of course, and her husband angry.

"Where have you been?" he demanded.

"Out," replied Lha-mo. ❖

recoiled—to shrink or spring back from fear

ON THE JOB
WILDLIFE MANAGER

Wildlife managers perform conservation work in wildlife refuges, public forests, and hunting grounds. They organize surveys to identify the kind and number of animals, birds, and fish located in their territory. They also restock species of fish and game whose population has decreased. Useful course work includes biology, botany, animal ecology, chemistry, math, and physics. Some colleges offer degree programs in wildlife management, usually in the school of forestry.

The Snow Woman

UNDERSTANDING

1. How does Lha-mo contradict the stereotype of women right up to the end of the story? Does her behavior at the end disappoint you? Does it indicate weakness or strength? Why do you think the author ended the story the way she did? Write a new ending for this story in which Lha-mo befriends or betrays the snow woman and her child. *Workshop 1*

2. Lha-mo is in part a product of her environment. What characteristics does she possess because of the place in which she lives? Find evidence in the text to support your conclusions.

   Using Lha-mo's story as one example, write an essay in which you explain your view of the influence environment has on shaping a person's tastes (likes and dislikes), activities (hobbies, occupations), and values. *Workshop 8*

3. Find in the text passages which reveal the kind of mother Lha-mo is. With a group, create a list of the personality traits you think mothers and fathers must have to help children succeed in today's world. Using this information, write a personal essay explaining your idea of how parents or guardians should raise children. *Workshop 3*

CONNECTING

1. For generations, people have referred to "mother instinct," the supposedly in-born knowledge women possess that enables them to care for their children. Increasingly, however, people claim that this intuition, if it does exist, is not enough to prepare women to raise children. What kind of training do adults need to do a good job of parenting? Conduct a survey to discover views on the following: Is the mother instinct evident in all mothers? Can males develop a "mother" instinct? What training do parents need and where can they find it? Chart your findings, comparing men's and women's responses. Present your findings to the class. *Workshops 15 and 22*

2. Research the Bhutanese people using print and on-line references. What is their daily life like, what do they wear and eat, and how do they combat the harsh climate? Do your findings support or contradict the story? Write your discoveries in a documented report. *Workshop 21*

Deer Hunter and White Corn Maiden

EXPLORING

In all societies, people who violate tradition are often ostracized or punished in one way or another. For example, for many years in our society working mothers and stay-at-home husbands were frowned upon. This has changed. Do we have any traditions that are as strong now as they were when your parents were young? What is the purpose of tradition?

THEME CONNECTION... TRADITION AND REALITY

This legend was probably created by the Indian people to keep individuals from becoming so involved with each other that they neglect their duties to the tribe. Though the story is imaginary, its purpose was real and benefited tribal society.

TIME & PLACE

"Deer Hunter and White Corn Maiden" is a legend from the Tewa, a Pueblo tribe that lived in the area around Sante Fe, New Mexico. As with all legends, the author is unknown and the story was originally handed down orally. Its purpose was both to teach young people to respect traditions and customs and to explain the appearance of two distinct stars in the sky.

THE WRITER'S CRAFT

LEGEND

"Deer Hunter and White Corn Maiden" is a legend. A legend is a story that contains perhaps some historical truth and that is recited aloud. Parents tell the legend to their children, who eventually pass the story along to their own children. A legend contains an idea or insight that belongs to the group of people who created it. Eventually many legends are written down. They are usually brief, set in a distant time and place, and present actions and their consequences.

Deer Hunter and White Corn Maiden

Unknown

(American Indian—Tewa)

Long ago in the ancient home of the San Juan people, in a village whose ruins can be seen across the river from present-day San Juan, lived two magically gifted young people. The youth was called Deer Hunter because even as a boy, he was the only one who never returned empty-handed from the hunt. The girl, whose name was White Corn Maiden, made the finest pottery and embroidered clothing with the most beautiful designs of any woman in the village. These two were the handsomest couple in the village, and it was no surprise to their parents that they always sought one another's company. Seeing that they were favored by the gods, the villagers assumed that they were destined to marry.

And in time they did, and contrary to their elders' expectations, they began to spend even more time with each other. White Corn Maiden began to ignore her pottery-making and embroidery, while Deer Hunter gave up hunting, at a time when he could have saved many of his people from hunger. They even began to forget their religious obligations. At the request of the pair's worried parents, the tribal elders called a council. This young couple was ignoring all the traditions by which the tribe had lived and prospered, and the people feared that angry gods might bring famine, flood, sickness, or some other disaster upon the village.

But Deer Hunter and White Corn Maiden ignored the council's pleas and drew closer together, swearing that nothing would ever part them. A sense of doom pervaded the village, even though it was late spring and all nature had unfolded in new life.

Then suddenly White Corn Maiden became ill, and within three days she died. Deer Hunter's grief had no bounds. He refused to speak or eat, preferring to keep watch beside his wife's body until she was buried early the next day.

For four days after death, every soul wanders in and around its village and seeks forgiveness from those whom it may have wronged in life. It is a time of unease for the living, since the soul may appear in the form of a wind, a disembodied voice, a dream, or even in human shape. To prevent such a visitation, the villagers go to the dead person before burial and utter a soft prayer of forgiveness. And on the fourth day after death, the relatives gather to perform a ceremony releasing the soul into the spirit world, from which it will never return.

But Deer Hunter was unable to accept his wife's death. Knowing that he might see her during the four-day interlude, he began to wander around the edge of the

> ● ● ● ● ● ● ● ● ● ● ●
> **"This young couple was ignoring all the traditions by which the tribe had lived and prospered."**
> ● ● ● ● ● ● ● ● ● ● ●

FOCUS ON...
SOCIAL STUDIES

"Deer Hunter and White Corn Maiden" is a legend from the Tewa people, one of many Pueblo tribes that lived along the Rio Grande. Find out about the Tewa and other Pueblo tribes. Prepare a multimedia presentation about their history, way of life, culture and traditions, and oral folklore.

village. Soon he drifted farther out into the fields, and it was here at sundown of the fourth day, even while his relatives were gathering for the ceremony of release, that he spotted a small fire near a clump of bushes.

Deer Hunter drew closer and found his wife, as beautiful as she was in life and dressed in all her finery, combing her long hair with a cactus brush in preparation for the last journey. He fell weeping at her feet, imploring her not to leave but to return with him to the village before the releasing rite was **consummated**. White Corn Maiden begged her husband to let her go, because she no longer belonged to the world of the living. Her return would anger the spirits, she said, and anyhow, soon she would no longer be beautiful, and Deer Hunter would shun her.

He brushed her pleas aside by pledging his undying love and promising that he would let nothing part them. Eventually she relented, saying that she would hold him to his promise. They entered the village just as their relatives were marching to the shrine with the food offering that would release the soul of White Corn Maiden. They were horrified when they saw her, and again they and the village elders begged Deer Hunter to let her go. He ignored them, and an air of grim expectancy settled over the village.

The couple returned to their home, but before many days had passed, Deer Hunter noticed that his wife was beginning to have an unpleasant odor. Then he saw that her beautiful face had grown ashen and her skin dry. At first he only turned his back on her as they slept. Later he began to sit up on the roof all night, but White Corn Maiden always joined him. In time the villagers became used to the sight of Deer Hunter racing among the houses and through the fields with White Corn Maiden, now not much more than skin and bones, in hot pursuit.

Things continued in this way, until one misty morning a tall and imposing figure appeared in the small dance court at the center of the village. He was dressed in spotless white buckskin robes and carried the biggest bow anyone had ever seen. On his back was slung a great

consummated—
completed

SPOTLIGHT ON...
WORKING COOPERATIVELY

Because of their all-consuming love for each other, Deer Hunter and White Corn Maiden neglect their tribal duties and religious obligations. Most selfishly, Deer Hunter gave up hunting, and therefore brought hunger to many of his people. In any working relationship, beginning within the family, people must work as a team. As you continue to work on relationships at home and establish new ones at school and work, keep the following guidelines in mind:

1. Discuss expectations, goals, and tasks with team members.
2. Divide tasks evenly among team members.
3. Discuss and resolve problems as they occur.
4. Encourage each other and express your appreciation for each other's efforts.

◆ ◆ ◆ ◆ ◆ ◆ ◆ ◆ ◆ ◆ ◆ ◆ ◆ ◆ ◆ ◆ ◆ ◆ ◆

quiver with the two largest arrows anyone had ever seen. He remained standing at the center of the village and called, in a voice that carried into every home, for Deer Hunter and White Corn Maiden. Such was its authority that the couple stepped forward meekly and stood facing him.

The awe-inspiring figure told the couple that he had been sent from the spirit world because they, Deer Hunter and White Corn Maiden, had violated their people's traditions and angered the spirits; that because they had been so selfish, they had brought grief and near-disaster to the village. "Since you insist on being together," he said, "you shall have your wish. You will chase each other forever across the sky, as visible reminders that your people must live according to tradition if they are to survive." With this he set Deer Hunter on one arrow and shot him low into the western sky. Putting White Corn Maiden on the other arrow, he placed her just behind her husband.

That evening the villagers saw two new stars in the west. The first, large and very bright, began to move east across the heavens. The second, a smaller, flickering star, followed close behind. So it is to this day, according to the Tewa; the brighter one is Deer Hunter, placed there in the prime of his life. The dimmer star is White Corn Maiden, set there after she had died; yet she will forever chase her husband across the heavens. ❖

UNDERSTANDING

1.  Working with a group, find examples in the text that show how the young couple was viewed for violating tradition. How did people react to them? What did they say and do?

    How does our society deal with young people who ignore accepted customs and behavior? Together think up examples of how young people today displease their elders by ignoring conventional dress, manners, and language. How does society respond to those who disregard traditional customs? Prepare a speech explaining why young people should, or should not, honor the dress, manners, and language of their elders. *Workshop 23*

2. Deer Hunter and White Corn Maiden were so infatuated with each other that they did foolish things. What problems did their excessive attention to each other cause?

    What problems can modern teenagers cause for themselves and others if they become too involved with each other? Pretend you are the parent of a teenager. Write a letter to your teenage son or daughter explaining the dangers of spending too much time and attention on a girlfriend or boyfriend.

3. A magical figure from the spirit world visited the tribe to deal with Deer Hunter and White Corn Maiden. What did this figure look like and what did he do?

    Imagine a messenger arriving today to teach important lessons. What might this figure look like? What might he or she do to stop the problems plaguing teenagers? Write the story in the form of a legend. *Workshop 1*

CONNECTING

1.  "DEER HUNTER AND WHITE CORN MAIDEN" provides some information about burial practices and attitudes towards death. How do the practices and beliefs reflected in the legend compare with today's burial practices and beliefs about death in your area? Working with a partner, arrange an interview with a local funeral home director and tour a funeral home. Write a report on the information you gather. In your report, explain why you do, or do not, approve of society's way of handling death. *Workshops 21 and 24*

2. Research star formations. Are there two stars in the galaxy that may represent Deer Hunter and White Corn Maiden? What are their astronomical names? Create a chart that shows their location in the sky and their relation to other star formations.

> ## A LAST WORD
>
> Whose needs do you put first: your community's or family's, or your own? How might cooperative efforts bring satisfaction to all members of your community—including yourself?

from *An American Childhood*

EXPLORING

● ●

Children are often frightened by harmless things. Babies can be afraid of people with glasses or big hats. Thunder, sirens, garter snakes, and large beetles may cause alarm in some small children. Even Santa Claus and Disney and Sesame Street characters can frighten children at times. In many cases, the cause of fright is the unknown—if you cannot determine why something happened or what something is, you will experience fear. With your class, compare childhood fears generated by imagination. Brainstorm to discuss whether these fears helped or hindered you.

THEME CONNECTION...
FEAR AND IMAGINATION

Each of us is capable of imagining terrible things, and these imaginings often frighten us. Have you ever been home alone at night, for example, and felt afraid when you heard a peculiar noise? Once you identified the cause of the noise, your fear disappeared. Because fear—even imaginary fear—can be overwhelming. President Franklin D. Roosevelt (1882–1945) reassured Americans in his First Inaugural Address, "Let me assert my firm belief that the only thing we have to fear is fear itself."

TIME & PLACE

This essay is set in Pittsburgh in the 1950s. This is the age of "Leave It to Beaver" and "Father Knows Best," popular television shows that depicted "typical" American families in which Dad went to the office, Mom stayed home and cooked and cleaned in a pretty dress, and the two kids were polite and well mannered. In fact most wives did stay home while husbands went to work, and whole families sat down to dinner every night and ate meat, potatoes, and vegetables. Real life was not quite as simple as the television shows led one to believe, but home and family were the guiding principles of life, perhaps more so than they are in the 1990s.

THE WRITER'S CRAFT
PERSONAL ESSAY

An essay may be formal and objective, or it may be personal. Annie Dillard's essay is personal. It talks about her own personal experiences and uses these to arrive at a conclusion about the human condition. Dillard's personal essay proposes a central thesis, offers specific examples and anecdotes, and is logically organized.

● ●

from An American Childhood

Annie Dillard

hen I was five, growing up in Pittsburgh in 1950, I would not go to bed willingly because something came into my room. This was a private matter between me and it. If I spoke of it, it would kill me.

Who could breathe as this thing searched for me over the very corners of the room? Who could ever breathe freely again? I lay in the dark.

My sister Amy, two years old, was asleep in the other bed. What did she know? She was innocent of evil. Even at two she composed herself attractively for sleep. She folded the top sheet tidily under her prettily outstretched arm; she laid her perfect head lightly on an unwrinkled pillow, where her thick curls spread evenly in rays like petals. All night long she slept smoothly in a series of pleasant and serene, if artificial-looking, positions, a faint smile on her closed lips, as if she were posing for an ad for sheets.

There was no messiness in her, no roughness for things to cling to, only a charming and charmed innocence that seemed then to protect her, an innocence I needed but couldn't muster. Since Amy was asleep, furthermore, and since when I needed someone most I was afraid to stir enough to wake her, she was useless.

I lay alone and was almost asleep when the . . . thing entered the room by flattening itself against the open door and sliding in. It was a transparent, luminous oblong. I could see the door whiten at its touch; I could see the blue wall turn pale where it raced over it, and see the maple headboard of Amy's bed glow. It was a swift spirit; it was an awareness. It made noise. It had two joined parts, a head and a tail, like a **Chinese dragon.** It found the door, wall, and headboard; and it wiped them, charging them with its luminous glance. After its **fleet**, searching passage, things looked the same, but weren't.

I dared not blink or breathe; I tried to hush my whooping blood. If it found another awareness, it would destroy it.

Every night before it got to me it gave up. It hit my wall's corner and couldn't get past. It shrank completely into itself and vanished like a cobra down a hole. I heard the rising roar it made when it died or left. I still couldn't breathe. I knew—it was the worst fact I knew, a very hard fact—that it could return again alive that same night.

Sometimes it came back, sometimes it didn't. Most often, restless, it came back. The light stripe slipped in the door, ran searching over Amy's wall, stopped, stretched lunatic at the first corner, raced wailing toward my wall, and vanished into the second corner with a cry. So I wouldn't go to bed.

It was a passing car whose windshield reflected the corner streetlight outside. I figured it out one night.

About the Author

Annie Dillard (b. 1945) has a long list of published works, one of which, *Pilgrim at Tinker Creek,* won a Pulitzer Prize. She was born and raised in Pennsylvania and graduated from Hollins College in Virginia. She is considered one of America's best essayists. Some of Dillard's best-known work includes *Teaching a Stone to Talk, An American Childhood, Tickets for a Prayer Wheel, Living by Fiction, Encounters with Chinese Writers,* and *The Writing Life.*

Chinese dragon—costume worn by several people; used especially during Chinese New Year festivities

fleet—swift

Figuring it out was as memorable as the oblong itself. Figuring it out was a long and forced ascent to the very rim of being, to the membrane of skin that both separates and connects the inner life and the outer world. I climbed deliberately from the depths like a diver who releases the monster in his arms and hauls himself hand over hand up an anchor chain till he meets the ocean's sparkling membrane and bursts through it; he sights the sunlit, **becalmed** hull of his boat, which had **bulked** so ominously from below.

I recognized the noise it made when it left. That is, the noise it made called to mind, at last, my daytime sensations when a car passed—the sight and noise together. A car came roaring down hushed Edgerton Avenue in front of our house, stopped at the corner stop sign,

and passed on shrieking as its engine shifted up the gears. What, precisely, came into the bedroom? A reflection from the car's oblong windshield. Why did it travel in two parts? The window sash split the light and cast a shadow.

Night after night I labored up the same long chain of reasoning, as night after night the thing burst into the room where I lay awake and Amy slept prettily and my loud heart thrashed and I froze.

There was a world outside my window and **contiguous** to it. If I was so all fired bright, as my parents, who had **patently** no basis for comparison, seemed to think, why did I have to keep learning this same thing over and over? For I had learned it a summer ago, when men with jackhammers broke up Edgerton Avenue. I had watched them from the yard; the street came up in jagged slabs like **floes**. When I lay to nap, I listened. One restless afternoon I connected the new noise in my bedroom with the jackhammer men I had been seeing outside. I understood abruptly that these worlds met, the outside and the inside. I traveled the route in my mind: You walked downstairs from here, and outside from downstairs. "Outside," then, was conceivably just beyond my windows. It was the same world I reached by going out the front or the back door. I forced my imagination yet again over this route.

The world did not have me in mind; it had no mind. It was a coincidental collection of things and people, items, and I myself was one such item—a child walking up the sidewalk whom anyone could see or ignore. The things in the world did not necessarily cause my overwhelming feeling, the feelings were

ON THE JOB
CHILD-CARE PROVIDER

Child-care providers take care of young children in their own homes or at child-care centers. Their varied duties include preparing and serving meals; organizing and supervising exercise; and providing a stimulating social and educational environment for the children. High school students interested in working with children should take courses in art, drama, home economics, nutrition, psychology, and physical education. Valuable experiences include baby-sitting and summer camp counseling.

inside me, beneath my skin, behind my ribs, within my skull. They were even, to some extent, under my control.

I could be connected to the outside world by reason, if I chose, or I could yield to what amounted to a narrative fiction, to a tale of terror whispered to me by the blood in my ears, a show in light projected on the room's blue walls. As time passed, I learned to amuse myself in bed in the darkened room by entering the fiction deliber-ately and replacing it by reason delib-erately.

When the low roar drew nigh and the oblong slid in the door, I threw my own switches for pleasure. It's coming after me; it's a car outside. It's after me. It's a car. It raced over the wall, lighting it blue wherever it ran; it bumped over Amy's maple headboard in a rush, paused, slithered **elongate** over the corner, shrank, flew my way and vanished into itself with a wail. It was a car. ❖

elongate—
stretched

UNDERSTANDING

1. What did Dillard's monster look like? Describe it as though you were a scientist or detective recording every detail about the creature.
   When you were a child, did you experience imaginary fears? With your group, brainstorm the kinds of things that sparked your imagination into frightening you. Did you imagine monsters under your bed, for example, or intruders hidden in closets? With a partner, collaborate to write a story inspired by your recollections of imaginary childhood fears. Read your story to the rest of the class. *Workshops 1 and 10*

2. Dillard finally figured out what caused the monster. Locate in the text the criti-cal point that brought understanding?
   Some experts say when you feel in control, you can eliminate fear. One way to feel control is to face your fear. Think about what you fear most. Then imagine the worst thing that could possibly happen—a worst-case scenario. Having imagined the worst thing that could happen, solve the problem: that is, figure out how to deal with it. In a paragraph, describe something that you fear right now. Next identify a worst-case scenario. What is the worst thing that could happen? Having done this exercise, describe it to a group of your class-mates. Together, discuss the effectiveness of the worst-case scenario. Does it work? *Workshop 10*

3. Dillard uses personification in this essay (giving human characteristics to nonliving things). Cite some examples of personification that occur in the selection.

Become the monster in Dillard's room. Using the first person, write a short personal essay telling how you feel about entering the room each night. What do you see? Why do you dissolve in the corner? What are your intentions? Be sure to have a central theme, or point that your description supports. *Workshop 8*

CONNECTING

1. Authorities believe that most prejudice in the world is caused by fear of the unknown. If we don't know about or understand a person from a different race or culture, we may prejudge or fear that person. Work with a group to write a proposal to your school principal for a multicultural fair. Include in your proposal suggestions for displays and presentations intended to teach students about different cultures. *Workshop 13*

2. Stage fright is a common fear afflicting speakers and performers. Shaky hands, knocking knees, loss of voice, and blank mind are a few of the symptoms. Research ways to conquer stage fright by talking to people who give speeches regularly and by reading books and articles on the subject. Compose a list of methods to relieve or prevent stage fright. Write a feature article for your school newspaper. Include what stage fright is, what causes it, and ways to relieve it or prevent it from happening. *Workshop 17*

A LAST WORD

In the excerpt from her autobiography, Dillard clearly describes the awakening of her imagination through a puzzling and frightening childhood experience. What stirred your childhood imagination? When were you first aware of your mind at work?

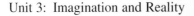

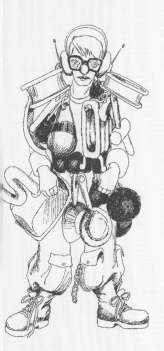

Harrison Bergeron

EXPLORING

Americans believe in equality. Our constitutional rights are based on the principle of equality, and the promise of equal opportunity for all reverberates through our schools and court-rooms. What is "equality"? In doing so, consider the difference between saying that everyone has identical rights and saying that everyone has identical abilities. Do you think all human beings are equally valuable and that they should therefore have the same rights? Do you think each person's talents are, or ought to be, the same?

THEME CONNECTION...
THE NATURE OF EQUALITY

Imagine that society deplored excellence and instead pro-moted mediocrity so that each person would be like everyone else. In such a world, anything that distinguishes an individual would be suppressed, particularly the ability to think indepen-dently. Vonnegut imagines such oppres-sive conformity in "Harrison Bergeron." He encourages us to laugh at the conse-quences of such absurd conformity.

TIME & PLACE

Vonnegut wrote this story in 1961, which was about the time people began talking seriously about achieving civil rights for all—championing the under-dog and punishing those who exploited others. As women, African Americans, Native Americans, the physically chal-lenged, and other groups demanded equal rights, the country came closer to the interpretation of the Constitution and the Bill of Rights the founders of our country envisioned: equal treatment under the law.

THE WRITER'S CRAFT

SATIRE

Satire seeks to improve the human condition by making fun of it. Satire may gently poke fun at human foolishness, or it may provoke laughter by sternly denouncing human corruption and evil. Vonnegut's satire makes fun of the point of view that no one person's excellent achievements should receive special acclaim or attention. On the contrary, we should all strive to be mediocre.

Harrison Bergeron

Kurt Vonnegut

The year was 2081, and everybody was finally equal. They weren't only equal before God and the law. They were equal every which way. Nobody was smarter than anybody else. Nobody was better looking than anybody else. Nobody was stronger or quicker than anybody else. All this equality was due to the 211th, 212th, and 213th Amendments to the Constitution, and to the unceasing vigilance of agents of the United States Handicapper General.

Some things about living still weren't quite right, though. April, for instance, still drove people crazy by not being springtime. And it was in that clammy month that the H-G men took George and Hazel Bergeron's fourteen-year-old son, Harrison, away.

It was tragic, all right, but George and Hazel couldn't think about it very hard. Hazel had a perfectly average intelligence, which meant she couldn't think about anything except in short bursts. And George, while his intelligence was way above normal, had a little mental-handicap radio in his ear. He was required by law to wear it at all times. It was tuned to a government transmitter. Every twenty seconds or so, the transmitter would send out some sharp noise to keep people like George from taking unfair advantage of their brains.

George and Hazel were watching television. There were tears on Hazel's cheeks, but she'd forgotten for the moment what they were about.

On the television screen were ballerinas.

A buzzer sounded in George's head. His thoughts fled in panic, like bandits from a burglar alarm.

"That was a real pretty dance, that dance they just did," said Hazel.

"Huh?" said George.

"That dance—it was nice," said Hazel.

"Yup," said George. He tried to think a little about the ballerinas. They weren't really very good—no better than anybody else would have been, anyway. They were burdened with sash weights and bags of birdshot, and their faces were masked, so that no one, seeing a free and graceful gesture or a pretty face, would feel like something the cat drug in. George was toying with the vague notion that maybe dancers shouldn't be handicapped. But he didn't get very far with it before another noise in his ear radio scattered his thoughts.

George winced. So did two out of the eight ballerinas.

Hazel saw him wince. Having no mental handicap herself, she had to ask George what the latest sound had been.

"Sounded like somebody hitting a milk bottle with a ball-peen hammer," said George.

"I'd think it would be real interesting, hearing all the different sounds," said

Hazel, a little envious. "All the things they think up."

"Um," said George.

"Only, if I was Handicapper General, you know what I would do?" said Hazel. Hazel, as a matter of fact, bore a strong resemblance to the Handicapper General, a woman named Diana Moon Glampers. "If I was Diana Moon Glampers," said Hazel, "I'd have chimes on Sunday—just chimes. Kind of in honor of religion."

"I could think, if it was just chimes," said George.

"Well—maybe make 'em real loud," said Hazel. "I think I'd make a good Handicapper General."

"Good as anybody else," said George.

"Who knows better'n I do what normal is?" said Hazel.

"Right," said George. He began to think glimmeringly about his abnormal son who was now in jail, about Harrison, but a twenty-one-gun salute in his head stopped that.

"Boy!" said Hazel, "that was a doozy, wasn't it?"

It was such a doozy that George was white and trembling, and tears stood on the rims of his red eyes. Two of the eight ballerinas had collapsed to the studio floor, were holding their temples.

"All of a sudden you look so tired," said Hazel. "Why don't you stretch out on the sofa, so's you can rest your handicap bag on the pillows, honeybunch." She was referring to the forty-seven pounds of birdshot in a canvas bag, which was padlocked around George's neck. "Go on and rest the bag for a little while," she said. "I don't care if you're not equal to me for a while."

George weighed the bag with his hands. "I don't mind it," he said, "I don't notice it any more. It's just a part of me."

"You been so tired lately—kind of wore out," said Hazel. "If there was just some way we could make a little hole in the bottom of the bag, and just take out a few of them lead balls. Just a few."

"Two years in prison and two thousand dollars fine for every ball I took out," said George. "I don't call that a bargain."

"If you could just take a few out when you came home from work," said Hazel. "I mean—you don't compete with anybody around here. You just set around."

> ● ● ● ● ● ● ●
> ## "Everyone was finally equal. They were equal every which way."
> ● ● ● ● ● ● ●

"If I tried to get away with it," said George, "then other people'd get away with it—and pretty soon we'd be right back to the dark ages again, with everybody competing against everybody else. You wouldn't like that, would you?"

"I'd hate it," said Hazel.

"There you are," said George. "The minute people start cheating on laws, what do you think happens to society?"

If Hazel hadn't been able to come up with an answer to this question, George couldn't have supplied one. A siren was going off in his head.

"Reckon it'd fall all apart," said Hazel.

"What would?" said George blankly.

"Society," said Hazel uncertainly. "Wasn't that what you just said?"

"Who knows?" said George.

FOCUS ON...
GOVERNMENT

In "Harrison Bergeron," the government passes a series of constitutional amendments and squelches every unique aspect of the individual, from talent and intelligence to weight and height. Research the United States Constitution and the Bill of Rights. What is the intent of these documents? What guarantees of equality are made by these documents? In what ways are laws in the United States meant to uphold individual freedoms? Prepare a three-minute speech to present your thoughts and findings.

◆ ◆

The television program was suddenly interrupted for a news bulletin. It wasn't clear at first as to what the bulletin was about, since the announcer, like all announcers, had a serious speech impediment. For about half a minute, and in a state of high excitement, the announcer tried to say, "Ladies and gentlemen—"

He finally gave up, handed the bulletin to a ballerina to read.

"That's all right—" Hazel said of the announcer, "he tried. That's the big thing. He tried to do the best he could with what God gave him. He should get a nice raise for trying so hard."

"Ladies and gentlemen—" said the ballerina, reading the bulletin. She must have been extraordinarily beautiful, because the mask she wore was hideous. And it was easy to see that she was the strongest and most graceful of all the dancers, for her handicap bags were as big as those worn by two-hundred-pound men.

And she had to apologize at once for her voice, which was a very unfair voice for a woman to use. Her voice was a warm, luminous, timeless melody. "Excuse me—" she said, and she began again, making her voice absolutely uncompetitive.

"Harrison Bergeron, age fourteen," she said in a grackle squawk, "has just escaped from jail, where he was held on suspicion of plotting to overthrow the government. He is a genius and an athlete, is underhandicapped, and should be regarded as extremely dangerous."

A police photograph of Harrison Bergeron was flashed on the screen—upside down, then sideways, upside down again, then right side up. The picture showed the full length of Harrison against a background calibrated in feet and inches. He was exactly seven feet tall. The rest of Harrison's appearance was Halloween and hardware. Nobody had ever borne heavier handi-

caps. He had outgrown hindrances faster than the H-G men could think them up. Instead of a little ear radio for a mental handicap, he wore a tremendous pair of earphones, and spectacles with thick wavy lenses. The spectacles were intended to make him not only half blind, but to give him whanging headaches besides.

Scrap metal was hung all over him. Ordinarily, there was a certain symmetry, a military neatness to the handicaps issued strong people, but Harrison looked like a walking junkyard. In the race of life, Harrison carried three hundred pounds.

And to offset his good looks, the H-G men required that he wear at all times a red rubber ball for a nose, keep his eyebrows shaved off and cover his even white teeth with black caps at snaggle-tooth random.

"If you see this boy," said the ballerina, "do not—I repeat, do not—try to reason with him."

There was the shriek of a door being torn from its hinges.

Screams and barking cries of consternation came from the television set. The photograph of Harrison Bergeron on the screen jumped again and again, as though dancing to the tune of an earthquake.

George Bergeron correctly identified the earthquake, and well he might have—for many was the time his own home had danced to the same crashing tune. "That must be Harrison!"

The realization was blasted from his mind instantly by the sound of an automobile collision in his head.

When George could open his eyes again, the photograph of Harrison was gone. A living, breathing Harrison filled the screen.

Clanking, clownish, and huge, Harrison stood in the center of the studio. The knob of the uprooted studio door was still in his hand. Ballerinas, technicians, musicians, and announcers cowered on their knees before him, expecting to die.

"I am the Emperor!" cried Harrison. "Do you hear? I am the Emperor! Everybody must do what I say at once!" He stamped his foot and the studio shook.

"Even as I stand here—" he bellowed, "crippled, hobbled, sickened—I am a greater ruler than any man who ever lived! Now watch me become what I can become!"

Harrison tore the straps of his handicap harness like wet tissue paper, tore straps guaranteed to support five thousand pounds.

Harrison's scrap-iron handicaps crashed to the floor.

Harrison thrust his thumbs under the bar of the padlock that secured his head harness. The bar snapped like celery. Harrison smashed his headphones and spectacles against the wall.

He flung away his rubber-ball nose, revealed a man that would have awed Thor, the god of thunder.

"I shall now select my Empress!" he said, looking down on the cowering people. "Let the first woman who dares rise to her feet claim her mate and her throne!"

A moment passed, and then a ballerina arose, swaying like a willow.

Harrison plucked the mental handicap from her ear, snapped off her physical handicaps with marvelous delicacy. Last of all, he removed her mask.

She was blindingly beautiful.

"Now—" said Harrison, taking her hand, "shall we show the people the meaning of the word *dance?* Music!" he commanded.

The musicians scrambled back into their chairs, and Harrison stripped them of their handicaps, too. "Play your best," he told them, "and I'll make you barons and dukes and earls."

The music began. It was normal at first—cheap, silly, false. But Harrison snatched two musicians from their chairs, waved them like batons as he sang the music as he wanted it played. He slammed them back into their chairs.

The music began again and was much improved.

Harrison and his Empress merely listened to the music for a while—listened gravely, as though synchronizing their heartbeats with it.

They shifted their weights to their toes.

Harrison placed his big hands on the girl's tiny waist, letting her sense the weightlessness that would soon be hers.

And then, in an explosion of joy and grace, into the air they sprang!

Not only were the laws of the land abandoned, but the law of gravity and the laws of motion as well.

Unit 3: Imagination and Reality

They reeled, whirled, swiveled, flounced, capered, **gamboled**, and spun.

They leaped like deer on the moon. The studio ceiling was thirty feet high, but each leap brought the dancers nearer to it.

It became their obvious intention to kiss the ceiling.

They kissed it.

And then, neutralizing gravity with love and pure will, they remained suspended in air inches below the ceiling, and they kissed each other for a long, long time.

It was then that Diana Moon Glampers, the Handicapper General, came into the studio with a double-barreled ten-gauge shotgun. She fired twice, and the Emperor and the Empress were dead before they hit the floor.

Diana Moon Glampers loaded the gun again. She aimed it at the musicians and told them they had ten seconds to get their handicaps back on.

It was then that the Bergerons' television tube burned out.

Hazel turned to comment about the blackout to George. But George had gone out into the kitchen for a can of beer.

George came back in with the beer, paused while a handicap signal shook him up. And then he sat down again. "You been crying?" he said to Hazel.

"Yup," she said.

"What about?" he said.

"I forget," she said, "Something real sad on television."

"What was it?" he said.

"It's all kind of mixed up in my mind," said Hazel.

"Forget sad things," said George.

"I always do," said Hazel.

"That's my girl," said George. He winced. There was the sound of a riveting gun in his head.

"Gee—I could tell that one was a doozy," said Hazel.

"You can say that again," said George.

"Gee—" said Hazel, "I could tell that one was a doozy." ❖

gamboled— skipped or leaped about, as if in play

UNDERSTANDING

1. In the story, how does the state prevent superior intelligence from overshadowing the average?

   Schools celebrate top athletes and scholars by providing special awards and organizations for them. Does this violate the rights of people who are not specially endowed with intelligence or athletic ability? Should such special attention be banned in public schools so as not to offend the less talented? Write an opinion essay on this topic, giving good reasons for your feelings. *Workshop 13*

2. The Handicapper General's goal is to stamp out competition. What are some of her methods?

   Competition in our society has both positive and negative effects. In a small group, create a two-column chart. Brainstorm the positive effects of competition and write them in one column. Write the negative effects in the other column. Using the points from the lists, write two persuasive paragraphs, one for each side, regardless of your own point of view. This activity will help you see both sides of the issue. *Workshop 13*

3. The dance Harrison and the ballerina engage in demonstrates the beauty of using talents as they were meant to be used. Describe their dance. In what ways do they defy all laws?

   What do you believe the purpose of laws or rules should be? Why do laws exist? In a small group, discuss these questions. Then, produce a set of criteria for effective and fair laws to govern your classroom.

4. Vonnegut uses strong, active verbs—sometimes three or more in one sentence—which give his sentences power and clarity. List at least 20 of his strongest verbs.

   Examine the paragraphs you wrote in question #1 or in another writing assignment. Underline the verbs in your sentences. Are they strong verbs? Have you used the active voice? If not, rewrite your paragraphs—strengthen sentences with strong verbs and the active voice. *Workshop 7*

A LAST WORD

"Harrison Bergeron" satirizes a society in which it is the government's goal to make everyone the same. Differences among people should be celebrated. How might we embrace and honor our differences?

CONNECTING

1. Sometimes laws do more harm than good. Investigate the laws of your city and state. Talk to people about the laws they like and those they feel are unnecessary or too restrictive. Once you have gathered information on laws people dislike, choose one you strongly oppose and write a letter to your state representative requesting a reconsideration of the law. ***Workshops 13 and 18***

2. Many schools have adopted a strict dress code requiring all students to wear uniforms. Does your school have a school uniform? Survey students and teachers in your school to determine their views on requiring uniforms at school. Prepare a chart illustrating your findings and write an interpretation to accompany it. Present your information to a school audience such as a faculty, student council, or school board meeting. ***Workshops 22 and 23***

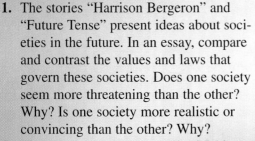

WRAP IT UP

UNIT 3

1. The stories "Harrison Bergeron" and "Future Tense" present ideas about societies in the future. In an essay, compare and contrast the values and laws that govern these societies. Does one society seem more threatening than the other? Why? Is one society more realistic or convincing than the other? Why?

2. The speaker in the poem "I'm Making You Up" imagines her grandmother and the relationship they might have had. In "The Snow Woman," the main character chooses to keep secret her discovery of the yeti. The myth "Deer Hunter and White Corn Maiden" has been handed down by the Tewa tribe and tells the story of the consequences of abandoning tradition. The five-year-old narrator in the excerpt from *An American Childhood* tells herself all sorts of stories and possible explanations for "it." What is the role of imagination in each of these stories? How is imagination used to account for or explain reality? What is the significance of each of these stories to its teller?

UNIT
④
MAKING DISCOVERIES

As we grow, we make many discoveries about ourselves and the people around us. For example, most of us discover that hard work is rewarding. Some of us learn painful lessons, such as that reaching a long-sought goal can be an empty victory.

It's never too early or too late in life to make discoveries. The more discoveries we make, the more we learn about ourselves and our world. We don't need microscopes or test tubes to make these discoveries. We just need to be open minded and observant.

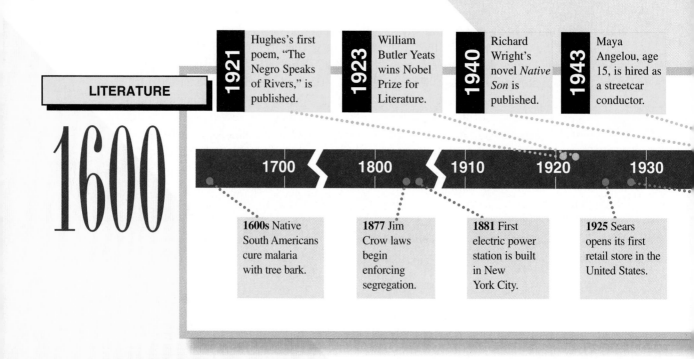

LITERATURE

1921 Hughes's first poem, "The Negro Speaks of Rivers," is published.

1923 William Butler Yeats wins Nobel Prize for Literature.

1940 Richard Wright's novel *Native Son* is published.

1943 Maya Angelou, age 15, is hired as a streetcar conductor.

1600

1700   1800   1910   1920   1930

1600s Native South Americans cure malaria with tree bark.

1877 Jim Crow laws begin enforcing segregation.

1881 First electric power station is built in New York City.

1925 Sears opens its first retail store in the United States.

1959 Candice Ransom writes her first novel, at age seven.

1989 Catherine Lim publishes *Little Ironies and Stories of Singapore*.

1993 Bessie (age 102) and Sadie (104) Delany write a best-seller.

1994 Lou Willett Stanek publishes *So You Want to Write a Novel*.

1950   1960   1970   1980   1990

2000

1929 Great Depression begins in the United States.

1940 A man born this year was expected to live to be 60.8 years.

1957 Gamblers Anonymous is founded.

1964 Civil Rights Act bans discrimination in hiring.

LIFE and WORK

Two Paths
to Discovery

- *The Library Card*
- *Dream Variations*

EXPLORING

From time to time each one of us makes discoveries that increase self-knowledge. With a group, compare moments of insight when you learned something that changed your attitude, point of view, or desires. Perhaps overhearing a friend's remark, reading a book, or talking to an adult changed your understanding of yourself.

THEME CONNECTION...
SELF-DISCOVERY

The ancient Greek philosopher Socrates said, "The unexamined life is not worth living." In "The Library Card," Richard Wright describes how study and experience increased his self-knowledge and led to discoveries that changed his personal outlook and ambitions. Langston Hughes, in his poem, "Dream Variations," expresses a longing that arises from self-knowledge.

TIME & PLACE

Authors Richard Wright and Langston Hughes were born in Mississippi and Missouri respectively at a time when discrimination against African Americans was open and accepted practice. Both men moved to the North in the hope of escaping racial prejudice and to find opportunities to develop their talents. Wright died in 1960 and Hughes in 1967, during the decade when the civil rights movement called for true equality.

THE WRITER'S CRAFT

THEME

Any good novelist or poet writes to express ideas, called "Themes." For example, one of Richard Wright's themes in this selection is the power of books to show readers new ways to think and feel. Poet Langston Hughes conveys as his theme a longing for joyful activity followed by serene evenings. Talented authors may present an entirely original theme, or they may present familiar ideas in new and striking ways.

The Library Card

Richard Wright

ne morning I arrived early at work and went into the bank lobby where the Negro porter was mopping. I stood at a counter and picked up the Memphis *Commercial Appeal* and began my free reading of the press. I came finally to the editorial page and saw an article dealing with one H. L. Mencken. I knew by hearsay that he was the editor of the *American Mercury,* but aside from that I knew nothing about him. The article was a furious **denunciation** of Mencken, concluding with one, hot, short sentence: Mencken is a fool.

I wondered what on earth this Mencken had done to call down upon him the scorn of the South. The only people I had ever heard denounced in the South were Negroes, and this man was not a Negro. Then what ideas did Mencken hold that made a newspaper like the *Commercial Appeal* **castigate** him publicly? Undoubtedly he must be **advocating** ideas that the South did not like. Were there, then, people other than Negroes who criticized the South? I knew that during the Civil War the South had hated Northern whites, but I had not encountered such hate during my life. Knowing no more of Mencken than I did at that moment, I felt a vague sympathy for him. Had not the South, which had assigned me the role of a non-man, cast at him its hardest words?

Now, how could I find out about this Mencken? There was a huge library near the riverfront, but I knew that Negroes were not allowed to patronize its shelves any more than they were the parks and playgrounds of the city. I had gone into the library several times to get books for the white men on the job. Which of them would now help me to get books? And how could I read them without causing concern to the white men with whom I worked? I had so far been successful in hiding my thoughts and feelings from them, but I knew that I would create hostility if I went about the business of reading in a clumsy way.

I weighed the personalities of the men on the job. There was Don, a Jew; but I distrusted him. His position was not much better than mine and I knew that he was uneasy and insecure; he had always treated me in an offhand, bantering way that barely concealed his contempt. I was afraid to ask him to help me get books; his frantic desire to demonstrate a racial solidarity with the whites against Negroes might make him betray me.

Then how about the boss? No, he was a Baptist and I had the suspicion that he would not be quite able to comprehend why a black boy would want to read Mencken. There were other white men on the job whose attitudes showed clearly that they were **Kluxers** or sympathizers, and they were out of the question.

denunciation— public condemnation

castigate— punish

advocating— supporting

Kluxers— members of the Ku Klux Klan

imponderable—
incapable of
being evaluated

There remained only one man whose attitude did not fit into an anti-Negro category, for I had heard the white men refer to him as a "Pope lover." He was an Irish Catholic and was hated by the white Southerners. I knew that he read books, because I had got him volumes from the library several times. Since he, too, was an object of hatred, I felt that he might refuse me but would hardly betray me. I hesitated, weighing and balancing the **imponderable** realities.

One morning I paused before the Catholic fellow's desk.

"I want to ask you a favor," I whispered to him.

"What is it?"

"I want to read. I can't get books from the library. I wonder if you'd let me use your card?"

He looked at me suspiciously.

"My card is full most of the time," he said.

"I see," I said and waited, posing my question silently.

"You're not trying to get me into trouble, are you, boy?" he asked, staring at me.

"Oh, no, sir."

"What book do you want?"

"A book by H. L. Mencken."

"Which one?"

"I don't know. Has he written more than one?"

"He has written several."

"I didn't know that."

"What makes you want to read Mencken?"

"Oh, I just saw his name in the newspaper," I said.

"It's good of you to want to read," he said. "But you ought to read the right things."

I said nothing. Would he want to supervise my reading?

"Let me think," he said. "I'll figure out something."

I turned from him and he called me back. He stared at me quizzically.

"Richard, don't mention this to the other white men," he said.

"I understand," I said. "I won't say a word."

A few days later he called me to him.

"I've got a card in my wife's name," he said. "Here's mine."

"Thank you, sir."

"Do you think you can manage it?"

"I'll manage fine," I said.

"If they suspect you, you'll get in trouble," he said.

"I'll write the same kind of notes to the library that you wrote when you sent me for books," I told him. "I'll sign your name."

He laughed.

"Go ahead. Let me see what you get," he said.

That afternoon I addressed myself to forging a note. Now, what were the names of books written by H. L. Mencken? I did not know any of them. I finally wrote what I thought would be a foolproof note: *Dear Madam: Will you please let this nigger boy*—I used the word "nigger" to make the librarian feel that I could not possibly be the author of the note—*have some books by H. L. Mencken?* I forged the white man's name.

I entered the library as I had always done when on errands for whites, but I

> • • • • • • • •
> ## "I can't get books from the library."
> • • • • • • • •

felt that I would somehow slip up and betray myself. I **doffed** my hat, stood a respectful distance from the desk, looked as unbookish as possible, and waited for the white patrons to be taken care of. When the desk was clear of people, I still waited. The white librarian looked at me.

"What do you want, boy?"

As though I did not possess the power of speech, I stepped forward and simply handed her the forged note, not parting my lips.

"What books by Mencken does he want?" she asked.

"I don't know, ma'am," I said, avoiding her eyes.

"Who gave you this card?"

"Mr. Falk," I said.

"Where is he?"

"He's at work, at the M—— Optical Company," I said. "I've been in here for him before."

"I remember," the woman said. "But he never wrote notes like this."

Oh, God, she's suspicious. Perhaps she would not let me have the books? If she had turned her back at that moment, I would have ducked out the door and never gone back. Then I thought of a bold idea.

"You can call him up, ma'am," I said, my heart pounding.

"You're not using these books, are you?" she asked pointedly.

"Oh, no, ma'am. I can't read."

"I don't know what he wants by Mencken," she said under her breath.

I knew now that I had won; she was thinking of other things and the race question had gone out of her mind. She went to the shelves. Once or twice she looked over her shoulder at me, as though

she was still doubtful. Finally she came forward with two books in her hand.

"I'm sending him two books," she said. "But tell Mr. Falk to come in next time, or send me the names of the books he wants. I don't know what he wants to read."

I said nothing. She stamped the card and handed me the books. Not daring to glance at them, I went out of the library, fearing that the woman would call me back for further questioning. A block away from the library I opened one of the books and read a title: *A Book of Prefaces.* I was nearing my nineteenth birthday and I did not know how to pronounce the word "preface." I thumbed the pages and saw strange words and strange names. I shook my head, disappointed. I looked at the other book; it was called *Prejudices.* I knew what that word meant; I had heard it all my life. And right off I was on guard against Mencken's books. Why would a man want to call a book *Prejudices?* The word was so stained with all my memories of racial hate that I could not conceive of anybody using it for a title. Perhaps I had made a mistake about Mencken? A man who had prejudices must be wrong.

When I showed the books to Mr. Falk, he looked at me and frowned.

"That librarian might telephone you," I warned him.

"That's all right," he said. "But when you're through reading those books, I want you to tell me what you get out of them."

That night in my rented room, while letting the hot water run over my can of pork and beans in the sink, I opened *A*

doffed—took off

SPOTLIGHT ON... FINDING INFORMATION

Libraries contain many different sources of information. Knowing how to use these resources can help you find what you need for class assignments or work-related projects. Following is a list of general reference works and the kinds of information included in each.

1. *Encyclopedias:* contain general information on a variety of topics
2. *Almanacs and yearbooks:* provide statistics, lists, and detailed information on recent issues
3. *Atlases:* provide collections of maps, including special maps on climate, land use, history, and other features
4. *Biographical reference works:* include brief life histories of noteworthy individuals

◆◆◆◆◆◆◆◆◆◆◆◆◆◆◆◆◆◆

extolling—
praising

Book of Prefaces and began to read. I was jarred and shocked by the style, the clear, clean, sweeping sentences. Why did he write like that? And how did one write like that? I pictured the man as a raging demon, slashing with his pen, consumed with hate, denouncing everything American, **extolling** everything European or German, laughing at the weaknesses of people, mocking God, authority. What was this? I stood up, trying to realize what reality lay behind the meaning of the words . . . Yes, this man was fighting, fighting with words. He was using words as a weapon, using them as one would use a club. Could words be weapons? Well, yes, for here they were. Then, maybe, perhaps, I could use them as a weapon? No. It frightened me. I read on and what amazed me was not what he said, but how on earth anybody had the courage to say it.

Occasionally I glanced up to reassure myself that I was alone in the room.

Who were these men about whom Mencken was talking so passionately? Who was Anatole France? Joseph Conrad? Sinclair Lewis, Sherwood Anderson, Dostoevski, George Moore, Gustave Flaubert, Maupassant, Tolstoy, Frank Harris, Mark Twain, Thomas Hardy, Arnold Bennett, Stephen Crane, Zola, Norris, Gorky, Bergson, Ibsen, Balzac, Bernard Shaw, Dumas, Poe, Thomas Mann, O. Henry, Dreiser, H. G. Wells, Gogol, T. S. Eliot, Gide, Baudelaire, Edgar Lee Masters, Stendhal, Turgenev, Huneker, Nietzsche, and scores of others? Were these men real? Did they exist or had they existed? And how did one pronounce their names?

I ran across many words whose meanings I did not know, and I either looked them up in a dictionary or, before I had a chance to do that, encountered the word in a context that made its meaning clear. But what strange world was this? I concluded the book with the conviction that I had somehow overlooked something terribly important in life. I had once tried to write, had once reveled in feeling, had let my crude imagination roam, but the impulse to dream had been slowly beaten out of me by experience. Now it surged up again and I hungered for books, new ways of looking and seeing. It was not a matter of believing or disbelieving what I read, but of feeling something new, of being affected by something that made the look of the world different.

As dawn broke I ate my pork and beans, feeling dopey, sleepy. I went to work, but the mood of the book would not die; it lingered, coloring everything I saw, heard, did. I now felt that I knew what the white men were feeling. Merely because I had read a book that had spoken of how they lived and thought, I identified myself with that book. I felt vaguely guilty. Would I, filled with bookish notions, act in a manner that would make the whites dislike me?

I forged more notes and my trips to the library became frequent. Reading grew into a passion. My first serious novel was Sinclair Lewis's *Main Street.* It made me see my boss, Mr. Gerald, and identify him as an American type. I would smile when I saw him lugging his golf bags into the office. I had always felt a vast distance separating me from the boss, and now I felt closer to him, though still distant. I felt now that I knew him, that I could feel the very limits of his narrow life. And this had happened because I had read a novel about a mythical man called George F. Babbitt.

The plots and stories in the novels did not interest me so much as the point of view revealed. I gave myself over to each novel without reserve, without trying to criticize it; it was enough for me to see and feel something different. And for me, everything was something different. Reading was like a drug, a dope. The novels created moods in which I lived for days. But I could not conquer my sense of guilt, my feeling that the white men around me knew that I was changing, that I had begun to regard them differently.

Whenever I brought a book to the job, I wrapped it in newspaper—a habit that was to persist for years in other cities and under other circumstances. But some of the white men pried into my packages when I was absent and they questioned me.

"Boy, what are you reading those books for?"

"Oh I don't know, sir."

"That's deep stuff you're reading, boy."

"I'm just killing time, sir."

"You'll addle your brains if you don't watch out."

I read Dreiser's *Jennie Gerhardt* and *Sister Carrie* and they revived in me a vivid sense of my mother's suffering; I was overwhelmed. I grew silent, wondering about the life around me. It would have been impossible for me to have told anyone what I derived from these novels, for it was nothing less than a sense of life itself. All my life had shaped me for the realism, the naturalism of the modern novel, and I could not read enough of them.

Steeped in new moods and ideas, I bought a ream of paper and tried to write;

but nothing would come, or what did come was flat beyond telling. I discovered that more than desire and feeling were necessary to write and I dropped the idea. Yet I still wondered how it was possible to know people sufficiently to write about them. Could I ever learn about life and people? To me, with my vast ignorance, my Jim Crow station in life, it seemed a task impossible of achievement. I now knew what being a Negro meant. I could endure the hunger. I had learned to live with hate. But to feel that there were feelings denied me, that the very breath of life itself was beyond my reach, that more than anything else hurt, wounded me. I had a new hunger.

In buoying me up, reading also cast me down, made me see what was possible, what I had missed. My tension returned, new, terrible, bitter, surging, almost too great to be contained, I no longer *felt* that the world about me was hostile, killing; I *knew* it. A million times I asked myself what I could do to save myself, and there were no answers. I seemed forever condemned, ringed by walls.

I did not discuss my reading with Mr. Falk, who had lent me his library card; it would have meant talking about myself and that would have been too painful. I smiled each day, fighting desperately to maintain my old behavior, to keep my disposition seemingly sunny. But some of the white men discerned that I had begun to brood.

"Wake up there, boy!" Mr. Olin said one day.

"Sir!" I answered for the lack of a better word.

"You act like you've stolen something," he said.

I laughed in the way I knew he expected me to laugh, but I resolved to be more conscious of myself, to watch my every act, to guard and hide the new knowledge that was dawning within me.

If I went north, would it be possible for me to build a new life then? But how could a man build a life upon vague, unformed yearnings? I wanted to write and I did not even know the English language. I bought English grammars and found them dull. I felt that I was getting a better sense of the language from novels than from grammars. I read hard, discarding a writer as soon as I felt that I had grasped his point of view. At night the printed page stood before my eyes in sleep.

Mrs. Moss, my landlady, asked me one Sunday morning:

"Son, what is this you keep on reading?"

ON THE JOB
LIBRARIAN

Public librarians make information available to the community they serve. They work with information in a variety of forms, including books, compact discs, audiotapes or videotapes, and computer software. Librarians' duties vary according to their area of specialty. Reference librarians in particular work closely with library users, helping them research information. They are familiar with and use a variety of computerized information services to provide answers to questions.

"Oh, nothing. Just novels."

"What you get out of 'em?"

"I'm just killing time," I said.

"I hope you know your own mind," she said in a tone which implied that she doubted if I had a mind.

I knew of no Negroes who read the books I liked and I wondered if any Negroes ever thought of them. I knew that there were Negro doctors, lawyers, newspapermen, but I never saw any of them. When I read a Negro newspaper I never caught the faintest echo of my pre-occupation in its pages. I felt trapped and occasionally, for a few days, I would stop reading. But a vague hunger would come over me for books, books that opened up new avenues of feeling and seeing, and again I would forge another note to the white librarian. Again I would read and wonder as only the naïve and unlettered can read and wonder, feeling that I carried a secret, criminal burden about with me each day.

That winter my mother and brother came and we set up housekeeping, buying furniture on the installment plan, being cheated and yet knowing no way to avoid it. I began to eat warm food and to my surprise found that regular meals enabled me to read faster. I may have lived through many illnesses and survived them, never suspecting that I was ill. My brother obtained a job and we began to save toward the trip north, plotting our time, setting tentative dates for departure. I told none of the white men on the job that I was planning to go north; I knew that the moment they felt I was thinking of the

North they would change toward me. It would have made them feel that I did not like the life I was living, and because my life was completely conditioned by what they said or did, it would have been **tantamount** to challenging them.

I could calculate my chances for life in the South as a Negro fairly clearly now.

I could fight the southern whites by organizing with other Negroes, as my grandfather had done. But I knew that I could never win that way; there were many whites and there were but few blacks. They were strong and we were weak. Outright black rebellion could never win. If I fought openly I would die and I did not want to die. News of lynchings were frequent.

I could submit and live the life of a **genial** slave, but that was impossible. All of my life had shaped me to live by my own feelings, and thoughts. I could make up to Bess and marry her and inherit the house. But that, too, would be the life of a slave; if I did that, I would crush to death something within me, and I would hate myself as much as I knew the whites already hated those who had submitted. Neither could I ever willingly present myself to be kicked, as Shorty had done. I would rather have died than do that.

I could drain off my restlessness by fighting with Shorty and Harrison. I had seen many Negroes solve the problem of being black by transferring their hatred of themselves to others with a black skin and fighting them. I would have to be cold to do that, and I was not cold and I could never be.

"But a vague hunger would come over me for books."

tantamount—equivalent

genial—happy, friendly

I could, of course, forget what I had read, thrust the whites out of my mind, forget them; and find release from anxiety and longing in sex and alcohol. But the memory of how my father had conducted himself made that course **repugnant.** If I did not want others to violate my life, how could I voluntarily violate it myself?

I had no hope whatever of being a professional man. Not only had I been so conditioned that I did not desire it, but the fulfillment of such an ambition was beyond my capabilities. Well-to-do Negroes lived in a world that was almost as alien to me as the world inhabited by whites.

What, then, was there? I held my life in my mind, in my consciousness each day, feeling at times that I would stumble and drop it, spill it forever. My reading had created a vast sense of distance between me and the world in which I lived and tried to make a living, and that sense of distance was increasing each day. My days and nights were one long, quiet, continuously contained dream of terror, tension, and anxiety. I wondered how long I could bear it. ❖

ACCENT ON...
LIBRARY TECHNOLOGY
• •

In this excerpt from *Black Boy,* Richard Wright wonders who the men are that H. L. Mencken mentions: Joseph Conrad, Sinclair Lewis, Nikolay Gogol, and many others. About who would you like to read? Richard Wright, perhaps? Make your own personal reading list. Start by listing three or more authors whose biography or work you would like to read; for example, Richard Wright, Mark Twain, William Shakespeare, and Maya Angelou. Then use the on-line card catalog at your school or local library to identify at least 10 titles of books, periodicals, CD-ROMs, and videos for each author. Compile your listings on a disk, then print out a copy of your personal reading bibliography.

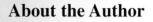

Dream Variations
Langston Hughes

To fling my arms wide
In some place of the sun,
To whirl and to dance
Till the white day is done.
Then rest at cool evening
Beneath a tall tree
While night comes on gently,
   Dark like me—
That is my dream!

To fling my arms wide
In the face of the sun,
Dance! Whirl! Whirl!
Till the quick day is done.
Rest at pale evening . . .
A tall, slim tree . . .
Night coming tenderly
   Black like me. ❖

About the Author

Langston Hughes was born in Joplin, Missouri, in 1902. Much later he came to be known as "the poet laureate of Harlem." He wrote novels and plays as well as poetry, and also lectured at colleges to motivate young black authors. One of his novels, *Not Without Laughter,* won the Harmon gold medal for literature in 1930. He spent most of his time in New York City, where he died in 1967.

FOCUS ON...
SOCIAL STUDIES

In "The Library Card," Richard Wright was prohibited from owning a library card or freely using the public library because he was an African American. Laws such as this were called Jim Crow Laws. They enforced racial segregation in the South from 1877 to the 1950s. Find out what the term *Jim Crow* means, how Jim Crow legislation was passed in the southern states, what the laws required, the effects of the laws on people's lives, and how the laws were eventually declared unconstitutional. Present your findings in a three- to five-minute speech to the class.

◆ ◆ ◆ ◆ ◆ ◆ ◆ ◆ ◆ ◆ ◆ ◆ ◆ ◆ ◆ ◆

UNDERSTANDING

1. Hughes's poem expresses his dream, his longing to experience joy and peace. Locate in the poem the actions Hughes connects with joy and the words he uses to convey a calm evening. Brainstorm a list of actions that you associate with happiness and joy. Make a second list of words that describe a peaceful, quiet, serene evening.

   It could be argued that Hughes's poem is about more than dreaming of experiencing a joyful day and a calm evening. Write a brief essay in which you identify passages in the poem and argue that they might mean more than a first glance suggests. ***Workshops 8 and 13***

2. Through reading, Wright made several major discoveries. Locate in the text passages that show what he discovered.

   What would life be like if you could not read at all? Write a short story about a central character who cannot read. ***Workshop 1***

3.  Working with a group, list the titles of the books Wright read and indicate whether they are fiction or nonfiction. Then together agree on a list of five novels you have read that you would recommend to others. Write a letter recommending these novels to an acquaintance. Comment on action, suspense, the qualities of the central figures, and themes. ***Workshops 1, 3, and 18***

CONNECTING

1.  Working with a group, collect information about the authors Wright mentions in his story. The library can refer you to various biographical reference books and databases containing useful facts. Locate, too, information about the kinds of writing each author produces. Prepare, summaries, posters, and visual aids that share your knowledge with the class. ***Workshops 16 and 22***

2. "The Library Card" is an excerpt from the book *Black Boy,* Richard Wright's autobiographical novel. Locate the book, read it, and write a book report to be shared with other students.

3.  With a group, do research on the Civil Rights Act of 1964. Write a documented report about this Act, explaining how it came to be, when the legislation passed, and what it provides. You may also wish to comment on the impact today of the Civil Rights Act on the thinking of the general public. Are people today concerned about freedom and liberty for all? Present your findings to the class. ***Workshops 21 and 23***

A LAST WORD

In "The Library Card," Richard Wright says, "Reading grew into a passion." How important is reading to you? How might your reading skills be related to your writing and thinking skills?

Late Discoveries

- *from The Delany Sisters' Book of Everyday Wisdom*
- *The Old Men Admiring Themselves in the Water*

EXPLORING

● ● ● ● ● ● ● ● ● ● ● ● ● ● ● ● ● ● ●

Just as people generalize about all teenagers, so they generalize about the elderly. With a group, brainstorm about common images we seem to have of the elderly. How do we think older people behave? Are they physically active? Are they mentally alert? Are they good natured? Tolerant? Consider not only how society thinks about old age, but also how it treats the elderly. Compare your conclusions with those of others in your class.

THEME CONNECTION...
DISCOVERY, THE REWARD FOR CURIOSITY

Discovery does not belong only to infants and explorers; it is every individual's reward for curiosity—for not accepting everything at face value but, instead, looking behind the obvious. The wisdom of age comes from the many discoveries made along the way.

TIME & PLACE

The Delany sisters survived two world wars, a serious economic depression, and a major civil rights revolution that brought about equal rights for African Americans. Amazingly hardy, outliving the life span for American females by dozens of years, they have gleaned the secret of long life—perspective and calm.

W. B. Yeats was a revolutionary at heart. His plays and poems, written in the late 1800s and early 1900s, have themes of freedom and unity.

THE WRITER'S CRAFT

STYLE

Style is the way a writer expresses himself or herself, through word choice, expressions, and organization. The Delany sisters' book is oral history. They told their experiences to an interviewer who later wrote down their spoken words. As a result, their style is natural and conversational, not premeditated or shaped. The poem by William Butler Yeats, however, shows careful attention to each detail. Yeats carefully chose each word to create an artistic effect.

from *The Delany Sisters' Book of Everyday Wisdom*

Sarah (Sadie) and
A. Elizabeth (Bessie) Delany

About the Author

Bessie Delany once said, "When you get real old, honey, you lay it all on the table." In 1993, at the age of 102, Bessie and her 104-year-old sister wrote *Having Our Say: The Delany Sisters' First 100 Years.* Their memoir was an instant best-seller. Daughters of a former slave who became the nation's first African-American Episcopal bishop, Sadie and Bessie Delany and their eight siblings grew up in North Carolina. After World War I, the two sisters moved to the North to pursue their careers in dentistry and teaching. Bessie Delany died in 1995 at the age of 104.

The Hard Way

Bessie: I have gotten smarter about a few things in my old age, things like taking chances. Now, I know there are folks who are afraid to try anything new, and that's a big problem for them. But me, I was never afraid of anything. I mean, I was always absolutely fearless! Naturally that meant that I didn't always use good sense.

When I was young, we were just getting electricity at Saint Aug's, and Papa warned us not to touch the light fixtures. But I just had to see what all the fuss was about. So I climbed up on a chair and reached for that socket. Next thing I knew, I was glued to it! After a moment, I crashed to the floor. I was lucky I didn't get badly hurt.

Another thing we were told to stay away from was snakes. Of course, we had plenty of snakes in North Carolina, and I knew that many of them were dangerous. But that didn't stop me, no, sir! One day we came across a big old snake and, naturally, I had to go and pick it up. Well, it didn't bite me but it oozed something slimy on my hand and about scared me to death. It was horrible.

I guess I always had to learn things the hard way. I don't know how Mama and Papa put up with it. If there's one lesson I'd like to pass on it's this: Each of us doesn't have to reinvent the world. You don't have to try to do everything yourself. You can learn just as much by watching and listening as by doing.

Don't Assume

Sadie: When you get old, everyone starts to worry about you. They say, "Don't do this, don't do that." It drives us plumb jack crazy. Bessie always says, "If I break my fool neck falling down the stairs while I'm feeding my little dog, well, so be it."

Folks think that because you're old, you're unable to do for yourself. Well, look at us! One time about ten years ago, when we were in our nineties, we needed to move an icebox from storage in the attic to the kitchen. We had hired two men to do it, but days and days passed and they never got around to it. Well, we just up and moved that icebox ourselves. That's right! Me and Bessie. We were slow and careful about it—the hardest part was all those stairs—but we did it. Those two men finally came by and said, "Okay, we're

> ● ● ● ● ● ● ● ● ●
> "You can learn just as much by watching and listening as by doing."
> ● ● ● ● ● ● ● ● ●

SPOTLIGHT ON... INTERVIEWING

In their books, Sadie and Bessie Delany make the point that older people have many stories to pass along, if only people would ask to hear them. One way to find out about a person is to conduct an interview. Here are some interview tips to keep in mind:

1. Make a list of details you already know about the person you'll be interviewing.
2. Make a list of questions you hope to have answered during the interview.
3. Make an appointment with the person for a convenient interview time. Request permission to tape the interview.
4. Take notes during the interview. Note the person's mood or tone of voice, humor, and so on.
5. Write a summary of the interview.
6. Thank the person for meeting with you.

ready to move the refrigerator now." And we said, "You're too late!" They couldn't believe that these two old ladies had moved it themselves. We didn't need those men!

Now, I'm not saying that older folks should try to do it all without help. All I mean is that you can't let folks assume that you're nothing but a helpless old fool.

But you do have to be honest about your limitations. If you don't do that, well, your clock's not ticking right! ❖

The Old Men Admiring Themselves in the Water

William Butler Yeats

I heard the old, old men say,
'Everything alters,
And one by one we drop away.'
They had hands like claws, and their knees
Were twisted like the old thorn-trees
By the waters.
I heard the old, old men say,
'All that's beautiful drifts away
Like the waters.' ❖

About the Author

Born near Dublin, Ireland, William Butler Yeats (1863–1939) wanted to become an artist like his father and brother. He changed his mind at age 21 when he took up writing and editing. His first works were plays written for the Irish Literary Theatre. Yeats was influenced by reading about the supernatural and about Irish legends. In 1923, he won the Nobel Prize for Literature, a prestigious award given to writers whose works have benefited humankind in some profound way.

UNDERSTANDING

1. What did Bessie learn the hard way? What was the final lesson regarding the episodes—the lesson she wishes to pass on?

    Think over the many things you have learned in your lifetime. What did you learn the hard way? How could you have learned it otherwise? Write a narrative about a personal experience of learning the hard way. *Workshop 9*

2. Which sister is the calmer, more easygoing of the two? On what examples from the text do you base this opinion?

    "Never assume" is a caution often heard today. In other words: don't guess; find out the truth. Brainstorming with a small group, write a list of ten things one should never assume when entering high school. Pretend you are writing it for new ninth-graders. An example might be: "Never assume that five minutes is plenty of time to get from one class to another."

3. How does the title "The Old Men Admiring Themselves in the Water" relate to the theme of the poem? What is the theme of the poem? Support your position with evidence from the text.

    Write a persuasive essay agreeing or disagreeing with the poem's theme. Be sure to offer sufficient support for your opinion. *Workshop 13*

CONNECTING

1. In our society, the elderly are often treated disrespectfully and discriminated against. In a small group, interview four elderly people to see what they think about how they are treated. Present your findings in an oral presentation using appropriate charts, graphs, and photographs. *Workshops 22 and 23*

2. Predicting change is a key factor in running a business. Imagine you are the owner of a chain of retail stores catering to teenagers. How would you keep up with the changing tastes of American teenagers? What methods might you use to keep up-to-date? Discuss this in a small group. With your group, write an action plan that describes the tactics the business will use.

3. Secure a copy of the 1990 census for your community. In what age group does the largest percentage of the population fall? The smallest percentage? How many females? Males? What economic level are the majority of people? Chart your findings on a graph and prepare a written description of the dominant characteristics of your community. *Workshops 10 and 22*

> ### A LAST WORD
> What stories do you know about your grandparents' or parents' childhood? How might their stories help you gain a better understanding of yourself?

Imagining
Characters

- *The Man on Stilts*
- *from So You Want to Write a Novel*

EXPLORING

● ●

When an author begins to write a story, he or she begins a voyage of discovery. Who are these people who inhabit the tale? The author must try to know them as well as close relatives—perhaps even better. What are their personal histories? What are their likes and dislikes, strengths and weaknesses? Writing a novel or short story involves a great deal of thinking time well before the first word hits the page. What do you think might be the steps in writing a novel or story?

THEME CONNECTION...
DISCOVERY IN WRITING

"How do I know what I think until I write it down?" someone once said. Your own writing can be an adventure. You might discover new things about yourself as you write in a journal, and your imaginative writing can take you to worlds you've never seen. In the imagination, the extent of discovery is unlimited.

TIME & PLACE

"The Man on Stilts" refers to a time in American history known as the Great Depression, when 40 percent of the American people were out of work, many hungry and homeless. The author's stepfather encountered a man who used a clever method to gain attention and earn money during this time when jobs were practically nonexistent.

THE WRITER'S CRAFT
EXPOSITORY ESSAY

Expository writing explains something. Both writers in this lesson have explained how to develop a character in fiction; each has used a different approach. One offers a straightforward explanation of "how-to"; the other uses personal experience as instruction.

● ●

The Man on Stilts

Candice F. Ransom

He came down the dusty road, impossibly long-legged, tall enough to touch telephone wires. Around him, ox-eye daisies drooped in the late September heat and pumpkins lolled in the cornfields like fallen harvest moons.

The boy watched the man's perky progress, one thumb hooked through the strap of his patched overalls. Strangers seldom came this way. The boy's grandfather claimed he had once seen General Tom Thumb when Barnum's Expedition dazzled the hamlet of Centreville shortly before the War of Northern Aggression, nearly eighty years before. Still, Pap had never mentioned anything about giants.

As the man drew closer, the boy saw his secret. Stilts! He walked on stilts that lifted him three feet off the ground.

"Is that hard to do?" the boy called.

"Not if you want to make a buck." A placard hung around the stranger's neck, extolling the virtues of Little Tavern hamburgers.

"You walk all the way from Washington?" the boy marveled. He had never been to the nation's capital. His father had worked downtown as a trolley car conductor but that was before the Great Trouble that shadowed the land. His father had been out of work now for months, and the boy had abandoned his dreams of ever seeing the magical domes and spires of the District of Columbia.

"Where you headin'?" the boy asked as the stranger passed.

"Don't know." There was a lot of that going around, it seemed. Aimlessness had become a national disease.

"Could I do that?"

"Try it. Great way to see the world." With a jaunty wave, the man on stilts stalked down the road.

The boy watched the shrinking figure, until the fields turned wine dark, with only hints of remembered amber.

My stepfather was that boy. And, of all his stories about the Depression, I like best the one about the man on stilts. Times were difficult for my stepfather's family—his descriptions of those days are peppered with accounts of lard-biscuit lunches carried to school in a molasses pail and short-term jobs that involved walking nine miles each way for ten-cent wages.

After the stranger left, my stepfather made himself a pair of stilts and stumbled through the orchards, struggling to master the art of walking with wooden sticks. He slipped off hundreds of times and his father, temper quickened by bad times, busted the stilts into kindling. But my stepfather, fired by some inner desire to see the world from **rarefied** heights, made another pair. He staggered through the orchards where yellow jackets hovered over ripening peaches and green apples sagged from bowed branches, his perception changed, the dreary days altered by his new sight.

About the Author

At the age of seven, Candice F. Ransom wrote her first novel on the long bus ride home from school. Through junior high and high school, Ransom kept writing. After high school, she worked as a secretary and longed to be a writer. Ransom says, "I *had* to write. And I did." She draws much of her material from her own experiences growing up in rural Fairfax County, Virginia. Ransom has written dozens of books for young adults.

rarefied—
relating to a
select group

Years later, when he traded his stilts for a ready-made family, he lifted me, a skinny, nondescript kid, up to his special stilt-high perspective, much the way his clumsy stilts had raised him above the dingy moonscape of his own childhood.

I tagged behind him while he did his chores, yet he was never too busy for me. Autumn was brush-thinning time. My stepfather swung the ax and I perched on a log, huge as a felled brontosaurus, scribbling stories in my notebook. When we both got tired, he would tell me the difference between a red oak and a white oak. Once he stopped to heft a rotted log. Underneath were two leopard-spotted slugs, big as puppies.

During spring plowing, I clung to the seat of his old Ford tractor, half-leaning against the chipped fender and half-resting against my stepfather's shoulder. From that noble chariot, he showed me how to read the clouds. Occasionally, the plow blades turned up a white quartz arrowhead, glittering against the red earth like the Hope Diamond. On each pass around the garden, I longed to grab my notebook to write down each new discovery.

I learned to see a peach as it really was—the essence of August contained within a dawn-tinted, velvety globe. The blunted ends of cut cornshocks reminded me of circus tent pegs driven into the ground. Golden gourds lying curled along tangles of morning-glory vines were like secrets waiting to be passed on to the slumbering pumpkins.

I graduated from notebook-scribbling to writing for a living,

concentrating my efforts on fiction for children and teenagers.

When my editor asked me to try a historical novel for young adults, I quaked with uncertainty. What did I know about traveling the Oregon Trail in 1846? I had never been any farther west than Kentucky, and an on-site research trip was out of the question. A three-month stint in libraries provided a factual framework for my book, but I couldn't elevate my characters above the black-and-white landscape I had created. They limped through the story. Their actions and motivation lay flat and lifeless on the pages, as if my chapters had been sprayed with the same gray wash that colored the sky during the Depression.

Then, just as the giant once freed a little boy from the tedium of poverty, my stepfather arrived on his homemade stilts to rescue my story. Slumped over my typewriter, I held an imaginary conversation with him.

"How do I know what the trail *looks* like?" I said in despair. "I've never *been* out West."

"So?" My stepfather hobbled around my office. "I'd never been to Washington either. But that didn't stop me from picturing Lincoln in his great stone chair or the towering majesty of the Washington Monument . . . . I saw those things because suddenly I believed I *could*. You can, too."

My anxiety eased somewhat. "Will you come with me?" I asked. And so a man on stilts accompanied my fictional wagon train.

Right away he pointed out the necessity to give my

● ● ● ● ● ● ● ●
"I longed to grab my notebook to write down each new discovery."
● ● ● ● ● ● ● ●

heroine a sense of family history. Tying Amanda to a heritage she left behind engaged reader sympathy from the onset and made the enormity of her journey more pronounced. From my stepfather's stilts I saw an ordinary trunk become a precious Pennsylvania Dutch wedding chest. When it is left behind in the dust, Amanda realizes how truly homeless she is, trapped between the known and the unknown. She feels the loss of cholera-stricken friends, not through the pathetic trailside grave crosses, but through the sight of a sweet briar cutting, which had been carefully nurtured across the plains, angrily tossed away to wither in the sun. My stepfather remarked that the smaller, more specific incident would have more impact than the passive line of graves.

With my stepfather's guidance, I was able to write descriptions that brought vague images into sharp focus: "The plains curved to the horizon in all directions, with the sun beating down, making them feel as though they were traveling in the bottom of a bowl. The sun flattened the life out of Amanda, filled her eyes with the color of blood, made her feel baked to the bone, her skin as taut as a crudely stitched leather moccasin."

I nearly faltered when I came to the Snake River portion of the trail—vaulting bluffs and deep-channeled gorges through which the Snake River writhed—country alien to eyes accustomed to the gentle slopes of the Blue Ridge Mountains.

"Suppose you sent Amanda down the cliff," my stepfather suggested, teetering on his stilts. "Imagine what she'd see, how she'd feel. Don't just describe the scenery, put her in it."

I hesitated. Having my heroine scale a hundred-foot gorge was as foolish as striding the Oregon Trail on stilts. Yet my stepfather was right: this was dramatic territory; it called for dramatic action. I sent Amanda down into the canyon to get water: "With a strange weightless feeling, as though her stomach were floating, she let go of the brush, digging her fingers into the rockface as she inched her way down. . . . Her fingers were cramped into claws, every nail broken to the quick. After a few moments she dared to look up. The top of the cliff soared above her. . . . Beyond the ragged line of stone, the sky unfurled an endless blue banner. Blue sky. Blue water. . . . The world seemed reversed somehow. Which way should she climb?"

Like Amanda, I looked to the sky and earth throughout my novel, aided by the keen perception my stepfather helped me to develop. In subsequent historical books for teens, I employed the same technique, striving to make my heroines' observations heartland-true, and allowing my characters to follow their various paths as accurately as geese vee southward in the fall.

But even as I write about subjects as diverse as the American Revolution and the sinking of the *Titanic,* I am already taking notes for a book, this one featuring a young boy in overalls, standing in an orchard and watching a giant coming toward him.

Going back in time is much easier with my stepfather's legacy. By highlighting details as rich and purple as clusters of pokeberries dangling over a stone wall, my characters transcend the centuries; their struggles and problems become sharp as star-pointed sweet gum leaves. Their stories, patient as pumpkins dreaming in the sun, wait for me to write them down. All I have to do is open my eyes. The man on stilts was right. It's a great way to view the world. ❖

from So You Want to Write a Novel
Your Character

Lou Willett Stanek

About the Author

Lou Willett Stanek is a novelist, teacher, and businesswoman. Born in Vandalia, Illinois, she now lives in New York City, where she is director of the Women in Management Program at Marymount Manhattan College. Stanek is the author of many articles and reviews, as well as *Gleanings,* a novel for young adults.

reating a character won't be difficult. Think of the experience you have had.

When you have a new boss, you meet an eligible someone at a party, a new member joins your club or organization, a new neighbor moves next door, your brother drops in for dinner with a new date, you hire a new employee or baby-sitter, your child introduces you to the person she is going to marry, you change barbers or hairdressers, what do you try to detect immediately? Make a list of the things you want to know about these people.

That list is a start for what you will have to learn about your character. You will certainly want to know if you can trust your boss, how the eligible someone feels about his mother, if the new member of your group is a giver or a taker, if the neighbor is nosy, if your brother's date likes Chinese take-out, if the new employee resents authority, if this person who is going to marry your child has a mean streak, if your barber is a Yankees fan. You have to grasp all those aspects of your character—and more.

What do you need to know about your character? Enough to write her biography. Actors call it the *backstory.* Who and where was the character before the curtain opens? Knowing what has happened to her before your story begins will be the energy propelling your novel.

Even if a match is never struck in your plot, you must understand how your character would behave in a burning theater and why. In your story, he might be in a plane crash, and you will have to realize beyond a reasonable doubt if he would walk over people to save himself, or make a heroic effort to rescue the trapped toddler in 12C.

If you want to write a novel, it is essential to understand your character as well as you do your best friend, father, lover, spouse, alter ego.

How do you do that?

How did you come to know your wife, boss, mother, college roommate, sister, doorman, stockbroker, father-in-law, house painter? Make a list of things that influenced your judgment. Have you been swayed more by what these people say or do? How much credence do you pay to other people's opinions or reactions to them? When you listen to one of them speak, do you translate what she says into what you think she means? Write down why you do that. Write down the most revealing thing you have ever seen anyone do.

Say at his wedding, when the minister asked your college roommate if he took Shelly to be his lawfully wedded wife, he hesitated so long the guests, the bride, the parents, and the preacher panicked. Was it one incident in a pattern showing he had doubts about Shelly, or simply another example of how this guy never could make up his mind about anything—what classes to take, what to order for lunch?

Your friend has spoiled her child, indulging her every whim. Why? Has she done it because she hasn't the self-confidence to think her daughter would love her if she were a strict parent? Is she compensating for the stern way she was raised? Is this a cowardly pattern that has allowed most people to dominate her?

These exercises are meant to help you organize the skills you have been using all your life to understand people. They will serve you well as a writer.

Exercises
- Name things that reveal someone's taste.
- List things that show somebody's values.
- How or when is an individual most apt to show her weaknesses, strengths?

Your Character
- What gives you clues about a person's self-confidence?
- What indicates someone's sense of entitlement?
- How do you judge presence?
- Make a list of possessions and property that are character revealing.
- What do a person's friends expose about him?
- What does somebody's home disclose?
- Name things you can understand about someone by learning how she feels about her family background.
- How do you discover if a person is intelligent?
- What indicates obsessive behavior?
- What does a person's laugh tell you?
- What do manners disclose?
- What aspects of someone's physical appearance are character revealing?
- What clues does political party loyalty give you about someone?

- To understand someone, is it important to know her religious persuasion or lack of?
- How does a person show stinginess?
- What do you learn from looking at an individual's bookshelves?
- How could the good causes someone serves be character revealing?
- What do you learn by observing the way people treat those who serve them?
- What type of individuals indulge themselves with massages, manicures, pedicures, facials, make-overs, expensive hair styles, costly cosmetics?

You will develop your character the way you have come to know your friends, family, enemies, and colleagues: by his actions, thoughts, conversation, tastes, values, dilemmas, conflicts, choices, fears, fetishes, shames; by the way he solves problems, the way other people respond to him. But first you will want to find a character you like, or who interests you enough to spend a year with him on a small sailboat.

If you find the right character, she will write your novel for you. ❖

UNDERSTANDING

1. How is a writer like a person on stilts? Imagine you are a spider that is calmly looking down on your classroom from its web in the upper corner of the room. Describe what you see from the spider's vantage point. Strive for clear, descriptive details using strong verbs and nouns. Exchange papers with a classmate and share constructive comments on each other's work. *Workshop 10*

2. Ransom's stepfather showed her how to get into the heads and hearts of characters, seeing and feeling what they did. Give examples of how the author's writing shows the thoughts and feelings of characters.

   It's hard to see from the point of view of a person you dislike. Select a celebrity politician, athlete, or actor whom you personally do *not* admire. Pretending you are this person, write a first-person (using the pronoun *I*) essay in which you reveal the main qualities he or she possesses. *Workshop 8*

3. What is a character's "backstory"? Select a character from a popular television show and write a backstory for him or her. Chances are, you won't know much about him or her, because television characters are rarely well developed. Make up the character's backstory as if you were the character's creator.

A LAST WORD

A seemingly small specific detail can reveal a great deal about a person or character. What specific details might a writer use to describe your personality?

CONNECTING

1. Every community has writers, whether they freelance or are on the staff of a local newspaper or magazine. Invite four writers to participate in a Writers' Forum at your school. Have them sit as panel members and as them to respond to a set of questions about making a living as a writer. Working with a group, prepare these questions well in advance.

2. Write a letter to the author of a book you have read. Send the letter in care of the book's publisher; the publisher's address is generally given on the copyright page of the book. You may wish to tell the author what you particularly like about his or her writing, or ask questions that the book may leave unanswered. You might ask for advice on your own writing. Either business or personal letter format is acceptable depending on how you want to approach the writer. Absolute accuracy is necessary, however. *Workshop 18*

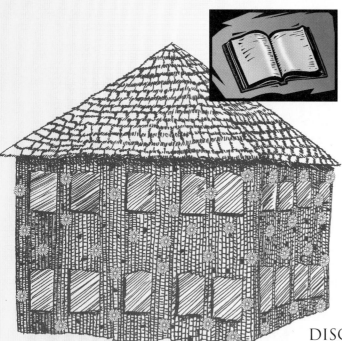

Paper

EXPLORING

• •

One thing about dreams is that they are not guaranteed to come true, especially when people try to attain them through luck or magic. Hard work is usually needed to make dreams come true. Those who depend on winning the lottery or cleaning up in the stock market to meet their goals usually suffer disappointment. Why do so many people still hope to get something for nothing? Is it human nature? For example, what drives the gambler?

THEME CONNECTION...
DISCOVERING FAILURE

Few things hurt more than discovering you have invested in a lost cause. You might face the loss of money, time, friendship, family, or perhaps life itself. Some things are worth taking risks for; others are not.

TIME & PLACE

"Paper" describes a fictional situation in Singapore similar to that in 1929 in the United States. A major stock market crash—a massive wave of selling at low prices, with no buying taking place—sent the country reeling into the Great Depression. For 10 years, the country struggled with the worst economic conditions it had ever known. Part of the cause of this terrible situation was what people called a "speculation frenzy," a situation in which thousands of people invested their savings and all they owned in stocks that did not pay off.

THE WRITER'S CRAFT
IRONY OF SITUATION

Irony of situation occurs when something very different from what is expected happens. In this case, Tay Soon finally gets the beautiful house of which he had always dreamed—but it was made only of paper, just as his fortune had been.

Paper

Catherine Lim

He wanted it, he dreamed of it, he hankered after it, as an addict after his **opiate**. Once the notion of a big beautiful house had lodged itself in his imagination, Tay Soon nurtured it until it became the consuming passion of his life. A house. A dream house such as he had seen on his drives with his wife and children along the roads bordering the prestigious housing estates on the island, and in the glossy pages of *Homes* and *Modern Living*. Or rather, it was a house which was an **amalgam** of the best, the most beautiful aspects of the houses he had seen. He knew every detail of his dream house already, from the aluminum sliding doors to the actual shade of the dining room carpet to the shape of the swimming pool. Kidney. He rather liked the shape. He was not ashamed of the enthusiasm with which he spoke of the dream house, an enthusiasm that belonged to women only, he was told. Indeed, his enthusiasm was so great that it had infected his wife and even his children, small though they were. Soon his wife Yee Lian was describing to her sister Yee Yeng the dream house in all its perfection of shape and decor, and the children were telling their cousins and friends, "My daddy says that when our house is ready . . ."

They talked of the dream house endlessly. It had become a reality stronger than the reality of the small terrace house which they were sharing with Tay Soon's mother, to whom it belonged. Tay Soon's mother, whose little business of selling bottled curries and vegetable preserves which she made herself left her little time for dreams, clucked her tongue and shook her head and made sarcastic remarks about the ambitiousness of young people nowadays.

"What's wrong with this house we're staying in?" she asked **petulantly**. "Aren't we all comfortable in it? . . . "

The house—the dream house—it would be a far cry from the little terrace house in which they were all staying now, and Tay Soon and Yee Lian talked endlessly about it, and it grew magnificently in their imaginations, this dream house of theirs with its timbered ceiling and paneled walls and sunken circular sitting room which was to be carpeted in rich amber. It was no empty dream, for there was much money in the bank already. Forty thousand dollars had been saved. The house would cost many times that, but Tay Soon and Yee Lian with their good salaries would be able to manage very well. Once they took care of the down payment, they would be able to pay back monthly over a period of ten years—fifteen, twenty—what did it matter how long it took as long as the dream house was theirs? It had become

About the Author

Catherine Lim is Singapore's foremost storyteller. A full-time writer, Lim describes herself as a "true chronicler of the human condition. True and caring." Lim holds a degree in applied linguistics and has worked as a teacher of the English language and of English literature. Lim has had a novel, numerous collections of short stories, and a book of poems translated into Chinese, Japanese, and Tagalog.

opiate—a substance containing opium, causing dullness and inactivity

amalgam—a mixture of a number of things, ideas, and so on

petulantly—rudely, with ill humor

broking houses—stock exchanges; places where security trading is conducted with an organized system

the symbol of the peak of earthly achievement, and all of Tay Soon's energies and devotion were directed towards its realization. His mother said, "You're a show-off; what's so grand about marble flooring and a swimming pool? Why don't you put your money to better use?" But the forty thousand grew steadily, and after Tay Soon and Yee Lian had put in every cent of their annual bonuses, it grew to forty-eight thousand, and husband and wife smiled at the smooth way their plans were going.

It was a time of growing interest in the stock market. The quotations for stocks and shares were climbing the charts, and the crowds in the rooms of the **broking houses** were growing perceptibly. Might we not do something about this? Yee Lian said to her husband. Do you know that Dr. Soo bought Rustan Banking for four dollars and today the shares are worth seven dollars each? The temptation was great. The rewards were almost immediate. Thirty thousand dollars' worth of NBE became fifty-five thousand almost overnight. Tay Soon and Yee Lian whooped. They put their remaining eighteen thousand in Far East Mart. Three days later the shares were worth twice that much. It was not to be imagined that things could stop here. Tay Soon secured a loan from his bank and put twenty thousand in OHTE. This was a particularly lucky share; it shot up to four times its value in three days.

"Oh, this is too much, too much," cried Yee Lian in her ecstasy, and she sat down with pencil and paper, and found after a few minutes' calculation that they had made a cool one hundred thousand in a matter of days.

And now there was to be no stopping. The newspapers were full of it, everybody was talking about it, it was in the very air. There was plenty of money to be made in the stock exchange by those who had guts—money to be made by the hour, by the minute, for the prices of stocks and shares were rising faster than anyone could keep track of them! Dr. Soo was said—he laughingly dismissed it as a silly rumor—Dr. Soo was said to have made two million dollars already. If he sold all his shares now, he would be a millionaire twice over. And Yee Yeng, Yee Lian's sister, who had been urged with sisterly good will to come join the others make money, laughed happily to find that the shares she had bought for four twenty on Tuesday had risen to seven ninety-five on Friday—she laughed and thanked Yee Lian who advised her not to sell yet, it was going further, it would hit the ten dollar mark by next week. And Tay Soon both laughed and cursed—cursed that he had failed to buy a share at nine dollars which a few days later had hit seventeen dollars! Yee Lian said reproachfully, "I thought I told you to buy it, darling," and Tay Soon had beaten his forehead in despair and said, "I know, I know, why didn't I! Big fool that I am!" And he had another reason to curse himself—he sold five thousand West Parkes at sixteen twenty-three per share, and saw, to his horror, West

● ● ● ● ● ● ● ●
"And now there was to be no stopping."
● ● ● ● ● ● ● ●

Parkes climb to eighteen ninety the very next day!

"I'll never sell now," he vowed. "I'll hold on. I won't be so foolish." And the frenzy continued. Husband and wife couldn't talk or think of anything else. They thought fondly of their shares—going to be worth a million altogether soon. A million! In the peak of good humor, Yee Lian went to her mother-in-law, forgetting the past insults, and advised her to join the others by buying some shares; she would get her broker to buy them immediately for her, there was sure money in it. The old lady refused curtly, and to her son later, she showed great annoyance, scolding him for being so foolish as to put all his money in those worthless shares. "Worthless!" exploded Tay Soon. "Do you know, Mother, if I sold all my shares today, I would have the money to buy fifty terrace houses like the one you have?"

His wife said, "Oh, we'll just leave her alone. I was kind enough to offer to help her make money. But since she's so nasty and ungrateful, we'll leave her alone." The comforting, triumphant thought was that soon, very soon, they would be able to purchase their dream house; it would be even more magnificent than the one they had dreamed of, since they had made almost a—Yee Lian preferred not to say the sum. There was the old superstitious fear of losing something when it is too often or too directly referred to, and Yee Lian had cautioned her husband not to make mention of their gains.

"Not to worry, not to worry," he said jovially, not superstitious like his wife, "After all, it's just paper gains so far."

The downward slide, or the bursting of the bubble as the newspapers dramatically called it, did not initially cause much alarm, for the speculators all expected the shares to bounce back to their original strength and **thence** continue the phenomenal growth. But that did not happen. The slide continued.

Tay Soon said nervously, "Shall we sell? Do you think we should sell?" but Yee Lian said stoutly, "There is talk that this decline is a technical thing only—it will be over soon, and then the rise will continue. After all, see what is happening in Hong Kong and London and New York. Things are as good as ever."

"We're still making, so not to worry," said Yee Lian after a few days. Their gains were pared by half. A few days later their gains were pared to marginal.

There is talk of a recovery, insisted Yee Lian. Do you know, Tay Soon, Dr. Soo's wife is buying up some OHTE and West Parkes now? She says these two are sure to rise. She has some inside information that these two are going to climb past the forty-dollar mark—

Tay Soon sold all his shares and put the money in OHTE and West Parkes. OHTE and West Parkes crashed shortly afterwards. Some began to say the shares were not worth the paper of the certificates.

"Oh, I can't believe, I can't believe it," gasped Yee Lian, pale and sick. Tay Soon looked in mute horror at her.

"All our money was in OHTE and West Parkes," he said, his lips dry.

"That stupid Soo woman!" shrieked Yee Lian. "I think she deliberately led me astray with her advice! She's always been jealous of me—ever since she

thence—from there

Singapore is the capital city of the Republic of Singapore. Located on the strait between the Indian Ocean and the South China Sea, Singapore is the largest port in Southeast Asia and one of the world's greatest commercial centers. Find out about Singapore's economic activities after World War II. Why have they been so successful? What impact has economic success had on Singapore and its people? Write your findings in a one- to two-page report.

◆ ◆ ◆ ◆ ◆ ◆ ◆ ◆ ◆ ◆ ◆ ◆ ◆ ◆

knew we were going to build a house grander than hers!"

"How are we going to get our house now?" asked Tay Soon in deep distress, and for the first time he wept. He wept like a child, for the loss of all his money, for the loss of the dream house that he had never stopped loving and worshipping.

The pain bit into his very mind and soul, so that he was like a madman, unable to go to his office to work, unable to do anything but haunt the broking houses, watching with frenzied anxiety for OHTE and West Parkes to show him hope. But there was no hope. The decline continued with gleeful rapidity. His broker advised him to sell, before it was too late, but he shrieked angrily, "What! Sell at a fraction at which I bought them! How can this be tolerated!"

And he went on hoping against hope.

He began to have wild dreams in which he sometimes laughed and sometimes screamed. His wife Yee Lian was

afraid and she ran sobbing to her sister who never failed to remind her curtly that all her savings were gone, simply because when she had wanted to sell, Yee Lian had advised her not to.

"But what is your sorrow compared to mine," wept Yee Lian, "see what's happening to my husband. He's cracking up! He talks to himself, he doesn't eat, he has nightmares, he beats the children. Oh, he's finished!" Her mother-in-law took charge of the situation, while Yee Lian, wide-eyed in mute horror at the terrible change that had come over her husband, shrank away and looked to her two small children for comfort. Tight-lipped and grim, the elderly woman made herbal medicines for Tay Soon, brewing and straining for hours, and got a Chinese medicine man to come to have a look at him.

"There is a devil in him," said the medicine man, and he proceeded to make him a drink which he mixed with the ashes of a piece of prayer paper. But

Tay Soon grew worse. He lay in bed, white, haggard, and delirious, seeming to be beyond the touch of healing. In the end, Yee Lian, on the advice of her sister and friends, put him in hospital.

"I have money left for the funeral," whimpered the frightened Yee Lian only a week later, but her mother-in-law sharply retorted, "You leave everything to me! I have the money for his funeral, and I shall give him the best! He wanted a beautiful house all his life; I shall give him a beautiful house now!"

She went to the man who was well-known on the island for his beautiful houses, and she ordered the best. It would come to nearly a thousand dollars, said the man, a thin, wizened fellow whose funereal gauntness and pallor seemed to be a concession to his calling.

That doesn't matter, she said, I want the best. The house is to be made of superior paper, she instructed, and he was to make it to her specifications. She recollected that he, Tay Soon, had often spoken of marble flooring, a timbered ceiling, and a kidney-shaped swimming pool. Could he simulate all these in paper?

The thin, wizened man said, "I've never done anything like that before. All my paper houses for the dead have been the usual kind—I can put in paper furniture and paper cars, paper utensils for the kitchen and paper servants, all that the dead will need in the other world. But I shall try to put in what you've asked for. Only it will cost more."

The house when it was ready was most beautiful to see. It stood six feet tall, a delicate framework of wire and thin bamboo strips covered with finely worked paper of a myriad colors. Little silver flowers, scattered liberally throughout the entire structure, gave a carnival atmosphere. There was a paper swimming pool (round, as the man had not understood "kidney") which had to be fitted inside the house itself, as there was no provision for a garden or surrounding grounds. Inside the house were paper figures; there were at least four servants to attend to the needs of the master who was posed beside two cars, one distinctly a Chevrolet and the other a Mercedes.

At the appointed time, the paper house was brought to Tay Soon's grave and set on fire there. It burned brilliantly, and in three minutes was a heap of ashes on the grave. ❖

ON THE JOB
SECURITIES BROKER

Securities brokers act as the link between the consumer and the stock market. They advise consumers on financial investments and arrange for the purchase or sale of stocks, bonds, and other securities. Brokers need to be able to communicate well with each client and understand each client's specific needs. High school courses in math, economics, and business are helpfu preparation. To become a broker, you must have a college education with a major in economics, finance, or business.

UNDERSTANDING

1. Tay Soon might have benefited from the old saying "Quit while you're ahead." Cite places in the story where he would have been wise to settle for what he had instead of going for more.

   Greed motivates those who are never satisfied with what they have. Write a definition paper on the word *greed*. How do you define it? Give good examples to illustrate the term.

2.  Find examples in the text that show the different philosophies of Tay Soon and his mother. What does the dream house mean to them?

   Working with a group, construct a model or draw a floor plan of a dream house. Attach a description of each room, giving color of walls, carpets, and type of flooring and furniture. Also provide a description of the outside—the siding, the roofing, and the landscaping. *Workshop 10*

3. The medicine man said Tay Soon had a "devil in him." What do you think this "devil" might be? How would a Western doctor or psychiatrist describe his condition?

   Brainstorm in a small group what Tay Soon might do to overcome his affliction. Then write out a set of directions for Tay Soon to follow to get his life back together. *Workshop 12*

CONNECTING

1. Working with a group, imagine you have $5,000 to put into the stock market. In the business section of the Sunday newspaper, select companies in which to "buy" stock and determine how many shares you can buy. Using the Sunday paper or the Internet, keep track of the stock you "bought." At the end of a month, determine how much money your group gained or lost. Keep chart graphing your investment activities to share with the class. *Workshop 22*

2. Research the stock market crash of 1929. What were its causes and effects? Write a documented report on your findings. *Workshops 14 and 21*

from I Know Why the Caged Bird Sings

EXPLORING

Persistence is an important quality. Even when the odds are against you, if you persist and keep trying, you'll often end up with the job, the possession, the date, or the school you want. Sometimes, however, once we attain a goal, we may be disappointed in it. Have you ever had this kind of experience? Have you ever worked hard to achieve something only to discover the fulfillment of the goal is unsatisfying or disappointing?

THEME CONNECTION... DISCOVERY AT THE END OF EXPERIENCE

Our imaginations picture what it would be like to do something or own something. The actual experience, however, may be very different from what we imagine. The discovery that follows experience may be that reality is nothing like our expectations.

TIME & PLACE

The story takes place in San Francisco, California the mid-1940s, while the United States was involved in World War II. Thousands of young men were overseas—fighting in Europe and in the Pacific islands, such as Guam. Because many factories were working around the clock to produce war matériel—weapons, uniforms, and foodstuffs for soldiers—there were many, many jobs available in the United States.

San Francisco is famous for its cable cars. They have been rumbling up and down its steep streets since 1873. Open to the fresh air, they give passengers an opportunity to enjoy the sights of San Francisco.

THE WRITER'S CRAFT

APHORISM

An aphorism, or wise saying, is defined as "a concise statement of a principle; a terse formulation of a truth or sentiment." Angelou's mother knew an aphorism to fit every situation. Many of them helped her daughter cope with life's problems.

from *I Know Why the Caged Bird Sings*

Getting a Job

Maya Angelou

About the Author

Maya Angelou (b. 1928) is an African-American poet, playwright, performer, composer, and author of several autobiographical works—*I Know Why the Caged Bird Sings* is just one of them. She grew up in the care of her grandmother in Stamps, Arkansas, a small segregated community. Angelou was invited to write and read a poem for President Clinton's inauguration in 1992. She also appears in present-day movies and television shows as an actor and a guest.

 y room had all the cheeriness of a dungeon and the appeal of a tomb. It was going to be impossible to stay there, but leaving held no attraction for me either. The answer came to me with the suddenness of a collision. I would go to work. Mother wouldn't be difficult to convince; after all, in school I was a year ahead of my grade and Mother was a firm believer in self-sufficiency. In fact, she'd be pleased to think that I had that much gumption, that much of her in my character. (She liked to speak of herself as the original "do-it-yourself girl.")

Once I had settled on getting a job, all that remained was to decide which kind of job I was most fitted for. My intellectual pride had kept me from selecting typing, shorthand, or filing as subjects in school, so office work was ruled out. War plants and shipyards demanded birth certificates, and mine would reveal me to be fifteen, and ineligible for work. So the well-paying defense jobs were also out. Women had replaced men on the streetcars as conductors and motormen, and the thought of sailing up and down the hills of San Francisco in a dark-blue uniform, with a money changer at my belt, caught my fancy.

Mother was as easy as I had anticipated. The world was moving so fast, so much money was being made, so many people were dying in Guam and Germany that hordes of strangers became good friends overnight. Life was cheap and death entirely free. How could she have the time to think about my academic career!

To her question of what I planned to do, I replied that I would get a job on the streetcars. She rejected the proposal with "They don't accept black people on the streetcars."

I would like to claim an immediate fury that was followed by the noble determination to break the restricting tradition. But the truth is, my first reaction was one of disappointment. I'd pictured myself dressed in a neat blue serge suit, my money changer swinging jauntily at my waist, and a cheery smile for the passengers that would make their own work day brighter.

From disappointment I gradually ascended the emotional ladder to haughty indignation, and finally to that state of stubbornness where the mind is locked like the jaws of an enraged bulldog.

I would go to work on the streetcars and wear a blue serge suit. Mother gave me her support with one of her usual terse asides: "That's what you want to do? Then nothing beats a trial but a failure. Give it everything you've got. I've told you many times, 'Can't Do is like Don't Care.' Neither of them has a home."

Translated, that meant there is nothing a person can't do, and there should be nothing a human being doesn't care about. It was the most positive encouragement I could have hoped for.

In the offices of the Market Street Railway Company, the receptionist seemed as surprised to see me there as I was surprised to find the interior dingy and drab. Somehow I had expected waxed surfaces and carpeted floors. If I had met no resistance, I might have decided against working for such a poor-mouth-looking concern. As it was, I explained that I had come to see about a job. She asked, was I sent by an agency, and when I replied that I was not, she told me they were only accepting applicants from agencies.

The classified pages of the morning papers had listed advertisements for motorettes and conductorettes, and I reminded her of that. She gave me a face full of astonishment that my suspicious nature would not accept.

"I am applying for the job listed in this morning's *Chronicle,* and I'd like to be presented to your personnel manager." While I spoke in **supercilious** accents and looked at the room as if I had an oil well in my own backyard, my armpits were being pricked by millions of hot pointed needles. She saw her escape and dived into it.

"He's out. He's out for the day. You might call him tomorrow, and if he's in,

I'm sure you can see him." Then she swiveled her chair around on its rusty screws, and with that I was supposed to be dismissed.

"May I ask his name?"

She half turned, acting surprised to find me still there.

"His name? Whose name?"

"Your personnel manager."

We were firmly joined in the **hypocrisy** to play out the scene.

"The personnel manager? Oh, he's Mr. Cooper, but I'm not sure you'll find him here tomorrow. He's . . . oh, but you can try."

"Thank you."

"You're welcome."

And I was out of the musty room and into the even mustier lobby. In the street I saw the receptionist and myself going faithfully through paces that were stale with familiarity, although I had never encountered that kind of situation before and, probably, neither had she. We were like actors who, knowing the play by heart, were still able to cry afresh over the old tragedies and laugh spontaneously at the comic situations.

The miserable little encounter had nothing to do with me, the me of me, any more than it had to do with that silly clerk. The incident was a recurring dream concocted years before by whites, and it eternally came back to haunt us all. The secretary and I were like people in a scene where, because of harm done by one ancestor to another, we were bound to duel to the death.

> "There should be nothing a human being doesn't care about."

supercilious—full of pride; haughty

hypocrisy—a situation in which one pretends to be something that he or she is not

SPOTLIGHT ON...
USING LOGIC

Fifteen-year-old Maya Angelou uses logic and reason to guide her in her decision to get a job. As you use logic to solve daily problems, practice the following guidelines:

1. Use available facts or information to draw logical conclusions about a situation.
2. When given a set of facts and conclusions, determine which conclusions logically follow from the facts.
3. Discover what links two or more objects, events, or people. Draw your conclusions from this information.

apertures—
openings

shuttlecock—
official name for
a badminton
"birdie"

Also, because the play must end somewhere.

I went further than forgiving the clerk; I accepted her as a fellow victim of the same puppeteer.

On the streetcar I put my fare into the box, and the conductorette looked at me with the usual hard eyes of white contempt. "Move into the car, please move on in the car." She patted her money changer.

Her Southern nasal accent sliced my meditation, and I looked deep into my thought. All lies, all comfortable lies. The receptionist was not innocent and neither was I. The whole charade we had played out in that waiting room had directly to do with me, black, and her, white.

I wouldn't move into the streetcar but stood on the ledge over the conductor, glaring. My mind shouted so energetically that the announcement made my veins stand out and my mouth tighten into a prune.

I WOULD HAVE THE JOB. I WOULD BE A CONDUCTORETTE AND SLING A FULL MONEY CHANGER FROM MY BELT. I WOULD.

The next three weeks were a honeycomb of determination with **apertures** for the days to go in and out. The black organizations to whom I appealed for support bounced me back and forth like a **shuttlecock** on a badminton court. Why did I insist on that particular job? Openings were going begging that paid nearly twice the money. The minor officials with whom I was able to win an audience thought me mad. Possibly I was.

Downtown San Francisco became alien and cold, and the streets I had loved in a personal familiarity were unknown lanes that twisted with malicious intent. My trips to the streetcar office were of the frequency of a person on salary. The struggle expanded. I was no longer in conflict only with the Market Street Railway but with the marble lobby of the building that housed its offices, and elevators and their operators.

During this period of strain, Mother and I began our first steps on the long path toward mutual adult admiration. She never asked for reports and I didn't offer any details. But every morning she made breakfast, gave me carfare and lunch money, as if I were going to work. She comprehended that in the struggle lies the joy. That I was no glory seeker was obvious to her, and that I had to exhaust every possibility before giving in was also clear.

On my way out of the house one morning she said, "Life is going to give you just what you put in it. Put your whole heart in everything you do, and pray; then you can wait." Another time she reminded me that "God helps those who help themselves." She had a score of **aphorisms** that she dished out as the occasion demanded. Strangely, as bored as I was with clichés, her inflection gave them something new and set me thinking for a little while at least. Later, when asked how I got my job, I was never able to say exactly. I only knew that one day, which was tiresomely like all the others before it, I sat in the Railway office, waiting to be interviewed. The receptionist called me to her desk and shuffled a bundle of papers to me. They were job application forms. She said they had to be filled in [in] triplicate. I had little time to wonder if I had won or not, for the

standard questions reminded me of the necessity for lying. How old was I? List my previous jobs, starting from the last job held and go backward to the first. How much money did I earn, and why did I leave the position? Give two references (not relatives). I kept my face blank (an old art) and wrote quickly the fable of Marguerite Johnson, aged nineteen, former companion and driver for Mrs. Annie Henderson (a White Lady) in Stamps, Arkansas.

I was given blood tests, aptitude tests, and physical coordination tests; then, on a blissful day, I was hired as the first black on the San Francisco streetcars.

Mother gave me the money to have my blue serge suit tailored, and I learned to fill out work cards, operate the money changer, and punch transfers. The time crowded together, and at an End of Days I was swinging on the back of the rackety trolley, smiling sweetly and persuading my charges to "step forward in the car, please."

For one whole semester the streetcars and I shimmied up and scooted down the sheer hills of San Francisco. I lost some of my need for the black ghetto's shielding-sponge quality as I clanged and cleared my way down Market Street, with its honky-tonk homes for homeless sailors, past the quiet retreat of Golden Gate Park, and along closed undwelled-in-looking dwellings of the Sunset District.

My work shifts were split so haphazardly that it was easy to believe that my superiors had chosen them maliciously. Upon mentioning my suspicions to Mother, she said, "Don't you worry about it. You ask for what you want, and

aphorisms—
short expressions of
principles or
wisdom

from I Know Why the Caged Bird Sings

you pay for what you get. And I'm going to show you that it ain't no trouble when you pack double."

She stayed awake to drive me out to the car barn at four-thirty in the mornings or to pick me up when I was relieved just before dawn. Her awareness of life's perils convinced her that while I would be safe on the public conveyances, she "wasn't about to trust a taxi driver with her baby."

When the spring classes began, I resumed my commitment to formal education. I was so much wiser and older, so much more independent, with a bank account and clothes that I had bought for myself, that I was sure I had learned and earned the magic formula that would make me a part of the life my contemporaries led.

Not a bit of it. Within weeks, I realized that my schoolmates and I were on paths moving away from each other. They were concerned and excited over the approaching football games. They concentrated great interest on who was worthy of being student body president and when the metal bands would be removed from their teeth, while I remembered conducting a streetcar in the uneven hours of the morning. ❖

ON THE JOB
LOCAL TRANSIT OPERATOR

Local transit operators provide transportation for the public on buses, subways, and trolleys. They drive their vehicles, give transfers, make refunds, and gather fares from passengers. Operators need a thorough knowledge of their routes and of the cities in which they work. They must have an excellent driving record and good eyesight. A few years of driving experience is highly recommended. Most states require transit operators to have a chauffeur's license.

UNDERSTANDING

1. Several factors stood in the way of the narrator getting the job with the street car company. Locate them in the text.

   Imagine your dream job—astronaut, jet pilot, movie star, lawyer, doctor, whatever has strong appeal for you. Now make a two-column table. In the first column, list all the factors that stand as barriers in the way of your getting that job today. In the second, list how you might overcome each barrier. Share your lists with a small group to see if they have additional insights.

2. The author sees the scene in the railway office as a play she and the receptionist acted out, one "concocted years before by whites." Discuss what she means.

   Write a dialogue between a store owner and a teenager who is applying for work in the store. Give the store owner the blindfold of prejudice. He can see the teenager as only young, unskilled, undependable, and dishonest. Read your dialogue aloud with a partner.

3. The narrator's mother knows many aphorisms. Cite examples of the wise sayings she recites to her daughter. How does each one apply to the narrator's experience in this story?

   Take one of the mother's aphorisms, or choose another one you've heard or read, and write a story illustrating how it applies to a personal experience of your own. *Workshops 1 and 7*

CONNECTING

1. Collect employment applications from three different companies. Compare them with applications collected by several classmates. Discuss their similarities and differences. Select one and complete it to the best of your ability. Invite a personnel manager to visit your class and to comment on these applications. After the visit, discuss what you learned with your class. *Workshop 25*

2. Interview five adults about their first jobs. How did they get their jobs? What did the work involve? Did they like it? Was it as they had anticipated when they applied? How long did they keep their jobs? Are their jobs today in the same occupational area? Combine your research with that of a partner. Together, create a chart that illustrates your findings. *Workshop 22*

from I Know Why the Caged Bird Sings

Family Traditions

- *Cooking a Mexican 'Sacrament'*
- *Abuela*

EXPLORING

•••••••••••••••••••••••

When you sit down to dinner this evening, look closely at the meal you eat. It may tell you about your cultural background or current lifestyle. How we cook our meals, what we cook, and when we eat are all part of our culture. For example, modern-day emphasis on saving time and money causes many people to eat "fast food." Does your immediate family cook and use food in a way that is different from your grandmother's way? Has food lost some of its meaning in our lives? Why have things changed?

THEME CONNECTION...
CULTURAL DISCOVERY

Interesting discoveries can be made in your own home and within your own family. What are your family traditions? How did they originate? Which have been maintained for many years? Have some been abandoned? You may find fascinating stories behind the traditions your family keeps.

TIME & PLACE

"Cooking a Mexican 'Sacrament'" mentions Mexico City, Mexico, which has a larger population than any other city in the world—about 20 million people. Though many parts of the city are beautiful and historic, the pollution levels are very high. Cuernavaca, Mexico, about 40 miles south of Mexico City, is a popular vacation and health resort.

Both the abuela and the author of "Abuela" are residents of the United States, one still immersed in the old culture, the other somewhere in between.

THE WRITER'S CRAFT
FEATURE STORY

The article by Juana Vazquez Gomez was originally a feature story in a large newspaper. Feature articles differ from news stories in that they deal with what is called "human interest." They are sometimes attached to the prominent news of the day but are not as newsworthy and can be written in a more creative manner.

"Abuela" could also be a feature story although it has not appeared in a newspaper. Neither story follows an inverted pyramid style (most important information first) as do most news stories, and both writers have inserted personal opinions and feelings.

Cooking a Mexican 'Sacrament'

Juana Vazquez Gomez

Food has been a topic, a hobby and an important obligation for generations of women in my family.

When I was a child I was shuffled back and forth between two homes. During the school year, I lived in my grandparents' home in Mexico City. For the holiday season, I would move to Cuernavaca, where my parents lived. This double life allowed me to learn both my grandma's and my mother's cooking.

I remember distinctly that in both homes, cooking began at 6 A.M. and the kitchen stayed open until the last member of the family came home. That often meant closing at midnight.

I won't even begin to talk about the quantity of dishes and the masses of people that traversed through the kitchen during birthdays, baptisms and weddings. Often, those dishes would take weeks to prepare.

For my grandmother, the kitchen was a sacred place. There she spent most of her time, cooking or teaching the cook how to prepare old and difficult Mexican dishes.

Thanks to her willingness to share those secret recipes, my mother and I can keep up the tradition of delicious, refined, and elaborate Mexican cuisine.

Top of the line

Given the **sanctity** that my grandmother **conferred** upon the kitchen, it was only natural that it occupied a huge, well-lit room.

It was extremely well equipped, too. My grandfather invested a very good slice of his salary to please my grandma. The best kitchen appliances were bought at Sears, Roebuck, which in the 1940s became the first American department store to open in Mexico and thus the symbol of modernity.

Her traditional side, however, demanded that the hardware and utensils came from known and reliable European labels. And, naturally, there were marvelous earthenware pots and casseroles from Puebla and Oaxaca.

The cook had to go to the market twice a day, the first time very early in the morning.

I remember her emptying an enormous basket filled with beef, fish, chicken, eggs, tortillas, *huitlacoche* (the corn fungus), *huauzontle* (a wild green), all kinds of fresh and dried chilies and pumpkin flowers, spices and herbs like anise and mint.

There were also the amazingly colorful and flavorful Mexican fruits: watermelon, mamey, guava, *tejocote*, avocado, mango, sugar cane. To prepare *aguas frescas* and lemonade, she bought *jamaica* flowers, chia seeds, oranges and limes.

About the Author

Juana Vazquez Gomez runs a Los Angeles translation service and is translating her book, *Compendium of Mexican Rulers 1325–1994*, into English.

UNITED STATES

MEXICO

MEXICO CITY

CUERNAVACA

sanctity—the quality or state of being holy or sacred

conferred—gave, bestowed

agave—a
tropical plant
with spiny
leaves and tall
spreading
flowers

Hacienda delivery

Every afternoon, a young man from a nearby hacienda would arrive on his horse, two big aluminum cans of unpasteurized milk hanging from his saddle. The arrival of the milkman meant that it was time to go back out to buy bread.

Sometimes grandmother, whom we called Nita, would allow me to go with the assistant to buy the bread. I really loved it. The smell of freshly baked bread was extraordinary: scents of cinnamon and recently sifted flour.

I went crazy buying the bread from the rich variety of the so-called Mexican *pan dulce* (literally, "sweet bread"): *gendarmes, palvorones, campechanas, pambazos, monos, semas, corbatas* and *conchas,* which later would be filled with *nata,* the creamy skin that formed on the milk as it was boiled for pasteurization.

The second most important room in my grandparents' home was the pantry. It was always locked, and my grandma kept the keys hidden in her apron pocket. The pantry had been built with a special system for ventilation and there she kept big sacks of sugar, salt, flour, coffee, rice, all kinds of beans, chilies, dried mushrooms, and spices.

Vast stores

There were also large shelves to keep the preserves for homemade Mexican desserts, like pine nut, almond, or walnut creams, pastes made of fruit, and *cajetas,* a thick, golden syrup made from cooked milk.

There were large bottles of olive oil and vinegar. Cases of wine, beer, and *pulque,* a Mexican beverage extracted from the **agave.** Pulque is essential in preparing many sophisticated Mexican dishes from the state of Hidalgo, where my grandmother's family was from.

My grandmother's generation grew up with the 20th century, but their costumes and habits had been shaped in the 19th century, when France was the model country.

By the time my mother married, Mexico, albeit very nationalistic, was beginning to look to the United States. Modernity was the rule; simplification the motto.

The nearness of the United States had created a new attitude in Mexican women.

Although my mother's kitchen was still high on ritual and the cook still went to the market twice a day and the number of hours devoted to cooking were still too many, early in her marriage my mother decided she would not remain in the kitchen all day long as my grandma had.

Helping hands

Fortunately for her, she was able to increase the number of people working in the kitchen, and the new kitchen equipment available then in Mexico made things easier.

Another difference between her kitchen and grandma's was in the variety of foods.

Grandma would rarely venture into other kinds of cooking—though Mexican cuisine is, of course, influenced by European cuisine. In my mother's house there was Mexican, French, Italian, and sometimes even Chinese cooking.

There was rarely a homemade preserve in my mother's house, and the big

FOCUS ON... LANGUAGE

The language expressed in "Cooking a Mexican 'Sacrament'" and "Abuela" uses Spanish words for many different Mexican foods and ingredients. Create a guide to foods and ingredients used in Mexican cooking, using words in these selections and others that you know or find. For each Spanish word, write a sample sentence in English and, if possible, add or create illustrations.

sacks of such staples as flour soon disappeared.

Perhaps the most dramatic difference between the households was the one between a hands-on cook like my grandma and a **laissez-faire** supervisor like my mother. Whereas my grandmother decided, directed, and even cooked every menu, my mother dictated the menu but let the cook prepare the meal, only occasionally going to the kitchen to teach something or prepare a very delicate dish.

On those occasions when she did go there, it was hard to decide who was the better cook, mother or grandma. Tasting the food, one would hardly notice a difference, either in ingredients or in preparation.

New priorities

Nowadays, although my mother enjoys cooking, she does not believe that taking charge of the kitchen is one of her most important duties. Perhaps this is natural, because she has twice been married to men who did not always appreciate a sophisticated dish.

My late father hated garlic and demanded "simple foods": grilled steaks with a good salsa and tortillas. Her second husband eats only because he has to; if he could discover the way to live without food, he would be happy.

I am like my mother: The kitchen is hardly sacred. First, I live in the United States, not in Mexico, and the pace of life here is very different. I work at home, and the kitchen is open only for about two hours a day. For me, cooking is not a full-time business.

While I cook, I listen to the news and run to answer the phone or the fax.

Furthermore, I have no helpers in the kitchen to assist me in preparing complicated and elaborate dishes.

On the weekends, however, cooking is still a ritual in my house. My husband not only enjoys eating good food but also loves to cook.

I like cooking, but it bores me, so I have tried to find ingenious ways to cook old recipes with new tools.

Melting pot meals

To simplify the recipes, I have had to change methods of preparation and ingredients, and I mix Mexican food

laissez-faire—
giving no
direction or
interference

with other national cuisines that add variety to the menus. My grandmother would have started a dish of black beans with *epazote,* a Mexican herb, by laboriously cleaning dried beans of husks and stones, and then boiling them for several hours in an earthenware casserole. I'm more likely to spice up canned beans with some *epazote* and a little crumbled *cotija* cheese.

For my grandmother, even something as simple as white rice was made by picking over the rice, washing it, soaking it, frying it in hot oil, draining it, and finally boiling it in homemade chicken broth. In my house, I use converted rice and it's ready in minutes.

Of course, she always made her tortillas from scratch.

ON THE JOB
• • • • • • • • • • • • • • • •
CATERER
• • • • • • • • • • • • • • • •

Caterers own their own businesses. They prepare and serve food for customers, usually specializing in providing food for special occasions such as parties, weddings, and banquets. Caterers must have good working relationships with a variety of customers. They must also know how to prepare or order good food at a competitive cost. Knowledge and experience in the food service field can be gained through work as a kitchen helper, cook, or chef. Many two-year colleges offer food service training.

For the most part, I do what could best be described as a very eclectic type of home cooking. Take, for instance, this menu: pasta, red snapper in a tomato-based sauce with capers, olives, lemons, and parsley and salad, with fruits and cheese for dessert.

When we have guests for dinner, I cook more complicated menus, and sometimes I even dare to prepare an elaborate dessert. But in preparing for a large party like a graduation or birthday, I call a catering service.

I remember, as if it were a nightmare, a farewell dinner for some friends who were going to live in Italy. I had promised them a good dessert from my grandmother's recipes and chose a corn tart that took me 12 hours to make, working nonstop. I followed the instructions closely, mixing, boiling, stirring each ingredient, and following the required times for each.

That night, as soon as I finished cooking the tart, I closed that little recipe book of old Mexican desserts forever.

It was a big success, and all the guests that came to dinner still remember grandmother's tart, but I will never again have the patience to spend 12 hours preparing one dish. ❖

Abuela

Rosa Elena Yzquierdo

My **Abuela** begins her daily ritual with "**Santa María, madre de Dios** . . ." She goes outside and waters the trailing plants surrounding the rickety old fence. **Yerbas** are growing profusely in Folger's coffee cans and an old Motorola. Abuela comes back inside and mixes flour, salt, and shortening to make tortillas for me. One of the tortillas cooking on the **comal** fills with air.

"That means you're going to get married," she says, then continues to knead and cook each tortilla with care, making sure to bless the first one of the stack.

"Abuela, I had a dream about fleas. What does it mean?"

"It means you're going to get some money, **mija.**"

"Abuela, my stomach hurts."

"Te doy un tesito mija?"

She picks the yerbas, prepares them, and makes a tea for me. No smell to it, but it tastes of milk of magnesia—maybe worse.

"Drink this tea every morning for nine days before breakfast, and your stomach-aches will disappear for one year."

She has always said to me, "Remember your dreams because they have special meaning. Remember the yerbas that grow in the wild, how they work, when to use them. Remember the cures for evil eye, fright, and fever.

"Sweep the herbs across the body and repeat three **Apostles' Creeds** to drive out evil spirits. Crack an egg in a glass of water and say three **Hail Marys** to take away evil eye and fever. Remember these things. They are all a part of you— a part of your heritage."

She said once, "**Yo soy mexicana; tu mamá es mexicana pero tú eres americana.**"

I just try to hold on. ❖

---

abuela—grandmother

Santa María . . . —a Roman Catholic prayer to the Virgin Mary

yerbas—a South American holly bush whose leaves are used in making a strong tea

comal—griddle or stove top

mija—term of endearment

Te doy . . . — Shall I give you some tea (medicinal)?

Apostles' Creed—a Christian statement of belief

Hail Mary—a Roman Catholic prayer to the Virgin Mary

Yo soy . . . —I am Mexican; your mother is Mexican, but you are American

UNDERSTANDING

1.  Gomez's mother's kitchen and cooking methods differ from her grandmother's. In what ways? How does the author's cooking differ from her mother's? Find evidence for your conclusions

    Convenience is important to modern families. Working in a group, compare several frozen or fast foods with traditional homemade dishes. Some items to compare are apple pie, macaroni and cheese casserole, burritos, pizza, and chili. Determine the criteria for comparison—such as flavor, appearance, texture, aroma, cost, and time to prepare—and devise a rating system. Create a chart that lists the criteria and the rating of each item you examine.

2. Why has the author of "Cooking a Mexican 'Sacrament'" closed her grandmother's recipe book forever? How does her attitude differ from the other author's closure, "I just try to hold on"?

    Talk to the cooks in your family. Ask if they have altered their methods of cooking, whether for everyday dinners or special occasions and if so, why. Make an oral report of your findings. ***Workshop 23***

3. Cooking, to one grandmother, was a "sacrament." Do you think the other grandmother felt the same way? Look up the definition of "sacrament." Is the author's use of this appropriate or not? What expressions, if any, do you identify as sacraments?

    Write a persuasive essay explaining why traditional ways are, or are not, preferable to new ways. ***Workshop 13***

A LAST WORD

Cooking plays a rich and delicious role in the heritage of the authors in this lesson. What foods are special to your family's heritage? How is life enhanced by preparing and sharing recipes passed down to us from earlier generations?

ACCENT ON... CULINARY ARTS

A Mexican garden wouldn't be complete without tomatillos, which look like small green tomatoes but are actually more closely related to the kiwi fruit. Working in pairs or small groups, create a cookbook devoted to the tomatillo. Find as many recipes as you can. In an introduction to your cookbook, write a descriptive paragraph about the tomatillo and its many uses in Mexican cooking. If possible, use a computer graphics program when making your cookbook. In addition to your recipes, include illustrations, quotations, information about the history of Mexican cooking, and other features to make your cookbook as creative as possible.

CONNECTING

1. With your family or with a group of friends, visit an authentic Mexican or other ethnic restaurant. Order something you've never tasted before. From the waiter or cook, acquire information on the ingredients and method of cooking. Write one of the following articles: 1) a review of the restaurant or 2) a detailed recipe for one of the dishes on the menu, with personal notes on appearance and flavor. *Workshop 17*

2. Bring a favorite family recipe from home to enter into the computer along with relevant comments about when or how the dish is prepared and eaten. Combine it with the recipes of other students to create a class recipe book. Desktop publish the book, perhaps with scanned photographs and computer graphics, and print a copy for each class member.

WRAP IT UP

UNIT 4

1. In the excerpt from Richard Wright's *Black Boy*, Wright heats a can of pork and beans with hot running tap water. In Ransom's essay, "The Man on Stilts," a young boy's poverty-stricken world is broken by the appearance of a man on stilts. As a reader, you make discoveries about a character by his or her actions or words. A large discovery can be made from the smallest detail. Explain in an essay what discoveries you made about Richard Wright and Ransom's stepfather from the seemingly small details included in these writings. How is it possible for a small detail to reveal so much about a human being?

2. People learn and make discoveries in a variety of ways. Bessie Delany, as she tells us in "Hard Way," had to learn everything for herself when she was young; she couldn't accept anyone else's advice or experience. For Maya Angelou, her path to discovery is grounded in logic and determination. Through their different methods, what do each of these authors discover about themselves? Use details from the selections to support your conclusions. Which of their methods is similar to your way of learning? Make a list of discoveries you have recently made about yourself and the world around you.

UNIT
⟨5⟩
FACING CHALLENGES

All day long we face challenges. Can we keep our tempers when someone puts us down? Can we answer the questions on a difficult test? Can we resist a classmate who wants to copy our answers? At the tryouts after school, are we good enough to make the team?

Challenges can be emotional, mental, ethical, physical—or a combination of all of these. Some people use challenges as an excuse to drop out, give in, or give up. Others thrive on challenges? What personal qualities help people meet challenges? The selections in this unit explore that question.

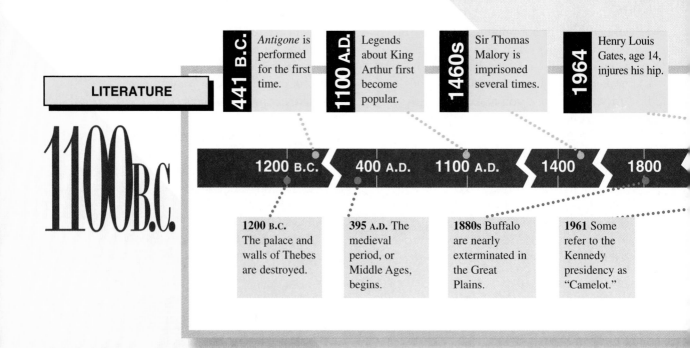

LITERATURE

1100 B.C.

441 B.C. *Antigone* is performed for the first time.

1100 A.D. Legends about King Arthur first become popular.

1460s Sir Thomas Malory is imprisoned several times.

1964 Henry Louis Gates, age 14, injures his hip.

| 1200 B.C. | 400 A.D. | 1100 A.D. | 1400 | 1800 |

1200 B.C. The palace and walls of Thebes are destroyed.

395 A.D. The medieval period, or Middle Ages, begins.

1880s Buffalo are nearly exterminated in the Great Plains.

1961 Some refer to the Kennedy presidency as "Camelot."

from **Antigone**
—Sophocles

from **The Once and Future King**
—T. H. White

from **Le Morte d'Arthur**
—Sir Thomas Malory

**Running Eagle: Woman Warrior
of the Blackfoot**
—Beverly Hungry Wolf

from **Policewoman**
—Dorothy Uhnak

Running Blind
—Thomas Fox Averill

It Happened in Montgomery
—Phil W. Petrie

A Giant Step
—Henry Louis Gates, Jr.

1973 Dorothy Uhnak writes *Law and Order.*

1980 Beverly Hungry Wolf writes *The Ways of My Grandmothers.*

1995 "Running Blind" is chosen for the book *Show Me a Hero.*

1950   1960   1970   1980   1990

2000

1963 *The Feminine Mystique* by Betty Friedan begins the Women's Movement.

1977 Rosa Parks receives the Humanitarian Award from Catholic Universities of America.

1992 Marla Runyon wins four gold medals in the Paralympics.

1992 More than 400,000 Americans receive artificial joints.

LIFE and WORK

from Antigone

EXPLORING

It has been said that each day presents challenges. Meeting these challenges, great and small, gives us opportunities to act responsibly and so to build character. Discuss the various challenges you and others face each day. Consider the qualities that help people meet challenges successfully.

THEME CONNECTION...
CHALLENGING AUTHORITY

Creon, king of Thebes, creates a new law. This law punishes with death anyone who buries Polyneices, a traitor who led an army against Thebes. The law follows tradition; Thebes has never allowed traitors to be buried. Antigone's love for her brother and her confidence that the gods desire his burial lead her to defy Creon. Certain that her cause is just, Antigone stands alone against Creon, determined to die rather than leave her brother unburied.

TIME & PLACE

Writing in Athens in the fifth century B.C., the Greek dramatist Sophocles tells his own version of an ancient myth about the distant past. His audience would have been very familiar with the facts surrounding Antigone. She, her sister Ismene, and her brothers Eteocles and Polyneices were the children of Oedipus, king of Thebes, and his wife, Jocasta. When his sons angered him, Oedipus cursed them, saying they would kill each other. After Oedipus's death, the two sons fought over the right to rule Thebes. Eteocles defeated Polyneices, who left Thebes, raised an army, and returned to attack Thebes. He and Eteocles killed each other in combat.

THE WRITER'S CRAFT
GREEK DRAMA

Initially, Greek drama consisted of a chorus, or dancing company, that recited and danced to celebrate military successes and honor the gods. Then someone, perhaps Thespis, added one actor who could converse with the chorus. The playwright Aeschylus later added a second actor to make conflict possible. Finally, Sophocles added a third actor to explore the complexities of relationships. He lessened the importance of the chorus, making it an anonymous crowd offering the average person's opinion about events.

from Antigone
Sophocles

Characters

Antigone, a daughter of Oedipus, former King of Thebes
Ismene, another daughter of Oedipus
Creon, king of Thebes, uncle of Antigone and Ismene
Haemon, Creon's son, engaged to be married to Antigone
Eurydice, wife of Creon
Teiresias, a blind prophet
Chorus, made up of about fifteen elders of Thebes
Choragos, leader of the Chorus
A Boy, who leads Teiresias
A Sentry
Guards
Servants
A Messenger

Scene: *Before the palace of Creon, king of Thebes. A central double door, and two doors at the side. A platform extends the length of the stage, and from this platform three steps lead down into the orchestra, or chorus-ground.*

Time: *Dawn of the day after the repulse of the Argive army from the assault on Thebes.*

Prologue

(*Antigone and Ismene enter from the central door of the palace.*)

[*Antigone asks Ismene if she has heard of Creon's new decree and says that she and Ismene must do something. Then follows this exchange:*] . . .

ANTIGONE. Listen, Ismene:
    Creon buried our brother **Eteocles**   15
    With military honors, gave him a soldier's funeral,
    And it was right that he should; but **Polyneices,**
    Who fought as bravely and died as miserably—
    They say that Creon has sworn
    No one shall bury him, no one mourn for him,   20
    But his body must lie in the fields, a sweet treasure
    For **carrion birds** to find as they search for food.
    This is what they say, and our good Creon is coming here
    To announce it publicly; and the penalty—
    Stoning to death in the public square!
                    There it is,   25

About the Author

Sophocles (c. 496–406 B.C.) was immensely popular, revered as a dedicated citizen of Athens and a brilliant playwright. Like all good Athenians, Sophocles was involved in public affairs. For instance, he was one of 10 generals in charge of the fleet that suppressed the revolt of Samos against Athens. Sophocles wrote 123 plays, 7 of which have survived. In these plays, Sophocles draws on ancient stories about gods, men, and women to examine the nature of justice and order in life.

Eteocles—
pronounced eh TEE uh cleez

Polyneices—
pronounced polly NIGH seez

carrion birds—
birds who do not kill their prey but feed on already dead animals

And now you can prove what you are:
A true sister, or a traitor to your family.

ISMENE. Antigone, you are mad! What could I possibly do?

ANTIGONE. You must decide whether you will help me or not.

ISMENE. I do not understand you. Help you in what?   30

ANTIGONE. Ismene, I am going to bury him. Will you come?

ISMENE. Bury him! You have just said the new law forbids it.

ANTIGONE. He is my brother. And he is your brother, too.

ISMENE. But think of the danger! Think what Creon will do!

ANTIGONE. Creon is not strong enough to stand in my way.   35

ISMENE. Ah sister!
Oedipus died, everyone hating him
For what his own search brought to light, his eyes
Ripped out by his own hand; and Jocasta died,
His mother and wife at once; she twisted the cords   40
That strangled her life; and our two brothers died,
Each killed by the other's sword. And we are left:
But oh, Antigone,
Think how much more terrible than these
Our own death would be if we should go against Creon   45
And do what he has forbidden! We are only women.
We cannot fight with men, Antigone!
The law is strong, we must give in to the law
In this thing, and in worse. I beg the dead
To forgive me, but I am helpless: I must yield   50
To those in authority. And I think it is dangerous business
To be always meddling.

ANTIGONE.   If that is what you think,
I should not want you, even if you asked to come.
You have made your choice, you can be what you want to be.
But I will bury him; and if I must die,   55
I say that this crime is holy: I shall lie down
With him in death, and I shall be as dear
To him as he to me . . . .

[*The conversation concludes with Ismene refusing to break Creon's law and Antigone insisting upon upholding the laws of the gods by burying her brother. Burial was deemed necessary to release a dead person's spirit from the body so that it could enter the afterlife. Spreading dust over the body counted as burial.*]

Scene 1

[*As soon as Creon finishes telling the Chorus that Polyneices must not be buried, the Sentry arrives to announce that someone has buried the body by covering it with light dust, enough to give peace to Polyneices's ghost. Creon attributes the burial to political anarchists, accuses the Sentry of accepting a bribe, and demands that the Sentry capture and bring him the lawbreaker. The Sentry accuses Creon of injustice and hastens away, eager for safety and vowing not to return.*]

Scene 2

(*Re-enter* Sentry *leading* Antigone.)

[*The Sentry arrives leading Antigone captive; he claims she buried Polyneices. An exchange follows between Creon and Antigone.*]

SENTRY. Here is the woman. She is the guilty one:
    We found her trying to bury him.   15
    Take her, then; question her; judge her as you will.
    I am through with the whole thing now, and glad of it.

CREON. But this is Antigone! Why have you brought her here?

SENTRY. She was burying him, I tell you!

CREON (*severely*).   Is this the truth?

SENTRY. I saw her with my own eyes. Can I say more?   20

CREON. The details: Come, tell me quickly!

SENTRY.   It was like this:
    After those terrible threats of yours, King,
    We went back and brushed the dust away from the body . . . .

    And then we looked, and there was Antigone!
    I have seen   35
    A mother bird come back to a stripped nest, heard
    Her crying bitterly a broken note or two
    For the young ones stolen. Just so, when this girl
    Found the bare corpse, and all her love's work wasted,
    She wept, and cried on heaven to damn the hands   40
    That had done this thing.
                      And then she brought more dust
    And sprinkled wine three times for her brother's ghost.

    We ran and took her at once. She was not afraid,
    Not even when we charged her with what she had done.
    She denied nothing.   45

like father—a
reference to
Antigone's
father, Oedipus,
the former king
of Thebes

And this was a comfort to me,
And some uneasiness: for it is a good thing
To escape from death, but it is no great pleasure
To bring death to a friend.
       Yet I always say
There is nothing so comfortable as your own safe skin!

CREON (*slowly, dangerously*). And you, Antigone,   50
  You with your head hanging—do you confess this thing?

ANTIGONE. I do. I deny nothing.

CREON (*to* Sentry).   You may go. (*Exit* Sentry.)
  (*to* Antigone) Tell me, tell me briefly:
  Had you heard my proclamation touching this matter?

ANTIGONE. It was public. Could I help hearing it?   55

CREON. And yet you dared defy the law.

ANTIGONE.   I dared.
  It was not God's proclamation. That final justice
  That rules the world below makes no such laws.

  Your edict, King, was strong,
  But all your strength is weakness itself against   60
  The immortal unrecorded laws of God.
  They are not merely now; they were, and shall be,
  Operative forever, beyond man utterly.

  I knew I must die, even without your decree:
  I am only mortal. And if I must die   65
  Now, before it is my time to die,
  Surely this is no hardship: can anyone
  Living, as I live, with evil all about me,
  Think death less than a friend? This death of mine
  Is of no importance; but if I had left my brother   70
  Lying in death unburied, I should have suffered.
  Now I do not.
      You smile at me. Ah Creon,
  Think me a fool, if you like; but it may well be
  That a fool convicts me of folly.

CHORAGOS. **Like father,** like daughter: both headstrong, deaf to reason.   75
  She has never learned to yield.

CREON.   She has much to learn.
  The inflexible heart breaks first, the toughest iron
  Cracks first, and the wildest horses bend their necks
  At the pull of the smallest **curb.**

SPOTLIGHT ON...
MAKING CHOICES

Several of the characters in *Antigone* make critical choices. Antigone chooses to break the law; Ismene decides not to do so. Haemon chooses to stand up to his father. Sophocles suggests that our significant choices make us what we are; they shape us.

In our daily lives, however, choices are usually about small matters. When you are making choices between two similar things, such as two classes or two backpacks, follow these steps to be sure you make a wise choice:

1. List the attributes or qualities of each item or thing you are considering.
2. Write down why you want each one.
3. List your criteria or requirements, such as cost, size, color, and other qualities. For example, if you are choosing between two backpacks, do you need it to hold a lot of stuff, or do you just need it to hold a book or two?
4. Compare your criteria with the lists of attributes to see which item meets your needs.

◆◆

                Pride? In a slave?

This girl is guilty of a double insolence,   80

Breaking the given laws and boasting of it.

Who is the man here,

She or I, if this crime goes unpunished?

Sister's child, or more than sister's child,

Or closer yet in blood—she and her sister   85

Win bitter death for this!

       (*to* Servants) Go, some of you,

Arrest Ismene. I accuse her equally.

Bring her: you will find her sniffling in the house there.

Her mind's a traitor: crimes kept in the dark

Cry for light, and the guardian brain shudders;   90

But how much worse than this

Is brazen boasting of barefaced anarchy!

ANTIGONE. Creon, what more do you want than my death?

CREON. Nothing.

  That gives me everything.

curb—a type of bit placed in a horse's mouth to control it

ANTIGONE.   Then I beg you: kill me.
        This talking is a great weariness: your words   95
        Are distasteful to me, and I am sure that mine
        Seem so to you. And yet they should not seem so:
        I should have praise and honor for what I have done.
        All these men here would praise me
        Were their lips not frozen shut with fear of you.   100
        (*bitterly*) Ah the good fortune of kings,
        Licensed to say and do whatever they please!

CREON. You are alone here in that opinion.

ANTIGONE. No, they are with me. But they keep their tongues in leash.

CREON. Maybe. But you are guilty, and they are not.   105

ANTIGONE. There is no guilt in reverence for the dead.

CREON. But Eteocles—was he not your brother too?

ANTIGONE. My brother too.

CREON.   And you insult his memory?

ANTIGONE (*softly*). The dead man would not say that I insult it.

CREON. He would: for you honor a traitor as much as him.   110

ANTIGONE. His own brother, traitor or not, and equal in blood.

CREON. He made war on his country. Eteocles defended it.

ANTIGONE. Nevertheless, there are honors due all the dead.

CREON. But not the same for the wicked as for the just.

ANTIGONE. Ah Creon, Creon,   115
        Which of us can say what the gods hold wicked?

CREON. An enemy is an enemy, even dead.

ANTIGONE. It is my nature to join in love, not hate.

CREON (*finally losing patience*). Go join them, then; if you must have your love,
        Find it in hell! . . .   120

[*Ismene arrives, offers to share Antigone's punishment, and Antigone rebuffs her. Ismene reminds Creon that Antigone is engaged to his son, Haemon.*]

Scene 3

[*His arrival announced by Choragos, Haemon talks to his father, Creon.*] . . .
CREON.   —Son,
        You have heard my final judgment on that girl:
        Have you come here hating me, or have you come
        With deference and with love, whatever I do?

HAEMON. I am your son, Father, You are my guide.
    You make things clear for me, and I obey you.
    No marriage means more to me than your continuing wisdom.

CREON. Good. That is the way to behave: **subordinate**

    Everything else, my son, to your father's will.
    This is what a man prays for, that he may get
    Sons attentive and dutiful in his house,
    Each one hating his father's enemies,
    Honoring his father's friends. But if his sons
    Fail him, if they turn out unprofitably,

    What has he fathered but trouble for himself
    And amusement for the malicious?
                      So you are right
    Not to lose your head over this woman.   20
    Your pleasure with her would soon grow cold, Haemon,
    And then you'd have a hellcat in bed and elsewhere.
    Let her find her husband in hell!
    Of all the people in this city, only she
    Has had contempt for my law and broken it.   25

    Do you want me to show myself weak before the people?
    Or to break my sworn word? No, and I will not.
    The woman dies.
    I suppose she'll plead "family ties." Well, let her.
    If I permit my own family to rebel,   30
    How shall I earn the world's obedience?
    Show me the man who keeps his house in hand,
    He's fit for public authority.
                    I'll have no dealings
    With lawbreakers, critics of the government:
    Whoever is chosen to govern should be obeyed—   35
    Must be obeyed, in all things, great and small,
    Just and unjust! O Haemon,
    The man who knows how to obey, and that man only,
    Knows how to give commands when the time comes.
    You can depend on him, no matter how fast   40
    The spears come: he's a good soldier, he'll stick it out.

    Anarchy, anarchy! Show me a greater evil!
    This is why cities tumble and the great houses rain down,
    This is what scatters armies!
    No, no: good lives are made so by discipline.   45

subordinate—
make less
important

sheet—sail; the phrase means "fasten your sail firmly"

We keep the laws then, and the lawmakers,
And no woman shall seduce us. If we must lose,
Let's lose to a man, at least! Is a woman stronger than we?

CHORAGOS. Unless time has rusted my wits,
What you say, King, is said with point and dignity.   50

HAEMON (*boyishly earnest*). Father:

Reason is God's crowning gift to man, and you are right
To warn me against losing mine. I cannot say—
I hope that I shall never want to say!—that you
Have reasoned badly. Yet there are other men   55
Who can reason, too; and their opinions might be helpful.
You are not in a position to know everything
That people say or do, or what they feel:
Your temper terrifies them—everyone
Will tell you only what you like to hear.   60
But I, at any rate, can listen; and I have heard them
Muttering and whispering in the dark about this girl.
They say no woman has ever, so unreasonably,
Died so shameful a death for a generous act:
"She covered her brother's body. Is this indecent?   65
She kept him from dogs and vultures. Is this a crime?
Death?—She should have all the honor that we can give her!"

This is the way they talk out there in the city.

You must believe me:
Nothing is closer to me than your happiness.   70
What could be closer? Must not any son
Value his father's fortune as his father does his?
I beg you, do not be unchangeable:
Do not believe that you alone can be right.
The man who thinks that,   75
The man who maintains that only he has the power
To reason correctly, the gift to speak, the soul—
A man like that, when you know him, turns out empty.

It is not reason never to yield to reason!

In flood time you can see how some trees bend,   80
And because they bend, even their twigs are safe,
While stubborn trees are torn up, roots and all.
And the same thing happens in sailing:
Make your **sheet** fast, never slacken—and over you go,

Head over heels and under: and there's your voyage.   85
Forget you are angry! Let yourself be moved!
I know I am young; but please let me say this:
The ideal condition
Would be, I admit, that men should be right by instinct;
But since we are all too likely to go astray,   90
The reasonable thing is to learn from those who can teach.

CHORAGOS. You will do well to listen to him, King,
    If what he says is sensible. And you, Haemon,
    Must listen to your father—both speak well.

CREON. You consider it right for a man of my years and experience   95
    To go to school to a boy?

HAEMON.   It is not right.
    If I am wrong. But if I am young, and right,
    What does my age matter? . . .

[*The debate continues. Haemon insists that Creon's new law tramples on divine law. Creon threatens the boy, and Haemon leaves, vowing never to see his father again.*]

Summary of remaining events

[*In Scene 4, guards take Antigone away to be shut in a tomb and left to die. Antigone and the Chorus hold a brief exchange. Unlike Antigone, who supports divine law, the Chorus expresses its support for the King's law. In Scene 5, Teiresias, a blind prophet, warns Creon to retract his law, bury Polyneices, and free Antigone. He says that to forbid Polyneices's burial and to entomb Antigone are crimes that the gods will punish. Creon relents and gives the order to free Antigone and bury Polyneices.*]

Final scene

[*A Messenger reports that Antigone hanged herself. Inconsolable, Haemon stabs himself. Appalled to lose her son, Creon's wife, Eurydice, goes into the palace and commits suicide. The Messenger emerges from the palace announcing that she has killed herself. Creon laments that his pride has killed his son and wife and re-enters the palace in despair. Choragos concludes that wisdom involves not pride, but submission to the gods.*]

UNDERSTANDING

1. Ismene and Antigone react differently to Creon's new law. Locate lines that identify these differences. Find additional references to the conflicting claims of human law and divine law.

   Use this information to write a summary of Sophocles's view of human and divine law. Share your summary with a small group. Discuss whether you think that modern religious beliefs clash with city, state, federal, or international laws. ***Workshop 16***

2. Identify the beliefs and personality traits that Antigone and Creon reveal in Scene 2. They might have avoided catastrophe had they been able to see both sides of an argument. Choose one of the following statements. Write one argument supporting the statement and one argument against it. Be sure to include evidence.
   1. Federal laws should prevent transmission of indecent material over computer networks.
   2. Laws should hold parents responsible for the crimes their teenage children commit.

3. Haemon makes an impressive attempt to change Creon's mind. Find the lines in Scene 3 in which Haemon does each of the following: pledges devotion to Creon; praises Creon's power of reasoning; claims other men have reason, too; shares public opinion of Antigone; again pledges devotion; suggests Creon be flexible; encourages Creon to learn from others.

   Choose an issue between you and a parent. Develop an argument to persuade him or her to see your side of the issue. ***Workshop 13***

A LAST WORD

Antigone's courage and sense of self-worth led her to stand up for what she *knew* was right. How can we make sure that we have the qualities needed to stand up for what is right?

CONNECTING

1. Antigone views herself as strong enough to achieve her goal. Choose an athlete, performer, or anyone you know who has set goals and achieved them. Gather information about this person's career, and design a project that persuades people to share your admiration for your choice. Your project might be an essay, a poster, a magazine cover, a cereal box, and so on.

2. Creon and Antigone argued; they raged at each other. At school and at work, however, we must work effectively with people we don't necessarily enjoy. Invite a panel of three experts to explain how people can work together in spite of differences. Take careful notes. After the presentation, work with a group of classmates to develop a set of guidelines to use in your groups.

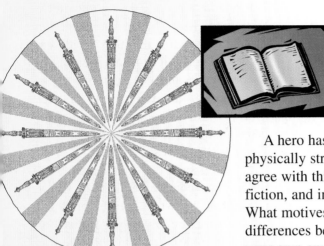

The Legends of Arthur

- *from* The Once and Future King
- *from* Le Morte d'Arthur

EXPLORING

● ● ● ● ● ● ● ● ● ● ● ● ● ● ● ● ● ●

A hero has been described as a person who is brave, moral, physically strong, and willing to stand up for others. Do you agree with this definition? Consider heroes on television, in fiction, and in news stories. What qualities do they possess? What motives do they have for their behavior? What are some differences between television heroes and real-life heroes? Using your own experience and observations, define the term *hero*.

THEME CONNECTION...
PHYSICAL AND ETHICAL CHALLENGES

White's Arthur mainly faces ethical challenges, and he triumphs because of values he learned from Merlyn the magician. Malory's Sir Launcelot mainly battles terrible enemies and wins because of superior physical strength and integrity. Malory and White agree that a true Arthurian hero is not only physically strong, but also virtuous.

TIME & PLACE

King Arthur was a common subject of medieval romances. The legend may be based on the life of a Celtic chieftain who lived during the sixth century. In T. H. White's story, England's king has died without an heir. Mysteriously, a sword stuck in an anvil on a flat stone has appeared. An inscription on the sword says that whoever can pull out the sword will be the next king of England.

In the excerpt from Sir Thomas Malory's version of the legend, King Arthur has brought peace to England and the knights have no more battles to fight. Sir Launcelot becomes bored with Camelot and leaves to search for adventure.

THE WRITER'S CRAFT

ROMANCE

When the term *romance* is applied to literature, it refers to exaggerated, unbelievable stories about incidents remote from ordinary life. Among the earliest romances were medieval stories about knights, kings, ladies in distress, enchantments, and adventures. Sir Thomas Malory's medieval romance *Le Morte d'Arthur* typically emphasizes chivalry, the supernatural, a quest, and love. T. H. White's novel *The Once and Future King* also contains elements of romance literature, such as magical episodes, quests, and adventure.

from *The Once and Future King*
Arthur Becomes King

T. H. White

About the Author

Influenced primarily by Malory, and writing 500 years later, T. H. White (1905–1964) wrote the most popular modern version of the Arthurian story, adding his own new episodes. Four of his five books retelling Arthurian legend are bound together as *The Once and Future King* (1958). The first volume, *The Sword in the Stone* (1938), focuses on Arthur's education, ending shortly after Arthur pulls the sword from the anvil.

SCOTLAND

IRELAND

ENGLAND

LONDON

FRANCE

Perhaps, if you happen not to have lived in the Old England of the **twelfth century,** or whenever it was, and in a remote castle on the borders of the **Marches** at that, you will find it difficult to imagine the wonders of their journey. . . .

They slept where they could, sometimes in the hut of some cottager who was prepared to welcome them, sometimes in the castle of a brother knight who invited them to refresh themselves, sometimes in the firelight and fleas of a dirty little hovel with a bush tied to a pole outside it—this was the sign board used at that time by inns—and once or twice on the open ground, all huddled together for warmth between their grazing **chargers.** Wherever they went and wherever they slept, the East wind whistled in the reeds, and the geese went over high in the starlight, honking at the stars.

London was full to the brim. If Sir Ector had not been lucky enough to own a little land in Pie Street, on which there stood a respectable inn, they would have been hard put to it to find a lodging. But he did own it, and as a matter of fact drew most of his **dividends** from that source, so they were able to get three beds among the five of them. They thought themselves fortunate.

On the first day of the tournament. If Sir Kay managed to get them on the way to the **lists** at least an hour before the jousts could possibly begin. He had lain awake all night, imagining how he was going to beat the best barons in England, and he had not been able to eat his breakfast. Now he rode at the front of the cavalcade, with pale cheeks, and Wart wished there was something he could do to calm him down.

For country people, who only knew the dismantled tilting ground of Sir Ector's castle, the scene which met their eyes was ravishing. It was a huge green pit in the earth, about as big as the arena at a **football** match. It lay ten feet lower than the surrounding country, with sloping banks, and the snow had been swept off it. It had been kept warm with straw, which had been cleared off that morning, and now the close-worn grass sparkled green in the white landscape. Round the arena there was a world of color so dazzling and moving and twinkling as to make one blink one's eyes. The wooden grandstands were painted in scarlet and white. The silk **pavilions** of famous people, pitched on every side, were **azure** and green and saffron and checkered. The **pennons** and pennoncels which floated everywhere in the sharp wind were flapping with every color of the rainbow, as they strained and slapped at their flagpoles, and the barrier down the middle of the arena itself was done in chessboard squares of black and white. Most of the combatants and their friends had not yet arrived, but one could see from those few who had come how the very people would turn the scene into a bank of flowers, and how the armor would flash, and the scalloped sleeves of the heralds jig in the wind, as they raised their brazen trumpets to their lips to shake the fleecy clouds of winter with **joyances** and fanfares.

"Good heavens!" cried Sir Kay. "I have left my sword at home."

"Can't joust without a sword," said Sir Grummore. "Quite irregular."

"Better go and fetch it," said Sir Ector. "You have time."

"My squire will do," said Sir Kay. "What a mistake to make! Here, squire, ride hard back to the inn and fetch my sword. You shall have a shilling if you fetch it in time."

The Wart went as pale as Sir Kay was, and looked as if he were going to strike him. Then he said, "It shall be done, master," and turned his ambling **palfrey** against the stream of newcomers. He began to push his way toward their **hostelry** as best he might.

"To offer me money" cried the Wart to himself. "To look down at this beastly little donkey-affair off his great charger and to call me squire! Oh, Merlyn, give me patience with the brute, and stop me from throwing his filthy shilling in his face."

When he got to the inn it was closed. Everybody had thronged to see the famous tournament, and the entire household had followed after the mob. Those were lawless days and it was not safe to leave your house—or even to go to sleep in it—unless you were certain that it was **impregnable.** The wooden shutters bolted over the downstairs windows were two inches thick, and the doors were double-barred.

"Now what do I do," asked the Wart, "to earn my shilling?"

He looked ruefully at the blind little inn, and began to laugh.

"Poor Kay," he said. "All that shilling stuff was only because he was scared and miserable, and now he has good cause to be. Well, he shall have a sword of some sort if I have to break into the Tower of London.

"How does one get hold of a sword?" he continued. "Where can I steal one? Could I waylay some knight even if I am mounted on an ambling **pad,** and take his weapons by force? There must be some swordsmith or armorer in a great town like this, whose shop would be still open."

He turned his mount and cantered off along the street. There was a quiet churchyard at the end of it, with a kind of square in front of the church door. In the middle of the square there was a heavy stone with an anvil on it, and a fine new sword was stuck through the anvil.

"Well," said the Wart, "I suppose it is some sort of war memorial, but it will have to do. I am sure nobody would grudge Kay a war memorial, if they knew his desperate straits."

He tied his reins round a post of the **lych-gate,** strode up the gravel path, and took hold of the sword.

"Come, sword," he said. "I must cry your mercy and take you for a better cause.

twelfth century— White chooses to make Arthur a medieval king, claiming that these events took place roughly in the twelfth century, "or whenever it was"

Marches— disputed boundaries with Wales

chargers— spirited horses used by knights

dividends—revenues; income

lists—arenas for jousting

football—White refers to a football (soccer) field to give his modern-day readers a sense of the size of the "huge green pit"

pavilions—tents

azure—sky-blue

pennons—a triangular flag; a pennoncel is a small pennon

joyances— delightful things

palfrey—a gentle horse (as opposed to a charger)

hostelry—inn

impregnable— incapable of being broken into

pad—a horse that moves at a slow pace

lych-gate—a gate covered by a roof

FOCUS ON...
HISTORY AND GEOGRAPHY

From the first through the fourth centuries, the Romans occupied Britain. The Romans introduced new ideas, such as towns, and roads that were something more than muddy tracks in the ground. Sir Ector, Sir Kay, and King Arthur may well have been traveling on a Roman road at times on their way to London. In a historical atlas, locate a map of Roman Britain that shows the Roman roads. Then find a modern-day map of Britain that shows major roads and highways. Now create your own map that shows the modern roads that follow the same route as the Roman roads once did. In several paragraphs, explain why you think these modern-day roads are so similar in location and route to the Roman roads.

◆ ◆ ◆ ◆ ◆ ◆ ◆ ◆ ◆ ◆ ◆ ◆ ◆ ◆ ◆ ◆ ◆

HOW ARTHVR DREW THE SWORD

---

lyew—a type of evergreen tree

pommel—the knob on the hilt or handle of a sword

consort—harmonious chord

"This is extraordinary," said the Wart. "I feel strange when I have hold of this sword, and I notice everything much more clearly. Look at the beautiful gargoyles of the church, and of the monastery which it belongs to. See how splendidly all the famous banners in the aisle are waving. How nobly that **yew** holds up the red flakes of its timbers to worship God. How clean the snow is. I can smell something like fetherfew and sweet briar—and is it music that I hear?"

It was music, whether of panpipes or of recorders, and the light in the churchyard was so clear, without being dazzling, that one could have picked a pin out twenty yards away.

"There is something in this place," said the Wart. "There are people. Oh, people, what do you want?"

Nobody answered him, but the music was loud and the light beautiful.

"People," cried the Wart, "I must take this sword. It is not for me, but for Kay. I will bring it back."

There was still no answer, and Wart turned back to the anvil. He saw the golden letters, which he did not read, and the jewels on the **pommel,** flashing in the lovely light.

"Come, sword," said the Wart.

He took hold of the handles with both hands, and strained against the stone. There was a melodious **consort** on the recorders, but nothing moved.

The Wart let go of the handles, when they were beginning to bite into the palms of his hands, and stepped back, seeing stars.

"It is well fixed," he said.

He took hold of it again and pulled with all his might. The music played more strongly, and the light all about the churchyard glowed like **amethysts;** but the sword still stuck.

"Oh, Merlyn," cried the Wart, "help me to get this weapon."

There was a kind of rushing noise, and a long chord played along with it. All round the churchyard there were hundreds of **old friends.** They rose over the church wall all together, like the Punch and Judy ghosts of remembered days, and there were badgers and nightingales and **vulgar** crows and hares and wild geese and falcons and fishes and dogs and dainty unicorns and solitary wasps and **corkindrills** and hedgehogs and **griffins** and the thousand other animals he had met. They loomed round the church wall, the lovers and helpers of the Wart, and they all spoke solemnly in turn. Some of them had come from the banners in the church, where they were painted in heraldry, some from the waters and the sky and the fields about—but all, down to the smallest shrew mouse, had come to help on account of love. Wart felt his power grow.

"Put your back into it," said a Luce (or pike) off one of the heraldic banners, "as you once did when I was going to snap you up. Remember that power springs from the nape of the neck."

"What about those forearms," asked a Badger gravely, "that are held together by a chest? Come along, my dear embryo, and find your tool."

A **Merlin** sitting at the top of the yew tree cried out, "Now then, Captain Wart, what is the first law of the foot? I thought I once heard something about never letting go?"

"Don't work like a stalling woodpecker," urged a Tawny Owl affectionately. "Keep up a steady effort, my duck, and you will have it yet."

A White-front said, "Now, Wart, if you were once able to fly the great North Sea, surely you can coordinate a few little wing muscles here and there? Fold your powers together, with the spirit of your mind, and it will come out like butter. Come along, Homo sapiens, for all we humble friends of yours are waiting here to cheer."

The Wart walked up to the great sword for the third time. He put out his right hand softly and drew it out as gently as from a scabbard.

There was a lot of cheering, a noise like a **hurdy-gurdy** which went on and on. In the middle of this noise, after a long time, he saw Kay and gave him the sword. The people at the tournament were making a frightful row.

"But this is not my sword," said Sir Kay.

"It was the only one I could get," said Wart. "The inn was locked."

"It is a nice-looking sword. Where did you get it?"

"I found it stuck in a stone, outside a church."

Sir Kay had been watching the tilting nervously, waiting for his turn. He had not paid much attention to his squire.

"That is a funny place to find one," he said.

amethysts— bluish-purple gemstones

old friends—a reference to Merlyn's education of Arthur, which involved turning Arthur into any number of different animals to learn from their habits and lifestyles

vulgar— common

corkindrills— fearful beasts, now thought to be crocodiles

griffins— mythical beasts that were half lion, half eagle

Merlin— European falcon

hurdy-gurdy—a musical instrument in which the sound is produced by turning a crank gouty—gout is a disease that causes joints to swell painfully

wote—archaic British word for "know"

wend—archaic British word for "thought"

seneschal—administrator

"Yes, it was stuck through an anvil."

"What?" cried Sir Kay, suddenly rounding upon him. "Did you just say this sword was stuck in a stone?"

"It was," said the Wart. "It was a sort of war memorial."

Sir Kay stared at him for several seconds in amazement, opened his mouth, shut it again, licked his lips, then turned his back and plunged through the crowd. He was looking for Sir Ector, and the Wart followed after him.

"Father," cried Sir Kay, "come here a moment."

"Yes, my boy," said Sir Ector. "Splendid falls these professional chaps do manage. Why, what's the matter, Kay? You look as white as a sheet."

"Do you remember that sword which the King of England would pull out?"

"Yes."

"Well, here it is. I have it. It is in my hand. I pulled it out."

Sir Ector did not say anything silly. He looked at Kay and he looked at the Wart. Then he stared at Kay again, long and lovingly, and said, "We will go back to the church."

"Now then, Kay," he said, when they were at the church door. He looked at his firstborn kindly, but straight between the eyes. "Here is the stone, and you have the sword. It will make you the King of England. You are my son that I am proud of, and always will be, whatever you do. Will you promise me that you took it out by your own might?"

Kay looked at his father. He also looked at the Wart and at the sword.

Then he handed the sword to the Wart quite quietly.

He said, "I am a liar. Wart pulled it out."

As far as the Wart was concerned, there was a time after this in which Sir Ector kept telling him to put the sword back into the stone—which he did—and in which Sir Ector and Kay then vainly tried to take it out. The Wart took it out for them, and stuck it back again once or twice. After this, there was another time which was more painful.

He saw that his dear guardian was looking quite old and powerless, and that he was kneeling down with difficulty on a **gouty** knee.

"Sir," said Sir Ector, without looking up, although he was speaking to his own boy.

"Please do not do this, Father," said the Wart, kneeling down also. "Let me help you up, Sir Ector, because you are making me unhappy."

"Nay, nay, my lord," said Sir Ector, with some very feeble old tears. "I was never your father nor of your blood, but I **wote** well ye are of a higher blood than I **wend** ye were."

"Plenty of people have told me you are not my father," said the Wart, "but it does not matter a bit."

"Sir," said Sir Ector humbly, "will ye be my good and gracious lord when ye are king?"

"Don't!" said the Wart.

"Sir," said Sir Ector, "I will ask no more of you but that you will make my son, your foster brother, Sir Kay, **seneschal** of all your lands?"

Kay was kneeling down too, and it was more than the Wart could bear.

"Oh, do stop," he cried. "Of course he can be seneschal, if I have got to be this king, and, oh, Father, don't kneel down like that, because it breaks my heart. Please get up, Sir Ector, and don't make everything so horrible. Oh, dear, oh, dear, I wish I had never seen that filthy sword at all."

And the Wart also burst into tears.

Later that day, Arthur replaces the sword and pulls it out again in front of all of the assembled knights and barons. Many of them accept Arthur immediately as their king. Some, who desired to be king themselves, are angry and refuse to swear their loyalty to this young boy. At that time, being king depended on having the support of local rulers who were loyal and obedient to the king. The new King Arthur fought in many battles with these local rulers who would not accept him as the rightful king.

The story resumes after many battles have taken place. Merlyn the magician has prepared Arthur for one more great battle, which is supposed to be the last one. Arthur looks toward a time in the future when the knights' energies might be used for good rather than for fighting battles.

The King of England painfully climbed the two hundred and eight steps which led to Merlyn's tower room, and knocked on the door. The magician was inside, with **Archimedes** sitting on the back of his chair, busily trying to find the square root of minus one. He had forgotten how to do it.

"Merlyn," said the king, panting, "I want to talk to you."

He closed his book with a bang, leaped to his feet, seized his wand of **lignum vitae,** and rushed at Arthur as if he were trying to shoo away a stray chicken.

"Go away!" he shouted. "What are you doing here? What do you mean by it? Aren't you the King of England? Go away and send for me! Get out of my room! I never heard of such a thing! Go away at once and send for me!"

"But I am here."

"No, you're not," retorted the old man resourcefully. And he pushed the king out of the door, slamming it in his face.

"Well!" said Arthur, and he went off sadly down the two hundred and eight stairs.

An hour later, Merlyn presented himself in the Royal Chamber, in answer to a summons which had been delivered by a page.

"That's better," he said, and sat down comfortably on a carpet chest.

"Stand up," said Arthur, and he clapped his hands for a page to take away the seat.

Merlyn stood up, boiling with indignation. The whites of his knuckles blanched as he clenched them.

"About our conversation on the subject of chivalry," began the king in an airy tone . . . .

"I don't recollect such a conversation."

"No?"

Archimedes— Merlyn's pet owl

lignum vitae— Latin meaning "wood of life"; a reference to the wood of Christ's cross

necromancer—
magician

kerns—common
foot soldiers

secret—Merlyn
had devised a
plan for winning
the battle

"I have never been so insulted in my life!"

"But I am the king," said Arthur. "You can't sit down in front of the king."

"Rubbish!"

Arthur began to laugh more than was seemly, and his foster brother, Sir Kay, and his old guardian, Sir Ector, came out from behind the throne, where they had been hiding. Kay took off Merlyn's hat and put it on Sir Ector, and Sir Ector said, "Well, bless my soul, now I am a **necromancer's** Hocus-Pocus." Then everybody began laughing, including Merlyn eventually, and seats were sent for so that they could sit down, and botttles of wine were opened so that it should not be a dry meeting.

"You see," he said proudly, "I have summoned a council."

There was a pause, for it was the first time that Arthur had made a speech, and he wanted to collect his wits for it.

"Well," said the king. "It is about chivalry. I want to talk about that."

Merlyn was immediately watching him with a sharp eye. His knobbed fingers fluttered among the stars and secret signs of his gown, but he would not help the speaker. You might say that this moment was the critical one in his career—the moment towards which he had been living backward for heaven knows how many centuries, and now he was to see for certain whether he had lived in vain.

"I have been thinking," said Arthur, "about Might and Right. I don't think things ought to be done because you are *able* to do them. I think they should be done because you *ought* to do them. After all, a penny is a penny in any case, how-

ever much Might is exerted on either side, to prove that it is or is not. Is that plain?"

Nobody answered.

"Well, I was talking to Merlyn on the battlements one day, and he mentioned that the last battle we had—in which seven hundred **kerns** were killed—was not so much fun as I had thought it was. Of course, battles are not fun when you come to think about them. I mean, people ought not to be killed, ought they? It is better to be alive.

"Very well. But the funny thing is that Merlyn was helping me to win battles. He is still helping me, for that matter, and we hope to win the battle of Bedegraine together, when it comes off."

"We will," said Sir Ector, who was in on the **secret.**

"That seems to me to be inconsistent. Why does he help me to fight wars, if they are bad things?"

There was no answer from anybody, and the king began to speak with agitation.

"I could only think," said he, beginning to blush, "I could only think that I—that we—that he—that he wanted me to win them for a reason."

He paused and looked at Merlyn, who turned his head away.

"The reason was—was it—the reason was that if I could be the master of my kingdom by winning these two battles, I could stop them afterwards and then do something about the business of Might. Have I guessed? Was I right?"

The magician did not turn his head, and his hands lay still in his lap.

"I was!" exclaimed Arthur.

And he began talking so quickly that he could hardly keep up with himself.

"You see," he said, "Might is not Right. But there is a lot of Might knocking about in this world, and something has to be done about it. It is as if People were half horrible and half nice. Perhaps they are even more than half horrible, and when they are left to themselves they run wild. You get the average baron that we see nowadays, people like Sir Bruce Sans Pitié, who simply go clod-hopping round the country dressed in steel, and doing exactly what they please, for sport. It is our **Norman** idea about the upper classes having a monopoly of power, without reference to justice. Then the horrible side gets uppermost, and there is thieving and plunder and torture. The people become beasts.

"But, you see, Merlyn is helping me to win my two battles so that I can stop this. He wants me to put things right.

"**Lot** and Uriens and Anguish and those—they are the old world, the old-fashioned order who want to have their private will. I have got to vanquish them with their own weapons—they force it upon me, because they live by force—and then the real work will begin. This battle at Bedegraine is the preliminary, you see. It is *after* the battle that Merlyn is wanting me to think about."

Arthur paused again for comment or encouragement, but the magician's face was turned away. It was only Sir Ector, sitting next to him, who could see his eyes.

"Now what I have thought," said Arthur, "is this. Why can't you harness Might so that it works for Right? I know it sounds nonsense, but, I mean, you can't just say

there is no such thing. The Might is there, in the bad half of people, and you can't neglect it. You can't cut it out, but you might be able to direct it, if you see what I mean, so that it was useful instead of bad."

The audience was interested. They leaned forward to listen, except Merlyn.

"My idea is that if we can win this battle in front of us, and get a firm hold of the country, then I will institute a sort of order of chivalry. I will not punish the bad knights, or hang Lot, but I will try to get them into our Order. We shall have to make it a great honor, you see, and make it fashionable and all that. Everybody must want to be in. And then I shall make the oath of the order that Might is only to be used for Right. Do you follow? The knights in my order will ride all over the world, still dressed in steel and whacking away with their swords—that will give an outlet for wanting to whack, you understand, an outlet for what Merlyn calls

> ● ● ● ● ● ● ● ●
> "Why can't you harness Might so that it works for Right?"
> ● ● ● ● ● ● ● ●

the foxhunting spirit—but they will be bound to strike only on behalf of what is good, to restore what has been done wrong in the past and to help the oppressed and so forth. Do you see the idea? It will be using the Might instead of fighting against it, and turning a bad thing into a good. There, Merlyn, that is all I can think of. I have thought as hard as I could, and I suppose I am wrong, as usual. But I did think. I can't do any better. Please say something!"

The magician stood up as straight as a pillar, stretched out his arms in both directions, looked at the ceiling and said the first few words of the **Nunc Dimittis.** ◆

Norman— peoples from Normandy, France, conquered England in 1066; this implies that Arthur is descended from these Norman conquerors

Lot—Lot is the leader of Uriens, Anguish, and other local rulers who have not sworn loyalty to Arthur

Nunc Dimittis— the first Latin words of the Song of Simeon from the Bible meaning, "Now Thou dost dismiss [thy servant] . . ." Simeon was an old man allowed by God to live long enough to see the infant Jesus. On seeing the child, Simeon declares that he is ready to die. Merlyn's use of these words indicates that his teachings have been worthwhile; Arthur has become a true king.

from *Le Morte d'Arthur*
Sir Launcelot du Lake

Sir Thomas Malory,
retold by Keith Baines

Le Morte d'Arthur—French for "The Death of Arthur"

prowess—strength and agility

fidelity—loyalty

hen King Arthur returned from Rome, he settled his court at Camelot and there gathered about him his knights of the Round Table, who diverted themselves with jousting and tournaments. Of all his knights one was supreme, both in **prowess** at arms and in nobility of bearing, and this was Sir Launcelot, who was also the favorite of Queen Gwynevere, to whom he had sworn oaths of **fidelity.**

One day Sir Launcelot, feeling weary of his life at the court and of only playing at arms, decided to set forth in search of adventure. He asked his nephew Sir Lyonel to accompany him and, when both were suitably armed and mounted, they rode off together through the forest.

At noon they started across a plain, but the intensity of the sun made Sir Launcelot feel sleepy, so Sir Lyonel suggested that they should rest beneath the shade of an apple tree that grew by a hedge not far from the road. They dismounted, tethered their horses, and settled down.

"Not for seven years have I felt so sleepy," said Sir Launcelot, and with that fell fast asleep, while Sir Lyonel watched over him.

Soon three knights came galloping past, and Sir Lyonel noticed that they were being pursued by a fourth knight, who was one of the most powerful he had yet seen. The pursuing knight overtook each of the others in turn and, as he did so, knocked each off his horse with a thrust of his spear. When all three lay stunned, he dismounted, bound them securely to their horses with the reins, and led them away.

Without waking Sir Launcelot, Sir Lyonel mounted his horse and rode after the knight, and as soon as he had drawn close enough, shouted his challenge. The knight turned about and they charged at each other, with the result that Sir Lyonel was likewise flung from his horse, bound, and led away a prisoner.

The victorious knight, whose name was Sir Tarquine, led his prisoners to his castle and there threw them on the ground, stripped them naked, and beat them with thorn twigs. After that he locked them in a dungeon where many other prisoners, who had received like treatment, were complaining dismally.

Meanwhile, **Sir Ector de Marys,** who liked to accompany Sir Launcelot on his adventures, finding him gone, decided to ride after him. Before long he came upon a forester.

"My good fellow, if you know the forest hereabouts, could you tell me in which direction I am most likely to meet with adventure?"

"Sir, I can tell you: Less than a mile from here stands a well-moated castle. On the left of the entrance, you will find a **ford** where you can water your horse and, across from the ford, a large tree from which hang the shields of many famous knights. Below the shields hangs a caldron, of copper and brass: strike it three times with your spear, and then surely you will meet with adventure—such, indeed, that if you survive it, you will prove yourself the foremost knight in these parts for many years."

"May God reward you!" Sir Ector replied.

The castle was exactly as the forester had described it, and among the shields Sir Ector recognized several as belonging to knights of the Round Table. After watering his horse, he knocked on the caldron, and Sir Tarquine, whose castle it was, appeared.

They jousted, and at the first encounter Sir Ector sent his opponent's horse spinning twice about before he could recover.

"That was a fine stroke; now let us try again," said Sir Tarquine.

This time Sir Tarquine caught Sir Ector just below the right arm and, having impaled him on his spear, lifted him clean out of the saddle and rode with him into the castle, where he threw him on the ground.

"Sir," said Sir Tarquine, "you have fought better than any knight I have encountered in the last twelve years; therefore, if you wish, I will demand no more of you than your **parole** as my prisoner."

"Sir, that I will never give."

"Then I am sorry for you," said Sir Tarquine, and with that he stripped and beat him and locked him in the dungeon with the other prisoners. There Sir Ector saw Sir Lyonel.

"Alas, Sir Lyonel, we are in a sorry plight. But tell me, what has happened to Sir Launcelot? For he surely is the one knight who could save us."

"I left him sleeping beneath an apple tree, and what has befallen him since I do not know," Sir Lyonel replied; and then all the unhappy prisoners once more bewailed their lot.

While Sir Launcelot still slept beneath the apple tree, four queens started across the plain. They were riding white mules and accompanied by four knights, who held above them, at the tips of their spears, a green silk canopy to protect them from the sun. The party was startled by the neighing of Sir Launcelot's horse and, changing direction, rode up to the apple tree, where they discovered the sleeping knight. And as each of the queens gazed at the handsome Sir Launcelot, so each wanted him for her own.

"Let us not quarrel," said Morgan le Fay. "Instead, I will cast a spell over him so that he remains asleep while we take him to my castle and make him our prisoner. We can then oblige him to choose one of us for his **paramour.**"

Sir Launcelot was laid on his shield and borne by two of the knights to the Castle Charyot, which was Morgan

Sir Ector de Marys—Launcelot's brother; not the Sir Ector who raised Arthur

ford—a place to cross a river or moat

parole—a promise in exchange for partial or complete freedom

paramour—mistress

champion—
fight for

ignominiously—
shamefully

le Fay's stronghold. He awoke to find himself in a cold cell, where a young noblewoman was serving him supper.

"What cheer?" she asked.

"My lady, I hardly know, except that I must have been brought here by means of an enchantment."

"Sir, if you are the knight you appear to be, you will learn your fate at dawn tomorrow." And with that the young noblewoman left him. Sir Launcelot spent an uncomfortable night, but at dawn the four queens presented themselves and Morgan le Fay spoke to him:

"Sir Launcelot, I know that Queen Gwynevere loves you, and you her. But now you are my prisoner, and you will have to choose: either to take one of us for your paramour, or to die miserably in this cell—just as you please. Now I will tell you who we are: I am Morgan le Fay, Queen of Gore; my companions are the Queens of North Galys, of Estelonde, and of the Outer Isles. So make your choice."

"A hard choice! Understand that I choose none of you, lewd sorceresses that you are; rather will I die in this cell. But were I free, I would take pleasure in proving it against any who would **champion** you that Queen Gwynevere is the finest lady of this land."

"So, you refuse us?" asked Morgan le Fay.

"On my life, I do," Sir Launcelot said finally, and so the queens departed.

Sometime later, the young noblewoman who had served Sir Launcelot's supper reappeared.

"What news?" she asked.

"It is the end," Sir Launcelot replied.

"Sir Launcelot, I know that you have refused the four queens, and that they wish to kill you out of spite. But if you will be ruled by me, I can save you. I ask that you will champion my father at a tournament next Tuesday, when he has to combat the King of North Galys, and three knights of the Round Table, who last Tuesday defeated him **ignominiously.**

"My lady, pray tell me, what is your father's name?"

"King Bagdemagus."

"Excellent, my lady, I know him for a good king and a true knight, so I shall be happy to serve him."

"May God reward you! And tomorrow at dawn I will release you and direct you to an abbey, which is ten miles from here, where the good monks will care for you while I fetch my father."

"I am at your service, my lady."

As promised, the young noblewoman released Sir Launcelot at dawn. When she had led him through the twelve doors to the castle entrance, she gave him his horse and armor and directions for finding the abbey.

"God bless you, my lady; and when the time comes, I promise I shall not fail you."

Sir Launcelot rode through the forest in search of the abbey, but at dusk had still failed to find it and, coming upon a red silk pavilion, apparently unoccupied, decided to rest there overnight and continue his search in the morning.

He had not been asleep for more than an hour, however, when the knight who owned the pavilion returned and got straight into bed with him. . . . Sir Launcelot awoke with a start and, seizing his sword, leaped out of bed and out of the pavilion, pursued closely by the other knight. Once in the open they

set to with their swords, and before long Sir Launcelot had wounded his unknown adversary so seriously that he was obliged to yield.

The knight, whose name was Sir Belleus, now asked Sir Launcelot how he came to be sleeping in his bed . . . adding: "But now I am so sorely wounded that I shall consider myself fortunate to escape with my life."

"Sir, please forgive me for wounding you; but lately I escaped from an enchantment, and I was afraid that once more I had been betrayed. Let us go into the pavilion and I will staunch your wound."

Sir Launcelot had just finished binding the wound when the young noblewoman who was Sir Belleus's paramour arrived, and seeing the wound, at once rounded in fury on Sir Launcelot.

"Peace, my love," said Sir Belleus. "This is a noble knight, and as soon as I yielded to him he treated my wound with the greatest care." Sir Belleus then described the events which had led up to the duel.

"Sir, pray tell me your name and whose knight you are," the young noblewoman asked Sir Launcelot.

"My lady, I am called Sir Launcelot du Lake."

"As I guessed, both from your appearance and from your speech; and indeed I know you better than you realize. But I ask you—in **recompense** for the injury you have done my lord, and out of the courtesy for which you are famous—to

recompense— payment, exchange

copse—a stand of trees at the edge of a field or plain

ninescore—a score is 20, so ninescore is 180

recommend Sir Belleus to King Arthur and suggest that he be made one of the knights of the Round Table. I can assure you that my lord deserves it, being only less than yourself as a man-at-arms and sovereign of many of the Outer Isles."

"My lady, let Sir Belleus come to Arthur's court at the next Pentecost. Make sure that you come with him, and I promise I will do what I can for him; and if he is as good a man-at-arms as you say he is, I am sure Arthur will accept him."

As soon as it was daylight, Sir Launcelot armed, mounted, and rode away in search of the abbey, which he found in less than two hours. King Bagdemagus's daughter was waiting for him, and as soon as she heard his horse's footsteps in the yard ran to the window, and, seeing that it was Sir Launcelot, herself ordered the servants to stable his horse. She then led him to her chamber, disarmed him, and gave him a long gown to wear, welcoming him warmly as she did so.

King Bagdemagus's castle was twelve miles away, and his daughter sent for him as soon as she had settled Sir Launcelot. The king arrived with his retinue and embraced Sir Launcelot, who then described his recent enchantment and the great obligation he was under to his daughter for releasing him.

"Sir, you will fight for me on Tuesday next?"

"Sire, I shall not fail you; but please tell me the names of the three Round Table knights whom I shall be fighting."

"Sir Modred, Sir Madore de la Porte, and Sir Gahalantyne. I must admit that last Tuesday they defeated me and my knights completely."

"Sire, I hear that the tournament is to be fought within three miles of the abbey. Could you send me three of your most trustworthy knights, clad in plain armor, and with no device, and a fourth suit of armor, which I myself shall wear? We will take up our position just outside the tournament field and watch while you and the King of North Galys enter into combat with your followers, and then, as soon as you are in difficulties, we will come to your rescue and show your opponents what kind of knights you command."

This was arranged on Sunday, and on the following Tuesday Sir Launcelot and the three knights of King Bagdemagus waited in a **copse,** not far from the pavilion which had been erected for the lords and ladies who were to judge the tournament and award the prizes.

The King of North Galys was the first on the field, with a company of **ninescore** knights; he was followed by King Bagdemagus, with fourscore knights, and then by the three knights of the Round Table, who remained apart from both companies. At the first encounter King Bagdemagus lost twelve knights, all killed, and the King of North Galys, six.

With that, Sir Launcelot galloped on to the field, and with his first spear unhorsed five of the King of North Galys's knights, breaking the backs of four of them. With his next spear he charged the king and wounded him deeply in the thigh.

"That was a shrewd blow," commented Sir Madore, and galloped onto the field to challenge Sir Launcelot. But he too was tumbled from his horse, and with such violence that his shoulder was broken.

Sir Modred was the next to challenge Sir Launcelot, and he was sent spinning over his horse's tail. He landed head first, his helmet became buried in the soil, and he nearly broke his neck, and for a long time lay stunned.

Finally Sir Gahalantyne tried; at the first encounter both he and Sir Launcelot broke their spears, so both drew their swords and hacked vehemently at each other. But Sir Launcelot, with mounting wrath, soon struck his opponent a blow on the helmet which brought the blood streaming from eyes, ears, and mouth. Sir Gahalantyne slumped forward in the saddle, his horse panicked, and he was thrown to the ground, useless for further combat. . . . The King of North Galys was forced to admit defeat, and the prize was awarded to King Bagdemagus.

That night Sir Launcelot was entertained as the guest of honor of King Bagdemagus and his daughter at their castle and before leaving was loaded with gifts.

"My lady, please, if ever again you should need my services, remember that I shall not fail you."

The next day Sir Launcelot rode once more through the forest and by chance came to the apple tree where he had previously slept. This time he met a young noblewoman riding a white palfrey.

"My lady, I am riding in search of adventure; pray tell me if you know of any I might find hereabouts."

"Sir, there are adventures hereabouts if you believe that you are equal to them; but, please tell me, what is your name?"

"Sir Launcelot du Lake."

"Very well, Sir Launcelot; you appear to be a sturdy enough knight, so I will tell you. Not far away stands the castle of Sir Tarquine, a knight who in fair combat has overcome more than sixty opponents whom he now holds prisoner. Many are from the court of King Arthur, and if you can rescue them, I will then ask you to deliver me and my companions from a knight who distresses us daily, either by robbery or by other kinds of outrage."

"My lady, please first lead me to Sir Tarquine; then I will most happily challenge this **miscreant** knight of yours."

When they arrived at the castle, Sir Launcelot watered his horse at the ford and then beat the caldron until the bottom fell out. However, none came to answer the challenge, so they waited by the castle gate for half an hour or so. Then Sir Tarquine appeared, riding toward the castle with a wounded prisoner slung over his horse, whom Sir Launcelot recognized as Sir Gaheris, Sir Gawain's brother and a knight of the Round Table.

"Good knight," said Sir Launcelot, "it is known to me that you have put to shame many of the knights of the Round Table. Pray allow your prisoner, who I see is wounded, to recover while I **vindicate** the honor of the knights whom you have defeated."

"I defy you, and all your fellowship of the Round Table," Sir Tarquine replied.

"You boast!" said Sir Launcelot.

At the first charge the backs of the horses were broken and both knights stunned. But they soon recovered and set to with their swords, and both struck so lustily that neither shield nor armor could resist, and within two hours they were cutting each other's flesh, from which the blood flowed liberally. Finally they paused for a moment, resting on their shields.

miscreant— evildoer

vindicate— defend

"Worthy knight," said Sir Tarquine, "pray hold your hand for a while and, if you will, answer my question."

"Sir, speak on."

"You are the most powerful knight I have fought yet, but I fear you may be the one whom in the whole world I most hate. If you are not, for the love of you I will release all my prisoners and swear eternal friendship."

"What is the name of the knight you hate above all others?"

"Sir Launcelot du Lake, for it was he who slew my brother, Sir Carados of the **Dolorous** Tower, and it is because of him that I have killed a hundred knights and maimed as many more, apart from the sixty-four I still hold prisoner. And so, if you are Sir Launcelot, speak up, for we must then fight to the death."

"Sir, I see now that I might go in peace and good fellowship or otherwise fight to the death; but being the knight I am, I must tell you: I am Sir Launcelot du Lake, son of King Ban of Benwick, of Arthur's court, and a knight of the Round Table. So defend yourself!"

"Ah! this is most welcome."

Now the two knights hurled themselves at each other like two wild bulls; swords and shields clashed together, and often their swords drove into the flesh. Then sometimes one, sometimes the other, would stagger and fall, only to recover immediately and resume the contest. At last, however, Sir Tarquine grew faint and unwittingly lowered his shield. Sir Launcelot was swift to follow up his advantages and, dragging the other down to his knees, unlaced his helmet and beheaded him.

Sir Launcelot then strode over to the young noblewoman: "My lady, now I am at your service, but first I must find a horse."

Then the wounded Sir Gaheris spoke up: "Sir, please take my horse. Today you have overcome the most formidable knight, excepting only yourself, and by so doing have saved us all. But before leaving, please tell me your name."

"Sir Launcelot du Lake. Today I have fought to vindicate the honor of the knights of the Round Table, and I know that among Sir Tarquine's prisoners are two of my brethren, Sir Lyonel and Sir Ector, also your own brother, Sir Gawain. According to the shields there are also: Sir Brandiles, Sir Galyhuddis, Sir Kay, Sir Alydukis, Sir Marhaus, and many others. Please release the prisoners and ask them to help themselves to the castle treasure. Give them all my greetings and say I will see them at the next Pentecost. And please request Sir Ector and Sir Lyonel to go straight to the court and await me there." ❖

ACCENT ON...
TRAVEL AND TOURISM

Suppose you work for a travel agency that is offering a "King Arthur" package. Research the area and create a package for a seven-day, six-night trip to England. In your package, include costs for round-trip airfare from a major airport near you, six nights' lodging in England, and train travel from London to the sites connected with the legend of Arthur: Cadbury, Glastonbury, and Tintagel. Use software to create an attractive brochure including descriptions of the English countryside.

UNDERSTANDING

1. Find passages in the first excerpt that reveal Sir Kay's personality. Based on this evidence, what is your opinion of him? Imagine that you have been asked to comment on how well Sir Kay might do as a fellow employee or team member. Write a memo to your employer or coach in which you evaluate Sir Kay's potential. *Workshop 19*

2. When Arthur calls his first council, he makes a speech. What problem does he identify in that speech and what solution does he propose? In your group, discuss whether or not Arthur's problem exists today. Provide examples to make your point. Do you think his solution could be useful today? Share your ideas with the class.

3. When exaggeration is so extreme that it cannot possibly be taken literally, it often serves to produce a comic effect. Exaggeration is an important element in Malory's writing. Identify places where he uses exaggeration and discuss its effect.

    Prepare a two- to three-minute speech that uses exaggeration to create humor and make a point. *Workshop 23*

4. Malory's Sir Launcelot and White's King Arthur are both heroes. In an essay, compare and contrast these heroes. What qualities and behaviors do the two heroes possess in the stories? *Workshop 15*

CONNECTING

1. Malory's tale has been called "escapist literature" of the 15th century. In other words, it provides only good fun and happy endings, not thought-provoking ideas. Escapist writing has always been popular, especially in times of social crisis. Audiences today also enjoy escapist movies that allow them to forget briefly the serious problems they face every day.

    In a small group, develop an annotated bibliography of 10 recent books and 10 G- or PG-rated movies that offer good fun and happy endings. Design a simple flyer to distribute. *Workshop 20*

2. Arthur indicates in his speech to his first council that he thinks people can achieve positive results by working together.

    Working with several classmates, identify a school or local problem that might be solved if people were to work together on it. Write a proposal to your principal identifying the problem and suggesting a collaborative approach to solving it. *Workshop 13*

A LAST WORD

Arthur wanted to pursue a path that allowed people to be heroes without having to fight wars. How can we be modern-day heroes without fighting or using force? Is a strong, nonviolent hero as much a hero as a fighting one?

Running Eagle: Woman Warrior of the Blackfoot

EXPLORING

Teenagers, senior citizens, children—we all set goals for ourselves. What factors help people reach the goals they set? What factors prevent them from attaining their life's ambitions? Consider the cases of adults you know or about whom you have heard. What helped them achieve their goals? What prevented them from having the career they wanted or the things they desired?

THEME CONNECTION...
CHALLENGING CONVENTION

Most people agree with conventional wisdom. Anyone who challenges society's ideas about how things are or how they should be is usually criticized. Running Eagle faced criticism from members of the Blackfoot Nation when she chose to become a hunter and warrior rather than do household work. She prevailed, however, earning the admiration of her tribe.

TIME & PLACE

Brown Weasel Woman, later known as Running Eagle, was a member of the Blackfoot Nation. Although the date of her birth is unknown, it is known that she was clubbed to death in 1850 during hand-to-hand combat. The Blackfoot Indians lived on the Great Plains in Canada and the United States. They consisted of three tribes: the Piegan; the Blood, to which the author belongs; and the Siksika, who lived chiefly in Canada. Warlike and adept at stealing horses while the enemy slept, they were also excellent trappers. Running Eagle's tribe occupied terrain just east of the Rocky Mountains.

THE WRITER'S CRAFT
BIOGRAPHY

Beverly Hungry Wolf has written a brief biography of Brown Weasel Woman, a Blackfoot so admired that she was honored with the name Running Eagle. A biography is the story of a person's life. It must present accurate facts, honestly interpret them, and provide a clear impression of the subject's personality. Wolf carefully separates fact from legend in her effort to portray Running Eagle's achievements.

Running Eagle: Woman Warrior of the Blackfoot

Beverly Hungry Wolf

 unning Eagle has become the most famous woman in the history of the Blackfoot Nation because she gave up the work of the household in exchange for the war trails usually followed by men. In fact, she became so successful on her war adventures that many men called her a chief and eagerly followed her whenever she would take them. She was finally killed during one of her war adventures. . . .

The popular story is that Running Eagle began life as an ordinary Blackfoot girl name Brown Weasel Woman. She had two brothers and two sisters, and her father was a well-known warrior. When she became of the age that boys begin to practice hunting, she asked her father to make a set of bow and arrows with which she could practice. He did so, though not without some argument from his wives. It is said that he even allowed her to go with him buffalo hunting, and that she learned to shoot well enough to bring some down.

It was during one of the buffalo hunts with her father that this unusual girl is said to have first shown her warrior's courage. There were only a few Blackfoot hunters in the party, and it was not far from the camps when an enemy war party attacked and chased it. As the people rode toward the camp at top speed, Brown Weasel Woman's father had his horse shot out from under him. One of the bravest deeds performed by warriors in the old days was to brave the enemy fire while riding back to rescue a companion who was left on foot. This is what the daughter did for her father, both of them making their escape on her horse, after she stopped to unload the fresh meat that was tied on behind her. When word of the attack reached the rest of the tribe, a great crowd of warriors rode out after the enemy, killing many of them and chasing the rest away. The young woman's name was mentioned for days and nights after, as the people recounted what had taken place during that particular fight. It is said that some of the people complained, and feared that the girl performing men's deeds would set a bad example which might lead other girls to give up their household ways.

However, when her mother became helplessly ill sometime later, the future warrior woman decided on her own to take up household work. Since she was the eldest child in the family, there was no one to do the cooking and tanning while her mother slowly withered away. So she worked hard to learn what she had been avoiding, and she taught her younger brothers and sisters to help out wherever they could. . . .

The turning point in the young woman's life came when her father was killed while on the war trail. News of his

About the Author

Beverly Hungry Wolf (b. 1950) grew up on Canada's largest reserve, the Blood Indian Reserve. She is married and is the mother of four sons and a daughter. Her deep respect for native women, especially those of her grandmother's generation, influences both her writing and the way in which she is raising her children.

death also killed his widow, in her weakened state. The young woman and her brothers and sisters suddenly were orphaned, and she decided at that point to devote herself to her dream power giving her directions to follow men's ways. She took a widow woman into the lodge to help with the household work, and she directed her brothers and sisters in doing their share. She even carried a rifle—inherited from her father—at a time when many men still relied mainly on their bows and arrows.

Her first war adventure came not long after she and her family had gotten over their initial mourning. A war party of men left the Blackfoot camps on the trail of Crow warriors who had come and stolen horses. When this party was well under way, one of its members noticed someone following behind, in the distance. It turned out to be the young woman, armed and dressed for battle. The leader of the party told her to go back, threatened her, and finally told her that he would take the whole party back home if she didn't leave them. She is said to have laughed and told him: "You can return if you want to; I will go on by myself." . . .

The war party with the young woman spent several days on the trail before they reached the enemy camps of the Crows. They made a successful raid, going in and out of the camp many times, by cover of night, to bring out the choice horses that their owners kept in front of the lodges. It is said that the woman and her cousin went in together and that she, by herself, captured eleven of the valuable runners. Before daylight they were mounted on their stolen horses

and headed back toward their own homeland, driving ahead of them the rest of the captured herd. The Crows discovered their loss in the morning and chased the party for some way. But the raiders were able to change horses whenever the ones they were riding became worn out, and in that way they soon left the enemy followers way behind.

However, the most exciting part of this first war adventure of the young Blackfoot woman was yet to come, according to the legend that has survived her. While the rest of the party rested and cooked in a hidden location, she kept watch on the prairie country from the top of a nearby **butte.** From there she saw the approach of two enemy riders, and before she could alert the rest of her party to the danger, the enemies were ready to round up the captured herd. It is said that she ran down the butte with her rifle and managed to grab the rope of the herd's lead horse, to keep the rest from running away. Then, as the enemies closed in on her, expecting no trouble from a woman, she shot the one who carried a rifle and forced the other one to turn and try an escape. Instead of reloading her own rifle, she ran and grabbed the one from the fallen enemy, and shot after the one getting away. She missed him, but others of the party went after him and shortly brought him down as well. Her companions were quite surprised and pleased at what she had done. Not only had she saved their whole herd from being captured, but she also killed an enemy and captured his gun. She even captured his horse and one of the others took his scalp and presented her with it. It is said that she didn't want it,

SPOTLIGHT ON... SETTING GOALS

The modern-day world does not call on us to be warriors, but we do set goals for ourselves. You can set and achieve goals—big or little—with some forward thinking and planning. Keep in mind the following:

1. Define the short-term and long-term goals that are most important to you.
2. Make each goal specific. For example, instead of "I will do better in school," your goal might be "I will improve my grades by making sure my homework is done."
3. List the steps you need to take to reach the goal. Check your progress at each step.
4. Acknowledge your achievement when you reach your goal.

◆ ◆

but she felt better when reminded that she had avenged her father's death.

Although the young woman's first war experience was quite successful, there were still many people who thought that the chiefs should make her stop following the ways of the men. However, the critical talking came to an end altogether after she followed the advice of wise elders and went out to **fast** and seek a vision. She spent four days and nights alone and the Spirits rewarded her with a vision that gave her the power that men consider necessary for leading a successful warrior's life. Such visions were not always received by those seeking them, and very seldom have women received them at all. By tribal custom, no one questioned her about the vision, nor did they doubt her right to follow the directions which she was thus given. From then on, the people

considered her as someone unusual, with special powers, whom only the Spirits could judge and guide.

The young woman's second war adventure took her west over the Rocky Mountains, to the camps of the Kalispell tribe. . . . This time, instead of wearing her buckskin dress, she had on a new suit of warrior's clothing, including leggings, shirt, and breechcloth. She also carried a fine rawhide war shield, that had been given to her by the man who married the widow woman who had moved into the orphan household some time before.

The second raid turned out quite successfully, although one member of the party was killed. They captured a herd of over six hundred horses, and killed a number of the enemy during a fight which followed their discovery during

fast—to abstain from food

the raiding. The young woman was shot at, and would have been killed, but the two arrows both struck her shield, instead of her body.

The next time that the tribe gathered for the annual medicine lodge ceremony, the young woman was asked to get up with the other warriors and tell the people about her war exploits. Other women had done so, but they had usually gone in the company of their husbands and had not accomplished such fearless deeds as she. When she finished her stories the people applauded with drumbeats and war whoops, as was the custom. Then the head chief of the tribe, a man named Lone Walker, is said to have honored her in a way never known to have been done for a woman. After a short talk and a prayer, he gave her a new name— Running Eagle—an ancient name carried by several famous warriors in the tribe before her. In addition, the Braves Society of young warriors invited her to become a member, which honor she is said to have accepted as well.

From that point on, Running Eagle, the young woman warrior, became the leader of the war parties she went with, no longer a follower. I cannot say how many such war raids she went on, nor how many horses she captured, nor enemies she killed. There are many different legends about them. There are also legends of men who could not accept that this proud woman wanted no husband, so they tried all the ways

● ● ● ● ● ● ● ● ●

"Running Eagle, the young woman warrior, became the leader of the war parties."

● ● ● ● ● ● ● ● ●

known of to make her change her mind about marriage. But the issue was settled when she explained that Sun had come in her vision and told her that she must belong only to him, and that she could not go on living if she broke such a commandment.

As Running Eagle lived by the war trail, so she died also. It was when she led a large party of warriors against the Flathead tribe in revenge for their killing of some men and women who had gone from the Blackfoot camps one morning to hunt and butcher buffalo. The revenge party was a very large one, and she led it right to the edge of the Flathead camp during the night. In the early morning, after waiting for the camp to be cleared of the prize horses by their herders, she gave the cry to attack. There followed a long-drawn-out battle in which many of the enemy were killed. After the initial shooting, the battle turned into a free-for-all in which clubs and knives were the main weapons. Running Eagle was attacked by a large enemy with a club, whom she killed, but another came up behind her and killed her with his club. One of Running Eagle's men in turn killed this man. When the battle was over, the members of her party found her, the large man in front, the other behind, and she dead in the middle. And so ended the career of the woman warrior whose life has become a legend among the Blackfoot. ❖

UNDERSTANDING

1.  Members of the tribe disapprove of Running Eagle for choosing a man's way of life over a woman's. Why do they disapprove? Support your answer with examples from the text.

   People often argue about the right way to do something. Imagine you are in the middle of a dispute between two friends. With a partner, brainstorm ways to help these friends settle their differences. What would you, as mediator—a neutral third party—ask them to discuss? Share your ideas with the class.

2. Find evidence in the text that the tribe finally accepts Running Eagle for what she is. What causes Running Eagle's tribe to stop judging her and instead to approve of her?

   Being receptive to how others think and feel, however, is necessary for success in any endeavor. In a narrative essay, tell about a time when your grasp or understanding of someone else's thoughts and feelings had a positive result. *Workshop 9*

3. In groups, find reasons given in the text for why the Blackfoot tribe fought other native people. Analyze these reasons. Consider the causes and effects of the Blackfoot's actions.

   Listen to three commercials on television or radio. Jot down any cause-effect relationships these commercials state directly or imply. Consider the logic of these connections. Do commercials portray genuine cause-effect connections? Write an opinion paper on this subject. *Workshop 6*

CONNECTING

1. The Blackfoot tribe had a system for honoring outstanding warriors. The warrior appeared in public to describe accomplishments, was given a new name, and was admitted into the Braves Society. Design and write down a system for honoring members of your class. In an oral presentation accompanied by appropriate handouts or overheads, explain this system. With your classmates, reach consensus about methods to be used to recognize notable performance. *Workshop 23*

2.  Working in small groups, investigate and develop an oral presentation concerning the roles of men and women of a specific Native American group. For your presentation, you may deliver a speech or role-play an episode, using a narrator to explain the action at various points. *Workshop 23*

> ## A LAST WORD
>
> When you see someone challenging society's conventions, what do you think? Instead of criticizing, we might do well to try to understand the person's motives. What is more important—agreement or acceptance?

from *Policewoman*

EXPLORING

You worked for weeks to build your model of the Capitol building and carry it proudly into the classroom. One of your outspoken classmates says, "But the dome is way too short; it isn't round enough." How did you respond? Have you ever accepted a challenge, done your very best to meet it, and then been told that your effort wasn't good enough? Have you ever been blamed for something you didn't do? Discuss ways to deal with criticism, just and unjust, and with unfair blame.

THEME CONNECTION...
TO CATCH A THIEF

Dorothy Uhnak describes two undercover police officers meeting the challenge of catching a thief. Working undercover, Dot and Hank show exemplary courage and determination when they chase a thief surprised in the act of stealing. A witness, however, criticizes the way they handle the difficult challenge of apprehending the criminal.

TIME & PLACE

Dorothy Uhnak describes a fictitious incident set in New York City during the early 1960s. Uhnak writes with authority; she was a police officer for 14 years. In this excerpt from her novel *Policewoman,* Dot and Hank are working together as undercover agents. Their assignment is to observe a window washer suspected of stealing from employees.

THE WRITER'S CRAFT
DESCRIPTION

In the novel *Policewoman,* Dorothy Uhnak makes excellent use of description. Descriptive words may appeal to any one of the five senses. They may show size, color, and shape, or reveal how something tastes or sounds. Uhnak's words help readers imagine realistic places, objects, people, and events. They see, for instance, the "fragile, needle-heeled high-style" shoes, and they hear Mr. Mac shouting as he "blasted forth" over the intercom and "thundered from the walls."

from *Policewoman*
Dorothy Uhnak

he window washer with the **light fingers** was due in the office sometime that day. He was finishing up the third floor and he always worked Kensington——it was his section. They didn't know exactly when he'd arrive, but I was hoping it would be soon.

Hank had asked why the girls hadn't complained to the man's boss, confront him with the accusation, even press charges, but the old man had insisted that he be caught in the act. Mr. Mac liked action, liked things done right, so there I sat at that crazy little pink typewriter and fooled around with the magic keys. Hank was in an adjoining office— the offices outside the executive suites were linked by airy, lacy white room dividers.

I did a few finger exercises to get the feel of the machine. I could see Hank looking over the sample shoes displayed on the wall-to-ceiling display case, fingering the fragile, needle-heeled high-style things with his large, unaccustomed hands. He held a shoe up to me, grinning; somebody's secretary, floating past, caught our amusement and froze in my direction, glancing quickly down. I tried to hide my feet but there they were on display under the glass desk. Then she raised her eyes to my face and looked right through me.

They spoke to each other in voices that were carpeted: soft, thick, and expensively trained at one of those how-to-succeed schools that I had learned Mr.

Mac insisted upon. He wanted them not only young but of a particular pattern. The only loud voice in the company was Mr. Mac's, and when he blasted forth on the small pink intercoms placed here and there on shelves about the room, everyone stood stock still, breathless, until he finished speaking. It seemed he had a technique all his own. Only when he finished the message would he announce the name of the person for whom it was intended. After an hour of these sudden pronouncements, I found myself listening intently, along with the others, as though it might be meant for me. "Those drawings are all smudges and smears and crummy, and I want the whole mess drawn up again. And play down the red edges. Marion!" "I want that showroom in one hundred percent perfect order and no speck of dust showing and those new slippers—the pink ones and the off-green ones in K-13 case—right now. Harold!" It was a little upsetting.

There was no conversation with these girls. I was someone who was just not there. They continued their quiet little gossipy huddles of office talk over drawings of shoes, pictures of shoes clipped from the best magazines—the kind that have a woman's face all over the page, sinking mysteriously into some kind of foggy background, and one word printed

About the Author
Dorothy Uhnak (b. 1933) spent 14 years as a New York City police-woman. Then, she made a career change in 1967 to mystery writer. Uhnak was an award-winning police officer and would become an award-winning writer. One of Uhnak's fictional detectives, Christy Opara, became the model for a television series, *Get Christy Love.* Her 1973 novel, *Law and Order,* became a best-seller and the basis of a television movie.

light fingers—an idiom describing a thief

depraved—
corrupted

jaded—dulled

Montauk—
Montauk Point,
the far eastern
tip of Long
Island, New
York

arduous—
needing great
effort

refinement—
elegance of
language,
manners,
and so on

neatly in a corner, the name of a firm manufacturing some cosmetic or miraculous rejuvenation lotion. They might have stepped from some similar fog, and with their veiled, mean little glances, have wondered where I had stepped from. They knew I was a policewoman and drew certain inferences from this—probably that I was **depraved** and **jaded** from contact with the unspeakables of some remote and barely existent world.

I was wearing a little black dress, my "nothing" dress, with one small gold pin—a little owl Tony had found in the sand at **Montauk**—that was all grubby and chipped but had "Tiffany—14 k" engraved near the safety catch. He had had it cleaned and polished for me, and that little pin gave me a certain courage even if their rigid poise and rightness were somewhat unnerving. They all had noticed my feet with my unacceptable shoes, just plain black pumps and not expensive, but none of them had even looked at my good little gold owl. I would have lasted about a day in that place. I could feel the delicate wallpaper and antique picture frames—placed around little shelves of silly-looking shoes—and the air of **arduous refinement** strangling me.

The window washer came in from the reception room, wordless, and went directly to his task. As had been prearranged, the girls vaporized soundlessly without any sign of emotion, like a bunch of cardboard dolls floating effortlessly away. Mr. Mac thundered from the walls for his secretary, and she glided over the carpet staring straight ahead, her notebook against her narrow, bony thigh. Hank was handling the shoes again, but

he was watching me now, and I knew that he would keep his eyes on me until he received a signal.

I was typing some paragraph from some shoe newspaper, fascinated by the weirdness of the machine. It was typing with a strange power of its own, barely relying on my fingers. My back was to the window, but there was a lovely, wide-framed mirror perched on one of the room dividers that gave me a perfect view of the suspect. I could glance up from my machine easily and observe him. He was smearing a squeegee over the pane of window from outside the building. He hadn't strapped on his safety belt and he seemed to hang by the tip of one finger. I could hear him making grunting noises as he hefted himself inside the window frame and sloshed his arm up and down. I kept my fingers on the keys and they clicked furiously, in a frenzy of noise and activity. He had his back to me, bending over his bucket and rags and equipment, straps and buckles hanging from all sides of him. He ran a dirty gray rag over the back of his neck, then stuffed it into a back pocket. He leaned heavily on the desk alongside of him, rested his hand on the surface of the desk, and without looking behind him, toward me, pocketed the diamond engagement ring that had been left next to the pink telephone.

As I touched my hair, my left hand on the clicking keys of the machine, Hank started for the room. The window washer reached into his shirt pocket, pulled out a cigarette and was placing it between his lips when Hank walked in and caught my nod and motion toward an imaginary pocket on my dress. I don't think Hank realized he was carrying the purple shoe in his left hand. He seemed a little surprised and let it drop to the floor as he took the window washer's arm and stuck his shield in the man's face.

Hank was a tall man, deceptively swift while appearing almost motionless. He had the suspect against a wall, or the latticework that passed for a wall, before I could even stand up.

"Put the bucket down, pal. Police."

Hank had one hand on the man's shoulder, and he jerked his head at the prisoner. "Okay, buddy, take the ring out of your pocket."

The man stared motionless, but there was a whiteness coming over his face. Hank pushed the man's chest. "Take out the cigarettes and the ring. C'mon, c'mon, put everything on the desk."

"I got no ring," the man said tensely, his eyes wandering around the room, then back to Hank's face. He bit his lip, seemed to be weighing things, making some decision. "Not me, pal, I'm not your man."

Hank reached roughly into the pocket, tossed the cigarettes on the desk, then fished the ring out and held it before the man's eyes. "This yours?" he asked softly.

Hank motioned to me; the suspect seemed surprised to see me. He hadn't even noticed me. "I'm a policewoman. I saw you take the ring from the desk and put it in your pocket."

The voice of Mr. Mac suddenly boiled into the room, seeming to come from the ceilings and the floors. He had apparently been tuned in on us, and he was howling furiously about what he was going to do to the "bum." In the instant it took us to realize what the sudden sound was, the prisoner shoved Hank into me and lunged across the room. He crashed into the room divider and through the glass doors of the reception room into the hallway. I raced after Hank, grabbing my pocketbook from the desk, and saw Hank catch the glass door on his shoulder, fighting it back open. I heard the commotion on the stairway, a sound of ugly scuffling. Hank was hanging onto the straps that were dangling from the window washer's pants, and the man kicked up with his heavy-booted feet at Hank's legs. The stairway was hard steel, fireproof, and dangerous, with sharp, point-edged steps. Hank had the man by the collar and I managed to grab a loose strap, but he shook me off with an elbow. I hadn't realized what a hugely powerful man he was, with arms and shoulders and back hardened by years of labor. He was a heavyset man with no scrap of fat on him, and he made thick, grunting sounds. Hank was tall and wiry, but in the scuffling he lost his footing and tumbled on the stairs. The three of us fell together, Hank on the bottom, the prisoner on top. I fell clear of the men, pulled along by the strap which had gotten tangled around my wrist. I was clutching my pocketbook as though it were part of me, and I felt no pain even though I was aware of being pulled down the stairs. We all stood up together, still clinging to each other in one way or another, and fell against the brass door that opened onto the lobby of the building.

We exploded into the lobby into the midst of startled office workers on their way to lunch: three grappling, grasping

SPOTLIGHT ON...
PAYING ATTENTION TO
DETAILS

As a police officer and as a writer, Dorothy Uhnak understands the importance of specific details. Specific details can bring alive for the reader a character, time or place, or event. Paying attention to details is a skill you practice every day. By paying attention to details, you may understand situations at home, school, and work more fully. Practice being observant by doing the following:

1. Watch carefully. As you watch, try to do so with an open mind. For example, think about how an event in a restaurant affects those directly involved and those at an adjoining table.
2. As you see details, try to connect them to other things that you already know.
3. Pay attention to numbers and statistics.

❖ ❖ ❖ ❖ ❖ ❖ ❖ ❖ ❖ ❖ ❖ ❖ ❖ ❖ ❖ ❖ ❖ ❖ ❖ ❖

figures. I had lost my shoes somewhere. I felt the cut on my leg. I heard the terrible sounds of blows—he was actually hitting me. My face felt the impact of the blow, but I felt no pain, just an awareness of having been struck. There was a terrible tangle of arms and legs; my hair was being pulled, and I felt a hand inside my mouth, roughly scraping the roof of it.

"The gun," Hank gasped, unable to reach his own. "For Pete's sake, Dot, pull the gun."

I let loose my hold of the strap and dug the gun out, dropped my pocketbook somewhere. Hank managed to shove the man against the wall with his shoulder, holding him, leaning against him, trying to hold himself up, and I pointed the gun in the man's face. But I could see that the glazed, pale eyes did not recognize

the weapon. It made no impression on him, and his blank, transparent expression was genuine.

"Sit still, you, or I'll shoot you!"

He managed a kick at Hank's shinbone. I held the gun flatly in my palm, the finger off the trigger, as I felt myself being shoved halfway across the lobby. I landed against a candy stand, and some face stuck itself in mine, some frantic candy-clerk face, saying words to me, hysterical words: "Lady, please lady, get off my merchandise. Lady, you're messing up my papers and my magazines." I heard the words and the voice and saw the sickening face, the arms outstretched over the shelves of candy bars and gum, the voice wailing in grief for his magazines and newspapers and nickel-and-dime merchandise. I saw all the faces all around us, a horrified, fascinated group of faces; open-mouthed, wide-eyed, drawing back, yet far too intrigued to move away—watching.

"Call the police!" I said in a thin, faraway, unknown voice. "We're police officers; for Pete's sake, someone make a call!"

Hank and the prisoner were grappling, and the powerful man, using the advantage of his weight and conditioned strength and those murderous dusty boots, delivered a terrific blow and kick at the same time. As Hank held on to him, pulling him down, too, I cracked the butt of my gun at the base of his skull as hard as I could. It was a horrible, loud, unimaginable sound, unreal. The window washer seemed to move in slow motion; he aimed a kick at Hank, missed his footing, slipped to his knees, swung his arm out wildly at Hank, who grabbed it and forced him down. The back of his head, balding but with thin strands of blond hair, began to ooze bright red from a long gash. I kicked at his stomach, the sharp pain telling me I didn't have any shoes on. He gave another animal lunge at me, and I slipped backward, my feet skidding along the slippery polished floor. I felt myself making contact with something, with someone, and some hands pushed me angrily away. I turned. A woman, standing in back of me, her face outraged, contorted, had pushed me. She was pregnant, I could see that, it registered, but I couldn't understand why she had pushed me. The prisoner and Hank were on the floor, each making motions reaching for the other. As I moved toward them, some man, some red-faced, tough-faced old man, some

skinny, wiry old guy in a bank guard's uniform shoved his face at me.

"Cop?" That's all he said. I nodded, and he reached down and gave the window washer a terrific punch in the face, and the prisoner settled down on the floor. Then the man caught Hank's arms and pulled him to a sitting position and pushed his own face at Hank.

"Okay? Okay, officer?"

Hank nodded, not seeing the face before him, just nodding, maybe just trying to shake it off, to focus. He reached for his handcuffs, but the old guy snatched them.

I'll do it, pal." Quickly, professionally, he slipped the handcuffs on the prisoner, who was reviving, twisting. He cuffed the man's hands behind his back, explaining as he did so, "Six years off the force and I haven't lost the old speed. Heard the commotion. I'm at First National—right in the building. You okay? Seventieth Precinct in Brooklyn last ten years on the job. Hey, you okay?"

I nodded, not looking at him but at the crowd, at the faces that were watching us, watching us, talking about us, pointing at us, at Hank and the prisoner and the bank guard and me. I saw the uniformed cops come in through the revolving doors—four of them, then three more, then a sergeant, a big, fat sergeant with great big cheeks.

The uniformed cops grabbed everyone; the sergeant had my arm. I was still holding my gun. "Policewoman—sergeant—that's my partner, and this man here, he helped us."

The spectators moved a little closer, wanting to hear some more of it. They knew nothing of what was happening.

Some woman, some woman from the crowd, whom I had never seen, kept calling to the sergeant, telling him she wanted to talk to someone in charge. She saw his stripes and kept on calling and calling until finally, with a heave of annoyance, he turned to her.

"Lady, what is it? Whassa matter—what d'ya want? C'mon, you men, get these people outta here—show's over—go to lunch." The woman, eyes blazing, pointed at us.

"I was a witness," she said in a high, shrill voice, and everyone came closer for a better look. "I want to know who to talk to here."

"Lady," the sergeant said, in his old-timer's growl, "what d'ya want?"

"I want to report an incident of police brutality," she said indignantly and shaking with rage. "I saw the whole thing: this girl hit that man on the head with a blackjack or a gun or something, and he was on his knees, helpless. Then this man, this bank guard, came and beat him mercilessly, and all the time his hands were handcuffed behind his back." ❖

ON THE JOB
POLICE OFFICER

Duties of police officers range from directing traffic to criminal investigation, from public safety to fingerprint identification. In all cases, good communication skills, the ability to work well with others, and attention to detail are critical to success on the job. Most police departments require applicants to pass a civil service examination as well as a physical examination. Applicants usually need a high school diploma, and most states have an age requirement of 21. For most law enforcement positions, college is not necessary. However, junior colleges and universities offer courses in law enforcement that may improve chances for success and advancement.

UNDERSTANDING

1. What is Dot's opinion of the women who work in the Kensington Shoe Company? Find evidence to justify your conclusions.

   Imagine that Dot's police work required her to spend a month working alongside the women at the Kensington Shoe Company. In groups, list steps that might be taken to create a working relationship between Dot and the shoe company employees.

2. Identify Mr. Mac's management style. What do you think of his style? What does he expect of his employees? How does he treat them? Support your views with passages in the text.

   Brainstorm with several classmates to identify the qualities an excellent supervisor would possess. Then role-play a scene similar to the shoe factory episode in the selection, but portray Mr. Mac as an excellent supervisor.

3. Does this story persuade you that women make good police officers? How effective is Dot? Base your response on the text.

   Write a letter of inquiry to your local police department asking for a police officer's job description and for information about the requirements for women who wish to become police officers. ***Workshop 18***

4. A good writer uses hints to prepare for a surprise ending. Did the author prepare you for this ending? Check the text. What did you think when you read it?

   With a partner, look up *irony*. Write a personal essay about an ironic experience you or a friend has had. ***Workshop 3***

CONNECTING

1. Gather information about careers in law enforcement. What does it take to become a police officer or FBI agent? Obtain job descriptions explaining what such work involves. Find out about salary and opportunity for advancement. Prepare an informative, attractive display for the classroom or for a career day.

2. Mr. Mac is an overbearing boss who imposes his will as he shouts commands. Today, many companies discourage such conduct. Gather information about how companies are managed today. Ask human resource representatives about the relationship between supervisors and employees. Based on your research, explain in a report how management style affects supervisor-employee relationships, the work environment, employee morale, and productivity. Include in your report any appropriate charts and visuals. ***Workshops 8 and 22***

Running Blind

EXPLORING

Society is providing more opportunities for the physically and mentally challenged to achieve their ambitions and lead satisfying lives. Discuss examples that illustrate the determination and ability of disabled people.

THEME CONNECTION... CHALLENGING YOURSELF

In this selection by Thomas Fox Averill, a blind man poses a challenge for himself: he decides to become a runner. Helped by a friend, he drives himself hard, practicing regularly and striving to excel. Eventually the blind runner becomes the true expert, faster than his friend and always working to increase his speed.

TIME & PLACE

Written in 1991, Averill's account is set in an unspecified town or city. The runners attempt increasingly challenging courses: the high school track, roads in the park, country roads, and finally an "intricate concrete course." Descriptions remind us that the running, done outdoors, begins in early spring. By week eight, early summer has arrived.

THE WRITER'S CRAFT

REPETITION

Repetition of words and phrases adds emphasis and clarity to writing. When repetition occurs often enough to become predictable, readers enjoy looking forward to it. By withholding expected repetition, the author can emphasize a point. Repetition unifies four of the paragraphs here: "Week one, one mile: asphalt high-school track"; "Week eight, three miles: asphalt park roads"; "Week twelve, five miles: country roads"; "Week fifteen, 10k: downtown, . . ." The absence of this repetition in the fifth and final paragraph calls attention to the fact that the blind man has become the faster of the two runners.

Running Blind
Thomas Fox Averill

"Why do you do it?" he asks. I talk of feeling trim, breathing deep, of burned calories, heart rate, **endorphins,** of T-shirts—a lifetime supply after five years of organized runs. I talk of sky, sun, wind, earth, asphalt, concrete. "Will you take me sometime?" he asks. My friend is blind.

Week one, one mile: asphalt high-school track. His legs are longer than mine. We stutter, finding our stride, his hand at my elbow. I describe the curves, teach him to lean. By the back stretch he is winded. I close my eyes. "What's wrong?" he asks, but I say, "Nothing, you're just tired."

Week eight, three miles: asphalt park roads. We run faster now. I describe trees, the elegant rose garden, the zoo, the amphitheatre, the incredible blue of early summer sky, clouds billowing like runner's breath. Eyes on the road, I anticipate gradual rises and falls, corners, patches of loose gravel, dead limbs. "Just another half-mile," I say when his breath shortens and his hand loses my elbow for a second. He grunts: "Tell me in time. Time means more than distance." I say, "Okay, four minutes or so to go."

Week twelve, five miles: country roads. His hand pushes my elbow, begging for speed. We climb hills as steeply pitched as ladders. I call out the views, lush green, hazy with humidity. Downhills we run so fast I'm afraid for him. "Let go," he says, "Just let yourself move. Don't talk, I know where I am now." I breathe hard. We run faster than I ever have before.

Week fifteen, **10K:** downtown, intricate concrete course. "How fast?" I ask as we wait for the gun. He stretches his long, sinewy legs, says, "As fast as you can." He is calm, confident. I weave us through the congestion of bodies. We race. With two-tenths left he leans against me, asks, "Straightaway?" and I gasp, "Yes," and he passes me, sprinting. Someone stops him at the finish.

From then on: he runs with faster companions. He tells me: "Want to improve? Running's inside you. Don't watch what's around you, pay attention to what's inside." He's right, but free again, I slow down, enjoy the view. ❖

endorphins—proteins in the brain that naturally cause an insensitivity to pain

10K—a common distance for running courses; approximately 6.2 miles

ACCENT ON...
FITNESS

• • • • • • • • • • • • • • • • • • •

Develop a training schedule for an average, casual runner to follow to prepare for a 10K. Consider diet, warm-up and cool-down exercises, and how far and how fast the runner should go each day. Make your training schedule in table format on computer, leaving room to make comments about the runner's progress.

UNDERSTANDING

1. Two people may have different motives for doing the same thing. Find references to the differences in the motives of the narrator and his blind friend.

   In your journal, recall occasions when you assigned motives to people. Why did you think you knew what they were thinking? Were you ever wrong? What did you learn from guessing people's motives?

2.  The blind man chose to become skillful at running fast. To be successful in the workplace and in life, everyone needs to acquire certain basic academic and social skills. In groups, discuss what you think these skills might be and list them. Then, working on your own, choose one of these skills and write a paragraph explaining how you have used the skill at work, with friends, with family, or at school. *Workshop 8*

3. Find references in the text that indicate how the two men differ. Use your information to figure out the ideas the author wishes to convey.

   Write a character sketch of a person you admire. Try to give your character complexity by showing his or her private thoughts as well as appearance, actions, and words. *Workshop 10*

CONNECTING

1.  The narrator teaches the blind man how to run, and the blind man advises his mentor about how to increase his speed. Choose a practical skill you are good at, such as driving, spiking a volleyball, or making homemade bread. Write a process explanation for this skill. Then, share your explanation with a partner and arrange to teach your partner how to perform this skill. If possible, you and your partner may demonstrate your new skills to the class. *Workshop 12*

2. The blind man set a goal and, with the help of his friend, achieved it in spite of his disability. Gather information about agencies in your region that serve people with disabilities. Investigate assisted-care facilities, state-funded agencies, and school programs for students with disabilities. Your findings may indicate that your region does a superb job of assisting the disabled, or it may suggest deficiencies that need to be corrected. Prepare an oral presentation using visual aids to explain the results of your research and make appropriate recommendations. *Workshops 22 and 23*

A LAST WORD

Each of us has his or her own challenges. They may come to us unexpectedly, or we may create them ourselves. How can we challenge ourselves in ways that are healthy? How can we help others whose challenges may be greater than our own?

It Happened in Montgomery

EXPLORING

With your classmates, discuss the status of civil rights in America today. First decide what you mean by the term *civil rights*. Does civil rights mean the absence of racism and sexism, or does it mean more than that? Share what you know about ordinary people and public leaders who have in the past contributed to, or who are presently contributing to, the increase of civil rights for every American. What qualities do such people seem to possess?

THEME CONNECTION... SPONTANEOUS HEROISM

When Rosa Parks refused to get up and give a white man her seat on the bus, she did so out of fatigue. Petrie says, "she was tired that day. / Weariness was in her bones." Combined with this fatigue, however, was remarkable courage. Parks resisted authority and defied unjust laws, while the men merely "talked and talked and talked." When an unexpected challenge asks us to take a stand, what will *we* do?

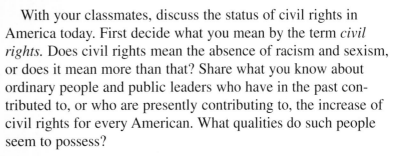

TIME & PLACE

"It Happened in Montgomery" describes a real event that took place in Montgomery, Alabama, in 1955. Rosa Lee Parks, a seamstress, decided to disregard a law. She sat in the front of the bus. When the bus driver ordered her to move so a white passenger could sit down, she refused. As a result, she was arrested and jailed for violating a city law decreeing that African Americans must sit at the back of the bus.

THE WRITER'S CRAFT

ALLITERATION

Alliteration occurs when words that are close together begin with the same consonant sound. Examples of alliteration are "**gr**uffly **gr**abbed," "**p**ulled and **p**ushed," and "**sh**arply **sh**oved." When a consonant sound in a position of emphasis is repeated, its music strikes the ear. The sound reverberates, underscoring ideas and unifying the poem.

It Happened in Montgomery

Phil W. Petrie

For Rosa Parks

Then he slammed on the brakes—
Turned around and grumbled.

But she was tired that day.
Weariness was in her bones.
And so the thing she's done yesterday,
And yesteryear,
On her workdays,
Churchdays,
Nothing-to-do-guess-I'll-go-and-visit
    Sister Annie Days—

She felt she'd never do again.

And he growled once more.
So she said:
No sir . . . I'm stayin' right here.

And he gruffly grabbed her,
Pulled and pushed her—
Then sharply shoved her through the doors.

The news slushed through the littered streets—
Slipped into the crowded churches,
Slimmered onto the **unmagnolied** side of town
While the men talked and talked and talked.

She—
Who was tired that day,
Cried and sobbed that she was glad she'd done it,
That her soul was satisfied.

That Lord knows,
A little walkin' never hurt anybody;

That in one of those unplanned, unexpected,
Unadorned moments—
A weary woman turned the page of
    History. ❖

slimmered—
created word
combining
slithered and
simmered to
suggest how the
news traveled

unmagnolied—
created word to
describe the
side of town
without
magnolia trees;
the unadorned,
poor, side
of town

UNDERSTANDING

1. How does Petrie create emphasis with rhythm? With a partner, take turns reading the lines aloud. Which ones have a swinging, lilting sound? Which syllables get a heavy beat? In what places does the beat add emphasis to the meaning?

   Since they can't rely on gestures and tone of voice to convey meaning, writers must achieve emphasis by other means. Identify various ways authors achieve emphasis. Imagine you are a displeased customer. Write a courteous but firm memo to the manager of a store or company. Use emphasis to make your complaint clear. *Workshop 19*

2. Why did Rosa Parks refuse to give her seat to a white man? Find evidence in the poem to support your conclusions.

   With several classmates, role-play for the class the history-making confrontation depicted in Petrie's poem. Collaborate to write and perform the scene. Write dialogue for Rosa Parks, the bus driver, and the white man. Other group members may be bus passengers or pedestrians reacting when Rosa steps off the bus. *Workshop 4*

3. How does Rosa Parks's behavior prove that one person can make a difference? In groups, think of situations in which one person's actions have made, and can make, a positive difference in your school or community. Then write an action plan for doing something *on your own* to solve a problem in your school or community.

CONNECTING

1. Rosa Parks's spontaneous action helped others remember their mission to gain equality and freedom. When a group shares a mission, it can accomplish far more than can one person acting alone.

   With your class, write a mission statement for students in your grade. Make a poster-sized version of it to hang in classrooms and attractive copies to go in students' notebooks.

2. Rosa Parks's behavior consisted in part of nonverbal communication. Nonverbal communication is body language that gives cues to others about what you are thinking. Brainstorm with the class to identify various kinds of socially acceptable nonverbal communication. Find pictures and make posters that illustrate nonverbal communication and post them in the classroom. On each poster, explain in writing the nonverbal behavior shown.

> **A LAST WORD**
>
> Amazing inventions have begun as laboratory failures. Great events can begin with just one person, one tired person. If you put your efforts into it, what great actions will you begin?

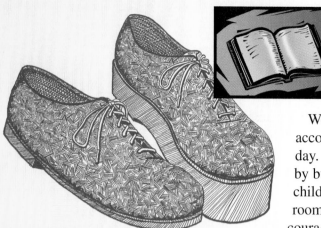

A Giant Step

EXPLORING

● ● ● ● ● ● ● ● ● ● ● ● ● ● ● ● ● ● ●

We have known, read about, or seen on television accounts of people who face difficult challenges every day. An elderly man may struggle to haul groceries home by bus; a young, single mother may care for her autistic child; a 14-year-old on a work permit may clean hotel rooms to help support his brothers and sisters. Discuss the courageous responses of friends to challenges they face as part of the ordinary business of getting through the day.

THEME CONNECTION...
STEADFAST COURAGE EVERY DAY

Henry Gates, Jr., explains in his personal narrative how at the age of 40 he finally came to be able to wear normal shoes. Without boasting of his courage or complaining of his misfortune, Gates tells about an injury he sustained at the age of 14 that resulted in living for 26 years with a painful hip condition.

When at last new hip-joint technology made possible an operation that would provide relief from his pain, Gates recalls the success of this operation.

TIME & PLACE

The injury that Henry Gates, Jr., had to live with the rest of his life happened to him in 1964. He was 14 years old and living in Piedmont, West Virginia, part of a poverty-stricken region known as Appalachia. His ball-and-socket hip joint broke, causing him excruciating agony. Gates was hospitalized and immobile for weeks; afterwards, he limped in spite of the special shoes he had to wear. The chronic pain from his injury and the disadvantages of growing up an African-American in rural West Virginia did not stop Gates from expanding his world, however.

THE WRITER'S CRAFT
POINT OF VIEW

Point of view is the perspective, or vantage point, an author uses to tell what happened. Authors customarily use either the first-person or third-person angle to tell about fiction or nonfiction events. Henry Gates, Jr., uses first person to describe what he and others do and say. Although Gates reveals his own thoughts, he does not say exactly what goes on in the minds of others.

● ●

A Giant Step

Henry Louis Gates, Jr.

"What's this?" the hospital janitor said to me as he stumbled over my right shoe.

"My shoes," I said.

"That's not a shoe, brother," he replied, holding it to the light. "That's a brick."

It *did* look like a brick, sort of.

"Well, we can throw these in the trash now," he said.

"I guess so."

We had been together since 1975, those shoes and I. They were **orthopedic** shoes built around molds of my feet, and they had a 2¼-inch lift. I had mixed feelings about them. On the one hand, they had given me a more or less even gait for the first time in 10 years. On the other hand, they had marked me as a "handicapped person," complete with cane and special license plates. I went through a pair a year, but it was always the same shoe, black, wide, weighing about four pounds.

It all started 26 years ago in Piedmont, W.Va., a backwoods town of 2,000 people. While playing a game of touch football at a Methodist summer camp, I **incurred** a hairline fracture. Thing is, I didn't know it yet. I was 14 and had finally lost the chubbiness of my youth. I was just learning tennis and beginning to date, and who knew where that might lead?

Not too far. A few weeks later, I was returning to school from lunch when, out of the blue, the ball-and-socket joint of my hip sheared apart. It was instant agony, and from that time on nothing in my life would be quite the same.

I propped myself against the brick wall of the schoolhouse, where the school delinquent found me. He was black as slate, twice my size, mean as the day was long and beat up kids just because he could. But the look on my face told him something was seriously wrong, and—bless him—he stayed by my side for the two hours it took to get me into a taxi.

"It's a torn ligament in your knee," the surgeon said. (One of the signs of what I had—a "slipped epithysis"—is intense knee pain I later learned.) So he scheduled me for a walking cast.

I was wheeled into surgery and placed on the operating table. As the doctor wrapped my leg with wet plaster strips, he asked about my schoolwork.

"Boy," he said, "I understand you want to be a doctor."

I said, "Yessir." Where I came from, you always said "sir" to white people, unless you were trying to make a statement.

Had I taken a lot of science courses?

"Yessir. I enjoy science."

"Are you good at it?"

"Yessir, I believe so."

"Tell me, who was the father of sterilization?"

"Oh, that's easy, Joseph Lister."

Then he asked who discovered penicillin.

orthopedic—intended to correct defects in the skeletal system

incurred—brought down upon oneself

psychosomatic
—physical
symptoms
caused by emo-
tional or mental
issues

pathology—
abnormal condi-
tion

Wimbledon—the
location in
England of an
annual interna-
tional tennis
tournament

calcified—hard-
ened, became
inflexible

atrophied—
wasted away

cordovan—fine-
grained leather

orthotics—shoes
containing sup-
ports for weak
muscles

Alexander Fleming.

And what about DNA?

Watson and Crick.

The interview went on like this, and I thought my answers might get me a pat on the head. Actually, they just confirmed the diagnosis he'd come to.

He stood me on my feet and insisted that I walk. When I tried, the joint ripped apart and I fell on the floor. It hurt like nothing I'd ever known.

The doctor shook his head. "Pauline," he said to my mother, his voice kindly but amused, "there's not a thing wrong with that child. The problem's **psychosomatic.** Your son's an over-achiever."

Back then, the term didn't mean what it usually means today. In Appalachia, in 1964, "overachiever" designated a sort of **pathology:** the overstraining of your natural capacity. A colored kid who thought he could be a doctor—just for instance—was headed for a breakdown.

What made the pain abate was my mother's reaction. I'd never, ever heard her talk back to a white person before. And doctors, well, their words were scripture.

Not this time. Pauline Gates stared at him for a moment. "Get his clothes, pack his bags—we're going to the University Medical Center," which was 60 miles away.

Not great news: the one thing I knew was that they only moved you to the University Medical Center when you were going to die. I had three operations that year. I gave my tennis racket to the delinquent, which he probably used to club little kids with. So I wasn't going to make it to **Wimbledon.** But at least I

wasn't going to die, though sometimes I wanted to. Following the last operation, which fitted me for a metal ball, I was confined to bed, flat on my back, immobilized by a complex system of weights and pulleys. It was six weeks of bondage—and bedpans. I spent my time reading James Baldwin, learning to play chess and quarreling daily with my mother, who had rented a small room—which we could ill afford—in a motel just down the hill from the hospital.

I think we both came to realize that our quarreling was a sort of ritual. We'd argue about everything—what time of day it was—but the arguments kept me from thinking about that traction system.

I limped through the next decade—through Yale and Cambridge . . . as far away from Piedmont as I could get. But I couldn't escape the pain, which increased as the joint calcified and began to fuse over the next 15 years. My leg grew shorter, as the muscle **atrophied** and the ball of the ball-and-socket joint migrated into my pelvis. Aspirin, then Motrin, heating pads and massages, became my traveling companions.

Most frustrating was passing store windows full of fine shoes. I used to dream about walking into one of those stores and buying a pair of shoes. "Give me two pairs, one black, one **cordovan,**" I'd say, "Wrap 'em up." No six-week wait as with the **orthotics** in which I was confined. These would be real shoes. Not bricks.

In the meantime, hip-joint technology progressed dramatically. But no surgeon wanted to operate on me until I was significantly older, or until the pain was so great that surgery was unavoidable. After all, a new hip would last only for 15 years, and I'd already lost too much bone. It wasn't a procedure they were sure they'd be able to repeat.

This year, my 40th, the doctors decided the time had come.

I increased my life insurance and made the plunge.

The nights before my operations are the longest nights of my life—but never long enough. Jerking awake, grabbing for my watch, I experience a delicious sense of relief as I discover that only a minute or two have passed. You never want 6 A.M. to come.

And then the door swings open. "Good morning, Mr. Gates," the nurse says. "It's time."

The last thing I remember, just vaguely, was wondering where **amnesiac** minutes go in one's consciousness, wondering if I experienced the pain and sounds, then forgot them, or if these were somehow blocked out, dividing the self on the operating table from the conscious self in the recovery room. I didn't like that idea very much. I was about to protest when I blinked.

"It's over, Mr. Gates," says a voice. But how could it be over? I had merely blinked. "You talked to us several times," the surgeon had told me, and that was the scariest part of all.

Twenty-four hours later, they get me out of bed and help me into a "walker." As they stand me on my feet, my wife bursts into tears. "Your foot is touching the ground!" I am afraid to look, but it is true: the surgeon has lengthened my leg with that gleaming titanium and chrome-cobalt alloy ball-and-socket-joint.

"You'll need new shoes," the surgeon says. "Get a pair of Dock-Sides; they have a secure grip. You'll need a ¾-inch lift in the heel which can be as discreet as you want."

I can't help thinking about those window displays of shoes, those elegant shoes that suddenly, I will be able to wear. Dock-Sides and sneakers, boots and loafers, sandals and brogues. I feel, at last, a furtive sympathy for **Imelda Marcos,** the queen of soles.

The next day, I walk over to the trash can, and take a long look at the brick. I don't want to seem ungracious or unappreciative. We have walked long miles together. I feel disloyal, as if I am abandoning an old friend. I take a second look.

Maybe I'll have them bronzed. ❖

amnesiac—the memory gap caused by loss of consciousness during surgery

Imelda Marcos—wife of former Philippine president, Ferdinand Marcos, whose huge shoe collection made the headlines

ON THE JOB
PHYSICAL THERAPIST

Physical therapists (PTs) and PT assistants work with accident victims, post-surgical patients, and stroke victims to help them strengthen weak or injured muscles and joints. Methods of therapy range from water aerobics to massage to repetitive movement of a joint. Patience, compassion, and an ability to clearly explain therapy so that patients can understand are vital skills. PTs study anatomy, biology, and psychology as well as specific physical therapy techniques.

UNDERSTANDING

1. Find references in the text that indicate how Gates regards his shoes. With several classmates, discuss the various associations the shoes might have for Gates.

    Just as an object may take on special meaning, so words and visual designs also assume special meanings. From magazines or newspapers, choose colorful advertisements that use either a single word or phrase to suggest meaning. Choose other advertisements that use a visual design such as a company logo to convey a significant message. With your classmates, discuss which advertisements best express an idea or feeling and why.

2. Use events in the story to reach conclusions about the significance of the title "A Giant Step."

    What "giant step" have you taken or would you like to take? Write a personal essay describing this giant step in your life. ***Workshop 3***

3.  Use passages in Gates's essay to explain the West Virginia doctor's personality traits. In groups, decide what kind of neighbor he would be.

    Suppose someone like the doctor, possessing his undesirable traits, joined a group at school that required its members to work well together. With your group, brainstorm and list the principles of teamwork that you would need to teach this person. Share your list with the class.

4. What is your impression of Gates's mother? Identify details in the narrative that give you this impression.

    Rewrite Henry Gates's story from his mother's point of view. Enter only her mind and give only her perspective on people and events. ***Workshops 3 and 7***

CONNECTING

1. When he was 14, Henry Louis Gates, Jr., wanted to be a medical doctor. Later he became a doctor of philosophy instead. Probably as he came to know himself, he recognized that his talents and skills suited him to teach college and write books rather than to diagnose and treat medical problems. What are your vocational interests? What jobs exist that would satisfy these interests?

With a partner, collect information about specific jobs in one of the following general fields: the arts, communication, engineering, health services, computers, transportation, natural resources. Discover the jobs that exist, the education and training they require, and where to apply for these jobs. Prepare an informative display for a career day to share information about jobs in your chosen vocational field.

2.  Gates said he got "as far away from Piedmont [West Virginia] as I could get." Collaborate with several other students to gather information about West Virginia. Analyze the types of work people do there and the standard of living. Consider West Virginia's assets, or good points. Which ones are unique? Write and design a pamphlet to promote West Virginia as a place to which to move a business. *Workshop 14 and 20*

WRAP IT UP

UNIT 5

1. The blind runner in "Running Blind" made discoveries that caused him to challenge himself. Henry Gates, Jr., did not allow constant pain to stop him from moving beyond poverty to pursue an education. Infer from "Running Blind" and "A Giant Step" the kinds of *physical* challenges these two men must have faced. Based on your inferences, draw conclusions about the personal qualities and characteristics of the two men.

2. Examine the characters of Antigone, Running Eagle, and Rosa Parks. In an essay, compare and contrast the ways in which they stood up for themselves and what they believed was right.

3. Consider King Arthur's plan to use Might for Right. How can we put the "bad half" of people—the half that goes around whacking at things—to good use? Devise a plan to put King Arthur's plan to work in the modern-day world. Create a pamphlet, proposal, or multimedia presentation to introduce your "Might for Right" program to the school or community.

UNIT
6
NATURE AND TECHNOLOGY

When you listen to the news today, you will probably notice that both nature and technology receive a lot of attention. Some people think that technology may eventually provide everything we need to live. For instance, experiments are being made to grow plants without sunlight, create building materials from trash, and replace wood and paper with synthetic materials. Others, however, believe that it is a great mistake to trust in technology. They argue that nature alone can support human life. They believe that too much technology will destroy the earth's ability to sustain life. The selections in this unit invite you to weigh the claims of nature and technology.

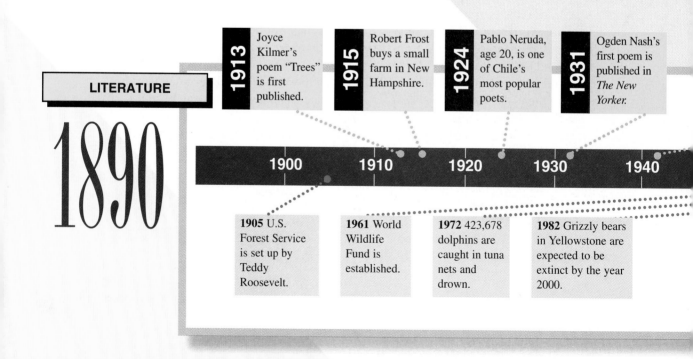

LITERATURE

1890

1913 Joyce Kilmer's poem "Trees" is first published.

1915 Robert Frost buys a small farm in New Hampshire.

1924 Pablo Neruda, age 20, is one of Chile's most popular poets.

1931 Ogden Nash's first poem is published in *The New Yorker.*

1900 1910 1920 1930 1940

1905 U.S. Forest Service is set up by Teddy Roosevelt.

1961 World Wildlife Fund is established.

1972 423,678 dolphins are caught in tuna nets and drown.

1982 Grizzly bears in Yellowstone are expected to be extinct by the year 2000.

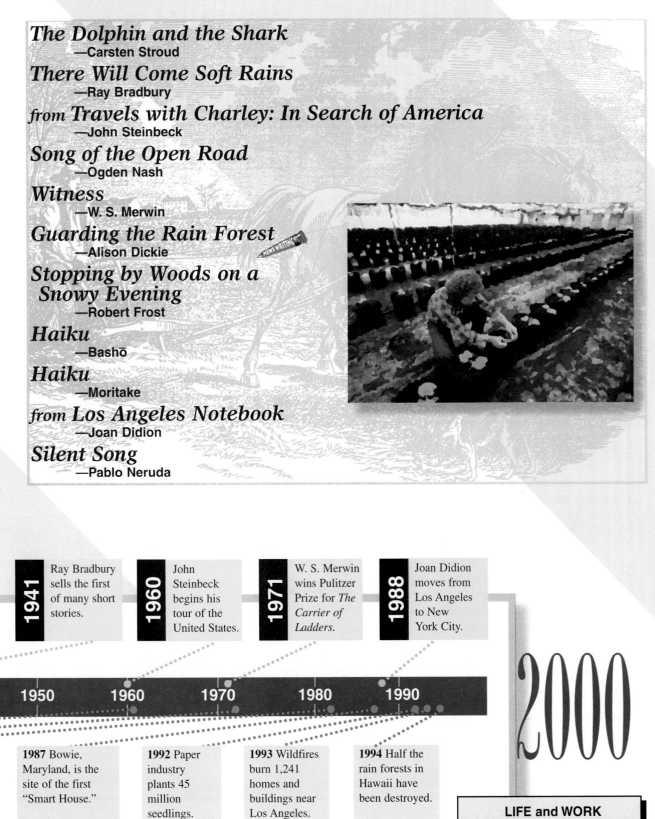

1941 Ray Bradbury sells the first of many short stories.

1960 John Steinbeck begins his tour of the United States.

1971 W. S. Merwin wins Pulitzer Prize for *The Carrier of Ladders.*

1988 Joan Didion moves from Los Angeles to New York City.

1950   1960   1970   1980   1990

2000

1987 Bowie, Maryland, is the site of the first "Smart House."

1992 Paper industry plants 45 million seedlings.

1993 Wildfires burn 1,241 homes and buildings near Los Angeles.

1994 Half the rain forests in Hawaii have been destroyed.

LIFE and WORK

The Dolphin
and the Shark

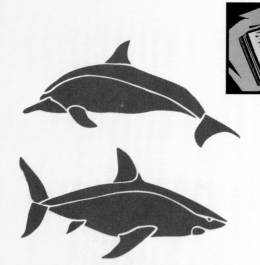

EXPLORING

Humans are a long way from understanding all the mysteries of nature. Unlike machines, living things are unpredictable. Just when we think we fully understand one of nature's creatures, it will surprise us by doing something unexpected. Have you ever been startled by the unexpected behavior of an animal or even a plant?

THEME CONNECTION...
THE WORLD BENEATH THE SEA

Beneath the surface of the ocean, another world exists. Scuba divers are intruders there, attracted by the beauty of unexpected surroundings. In a world that may not always be friendly, where it is sometimes hard to tell friend from foe, human beings are at a disadvantage. Scuba divers may encounter not only inspiring beauty, but also sudden threats.

TIME & PLACE

The scuba divers in the story are diving off the coast of the Yucatan Peninsula, which separates the Gulf of Mexico from the Caribbean Sea. The area is warm year-round, with an average annual temperature above 78 degrees Fahrenheit. For this reason and for the beautiful scenery, it is a popular vacation spot for tourists from the United States, Western Europe, and Japan. Warm waters and an abundance of sea life make the area a superb place to scuba dive.

THE WRITER'S CRAFT
CHRONOLOGICAL ORDER

This article is organized in chronological order, the minute by minute, hour by hour, day by day order in which things happen. Events in this article occur between 3 P.M. and 3:10 P.M. Writer's often relate a story exactly as it happened from beginning to end. Following chronological order creates suspense and is easy to follow.

The Dolphin and the Shark

Carsten Stroud

long the windward shore of the popular resort island of Cozumel, off Mexico's Yucatan Peninsula, my wife Linda and I discovered a small, reef-bound lagoon. It was isolated, reachable only by Jeep on a spine-cracking road through jungle palms, but it was ideal for scuba diving. A rocky spur ran down the beach at the northern edge, curving out into the sea for almost 300 yards. It stopped at a deep-water trench that had been cut away by a rapid tidal flow, leaving a sea gate about 30 feet wide. The circle was completed by a ragged chain of limestone rocks. The area contained by this natural breakwater was close to 400 yards across, and reached a depth of 52 feet. Beyond the reef, the waves boomed and crashed, but within, all was calm.

At least on the surface; underneath, the lagoon was filled with the bizarre flora and fauna of tropical oceans. Most of the larger predators—the barracuda and sharks—were kept out by the sea walls. This tidal pool was teeming with life. In it, we became completely involved in the visual and spiritual delight of tropical diving.

At three o'clock on the afternoon of March 18, we were finning along in 33 feet of water just inside the mouth of the lagoon. A few minutes before, I had been pulled through the sea gate by the tide. Linda, always a cool head in a crisis, had braced herself in a seam and dragged me back in. The whole action hadn't taken thirty seconds, but I had blown a fair amount of air in my fright, and my lungs were still laboring.

People are less alert after such an incident, so neither Linda nor I realized what was happening when a large, dark shape hurtled by us, putting out a pressure wave strong enough to send us spinning. My mind screamed *Shark!* as I fumbled for the shark **billy** I always carry. At that moment a smaller form rocketed through the sea gate.

Instinctively, Linda and I lined up back to back, scanning the waters for whatever it was that had buzzed us. Forty yards away, swimming in a tight, agitated circle, were a bottle-nosed dolphin and her pup. We could hear their high-pitched, chattering squeals through the water and, when the pup turned, we saw a cut that was trailing a dark mist just back of the blowhole.

I wondered why the pair had strayed so far from their school, and then a slow chill gathered around the back of my neck. Linda and I moved closer to each other, and I pulled her to the bottom of the lagoon. Somewhere nearby, and closing fast, there must be a shark.

In the **taut** seconds that followed, local marine life slowed into a profound silence. Just beyond the sea gate, something was moving up the incline of the

About the Author

Award-winning Canadian journalist Carsten Stroud has traveled to the United States, Mexico, Central America, and other places around the world in pursuit of a story. His first book, *Sniper's Moon,* won an award for best first novel from Crime Writers of Canada. Among his numerous books are *Lizardskin; Close Pursuit;* and *Iron Bravo: Hearts, Minds, and Sergeants in the U.S. Army.*

billy—similar to a policeman's billy club, a stick with a handle; unlike a billy club, the shark billy has a somewhat sharpened blade rather than a blunt club

taut—tense

sea floor—a dark flicker of **sinuous** motion. My breath stopped, and a vein began to pound in my right temple. Suddenly, a 13-foot-long tiger shark with a mass of perhaps 550 pounds cruised through the gate, head moving from side to side as it sensed the waters. A school of pilot fish clustered around its flanks and we could make out the markings, dirty brown on top, with faint shadowy stripes, a notched **dorsal** fin, and a gray-white belly. As it passed by, no more than 20 feet away, one black eye tracked us. Its jaws were open slightly, its gills were distended, and its tail fin was stroking; its nostrils stirred with the blood scent of the wounded dolphin pup.

If the shark ran true to form, concentrating on the bleeding prey, we might be able to bottom-crawl to the shallows and—with luck—get out of the water safely.

I hooked into Linda's weight belt (she would guide us while I watched the rear), and we began moving slowly along the bottom. We covered a hundred

yards without seeing either the shark or the dolphins . . . . Where was it? What was it doing?

Something moved to our right. I snapped my head around and saw a thick, black shadow rippling over the sandy bottom. Flipping over on my back, I got my shark billy up barely in time to plant the spikes in the shark's gills. It was on top of us, massive jaws pushed open, jagged rows of triangular teeth inches from my face. With a hideous snaking twist it drove us down into a small trench.

I heard a muffled snap as its jaws closed on the water in front of my faceplate. They sprang open, and it snapped again and again at my chest, shredding my gear, held off by the flexing shaft of the shark billy, its sheer brute force driving it into the rocks at the base of the trench. Linda twisted underneath me, and sank her blade into the shark's throat. Blood began to darken the water. I heard a splitting crack, and the handle of the shark billy gave way. The tiger turned above me, jaws opening, and then something struck it heavily in the side, knocking it away from us.

Blood and sand swirled around us as we lay in the trench. Linda, her eyes wild behind her faceplate, put her hand out and ran it tentatively over my chest, unable to believe that I hadn't been bitten. My wet suit was in tatters, my flotation vest had been chewed away, but I was all right.

The tiger was within 30 feet, circling without rhythm, shudders rippling down its flanks as it jerked its head and bit at the water. Whatever had delivered that ferocious blow, knocking it away from the trench, had saved our lives—for the moment.

Then it turned to come in again—one obscene killing machine, jaws gaping between cold eyes. It got to within 15 feet of us when, with blurring speed, the female dolphin shot in from the right. She struck it with terrible force near its **pectoral** fin. A huge black bubble burst out of the shark's mouth, and it swerved to strike at its assailant. It was certainly hurting, but how badly it was impossible to guess.

FOCUS ON...
BIOLOGY

Coral reefs are made up chiefly of the dead skeletons of coral animals. The main reef-building corals thrive only in water that is at least 70 degrees Fahrenheit. Find out where the world's coral reefs are. What is a coral animal? What is the name for a single coral animal? How do coral animals live? Eat? Die? How do they make coral reefs? Find the answers to these questions and develop a model or illustration of the life cycle of one of the many types of coral.

The shark was now less than 2 yards away in the murk, rolling on its side to pursue the dolphin. We seized the moment to try to get into clear water again. While we were kicking out of the blood and **wrack,** expecting the tiger's bull-like snout to explode out of the mist in front of us, I ran out of air. I pulled the reserve rod and gave Linda the throat-cutting sign to let her know that I was now on emergency air. It might last three minutes.

Suddenly, the dolphin pup skimmed over us, taking the chance to run for the open sea. It flew past with eyes wide and beak shut tight, and was gone. With the pup safe, the mother might run for it. That would leave us roughly 25 yards from the beach, with the wounded tiger about 15 yards away. As we knelt on the sandy lagoon floor, it turned and headed for us again, passing overhead, looking like some lighter-than-air craft and trailing a steady stream of blood from the gills.

Out of the corner of my eye I saw the dolphin, swimming some distance to our right, moving roughly parallel and making a clicking sound with its blow-hole. The shark was at the edge of the shallows, between us and land. It stopped its erratic turns, and began to swim quickly along the shoreline. Then it gave a violent twist of its muscular torso and hurled itself away from the beach, right at us. I kicked up and away from Linda, holding out the splintered shaft of the shark billy. I think I had some idea of wedging it into its jaws. When it was within 2 yards of me, I struck out—and hit nothing. In less than a second the tiger had covered the distance separating us, dipped underneath me, and cut straight out for the gap in the sea wall. Within seconds it was out of sight. The dolphin circled us and flashed out to sea in the wake of the tiger shark.

For some seconds, Linda and I hung suspended in the water, minds blank.

wrack— the remains of something destroyed; evidently the shark's wounds have caused bits of tissue to be emitted from its gills, along with the blood

Then we blew out hard and kicked for the surface. When our heads broke into the air, we were 10 yards from shore. Wordlessly, we swam to the shallows, staggered up the beach, and collapsed on a rock facing the ocean. I was vaguely aware that the vein pounding in my temple was slowing its beat. Linda gave a short laugh, and showed me her watch. It was 3:10 P.M. The entire episode had lasted less than ten minutes.

That evening, we went down to the beach in front of our hotel room and tried to make some sense out of what had happened. Why the shark decided to attack us instead of its chosen prey, we can't imagine. I wouldn't care to speculate on why a shark does anything; I doubt they know themselves. I think that the mother dolphin took advantage of the shark's interest in us to try to eliminate the danger to herself and her pup. Linda sees it differently. She thinks the dolphin fought for us—that in the midst of all the cruelties of nature, there is room for kindness as well. ❖

ON THE JOB
OCEAN TECHNICIAN

Ocean technicians help scientists, or oceanographers, explore the oceans and study marine life. They also study the effects of pollution and how changes in the oceans and their currents affect weather. Some technicians help gather data for maps of the oceans and ocean floors. To perform their work, technicians use a variety of scientific and navigational equipment. High school courses in science, math, and biology are helpful preparation, and many two-year colleges offer programs in marine science.

UNDERSTANDING

1.  Find the line in the article that explains why the shark was pursuing the mother dolphin and her pup.

   Dolphins and sharks differ in several ways. Working with a group and using only the article, create a chart comparing the differences you can identify. Then, look up dolphins and sharks in an encyclopedia or on-line reference source and add more characteristics to your chart. **Workshop 22**

2. The divers use quick thinking and decision making skills to save their lives. What do they decide, and what actions do they take?

   Think of a situation in which quick thinking helped you avoid an unpleasant experience. Write a narrative describing the occurrence. What problem-solving strategies did you use? **Workshop 9**

3. What occurred that might have weakened and discouraged the shark?

   Research shark attacks on humans. When and why do they occur? How can they be prevented? Write a report, including a chart or graph, on your findings. **Workshops 21 and 22**

4. Both the author and Linda have theories as to why the mother dolphin attacked the shark. With whom do you agree? Give reasons for your opinion.

   The idea that animals have emotions and can demonstrate kindness, caring, and consideration is debatable. What do you believe? Write an opinion paper presenting your personal opinion on this issue, citing examples from your reading and from your own experience to support your thesis. **Workshop 13**

CONNECTING

1.  As the article shows, scuba diving has some dangers. Assume you must write advertising copy that will entice people to take up scuba diving. Working with a group, do some research on the sport and the frequency of injuries, and then word your copy and add artwork so as to relieve people's fears.

2. Animal rights advocates have protested the killing of dolphins by tuna fishers who catch both dolphins and tuna in their nets. This has resulted in the boycotting of major tuna canning companies. Research this problem. Write a feature story explaining how the dolphins are caught and why animal rights defenders are angry. Try to present both sides of the issue in your article. **Workshop 17**

A LAST WORD

The author and his wife took a risk scuba diving in the lagoon. Do you think they had fully considered the possible dangers or consequences of their adventure before diving? How might we be better prepared for possible dangers when taking risks?

There Will Come Soft Rains

EXPLORING

A volcano erupts and pours lava over forest and field. Within a short period of time, green sprouts rise out of the dead, gray remains. The same occurs after drought, fire, and flood. Life comes back. The artificial, however, does not return. Human-made objects cannot rejuvenate. If human life were suddenly blotted out, what would happen? Would all life on Earth end? How important are humans to the Earth? Are other forms of life dependent on us?

THEME CONNECTION...
TECHNOLOGY REPLACING HUMANS

Technology has replaced humans in many ways. Industry has installed robotics systems to do the work humans either do not want to do or cannot safely do. Scientists keep finding new ways to accomplish work without the presence of humans. From the bank to the gas station, we see machines making human work easier or taking it over completely.

TIME & PLACE

This story takes place in the year 2026. Bradbury, writing in 1950, has attempted to imagine what the world will be like by that time. When he wrote this story, nuclear warfare was an imminent—a very real and close—threat. Today, it no longer looms as dangerously as it did then because of events in the world that have lessened conflict between major political powers.

THE WRITER'S CRAFT
SCIENCE FICTION

Science fiction writers refer to actual scientific facts as they make up events that might happen in a future time or in some non-existent place. Though science fiction presents times and circumstances that do not exist, references to science persuade readers that these strange events might one day come into being. Though its setting is not realistic, science fiction often expresses profound truths about human nature.

There Will Come Soft Rains

Ray Bradbury

n the living room the voice-clock sang, *Tick-tock, seven o'clock, time to get up, time to get up, seven o'clock!* as if it were afraid that nobody would. The morning house lay empty. The clock ticked on, repeating and repeating its sounds into the emptiness. *Seven-nine, breakfast time, seven-nine!*

In the kitchen the breakfast stove gave a hissing sigh and ejected from its warm interior eight pieces of perfectly browned toast, eight eggs sunnyside up, sixteen slices of bacon, two coffees, and two cool glasses of milk.

"Today is August 4, 2026," said a second voice from the kitchen ceiling, "in the city of Allendale, California." It repeated the date three times for memory's sake, "Today is Mr. Featherstone's birthday. Today is the anniversary of Tilita's marriage. Insurance is payable, as are the water, gas, and light bills."

Somewhere in the walls, relays clicked, memory tapes glided under electric eyes.

Eight-one, tick-tock, eight-one o'clock, off to school, off to work, run, run, eight-one! But no doors slammed, no carpets took the soft tread of rubber heels. It was raining outside. The weather box on the front door sang quietly: "Rain, rain, go away; rubbers, raincoats for today . . ." And the rain tapped on the empty house, echoing.

Outside, the garage chimed and lifted its door to reveal the waiting car. After a long wait the door swung down again.

At eight-thirty the eggs were shriveled and the toast was like stone. An aluminum wedge scraped them into the sink, where hot water whirled them down a metal throat which digested and flushed them away to the distant sea. The dirty dishes were dropped into a hot washer and emerged twinkling dry.

Nine-fifteen, sang the clock, *time to clean.*

Out of **warrens** in the wall, tiny robot mice darted. The rooms were acrawl with the small cleaning animals, all rubber and metal. They thudded against chairs, whirling their mustached runners, kneading the rug nap, sucking gently at hidden dust. Then, like mysterious invaders, they popped into their burrows. Their pink electric eyes faded. The house was clean.

Ten o'clock. The sun came out from behind the rain. The house stood alone in a city of rubble and ashes. This was the one house left standing. At night the ruined city gave off a radioactive glow which could be seen for miles.

Ten-fifteen. The garden sprinklers whirled up in golden founts, filling the soft morning air with scatterings of brightness. The water pelted window-panes running down the charred west side where the house had been burned

warrens—passageways or cubbies

titanic—colossal; huge

Baal—an ancient god of the Semitic peoples considered by the Hebrews in the Bible to be a false god. The word has come to mean "evil" in general.

evenly free of its white paint. The entire west face of the house was black, save for five places. Here the silhouette in paint of a man mowing a lawn. Here, as in a photograph, a woman bent to pick flowers. Still farther over, their images burned on wood in one **titanic** instant, a small boy, hands flung into the air; higher up, the image of a thrown ball, and opposite him a girl, hands raised to catch a ball which never came down.

The five spots of paint—the man, the woman, the children, the ball—remained. The rest was a thin charcoaled layer.

The gentle sprinkler rain filled the garden with falling light.

Until this day, how well the house had kept its peace. How carefully it had inquired, "Who goes there? What's the password?" and, getting no answer from lonely foxes and whining cats, it had shut up its windows and drawn shades in an old-maidenly preoccupation with self-protection which bordered on a mechanical paranoia.

It quivered at each sound, the house did. If a sparrow brushed a window, the shade snapped up. The bird, startled, flew off! No, not even a bird must touch the house!

The house was an altar with ten thousand attendants, big, small, servicing, attending, in choirs. But the gods had gone away, and the ritual of the religion continued senselessly, uselessly.

Twelve noon.

A dog whined, shivering, on the front porch.

● ● ● ● ● ● ● ●
"Until this day, how well the house had kept its peace."
● ● ● ● ● ● ● ●

The front door recognized the dog voice and opened. The dog, once huge and fleshy, but now gone to bone and covered with sores, moved in and through the house, tracking mud. Behind it whirred angry mice, angry at having to pick up mud, angry at inconvenience.

For not a leaf fragment blew under the door but what the wall panels flipped open and the copper scrap rats flashed swiftly out. The offending dust, hair, or paper, seized in miniature steel jaws, was raced back to the burrows. There, down tubes which fed into the cellar, it was dropped into the sighing vent of an incinerator, which sat like evil **Baal** in a dark corner.

The dog ran upstairs, hysterically yelping to each door, at last realizing, as the house realized, that only silence was here.

It sniffed the air and scratched the kitchen door. Behind the door, the stove was making pancakes which filled the house with a rich baked odor and the scent of maple syrup.

The dog frothed at the mouth, lying at the door, sniffing, its eyes turned to fire. It ran wildly in circles, biting at its tail, spun in a frenzy, and died. It lay in the parlor for an hour.

Two o'clock, sang a voice.

Delicately sensing decay at last, the regiments of mice hummed out as softly as blown gray leaves in an electrical wind.

Two-fifteen.

The dog was gone.

In the cellar, the incinerator glowed suddenly and a whirl of sparks leaped up the chimney.

Two thirty-five.

Bridge tables sprouted from patio walls. Playing cards fluttered onto pads in a shower of pips. Martinis **manifested** on an oaken bench with egg-salad sandwiches. Music played.

But the tables were silent and the cards untouched.

At four o'clock the tables folded like great butterflies back through the paneled walls.

Four-thirty.

The nursery walls glowed.

Animals took shape: yellow giraffes, blue lions, pink antelopes, lilac panthers cavorting in crystal substance. The walls were glass. They looked out upon color and fantasy. Hidden films clocked through well-oiled sprockets, and the walls lived. The nursery floor was woven to resemble a crisp, cereal meadow. Over this ran aluminum roaches and iron crickets, and in the hot still air butterflies of delicate red tissue wavered among the sharp aroma of animal spoors! There was the sound like a great matted yellow hive of bees within a dark bellows, the lazy bumble of a purring lion. And there was the platter of **okapi** feet and the murmur of a fresh jungle rain, like other hoofs, falling upon the summer-starched grass. Now the walls dissolved into distances of parched weed, mile on mile, and warm endless sky. The animals drew away into thorn brakes and water holes.

It was the children's hour.

Five o'clock. The bath filled with clear hot water.

Six, seven, eight o'clock. The dinner dishes manipulated like magic tricks, and in the study of a *click.* In the metal stand opposite the hearth where a fire now blazed up warmly, a cigar popped out, half an inch of soft gray ash on it, smoking, waiting.

Nine o'clock. The beds warmed their hidden circuits, for nights were cool here.

Nine-five. A voice spoke from the study ceiling:

"Mrs. McClellan, which poem would you like this evening?"

The house was silent.

The voice said at last, "Since you express no preference, I shall select a poem at random." Quiet music rose to back the voice. "Sara Teasdale. As I recall, your favorite . . . ."

manifested—appeared

okapi—an African animal closely related to the giraffe but with a shorter neck

There Will Come Soft Rains

Picassos and Matisses—paintings by Pablo Picasso and Henry Matisse, early 20th-century European painters

*"There will come soft rains and the
    smell of the ground,
And swallows circling with their
    shimmering sound;*

*And frogs in the pools singing at
    night,
And wild plum-trees in tremulous white;*

*Robins will wear their feathery fire
Whistling their whims on a low
    fence-wire;*

*And not one will know of the war,
    not one
will care at last when it is done.*

*Not one would mind, either bird
    nor tree
If mankind perished utterly;*

*And Spring herself, when she woke
    at dawn,
Would scarcely know that we
    were gone."*

The fire burned on the stone hearth and the cigar fell away into a mound of quiet ash on its tray. The empty chairs faced each other between the silent walls, and the music played.

At ten o'clock the house began to die. The wind blew. A falling tree bough crashed through the kitchen window. Cleaning solvent, bottled, shattered over the stove. The room was ablaze in an instant!

"Fire!" screamed a voice. The house lights flashed, water pumps shot water from the ceilings. But the solvent spread on the linoleum, licking, eating under the kitchen door, while the voices took it up in chorus: "Fire, fire, fire!"

The house tried to save itself. Doors sprang tightly shut, but the windows were broken by the heat and the wind blew and sucked upon the fire.

The house gave ground as the fire in ten billion angry sparks moved with flaming ease from room to room and then up the stairs. While scurrying water rats squeaked from the walls, pistoled their water, and ran for more. And the wall sprays let down showers of mechanical rain.

But too late. Somewhere, sighing, a pump shrugged to a stop. The quenching rain ceased. The reserve water supply which had filled baths and washed dishes for many quiet days was gone.

The fire crackled up the stairs. It fed upon **Picassos and Matisses** in the upper halls, like delicacies, baking off the oily flesh, tenderly crisping the canvases into black shavings.

FOCUS ON...
SCIENCE

In "There Will Come Soft Rains," the house and all domestic activities are attended to by computerized robots. The invention of the computer was the most important 20th-century development for automation. Linking computer technology to machines led to the creation of modern industrial robots. Research how industrial robots are used in the world today. What kinds of tasks do they perform? In which industries are they most widely used? What are the positive and negative aspects of industrial robots in the workplace?

Now the fire lay in beds, stood in windows, changed the colors of drapes!

And then, reinforcements.

From attic trapdoors, blind robot faces peered down with faucet mouths gushing green chemical.

The fire backed off, as even an elephant must at the sight of a dead snake. Now there were twenty snakes whipping over the floor, killing the fire with a clear cold venom of green froth.

But the fire was clever. It had sent flame outside the house, up through the attic to the pumps there. An explosion! The attic brain which directed the pumps was shattered into bronze shrapnel on the beams.

The fire rushed back into every closet and felt of the clothes hung there.

The house shuddered, oak bone on bone, its bared skeleton cringing from the heat, its wire, its nerves revealed as if a surgeon had torn the skin off to let the red veins and capillaries quiver in the scalded air. Help, help! Fire! Run, run! Heat snapped mirrors like the first brittle winter ice. And the voices wailed Fire, fire, run, run, like a tragic nursery rhyme, a dozen voices, high, low, like children dying in a forest, alone, alone. And the voices fading as the wires popped their sheathings like hot chestnuts. One, two, three, four, five voices died.

In the nursery the jungle burned. Blue lions roared, purple giraffes bounded off. The panthers ran in circles, changing color, and ten million animals, running before the fire, vanished off toward a distant steaming river . . . .

Ten more voices died. In the last instant under the fire avalanche, other choruses, **oblivious,** could be heard announcing the time, playing music, cutting the lawn by remote-control mower, or setting an umbrella frantically out and in the slamming and opening front door, a thousand things happening, like a clock shop when each clock strikes the hour insanely before or after the other, a scene of maniac confusion, yet unity; singing, screaming, a few last cleaning mice darting bravely out to carry the horrid ashes away! And one voice, with

oblivious—
unaware or
unmindful of

sublime disregard for the situation, read poetry aloud in the fiery study, until all the film spools burned, until all the wires withered and the circuits cracked.

The fire burst the house and let it slam flat down, puffing out skirts of spark and smoke.

In the kitchen, an instant before the rain of fire and timber, the stove could be seen making breakfasts at a psychopathic rate, ten dozen eggs, six loaves of toast, twenty dozen bacon strips, which, eaten by fire, started the stove working again, hysterically hissing!

The crash. The attic smashing into kitchen and parlor. The parlor into cellar, cellar into subcellar. Deep freeze, armchair, film tapes, circuits, beds, and all like skeletons thrown in a cluttered mound deep under.

Smoke and silence. A great quantity of smoke.

Dawn showed faintly in the east. Among the ruins, one wall stood alone. Within the wall, a last voice said, over and over again and again, even as the sun rose to shine upon the heaped rubble and steam:

"Today is August 5, 2026, today is August 5, 2026, today is . . ." ❖

UNDERSTANDING

1. What has happened to the people who live in this house? What evidence leads you to this conclusion?

   With the fall of Communism in the Soviet Union, the threat of nuclear war has lessened. Rather than fear a nuclear attack, what do families of today fear? Discuss this in a small group, and then write a short essay describing the fears of today's families. *Workshop 8*

2. How does this house differ from your own? Do you like or dislike these differences?

   Look at the classified ads for houses in the local newspaper or in a realtor's flyer. Write an ad to sell the home described in this story. Based on today's prices, what would be the asking price of the house?

3. The story takes place in the year 2026. The story gives the reader an idea of what family life might be like by that time, according to the limited view of one 1950s writer. Write your own idea of daily life for a family living in 2026. Begin with their waking in the morning and continue as you imagine how their day would unfold. Your effort might be science fiction (imaginary but possible) or fantasy (imaginary but impossible). *Workshop 7*

CONNECTING

1. Investigate the effects of the atomic bombs dropped on Japan near the end of World War II. Compare what you discover in your research with details in this story, such as the silhouettes on the side of the building. Is the author accurate in his descriptions of the bomb's effects? In a report, compare and contrast the author's descriptions with those of the real bombs. Summarize your conclusions regarding the accuracy of the author. Keep in mind, however, that the author is describing hydrogen bomb results, reputed to be much worse than the aftermath of an atomic bomb explosion. *Workshop 15*

2. Working with a group, write to several peace organizations such as the Carnegie Endowment for International Peace, Amnesty International, or the United Nations to inquire about their efforts to promote peace and stop the production of nuclear weaponry. Follow business letter format. Ask your group to critique your letters. Revise and send it. *Workshop 18*

A LAST WORD

Bradbury describes a world in which the advances of science destroy human life rather than benefit it. In what ways are human beings helped by technological progress? How might this progress harm rather than benefit humans?

from *Travels with Charley: In Search of America*
Charley in Yellowstone

EXPLORING

All animals, including humans, display instinctual behavior. It can serve to motivate, invigorate, and protect. Think of the many ways instinct guides action—birds build nests and migrate, bears hibernate, mothers protect their young, turtles lay their eggs in the sand, and salmon battle upstream to spawn. Does instinct ever outwear its usefulness? Can you think of instinctual behaviors that no longer have a purpose?

THEME CONNECTION...
NATURAL INSTINCT

Animals and plants naturally know how to live their lives. Responding to their environments on cue, they are born, live, reproduce, and die. However, technology in the modern world has enhanced human knowledge well beyond instinct.

TIME & PLACE

In 1960, John Steinbeck, already an award-winning writer, set out on a tour of the United States. He traveled in a homemade camper that he called "Rocinante"—the same name as the old horse that the character Don Quixote rode as he imagined himself to be a brave knight. Steinbeck's only traveling companion was his standard poodle, Charley. The writer's goal was to discover the true America. He later shared his impressions of his travels and adventures in *Travels with Charley: In Search of America*.

THE WRITER'S CRAFT
TRAVEL WRITING

Many writers make their living writing travel articles and books. Often these pieces are no more than guides to the best restaurants and hotels. But some writers, like Steinbeck, make the places they visit come alive with vivid descriptions of the people and places they observe.

from *Travels with Charley: In Search of America*
Charley in Yellowstone

John Steinbeck

 I must confess to a laxness in the matter of National Parks. I haven't visited many of them. Perhaps this is because they enclose the unique, the spectacular, the astounding—the greatest waterfall, the deepest canyon, the highest cliff, the most stupendous works of man or nature. And I would rather see a good **Brady** photograph than Mount Rushmore. For it is my opinion that we enclose and celebrate the freaks of our nation and of our civilization. Yellowstone National Park is no more representative of America than is Disneyland.

This being my natural attitude, I don't know what made me turn sharply south and cross a state line to take a look at Yellowstone. Perhaps it was a fear of my neighbors. I could hear them say, "You mean you were that near to Yellowstone and didn't go? You must be crazy." Again it might have been the American tendency in travel. One goes, not so much to see but to tell afterward. Whatever my purpose in going to Yellowstone, I'm glad I went because I discovered something about Charley I might never have known.

A pleasant-looking National Park man checked me in, and then he said, "How about that dog? They aren't permitted in except on leash."

"Why?" I asked.

"Because of the bears."

"Sir," I said, "this is a unique dog. He does not live by tooth or fang. He respects the right of cats to be cats although he doesn't admire them. He turns his steps rather than disturb an earnest caterpillar. His greatest fear is that someone will point out a rabbit and suggest that he chase it. This is a dog of peace and tranquillity. I suggest that the greatest danger to your bears will be **pique** at being ignored by Charley."

The young man laughed. "I wasn't so much worried about the bears," he said. "But our bears have developed an intolerance for dogs. One of them might demonstrate his prejudice with a clip on the chin, and then—no dog."

"I'll lock him in the back, sir. I promise you Charley will cause no ripple in the bear world, and as an old bear-looker, neither will I."

> ● ● ● ● ● ● ●
> ## "This is a dog of peace and tranquillity."
> ● ● ● ● ● ● ●

"I just have to warn you," he said. "I have no doubt your dog has the best of intentions. On the other hand, our bears have the worst. Don't leave food about. Not only do they steal but they are

About the Author

John Steinbeck (1902–1968) won the 1962 Nobel Prize for Literature as well as the Pulitzer Prize in 1940 for his novel *The Grapes of Wrath* and the Drama Critics Award for the dramatization of his novel *Of Mice and Men* in 1938. One of the most revered and well-known American authors, Steinbeck wrote from experience, most of it in a variety of jobs among the people and places of central California.

Brady— Mathew Brady (1823?–1896), famous photographer of the Civil War

pique—irritation

house—
meaning the
camper

critical of anyone who tries to reform them. In a word, don't believe their sweet faces, or you might get clobbered. And don't let the dog wander. Bears don't argue."

We went on our way into the wonderland of nature gone nuts, and you will have to believe what happened. The only way I can prove it would be to get a bear.

Less than a mile from the entrance I saw a bear beside the road, and it ambled out as though to flag me down. Instantly a change came over Charley. He shrieked with rage. His lips flared, showing wicked teeth that have some trouble with a dog biscuit. He screeched insults at the bear, which hearing, the bear reared up and seemed to me to overtop Rocinante. Frantically I rolled the windows shut and, swinging quickly to the left, grazed the animal, then scuttled on while Charley raved and ranted beside me, describing in detail what he would do to that bear if he could get at him. I was never so astonished in my life. To the best of my knowledge Charley had never seen a bear and in his whole history had showed great tolerance for every living thing. Besides all this, Charley is a coward, so deep-seated a coward that he has developed a technique for concealing it. And yet he showed every evidence of wanting to get out and murder a bear that outweighed him a thousand to one. I don't understand it.

A little farther along two bears showed up, and the effect was doubled. Charley became a maniac. He leaped all over me, he cursed and growled, snarled and screamed. I didn't know he had the ability to snarl. Where did he learn it? Bears were in good supply, and the road became a nightmare. For the first time in his life Charley resisted reason, even resisted a cuff on the ear. He became a primitive killer lusting for the blood of his enemy, and up to this moment he had had no enemies. In a bearless stretch, I opened the cab, took Charley by the collar, and locked him in the **house.** But that did no good. When we passed other bears, he leaped on the table and scratched at the windows trying to get out at them. I could

hear canned goods crashing as he struggled in his mania. Bears simply brought out the Hyde in my Jekyll-headed dog. What could have caused it? Was it a pre-breed memory of a time when the wolf was in him? I know him well. Once in a while he tries a bluff, but it is a **palpable** lie. I swear that this was no lie. I am certain that if he were released he would have charged every bear we passed and found victory or death.

It was too nerve-wracking, a shocking spectacle, like seeing an old, calm friend go insane. No amount of natural wonders, of rigid cliffs and belching waters, of smoking springs could even engage my attention while that pandemonium went on. After about the fifth encounter I gave up, turned Rocinante about, and retraced my way. If I had stopped the night and bears had gathered to my cooking, I dare not think what would have happened.

At the gate the park guard checked me out. "You didn't stay long. Where's the dog?"

"Locked up back there. And I owe you an apology. That dog has the heart and soul of a bear-killer, and I didn't know it. Heretofore he has been a little tender-hearted toward an underdone steak."

"Yeah!" he said. "That happens sometimes. That's why I warned you. A bear dog would know his chances, but I've seen a Pomeranian go up like a puff of smoke. You know, a well-favored bear can bat a dog like a tennis ball."

I moved fast, back the way I had come, and I was reluctant to camp for fear there might be some unofficial nongovernment bears about. That night I spent in a pretty auto court near Livingston. I had my dinner in a restaurant, and when I had settled in with a drink and a comfortable chair and my bathed bare feet on a carpet with red roses, I inspected Charley. He was dazed. His eyes held a faraway look and he was totally exhausted, emotionally no doubt. Mostly he reminded me of a man coming out of a long, hard drunk—worn out, depleted, collapsed. He couldn't eat his dinner, he refused the evening walk, and once we were in he collapsed on the floor and went to sleep. In the night I heard him whining and yapping, and when I turned on the light his feet were making running gestures and his body jerked and his eyes were wide open, but it was only a night bear. I awakened him and gave him some water. This time he went to sleep and didn't stir all night. In the morning he was still tired. I wonder why we think the thoughts and emotions of animals are simple. ❖

palpable—
noticeable,
easily detected

ON THE JOB

PARK RANGER

Park rangers are employed by the National Park Service to protect and preserve our national parks. They prevent forest fires, help maintain an ecological balance, plan campsites, and regulate the number of park visitors. Skilled campers, park rangers also protect and educate park visitors. A love of nature and camping is the first requirement for becoming a park ranger. High school courses in biology, botany, geology, and ecology are helpful, as is experience in conservation work.

UNDERSTANDING

1. Steinbeck pokes fun at "the American tendency in travel. One goes, not so much to see but to tell afterward." What does this tell us about Steinbeck's attitude toward Americans?

    When you think of the most exciting place you have ever visited, does the pleasure come from reliving the experience or from telling others about it? Discuss this question in a small group. Then create a pamphlet to invite other tourists to visit this place. *Workshop 20*

2. Steinbeck writes about Charley as though he is a human, an old friend. Cite passages in which Steinbeck describes his friend Charley in human terms.

    The companionship of pets has been shown to enhance the mental and physical health of human beings. Find articles about how pets help reduce stress and loneliness in humans. Summarize two such articles and compare your findings with those of your classmates. *Workshop 16*

3. Steinbeck's sense of humor is evident in this story. Point out some examples of his humor.

    When we refer to animals as people, imagining their thoughts and putting them into human language, the result is humorous. Consider the success of such cartoon characters as Snoopy and Garfield, for example. With a partner, create a script presenting a conversation between a person and an animal. Making the animal talk and think like a human can be an opportunity for humor. Share your script with other teams, reciting it with good expression.

A LAST WORD

Why do humans tend to be surprised when animals exhibit complex or surprising behavior? What kinds of assumptions do humans tend to make about animals and their nature?

CONNECTING

1. Visit an animal shelter, talk to the workers, and pick up pamphlets and handouts. In a small group, brainstorm ideas for a project that will help the shelter, perhaps a spaying/neutering campaign or a campaign for pet adoption. Select a project, draw up a proposal, and carry out your plans. *Workshop 13*

2. Animals can be a problem in neighborhoods if they are allowed to run free. In a small group, brainstorm ideas for a neighborhood pet policy. Consider situations such as pets' leaving excrement in people's yards and parking areas, tipping over garbage cans, digging up gardens, and fighting in the middle of the night. Draft a set of rules for pets in the form of a neighborhood pet policy.

The Value of Trees

- *Song of the Open Road*
- *Witness*

EXPLORING

The value of a tree cannot be calculated. Living trees give us shade from the sun and edible produce. They remove carbon dioxide from the air and release valuable oxygen, necessary for humans to survive. Too often trees are taken for granted. How do trees affect your daily life? What programs do you know about that work for the preservation of trees? Think of ways to make sure trees continue to exist and are safeguarded.

THEME CONNECTION...
THE NATURE AND TECHNOLOGY OF TREES

Trees are the Earth's largest living organisms and one of our most valuable resources. Technology has introduced new ways to harvest, process, and use trees. Science has discovered the extent to which life on earth depends on living forests and living trees in jungles. It is important to balance the need for living forests with the need for the products technology makes from trees.

TIME & PLACE

Ogden Nash, a popular poet during the 1930s and 1940s especially, wrote amusing poems to make us laugh. Much of his wit satirizes American society. W. S. Merwin, a popular poet today, writes about nature, focusing attention on animals, plants, and various places. His poetry, too, comments on society. Merwin notes our tendency to neglect or destroy nature's wonders.

THE WRITER'S CRAFT

METER

Meter is the arrangement of stressed and unstressed syllables that produces a poem's rhythm. Even when we speak to one another, our words have meter—they consist of stressed and unstressed syllables. By carefully arranging words in syllable patterns according to certain rules, poets create meter. Sometimes the meter of a poem is varied, as in free verse, and sometimes it is fixed, as in limericks and nursery rhymes.

Song of the Open Road
Ogden Nash

I think that I shall never see
A billboard lovely as a tree.
Indeed, unless the billboards fall,
I'll never see a tree at all. ❖

FOCUS ON...
LITERATURE

In their poems, the poets Nash and Merwin celebrate the presence of nature and lament its abuse or disappearance. Working in pairs, find other poems by a variety of poets who also express a deep concern over nature's destruction. Then give a poetry reading of the four poems that you and your partner feel best express the conflict between nature and technology.

◆ ◆ ◆ ◆ ◆ ◆ ◆ ◆ ◆ ◆ ◆ ◆ ◆ ◆ ◆ ◆

Witness

W. S. Merwin

I want to tell what the forests
were like

I will have to speak
in a forgotten language ❖

About the Author

Poet, translator, and prose writer, W. S. Merwin (b. 1927) lives and works on Maui in the Hawaiian Islands. He was born in New York City and grew up in Union City, New Jersey, and Scranton, Pennsylvania. For several years, Merwin made his living as a translator of French, Spanish, Latin, and Portuguese. Among his many books of poetry are *A Mask for Janus, The Lice,* and *Travels.* For his poetry, Merwin has received a number of awards, including the Pulitzer Prize.

ACCENT ON...
RECYCLING TECHNOLOGY

Recycling paper has become a common practice for many businesses, schools, and households. How long has the *technology* for recycling paper existed? How do modern-day paper mills recycle paper? Find out what the process is and create a diagram with captioned illustrations that show how a used piece of paper becomes a new piece of paper. **Workshop 12**

UNDERSTANDING

1. Ogden Nash uses parody and humor to convey his meaning. How does his poem reflect society's attitudes? Base your answer on the text.

    The rhyme scheme and syllable count in each line in Nash's poem is simple and fixed. Write a poem modeled on this one. *Workshop 2*

2. Locate a copy of the poem, "Trees" by Joyce Kilmer. Why do you think Ogden Nash decided to make fun of this poem by writing a parody of it?

    Working with a group, brainstorm on the qualities you think make a good poem. Consider such things as vivid detail, fresh words, and clarity. *Workshop 2*

3. Merwin's poem uses direct statements to imply serious meaning. What are the statements he makes? What do they imply about our treatment of trees and of the environment in general?

    Working with a group, list examples from your community or state that support the concern for nature Merwin expresses in his poem. Prepare a speech explaining environmental problems and suggesting action to solve these problems. *Workshop 23*

A LAST WORD

The poets in this lesson lament the disappearance of trees. What happens if we come to recognize the value of nature too late?

CONNECTING

1. Working in a small group, create a display celebrating trees. Each member might select one variety of tree and gather information on it such as average size, location, products, appearance, and other relevant facts. When the research is done, organize the information and create a display complete with photos or drawings and written descriptions and headings. Create your final product on computer, if possible.

2. Working in a group, plan and carry out a tree planting day for your class or school. Find out where to purchase young trees, plan where and when to plant them, and find out how to secure the proper equipment. You may want to enlist the aid of a nursery in this project. At least two weeks before the event, write a press release to publicize your project and send it to local newspapers and television and radio stations. *Workshop 17*

Guarding the Rain Forest

EXPLORING
● ● ● ● ● ● ● ● ● ● ● ● ● ● ● ● ● ●

It seems hard to believe that the preservation or devastation of forests in Central and South America affects the entire world, but it does. These tropical rain forests are fragile and critically important to the well-being of this planet. They absorb carbon dioxide, too much of which in the atmosphere causes the greenhouse effect. They also produce and sustain millions of invaluable plants and animals. Corporations have cut down millions of acres of rain forest for profit, although many environmental groups are now working to stop this practice. How could the fate of forests in such faraway lands affect our lives? What can we do?

THEME CONNECTION...
KEY TO THE HEALTH OF THE PLANET

Rain forests, some of the most valuable natural areas in the world, are in danger. Essential to the health of the planet, their preservation is a major goal of environmental groups.

TIME & PLACE

Humans have significantly decreased the rain-forested areas on this planet. Between 19 and 50 million acres are being destroyed each year. "Guarding the Rainforest" gives readers a glimpse of one modern-day traveler's impressions as he visits a rain forest for the first time. His destination is Costa Rica, which lies in Central America between Nicaragua and Panama.

THE WRITER'S CRAFT

SCIENCE WRITERS

Science writers put scientific information into language and ideas the general public can understand. They write primarily for newspapers and popular magazines. This article is an example of writing that makes science interesting and understandable.

Guarding the Rain Forest

Alison Dickie

alking through a tropical rain forest is like finding yourself in a huge, tropical plant store, except that everything is oversized. You're surrounded by philodendrons, all kinds of palms and vines, and exotic flowers like hibiscus and bird of paradise," says Canadian nature lover David White.

"But I saw at least one plant you'd never find in North America. It's called a strangler fig, and it wraps itself round and round a tree until it kills it, leaving a hollow center where the old tree once lived."

After watching a documentary film about Costa Rica, in Central America, David White was determined to visit a rain forest. A year later he found himself hiking through the Monteverde Cloud Forest, a Costa Rican national park. More than half of the world's tropical rain forests are in Central and South America. Among them, Monteverde is unique. It is a cloud forest—so high in the mountains that it sits above the clouds. David found his first experience in a tropical cloud forest very mysterious, and even a little frightening.

"It felt as though we were being watched all the time," David says. "And there were lots of surprises in store. Once we heard an incredible growl which sounded exactly like a roaring

tiger. After feeling pretty shaky for a while, we learned it was a monkey."

In Monteverde, the rain falls constantly. There are small waterfalls and pools everywhere. The high leafy canopy is home to monkeys, fruit-eating bats, lizards, and insects of all shapes and sizes. Brilliant red- and green-feathered birds live there too, like parrots and macaws and quetzals. There are snakes, and slow-moving sloths; and big cats—ocelots and jaguars—who catch their prey and eat it up in the tall trees.

David didn't run into any dangerous animals, but he and his hiking group did find the trail of a tapir. This is a rare creature that lives only in rain forests. It looks a bit like a pig with a long curved snout, but actually it's a distant relative of both the horse and the rhinoceros. David followed his guide through a hollowed-out tunnel of vegetation up a mud-soaked slope trying to find one. But the tapir must have heard them coming, so it was nowhere to be seen.

A Fragile Environment

Tropical forests are home to the richest variety of plant and animal life anywhere on Earth. Although they cover only six percent of the Earth's surface, tropical forests contain two-thirds of all the world's species of plants and animals. For example, three square miles of rain forest in Peru, about the size of a very large city park, has been found to contain 525 species of birds.

Monteverde Cloud Forest is a beautiful place, so lush it looks as though it could sustain life forever. But, like all rain forests, it is really a very fragile environment. The trees grow very tall, with most of their leaves at the top of the trunk to compete with other trees for light. The soil, made up of decomposing leaves, is very thin, so that tree roots tend to hug the surface of the forest floor. This means that if the trees are cut down and the roots die, heavy rains will wash the unprotected soil away and leave a muddy desert.

Then even the rain can stop falling. This happens because the tree roots act like sponges, taking large amounts of water up into the leaves. The leaves then "breathe" this water back into the air, and the water given off by millions of trees begins to fall again as rain. When the trees are cut down, this cycle is broken, and the entire climate of the area changes. Dry deserts can be the result.

Destruction of Rain Forests

There are rain forests like Monteverde around the world, but they are all in danger. Why would anyone cut down these beautiful rain forests? Logging is one main reason. Tropical woods like mahogany are highly prized for their strength and lovely grains, and the lumber brings in lots of money when it's exported to countries like Japan, the U.S., France, and Britain.

Another reason why people cut down rain forests is to make pasture for beef cattle. The beef is then sold, most of it to fast-food restaurants in North America. In the Amazon area of Brazil, 2.64 million acres of rain forest have been burned for ranching purposes.

What happens when rain forests are destroyed? Scientists believe that the destruction of rain forest is a major cause of the greenhouse effect—also known as global warming. Forests normally absorb most of the air's carbon dioxide, the gas that is the main cause of the greenhouse effect. As the forests are cut down and burned, most of the carbon dioxide remains in the atmosphere, further raising global temperatures.

Another problem is the effect on wildlife. When rain forests are cut down, much of the surrounding vegetation dies. This in turn means the decline of the animal population. Many animals and birds are now on the endangered species list.

Plant species are disappearing quickly, too, and with them many potential medicines. Researchers are still experimenting with the tropical periwinkle, and it is now being used successfully in the treatment of childhood leukemia. But many plants that might have medical uses are dying before medical scientists even get a chance to examine them.

Since 1945, 40 percent of the world's rain forests have disappeared. If the present rate of destruction continues, a full half will be gone by the year 2000. Fifty acres of rain forest, the size of a small farm, disappear every hour, along with one species of plant or animal life.

How We Can Help

Environmental groups in many countries are making a major effort to stop the destruction of the world's tropical rain forests. To do this, organizations like World Wildlife Fund need to raise funds from individuals.

Someone had the great idea that they could raise money by offering certificates to help protect the rain forest. So now, if you donate $25, you can obtain a certificate for an acre of tropical forest and become a "Guardian of the Rain Forest." This doesn't mean that you actually own that acre, but you are paying for its protection.

The money goes toward protection of the rain forest. Wardens guard against poachers of rare animals, and nature stations are set up to monitor the wildlife. As well, model farms demonstrate farming techniques that don't cause erosion.

In just one year, Canadians like David White helped to protect about 20,000 acres of forest in the Monteverde Nature Reserve. This allowed World Wildlife Fund to raise two million dollars for the Costa Rican government in a "debt for nature" swap. The money helps poor countries like Costa Rica to pay off some of the big debts they owe to the U.S., Canada, or other countries. Now WWF has raised so much money through the "Guardian of the Rain Forest" program that over 200 projects can be funded.

The benefits of rain forest preservation will be felt even here in North America. For one thing, the greenhouse effect should start to slow down. But there are other examples. Birds which need to spend their winters in tropical forests, like the tiny hummingbird, will still be able to migrate to the U.S. and Canada for the summer. And the spectacular monarch butterfly, which travels 2,500 miles to spend the winter in Central America, will be saved.

But there is still a lot of work to be done. The battle to protect the world's rain forests is far from over. For more information on the rain forests, or to find out how you can become a guardian of the rain forest, contact World Wildlife Fund in Washington, D.C. ❖

ON THE JOB
• • • • • • • • • • • • • • • • • •
ENVIRONMENTALIST
• • • • • • • • • • • • • • • • • •

Environmentalists work to protect the air, land, and water from pollution or destruction. In their work, they strive to balance the needs of the natural environment with those of industries and workers. Environmentalists usually specialize in one aspect of the environment—such as acid rain, wildlife preservation, rain-forest preservation, land conservation, or toxic waste removal and disposal. High school courses in the natural sciences are a good beginning.

SPOTLIGHT ON...
READING CHARTS AND GRAPHS

An effective way to communicate information is through graphic aids or visuals, such as charts and graphs. They can convey complex information in an organized and easy-to-understand format. When reading a chart or graph, follow these guidelines:

1. Identify the form. Is it a chart, graph, flow chart, or timeline? Each form has a different format and a different use.
2. Read the titles and subtitles. In a chart or graph, the title will tell you what information is presented. Subtitles or labels will tell you what the categories of information are.
3. Figure out the symbols. If symbols are used in a chart or graph, their meanings are explained in a key or footnote.
4. Analyze the information. After you recognize the form and understand the information presented, you can analyze the information by making predictions, comparing and contrasting, understanding a process, or seeing parts of a whole.

Annual Rate of Tropical Deforestation, 1981–1990 (in millions of acres per year)

Central and South America are home to more than half of the world's tropical rain forests. The other rain forests are found in Africa and Asia. The pie chart at the right shows that although all rain forests are in danger, those in Latin America face the greatest threat. According to the pie chart, how many total acres of rain forest were deforested each year?

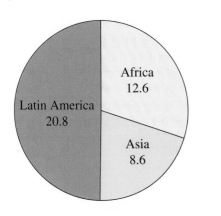

Original Rain Forest Remaining by 2010 in Latin America (projected percentages)

Environmentalists have raised many concerns about the future of our planet's rain forests. This bar graph shows projected data for the decrease in rain forest acreage in Latin America.

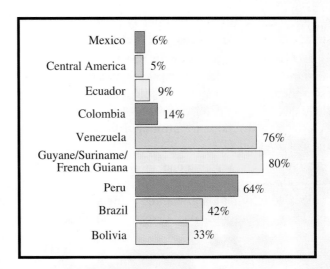

UNDERSTANDING

1. According to the text, what happens to the immediate area when trees in the rain forest are cut down?

   Native Americans think of the Earth as Mother and whatever hurts the mother hurts all the children. Write an essay in which you extend this metaphor to the rain-forest dilemma. Using this Native American view, state the case for preserving the rain forests. ***Workshop 3***

2. Why do companies cut down rain forests? What are their reasons?

   Write a letter to the chief executive officer of your favorite fast-food chain asking the company to explain if its policy supports cutting down rain forests for cattle-grazing purposes. ***Workshops 13 and 18***

3. According to the article, how does the world benefit from the amazing plants and trees found in the rain forest?

   Research the plants that grow in the rain forest to discover those that have come to be used as valuable medicines. What other uses have scientists found for these plants in addition to their value as objects of wonder and study? Write a documented report on the information you discover. ***Workshop 21***

A LAST WORD

The article "Guarding the Rain Forest" makes clear the need to preserve the rain forest. What are the many benefits of rain forest preservation? What can you do to help?

CONNECTING

1. Working in small groups, produce a four-page newsletter whose goals include such things as:

   • informing the public of the threat to rain forests

   • explaining the importance of rain forests

   • identifying organizations working to save rain forests

   • suggesting how readers can help prevent rain-forest destruction

   As a group, you will need to write three or more articles to achieve your goals in the newsletter. Research the articles thoroughly, brainstorm the best ways to present them, and plan and design the publication. You may also want to include advertisements for rain forest–friendly products. Use a computer to develop the final version for printing. Distribute your newsletter in your community. ***Workshop 17***

2. As a class, secure a map of the world and mark with a thumbtack or other device the location of each rain forest. For each forest, provide a text block of information giving the name and brief historical or geographical notes. Display your work on a class or school bulletin board or in a local business.

In Awe of Nature

- *Stopping by Woods on a Snowy Evening*
- *Two Haiku*

EXPLORING

Certain moments in nature profoundly affect us. Has looking at a waterfall, mountain, or open field, at a tree, butterfly, or bird ever caused you to think about things in an unexpected way? Sometimes people retreat to a pasture or hillside to think. Sometimes the sight of an animal gives them great pleasure. What experiences have you had in nature?

THEME CONNECTION... RESPONDING TO NATURE

In Frost's poem and the two Haiku, nature is vividly described, and nature's influence is also indicated. Robert Frost's narrator, for example, stops in the darkness during a snowstorm to look at the woods. Bashō also shows us a beautiful spectacle happening in darkness—lightning slashing through the sky—and its effect, in this case, on the heron. Moritake's Haiku shows a narrator recognizing that he has mistaken a butterfly for a flower.

TIME & PLACE

This lesson includes three poems written in different cultures and at different times. Moritake wrote in Japan during the late fifteenth and early sixteenth centuries. Bashō wrote during the seventeenth century, and the American Robert Frost lived and worked during the twentieth century. Each of these poets captures a scene in nature and communicates an emotion or thought prompted by this scene. Each of them helps the reader see nature and appreciate its influence on our daily lives.

THE WRITER'S CRAFT

HAIKU

The haiku is a special form of poetry developed by the Japanese. Consisting of only three lines, the haiku follows a strict pattern of syllables: five syllables in the first line, seven in the second, and five in the final line. As is the case with both haiku in this selection, such poems try to capture a precise moment and, in so doing, to imply meaning.

Stopping by Woods on a Snowy Evening

Robert Frost

Whose woods these are I think I know.
His house is in the village though;
He will not see me stopping here
To watch his woods fill up with snow.

My little horse must think it queer
To stop without a farmhouse near
Between the woods and frozen lake
The darkest evening of the year.

He gives his harness bells a shake
To ask if there is some mistake.
The only other sound's the sweep
Of easy wind and downy flake.

The woods are lovely, dark and deep,
But I have promises to keep,
And miles to go before I sleep,
And miles to go before I sleep. ❖

About the Author

Robert Frost (1874–1963) was born in San Francisco. His family moved to the East Coast when he was very young, and he grew up there. Frost briefly attended Harvard University, but his independent spirit and love of poetry caused him to abandon formal studies. For a time he lived and worked on poetry in England, and eventually he settled in New England, where he spent a great deal of his time. Frost's poems about New England life and personalities made him one of the most popular poets of this century. He also had the great honor of reading one of his poems at the inauguration of President John F. Kennedy.

Unit 6: Nature and Technology

Two Haiku

Bashō

The lightning flashes!
And slashing through the darkness,
  A **night-heron's** screech. ❖

Moritake

The falling flower
I saw drift back to the branch
Was a butterfly. ❖

About the Authors

Matsuo Bashō (1644–1694) is considered the master of haiku. Bashō wandered throughout Japan, and his travels are recorded in the 1688 book *Oi no kobumi*. The English translation, *The Records of a Travel-Worn Satchel*, was published in 1966.

Moritake's works still arouse strong feeling. A high-ranking Shinto priest, Moritake (1452–1540) found inspiration for his best work in religion and scripture.

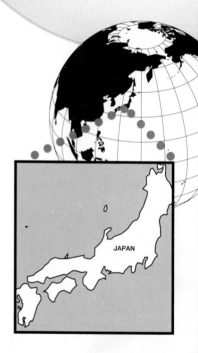

night-heron—a large wading bird with a long neck and long legs that is active at night

UNDERSTANDING

1.  Note the strong use of verbs and nouns in the two haiku. List these words and indicate what each denotes and connotes. With a group, develop a 5 line advertisement of some event or product. Use verbs and nouns heavily. Avoid adverbs and adjectives. After your advertisement, list the five words your group considers to be most effective. After each word, indicate both its denotation and its connotation. *Grammar Workshop: Parts of Speech Overview*

2.  Locate in Robert Frost's poem words that create the poem's dominant mood. Present your findings to your group, With your group, discuss whether you think the narrator's delay is normal and why he eventually decides to leave. Support your views with evidence from the text.

3. A haiku follows the pattern of 17 syllables arranged in three lines of 5,7,5 syllables. A haiku focuses on one moment and in so doing implies significance. What moment is captured by the two haiku in this lesson? What significance is expressed? Paraphrase one of the two haiku in a carefully constructed paragraph with a clear topic sentence. *Workshop 16*

A LAST WORD

The poems by Frost, Bashō, and Moritake each capture a moment of nature's beauty. Do you stop to observe and wonder at the beauty and mystery of the natural world? Why or why not?

CONNECTING

1.  Write two haiku. Discuss these with your group, and, as a result of this discussion, choose the one you like best. Contribute this haiku to a booklet consisting of the best haiku by all your classmates. Use a computer to produce the booklet. For the cover, generate an electronic piece of art or use other media. Assign each of the following roles to one or more students to complete the publishing process: designer, word processor, editor, proofreader, cover designer, cover artist.

2. Research President Kennedy's inauguration to discover which poem Frost chose to read. Compare it with the one Maya Angelou read at President Clinton's inauguration in 1992. Some political analysts claim that Clinton and Kennedy share similar ideals and goals. Do the two poems carry any similarities? Write a report on your conclusions. *Workshop 6*

from *Los Angeles Notebook*

EXPLORING

It seems some people never tire of talking about the weather. They complain, they groan, or they delight in it. They plan activities around the weather. How else does the weather affect our behavior? Can the weather cause people to do things they wouldn't ordinarily consider? Discuss how the changing weather affects your life.

THEME CONNECTION...
WEATHER'S EFFECTS

Though we believe we are in control of our lives, evidence shows that weather conditions can have pronounced effects on human behavior. Weather can affect outlook, temperament, and decisions. In this essay, Joan Didion describes the Santa Ana wind's effects on the residents of Los Angeles.

TIME & PLACE

Los Angeles, located on the coast of Southern California, is the center of a heavily populated urban area of about 11.5 million people. It is the second largest city in the United States and has one of the most diverse populations.

THE WRITER'S CRAFT
SENTENCE VARIETY

Joan Didion is one of America's most talented essay writers. One of her strengths is her ability to construct strong, clear sentences that vary in type and length. Notice that she inserts very short sentences—"The baby frets. The maid sulks."—for variety and to change the pace of the sentence flow. She also varies the openings of her sentences.

from *Los Angeles Notebook*

Joan Didion

About the Author

Joan Didion, born in 1934 in Sacramento, California, writes novels and essays that focus on contemporary American life, its complexities and problems. Most famous for her essay collections, she has written several on current topics. This excerpt is from *Slouching Toward Bethlehem.* Other collections include *The White Album* (1979) and *After Henry* (1992).

There is something uneasy in the Los Angeles air this afternoon, some unnatural stillness, some tension. What it means is that tonight a Santa Ana will begin to blow, a hot wind from the northeast whining down through the Cajon and San Gorgonio Passes, blowing up sandstorms out along Route 66, drying the hills and the nerves to the **flash point.** For a few days now we will see smoke back in the canyons, and hear sirens in the night. I have neither heard nor read that a Santa Ana is due, but I know it, and almost everyone I have seen today knows it too. We know it because we feel it. The baby frets. The maid sulks. I rekindle a waning argument with the telephone company, then cut my losses and lie down, given over to whatever it is in the air. To live with the Santa Ana is to accept, consciously or unconsciously, a deeply **mechanistic** view of human behavior.

I recall being told when I first moved to Los Angeles and was living on an isolated beach, that the Indians would throw themselves into the sea when the bad wind blew. I could see why. The Pacific turned ominously glossy during a Santa Ana period, and one woke in the night troubled not only by the peacocks screaming in the olive trees but by the eerie absence of surf. The heat was **surreal.** The sky had a yellow cast, the kind of light sometimes called "earthquake weather." My only neighbor would not come out of her house for days, and there were no lights at night, and her husband roamed the place with a machete. One day he would tell me that he had heard a trespasser, the next a rattlesnake.

"On nights like that," **Raymond Chandler** once wrote about the Santa Ana, "every booze party ends in a fight. Meek little wives feel the edge of the carving knife and study their husbands' necks. Anything can happen." That was the kind of wind it was. I did not know then that there was any basis for the effect it had on all of us, but it turns out to be another of those cases in which science bears out folk wisdom. The Santa Ana, which is named for one of the canyons it rushes through, is a *foehn* wind, like the *foehn* of Austria and Switzerland and the *hamsin* of Israel. There are a number of persistent **malevolent** winds, perhaps the best known of which are the *mistral* of France and the Mediterranean *sirocco,* but a *foehn* wind has distinct characteristics: it occurs on the leeward slope of a mountain range and, although the air begins as a cold mass, it is warmed as it comes down the mountain and appears finally as a hot dry wind. Whenever and wherever a *foehn* blows, doctors hear

flash point—temperature at which a volatile substance ignites with a flash

about headaches and nausea and allergies, about "nervousness," about "depression." In Los Angeles some teachers do not attempt to conduct formal classes during a Santa Ana, because the children become unmanageable. In Switzerland, the suicide rate goes up during the *foehn,* and in the courts of some Swiss **cantons** the wind is considered a **mitigating** circumstance for crime. Surgeons are said to watch the wind, because blood does not clot normally during a *foehn.* A few years ago an Israeli physicist discovered that not only during such winds, but for the ten or twelve hours which precede them, the air carries an unusually high ratio of positive to negative ions. No one seems to know exactly why that should be; some talk about friction and others suggest solar disturbances. In any case the positive ions are there, and what an excess of positive ions does, in the simplest terms,

is make people unhappy. One cannot get much more mechanistic than that.

Easterners commonly complain that there is no "weather" at all in Southern California, that the days and the seasons slip by relentlessly, numbingly bland. That is quite misleading. In fact the climate is characterized by infrequent but violent extremes: two periods of torrential subtropical rains which continue for weeks and wash out the hills and send subdivisions sliding toward the sea; about twenty scattered days a year of the Santa Ana which, with its **incendiary** dryness, invariably means fire. At the first prediction of a Santa Ana, the Forest Service flies men and equipment from Northern California into the southern forests, and the Los Angeles Fire Department cancels its ordinary nonfire-fighting routines. The Santa Ana caused Malibu to burn the way it did in 1956, and Bel Air in 1961, and Santa Barbara in 1964. In the winter of 1966–67 eleven men were killed fighting a Santa Ana fire that spread through the San Gabriel Mountains.

Just to watch the front-page news out of Los Angeles during a Santa Ana is to get very close to what it is about the place. The longest single Santa Ana period in recent years was in 1957, and it lasted not the usual three or four days but fourteen days, from November 21 until December 4. On the first day 25,000 acres of the San Gabriel Mountains were burning, with gusts reaching 100 miles an hour. In town, the wind reached Force 12, or hurricane force, on the Beaufort Scale; oil

mechanistic—an attempt to explain human behavior in terms of physical and chemical influences

surreal—unnatural; dreamlike

Raymond Chandler—(1888–1959) American author of Los Angeles–based detective novels

malevolent—bearing or doing evil

cantons—states of the Swiss Republic

mitigating—causing to become less harsh

incendiary—tending to inflame; relating to burning

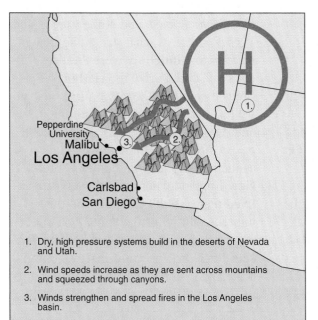

1. Dry, high pressure systems build in the deserts of Nevada and Utah.

2. Wind speeds increase as they are sent across mountains and squeezed through canyons.

3. Winds strengthen and spread fires in the Los Angeles basin.

FOCUS ON... SCIENCE

Joan Didion describes the Santa Ana wind as a "persistent malevolent wind." She names other winds of this nature: the *foehn* of Austria and Switzerland, the *hamsin* of Israel, the *mistral* of France, and the *sirocco* of the Mediterranean. Research these powerful winds. What causes them? How are they different? What effects do they have on people and the environment? Present your findings to the class, perhaps with the aid of a meteorological map or chart.

◆ ◆ ◆ ◆ ◆ ◆ ◆ ◆ ◆ ◆ ◆ ◆ ◆

Nathaniel West— (1903–1940) writer of a novel based in Los Angeles; at the end, an artist imagines a raging fire consuming the city

indelibly—in a way not able to be erased

apocalypse—the end of the world

derricks were toppled and people ordered off the downtown streets to avoid injury from flying objects. On November 22 the fire in the San Gabriels was out of control. On November 24 six people were killed in automobile accidents, and by the end of the week the Los Angeles *Times* was keeping a box score of traffic deaths. On November 26 a prominent Pasadena attorney, depressed about money, shot and killed his wife, their two sons, and himself. On November 27 a South Gate divorcée, twenty-two, was murdered and thrown from a moving car. On November 30 the San Gabriel fire was still out of control, and the wind in town was blowing 80 miles an hour. On the first day of December four people died violently, and on the third the wind began to break.

It is hard for people who have not lived in Los Angeles to realize how radically the Santa Ana figures in the local imagination. The city burning is Los Angeles's deepest image of itself: **Nathanael West** perceived that, in *The Day of the Locust,* and at the time of the 1965 Watts riots what struck the imagination most **indelibly** were the fires. For days one could drive the Harbor Freeway and see the city on fire, just as we had always known it would be in the end. Los Angeles weather is the weather of catastrophe, of **apocalypse,** and, just as the reliably long and bitter winters of New England determine the way life is lived there, so the violence and the unpredictability of the Santa Ana affect the entire quality of life in Los Angeles, accentuate its impermanence, its unreliability. The wind shows us how close to the edge we are. ❖

UNDERSTANDING

1. Didion calls the Santa Ana a *foehn* wind. What are its chief characteristics?

   Study the atlas or encyclopedia description of the weather in your region, writing down its major features. Next, interview three people who have lived in the area for at least 20 years. How does each of them describe the weather? How do their opinions compare to the official description? Write a summary of your work. ***Workshops 16 and 24***

2. Aside from causing bizarre human behavior, the Santa Ana sets off forest fires. What specifics about forest fires does Didion provide?

   A controversy exists concerning whether to allow forest fires to burn themselves out or to put out all forest fires. Through research or interview, find an authoritative answer to this question. Write a documented report on your findings. ***Workshop 21***

3. Comment on Didion's last few lines in the essay. Considering the reputation of Los Angeles, explain her references to the city's "impermanence," "unreliability," and "how close to the edge we are."

   Los Angeles, along with its surrounding area, is a major tourist attraction. Prepare a simple brochure highlighting several of the most attractive tourist sites in the area. ***Workshop 20***

A LAST WORD

How would you describe the weather in the place where you live? What effect does it have on human behavior?

CONNECTING

1. Invite a local weather forecaster to speak to the class. Prepare a list of questions ahead of time that address the work of a weather forecaster, the general weather of the region, and his or her opinion regarding the effects of weather conditions on humans. ***Workshops 18 and 24***

2. Conduct an experiment. Keep a two-week observational record, making note of the following information each day: (1) your own mood and behavior, (2) the moods and behaviors of the people around you, and (3) the weather conditions. At the end of your experiment, see if you can draw any conclusions regarding the effects of weather on mood and behavior. ***Workshop 6***

Silent Song

EXPLORING
● ●

The death of a living thing, particularly if it is beautiful and awe inspiring, is a terrible thing to watch. Powerful whales wash up on our beaches, injured racehorses are put to sleep, an enormous elk is brought down by a hunter's high-powered rifle. We note sadly that the death of many animals is the direct or indirect result of human action. Have you ever witnessed the death of an animal? Whatever the cause, how did you feel?

THEME CONNECTION...
DEATH: NATURAL AND UNNATURAL

Death is as much a part of life as birth, a natural act that eventually every living thing must undergo. Even when one animal kills another for food, it is natural. Senseless injury or death, however, is unnatural.

TIME & PLACE

The country of Chile where this story takes place is a land of diversity in climate and terrain. The north is dry and hot and, in fact, has places where rainfall has never been recorded. In the south the land is extremely rainy. In the middle is a strip that serves as a buffer between the two extremes. The land also varies, with flat valleys below the majestic Andes Mountains. There is little beach area because the mountains rise right up out of the Pacific Ocean.

THE WRITER'S CRAFT
VISUAL IMAGERY

Images in literature can appeal to all five of our senses. Neruda uses visual imagery to paint beautiful pictures in the mind's eye that we can see as vividly as we can see the real world. One example: "a snow boat with a neck packed, as it were, into a tight stocking of black silk. Orange-beaked, red-eyed."

● ●

Silent Song

Pablo Neruda

I'll tell you a story about birds. On Lake Budi some years ago, they were hunting down the swans without mercy. The procedure was to approach them **stealthily** in little boats and then rapidly—very rapidly—row into their midst. Swans like albatrosses have difficulty in flying; they must skim the surface of the water at a run. In the first phase of their flight they raise their big wings with great effort. It is then that they can be seized: a few blows with a **bludgeon** finish them off.

Someone made me a present of a swan: more dead than alive. It was of a marvelous species I have never seen anywhere else in the world: a black-throated swan—a snow boat with a neck packed, as it were, into a tight stocking of black silk. Orange-beaked, red-eyed.

This happened near the sea, in Puerto Saavedra, Imperial del Sur.

They brought it to me half-dead. I bathed its wounds and pressed little pellets of bread and fish into its throat; but nothing stayed down. Nevertheless the wounds slowly healed, and the swan came to regard me as a friend. At the same time, it was apparent to me that the bird was wasting away with nostalgia. So, cradling the heavy burden in my arms through the streets, I carried it down to the river. It paddled a few strokes, very close to me. I had hoped it might learn how to fish for itself, and pointed to some pebbles far below, where they flashed in the sand like the silvery fish of the South. The swan looked at them remotely, sad-eyed.

For the next twenty days or more, day after day, I carried the bird to the river and toiled back with it to my house. It was almost as large as I was. One afternoon it seemed more **abstracted** than usual, swimming very close and ignoring the lure of the insects with which I tried vainly to tempt it to fish again. It became very quiet; so I lifted it into my arms to carry it home again. It was breast high, when I suddenly felt a great ribbon unfurl, like a black arm encircling my face: it was the big coil of the neck, dropping down.

It was then that I learned **swans do not sing** at their death, if they die of grief. ❖

About the Author

Pablo Neruda is known all over the world for beautiful poetry and his dedication to the causes of peace and social reform. He was born July 12, 1904, in Parral, Chile. He became interested in writing poetry and later became active in politics, first as an anarchist, then a socialist. He spent time in Spain and served in the early part of the Spanish Civil War. He served as Chile's ambassador to France in 1971–1972 and died in 1973.

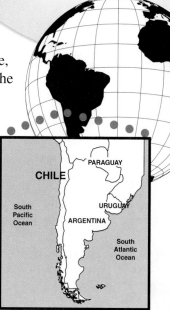

CHILE
PARAGUAY
URUGUAY
ARGENTINA
South Pacific Ocean
South Atlantic Ocean

steathily—slowly and secretly

bludgeon—a short stick used as a weapon

abstracted—preoccupied, absent-minded

swans do not sing—a reference to "swan song," the song of great sweetness said to be sung by a dying swan

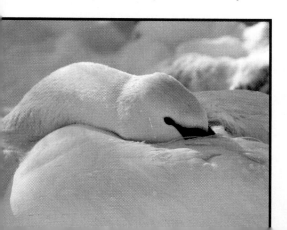

UNDERSTANDING

1. How did the swan come to be with the narrator? What was its condition?
   Have you had the experience of nursing a wounded animal back to health? After consulting a veterinarian on sick animal care, write a general set of guidelines for dealing with sick and injured animals or birds. ***Workshop 12***

2. Why do you think the swan died in spite of the narrator's efforts?
   Sometimes, regardless of our best efforts, we lose what we wish to keep or fail to reach a goal. In a personal essay, write about a disappointment you suffered after you had expended great effort to avoid it.

3. This essay reads almost like a poem. What elements seem to you to be poetic?
   Select an animal or bird you find to be particularly beautiful or interesting. Describe it, modeling your style on the strong visual imagery Neruda used in his essay. You may end up with either a poem or an essay. ***Workshops 2 and 3***

4. The swan did not sing at death because it died of grief. For what did it grieve?
   The two most heinous crimes, says M. Scott Peck, writer and sociologist, are to kill the spirit and to kill the physical self of an individual. In this case, the swan's spirit was killed. Write an expository essay in which you explain what it means to "kill the spirit" of a person or, in this case, an animal. Give examples and compare the act to the killing of a physical body. ***Workshop 8***

A LAST WORD

What causes one human being to kill animals and another to care for them? Is there some fundamental difference between individuals in their regard for nature and its creatures?

ON THE JOB
ANIMAL CARETAKER

Animal caretakers tend to the needs of animals in zoos, aquariums, or animal shelters. In addition to feeding and cleaning the animals, they make sure that the animals are in good health. Animal caretakers may also provide information to the public about the animals and protect the animals from possible harm. Animal caretakers must enjoy working with animals. High school courses in biology and experience working at a veterinarian's office are good preparation.

CONNECTING

1. Did you know it was against the law to beat an animal before it was illegal to beat one's child or spouse? Research the history of the American Society for the Prevention of Cruelty to Animals (ASPCA). Make a brief oral presentation to the class about the history and goals of the ASPCA. *Workshop 23*

2. Many animals are starved and neglected, used for experiments, and allowed to overpopulate to their own detriment. In small groups, brainstorm ways to promote responsible treatment of animals. Plan and implement a project to promote community awareness of animal cruelty.

3. Oil spills on the world's beaches from damaged oil tankers have killed and injured millions of coastal birds and animals. Write a letter to a major oil company calling for double hulls for tankers and other measures to eliminate oil spills. Research the problem before wording your letter to gather statistics to strengthen your argument. *Workshop 18*

WRAP IT UP

UNIT 6

1. Several of the selections present a situation in which the natural world is in conflict with the world of humans. The speaker in Merwin's poem "Witness" says that he will need to speak in a forgotten language to tell about the forests. Neruda, in "Silent Song," concludes that a swan does not sing when it dies of grief. Why does this conflict between nature and humans exist? What responsibilities do humans have toward protecting nature? How does the preservation of nature benefit humankind? Answer these questions in a persuasive essay.

2. Several of the poems and haiku have speakers who stop what they are doing to observe and note the beauty of nature. The speaker in "Stopping by Woods on a Snowy Evening" confuses his horse by stopping during his travels to admire the snowfall. Bashō describes a nightheron's screech, and Moritake mistakes a falling flower for a butterfly. Create an advertising campaign and a slogan that promote human observation of and appreciation for nature.

UNIT ⟨7⟩

COURAGE AND DETERMINATION

Some people risk their lives climbing mountains. Are they being courageous—or foolish? If a person rushes into a burning building to rescue strangers trapped inside, is he or she being courageous—or foolish?

In deciding whether to call acts courageous, we need to consider the reasons behind them and their probable outcomes. The characters in these selections all exhibit courage and determination. For some, showing courage brings success, admiration, or peace of mind. For others, a show of courage leads to death. Still others lack courage altogether. These selections invite you to examine courage—what it is, why it matters, and how it affects us.

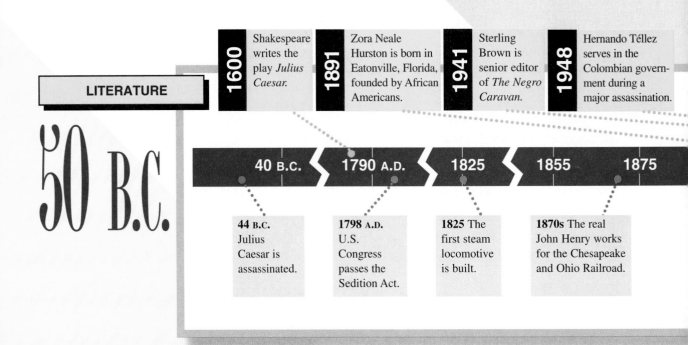

LITERATURE

1600 Shakespeare writes the play *Julius Caesar.*

1891 Zora Neale Hurston is born in Eatonville, Florida, founded by African Americans.

1941 Sterling Brown is senior editor of *The Negro Caravan.*

1948 Hernando Téllez serves in the Colombian government during a major assassination.

50 B.C.

40 B.C. · 1790 A.D. · 1825 · 1855 · 1875

44 B.C. Julius Caesar is assassinated.

1798 A.D. U.S. Congress passes the Sedition Act.

1825 The first steam locomotive is built.

1870s The real John Henry works for the Chesapeake and Ohio Railroad.

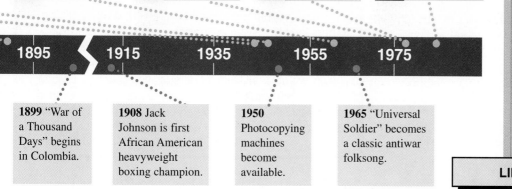

1958 Langston Hughes co-edits *The Book of Negro Folklore*.

1976 Jack Finney writes *The Body Snatchers*.

1976 Dahlia Ravikovitch writes *Dress of Fire*.

1982 Buffy Sainte-Marie wins an Oscar for her movie theme.

1895   1915   1935   1955   1975

1899 "War of a Thousand Days" begins in Colombia.

1908 Jack Johnson is first African American heavyweight boxing champion.

1950 Photocopying machines become available.

1965 "Universal Soldier" becomes a classic antiwar folksong.

1985

LIFE and WORK

from *The Tragedy of Julius Caesar*

EXPLORING

Persuasion can be powerful. A speaker or writer with some skill and with passion for his or her cause can convince people to believe certain things or act in certain ways. How do you use the power of persuasion in your life? Whom do you persuade, and for what reasons?

THEME CONNECTION...
DETERMINATION AND POWER

The Tragedy of Julius Caesar examines, among other things, human beings competing to gain power. Act III, scene ii, shows both Brutus and Antony determined to gain power by winning the citizens' support. Although at first Antony would seem to have little chance of seizing authority from Brutus, he succeeds in doing so. Determination and eloquence help him carry the day. Antony demonstrates the enormous power of words to sway a crowd, thus gaining control over them.

TIME & PLACE

The play is set in Rome in 44 B.C. Gaius Julius Caesar, a Roman general and statesman who was born around 100 B.C., had served as permanent head of the government since 49 B.C. Rome was a republic at the time, meaning that the citizens, as a body, voted on laws, elected officials, and held general power over their own fate. Strictly speaking, there was not supposed to be a "permanent head of the government." Some political leaders feared that Caesar would make himself king or emperor and defy those who supported the republic. These men, including Marcus Junius Brutus (85?–42 B.C.), himself a famous general and politician, assassinated Caesar on March 15, 44 B.C.

THE WRITER'S CRAFT
PERSUASIVE SPEAKING

Act III, scene ii, consists of two opposing speeches, both intended to persuade. It is possible to persuade people primarily by appealing to their emotions. It is also possible to persuade by relying on logical reasoning. Typically, speakers succeed best when they use both emotion and reason to move an audience. In this scene, Shakespeare shows two different kinds of persuasive speeches. Brutus's speech relies primarily on reason; his words are those of a logical teacher. Antony plays on the feelings of his listeners; his words are charged with emotion.

from *The Tragedy of Julius Caesar*

William Shakespeare

Characters

Julius Caesar (murdered in Act III, scene i)
Marcus Antonius (Mark Antony), a friend of Caesar's
Marcus Brutus, a conspirator against Caesar
Cassius, a conspirator against Caesar
Citizens of Rome
Servant

Act III, scene ii The Forum

[*Enter* BRUTUS *and goes into the pulpit,* CASSIUS, *and the citizens.*]

CITIZENS. We will be **satisfied**! Let us be satisfied!

BRUTUS. Then follow me and give me audience, friends.
Cassius, go you into the other street
And **part the numbers**.
Those that will hear me speak, let 'em stay here;
Those that will follow Cassius, go with him;
And public reasons shall be rendered
Of Caesar's death.

FIRST CITIZEN.   I will hear Brutus speak.

SECOND CITIZEN. I will hear Cassius, and compare their reasons
When **severally** we hear them rendered.

THIRD CITIZEN. The noble Brutus is ascended. Silence!

BRUTUS. Be patient till the last.
Romans, countrymen, and **lovers**, hear me for **my cause**, and be silent, that
you may hear. Believe me for mine honor, and **have respect** to mine honor,   15
that you may believe. **Censure** me in your wisdom and awake your senses,
that you may the better judge. If there be any in this assembly, any dear friend
of Caesar's, to him I say that Brutus' love to Caesar was no less than his. If
then that friend demand why Brutus rose against Caesar, this is my answer:
Not that I loved Caesar less, but that I loved Rome more. Had you rather   20
Caesar were living, and die all slaves, than that Caesar were dead, to live all

satisfied—
receive an
explanation

part the
numbers—
divide the
people

severally—
separately

freemen? As Caesar loved me, I weep for him; as he was fortunate, I rejoice at it; as he was valiant, I honor him; but as he was ambitious, I slew him. There is tears for his love; joy for his fortune; honor for his valour; and death for his ambition. Who is here so **base** that would be a **bondman**? If any, speak; for him I have offended. Who is here so **rude** that would not be a Roman? If any, speak; for him have I offended. Who is here so vile that will not love his country? If any, speak; for him I have offended. I pause for a reply. 25

ALL. None, Brutus, none!

BRUTUS. Then none have I offended. I have done no more to Caesar than you shall do to Brutus. The question of his death is **enrolled** in the Capitol; his glory not **extenuated**, wherein he was worthy; nor his offenses 30

enforced, for which he suffered death.

[*Enter* MARK ANTONY *and* others, with CAESAR'S *body.*]

Here comes his body, mourned by Mark Antony, who, though he had no hand in his death, shall receive the benefit of his dying, a place in the common- 35 wealth, as which of you shall not? With this I depart, that, as I slew my best lover for the good of Rome, I have the same dagger for myself when it shall please my country to need my death.

ALL. Live, Brutus! Live, live!

FIRST CITIZEN. Bring him with triumph home unto his house. 40

SECOND CITIZEN. Give him a statue with his ancestors.

THIRD CITIZEN. Let him be Caesar.

FOURTH CITIZEN.   Caesar's better parts
    Shall be crowned in Brutus.

FIRST CITIZEN. We'll bring him to his house with shouts and clamors.

BRUTUS. My countrymen—

SECOND CITIZEN.   Peace! Silence! Brutus speaks. 45

FIRST CITIZEN. Peace, ho!

---

lovers—used throughout to mean "dear friends"

my cause—Brutus's cause is freedom

have respect — remember

Censure—judge

base . . .—"Who is so low-born (**base**) that he would prefer to be a slave (**bondman**)?"

rude—uncivilized

enrolled—officially recorded

extenuated—understated

enforced—overstated

BRUTUS. Good countrymen, let me depart alone,
And for my sake, stay here with Antony.
Do grace to Caesar's corpse, and grace his speech
Tending to Caesar's glories which Mark Antony,
By our permission, is allowed to make.   50
I do entreat you, not a man depart,
Save I alone, till Antony have spoke.

[*Exit.*]

Do grace—treat
with respect

beholding—
indebted

interred—placed
in the grave or
tomb

answered it—
paid the penalty
for it

FIRST CITIZEN. Stay, ho! and let us hear Mark Antony.

THIRD CITIZEN. Let him go up into the public chair.
We'll hear him, noble Antony, go up.   55

ANTONY. For Brutus' sake I am **beholding** to you.

[ANTONY *goes into the pulpit.*]

FOURTH CITIZEN. What does he say of Brutus?

THIRD CITIZEN. He says for Brutus' sake
He finds himself beholding to us all.

FOURTH CITIZEN. 'Twere best he speak no harm of Brutus here!   60

FIRST CITIZEN. This Caesar was a tyrant.

THIRD CITIZEN.   Nay, that's certain.
We are blest that Rome is rid of him.

SECOND CITIZEN. Peace! Let us hear what Antony can say.

ANTONY. You gentle Romans—   65

ALL.   Peace, ho! Let us hear him.

ANTONY. Friends, Romans, countrymen, lend me your ears;
I come to bury Caesar, not to praise him.
The evil that men do lives, after them;
The good is oft **interred** with their bones.   70
So let it be with Caesar. The noble Brutus
Hath told you Caesar was ambitious.
If it were so, it was a grievous fault,
And grievously hath Caesar **answered it**.
Here under leave of Brutus and the rest   75
(For Brutus is an honorable man;
So are they all, all honorable men),
Come I to speak in Caesar's funeral.
He was my friend, faithful and just to me;
But Brutus says he was ambitious,   80
And Brutus is an honorable man.

He hath brought many captives home to Rome,
Whose ransoms did the **general coffers** fill.
Did this in Caesar seem ambitious?
When that the poor have cried, Caesar hath wept;   85
Ambition should be made of sterner stuff.
Yet Brutus says he was ambitious;
And Brutus is an honorable man.
You all did see that on the **Lupercal**
I thrice presented him a kingly crown,   90
Which he did thrice refuse. Was this ambition?
Yet Brutus says he was ambitious;
And, sure, he is an honorable man.
I speak not to disprove what Brutus spoke,
But here I am to speak what I do know.   95
You all did love him once, not without cause.
What cause withholds you, then, to mourn for him?
O judgment, thou art fled to brutish beasts,
And men have lost their reason! Bear with me.
My heart is in the coffin there with Caesar,
And I must pause till it come back to me.

FIRST CITIZEN. Methinks there is much reason in his
   sayings.

SECOND CITIZEN. If thou consider rightly of the matter,
   Caesar has had great wrong.

THIRD CITIZEN.   Has he, masters?

   I fear there will a worse come in his place.   105

FOURTH CITIZEN. Marked ye his words? He would
      not take the crown;
   Therefore 'tis certain he was not ambitious.

FIRST CITIZEN. If it be found so, some will **dear abide** it.   110

SECOND CITIZEN. Poor soul! His eyes are red as fire with weeping.

THIRD CITIZEN. There's not a nobler man in Rome than Antony.

FOURTH CITIZEN. Now mark him. He begins again to speak.

ANTONY. **But** yesterday the word of Caesar might   115
   Have stood against the world. Now lies he there,
   And **none so poor** to do him reverence.
   O masters! If I were disposed to stir

● ● ● ● ● ● ●
"And Brutus is
an honorable
man."
● ● ● ● ● ● ●

Your hearts and minds to mutiny and rage,
I should do Brutus wrong, and Cassius wrong,   120
Who, you all know, are honorable men.
I will not do them wrong. I rather choose
To wrong the dead, to wrong myself and you,
Than I will wrong such honorable men.
But here's a parchment with the seal of Caesar.   125
I found it in his closet; 'tis his will.
Let but the **commons** hear this testament,
Which (pardon me) I do not mean to read,
And they would go and kiss dead Caesar's wounds
And dip their **napkins** in his sacred blood;   130
Yea, beg a hair of him for memory,
And dying, mention it within their wills,
Bequeathing it as a rich legacy
Unto their issue.

FOURTH CITIZEN. We'll hear the will! Read it, Mark Antony.   135

ALL. The will, the will! We will hear Caesar's will!

ANTONY. Have patience, gentle friends; I must not read it.

commons—ordinary citizens

napkins—handkerchiefs

meet—
appropriate

o'ershot
myself—went
further than I
intended

hearse—bier

mantle—cloak;
specifically here,
a special toga
that signified
Caesar's status

Nervii—one of
many tribes
defeated by the
Romans in 57
B.C. during what
are called the
Gallic Wars

rent—tear or
hole; Antony did
not witness the
assassination,
but here assigns
specific wounds
to specific men
to arouse the
sympathy of the
citizens.

It is not **meet** you know how Caesar loved you.
You are not wood, you are not stones, but men;
And being men, hearing the will of Caesar,   140
It will inflame you, it will make you mad.
'Tis good you know not that you are his heirs;
For if you should, O, what would come of it!

FOURTH CITIZEN. Read the will! We'll hear it, Antony!
You shall read us the will, Caesar's will!   145

ANTONY. Will you be patient? Will you stay awhile?
I have **o'ershot myself** to tell you of it.
I fear I wrong the honorable men
Whose daggers have stabbed Caesar; I do fear it.

FOURTH CITIZEN. They were traitors. Honorable men!   150

ALL. The will! The testament!

SECOND CITIZEN. They were villains, murderers! The will! Read the will!

ANTONY. You will compel me then to read the will?
Then make a ring about the corpse of Caesar
And let me show you him that made the will.   155
Shall I descend? and will you give me leave?

ALL. Come down.

SECOND CITIZEN. Descend.

THIRD CITIZEN. You shall have leave.

[ANTONY *comes down.*]

FOURTH CITIZEN. A ring! Stand round.   160

FIRST CITIZEN. Stand from the **hearse**! Stand from the body!

SECOND CITIZEN. Room for Antony, most noble Antony!

ANTONY. Nay, press not so upon me. Stand far off.

ALL. Stand back! Room! Bear back!

ANTONY. If you have tears, prepare to shed them now.   165
You all do know this **mantle**. I remember
The first time ever Caesar put it on.
'Twas on a summer's evening in his tent,
That day he overcame the **Nervii**.
Look, in this place ran Cassius' dagger through.   170
See what a **rent** the envious Casca made.

Through this the well-beloved Brutus stabbed;
And as he plucked his cursed steel away,
Mark how the blood of Caesar followed it,
As rushing out of doors **to be resolved**   175
If Brutus so unkindly knocked or no;
For Brutus, as you know, was Caesar's **angel**.
Judge, O you gods, how dearly Caesar loved him!
This was the most unkindest cut of all;
For when the noble Caesar saw him stab,   180
Ingratitude, more strong than traitors' arms,
Quite vanquished him. Then burst his mighty heart;
And in his mantle muffling up his face,
Even at the base of **Pompey's** statue
(Which all the while ran blood) great Caesar fell.   185
O what a fall was there, my countrymen!
Then I, and you, and all of us fell down,
Whilst bloody treason flourished over us.
O, now you weep, and I perceive you feel
The **dint** of pity. These are **gracious drops**.   190
Kind souls, what, weep you when you but behold
Our Caesar's **vesture** wounded? Look you here!
Here is himself, **marred** as you see with traitors.

FIRST CITIZEN. O piteous spectacle!

SECOND CITIZEN. O noble Caesar!   195

THIRD CITIZEN. O woeful day!

FOURTH CITIZEN. O traitors, villains!

FIRST CITIZEN. O most bloody sight!

SECOND CITIZEN. We will be revenged.

ALL. Revenge! About! Seek! Burn! Fire! Kill! Slay!   200
    Let not a traitor live!

ANTONY. Stay, countrymen.

FIRST CITIZEN. Peace there! Hear the noble Antony.

SECOND CITIZEN. We'll hear him, we'll follow him, we'll die with him!

ANTONY. Good friends, sweet friends, let me not stir you up   205
    To such a sudden flood of mutiny.
    They that have done this deed are honorable.
    What **private griefs** they have, alas, I know not,

---

to be resolved—
to make certain

angel—favorite

Pompey—
Roman general
and son-in-law
of Caesar,
though the two
were political
enemies.
Caesar's army
finally defeated
Pompey's in 48
B.C.; Pompey
was assassi-
nated shortly
thereafter.

dint—
impression

gracious
drops—honor-
able tears

vesture—
garment

marred—
mutilated

private griefs—
personal griev-
ances or
complaints

The Tragedy of Julius Caesar   **313**

That made them do it. They are wise and honorable,
And will no doubt with reasons answer you.   210
I come not, friends, to steal away your hearts.
I am no orator, as Brutus is,
But (as you know me all) a plain blunt man
That love my friend; and that they know full well
That gave me **public leave** to speak of him.   215
For I have neither wit, nor words, nor worth,
Action, nor utterance, nor the power of speech
To stir men's blood. I only speak right on.
I tell you that which you yourselves do know,
Show you sweet Caesar's wounds, poor poor dumb **mouths**,   220
And bid them speak for me. But **were** I Brutus,
And Brutus Antony, there were an Antony
Would **ruffle up** your spirits, and put a tongue
In every wound of Caesar, that should move
The stones of Rome to rise and mutiny.   225

ALL. We'll mutiny.

FIRST CITIZEN. We'll burn the house of Brutus.

THIRD CITIZEN. Away then! Come, seek the conspirators.

ANTONY. Yet hear me, countrymen. Yet hear me speak.

ALL. Peace, ho! Hear Antony, most noble Antony!   230

ANTONY. Why friends, you go to do you know not what.
   Wherein hath Caesar thus deserved your loves?
   Alas, you know not! I must tell you then.

   You have forgot the will I told you of.

ALL. Most true! The will! Let's stay and hear the will.   235

ANTONY. Here is the will, and under Caesar's seal.
   To every Roman citizen he gives,
   To every several man, seventy-five **drachmas**.

SECOND CITIZEN. Most noble Caesar! We'll revenge his death.

THIRD CITIZEN. O royal Caesar!   240

ANTONY. Hear me with patience.

ALL. Peace, ho!

ANTONY. Moreover he hath left you all his walks,

His private arbors, and new-planted orchards,
On this side Tiber; he hath left them you, 245
And to your heirs for ever—common pleasures,
To walk abroad and recreate yourselves.
Here was a Caesar! When comes such another?

FIRST CITIZEN. Never, never! Come away, away!
We'll burn his body in the **holy place** 250
And with the **brands** fire the traitors' houses.
Take up the body.

SECOND CITIZEN. Go fetch fire!

THIRD CITIZEN. Pluck down benches!

FOURTH CITIZEN. Pluck down **forms**, **windows**, anything! 255

[*Exit* CITIZENS *with the body.*]

ANTONY. Now let it work. Mischief, thou art afoot,
Take thou what course thou wilt.
[*Enter* SERVANT.]
How now, fellow?

SERVANT. Sir, **Octavius** is already come to Rome.

ANTONY. Where is he? 260

SERVANT. He and **Lepidus** are at Caesar's house.

ANTONY. And thither will I straight to visit him.
He comes **upon a wish**. Fortune is merry,
And in this mood will give us anything.

SERVANT. I heard him say Brutus 265
and Cassius
Are **rid** like madmen through the gates of Rome.

ANTONY. **Belike** they had some **notice** of the people,
How I had **moved** them. Bring me to Octavius.

[*Exeunt.*] ❖

ACCENT ON...
ARCHITECTURE
· · · · · · · · · · · · · · · · · · · ·

Act III, scene ii, of *The Tragedy of Julius Caesar* is set at the Forum in Rome. In this setting, both Brutus and Mark Antony walk to the Forum's pulpit and deliver moving and persuasive speeches to the Roman citizens. Design a contemporary building that will be used primarily as a forum, a public meeting place for open discussion. Build a model of your design. Then write a brief essay explaining why you think your design effectively conveys the function of the building. Present your model and your essay to the class.

holy place—among the sacred temples of Rome

brands—coals from Caesar's funeral fire

forms . . .—long benches and shutters (**windows**)

Octavius—Caesar's 19-year-old great-nephew. In the will that Antony has, Caesar has officially adopted Octavius as his heir. After some struggles, Octavius becomes Caesar Augustus and rules Rome for 40 years.

Lepidus—For a time, Lepidus rules jointly with Octavius and Antony, though Lepidus is neither as strong nor as ambitious as the other two

upon a wish—just as I wished

rid—have ridden

Belike . . .—"Probably they had some early news (**notice**) of how I had swayed (**moved**) the people against them."

UNDERSTANDING

1. Outline the logical thinking that Brutus conveys in his speech.

   Brainstorm occasions when reason might be the best persuasive strategy you could use. Give a speech on something you believe in. Use reason to persuade readers to accept your point of view. ***Workshops 13 and 23***

2. What is the opinion of the crowd when Antony begins speaking? What does Antony do to arouse the crowd's emotions and to sway their opinions?

   Write a letter to an adult you know well. Use emotional strategies to persuade this person to change his or her mind about an issue. ***Workshop 13***

3. Analyze the crowd's reactions to the speeches. For each speech, create a two-column chart. Label one column "Reason" and the other "Emotion." List each reaction of the crowd under the appropriate category. Examine what the crowd is reacting to for each item you enter in the chart.

   Prepare a pamphlet for training political candidates. List the elements of an effective persuasive speech. Give tips on the best ways to sway listeners' opinions. ***Workshop 6***

A LAST WORD

How may power or authority be communicated through words? In what kinds of situations at school, home, or on the job might you need to use the powers of verbal persuasion?

CONNECTING

1. Bring to class two articles from newspapers or magazines that intend to persuade. In groups, share your articles. Analyze them to see if the authors use reason, emotion, or both.

   Collaborate to write an editorial to be sent to a newspaper or magazine in which you attempt to persuade those in authority to do something you think needs doing. To be effective, you will need to use reason. Research the issue to gain information to use in your logical argument. ***Workshop 13***

2. Working with several classmates, collect information about mob psychology. In addition to considering what psychologists say on this topic, look at examples of mob behavior in videotapes and in photographs from back issues of magazines such as *Life*. In a multimedia presentation involving overheads, enlarged photographs, and/or video clips, explain how mobs operate. ***Workshop 23***

3. Prepare and stage an informal debate for your classmates on a subject dividing your school or community. A panel of students in the class should judge the debate.

Courage Against the Odds

- *John Henry*
- *John Henry*
- *Strange Legacies*

EXPLORING

Downsizing, laying people off, has become common practice in the 1990s as companies replace employees with machines. What do you think about technology? Are some machines a mixed blessing, creating both possibilities and problems? What ordinary household work do machines now do? Are these machines really necessary? What mental and physical tasks do you perform that technology could handle just as easily?

TIME & PLACE

Although nobody knows for certain, it is thought that John Henry may have been an actual person who worked for the Chesapeake and Ohio Railroad, perhaps in the 1870s. Some say he used a long-handled hammer to make holes in rocks for explosives; others say he used a hammer to drive spikes into train rails, securing them to the ground. Whatever Henry's target, legend agrees that he wielded a massive hammer and that when challenged, John Henry agreed to compete with a steam-powered machine. He died attempting this impossible task.

THEME CONNECTION... REFUSING TO GIVE UP

In these three selections, the characters courageously face overwhelming adversity. Their refusal to give up serves as an inspiring example to people everywhere.

THE WRITER'S CRAFT

DIALECT

Dialect refers to any form of speech that departs from standard English. Various regions of the United States, such as New England and the southern states, are well known for their distinctive dialects. Using dialect helps writers portray specific places and times. Examples of dialect from the ballad "John Henry" include "Alabam," "it's wrote," "hammah," and "yoh" (for "your").

John Henry

Anonymous

Some say he's from Georgia,
Some say he's from Alabam,
But it's wrote on the rock at the Big
    Ben Tunnel,
John Henry's a East Virginia Man,
John Henry's a East Virginia Man.

John Henry he could hammah,
He could whistle, he could sing,
He went to the mountain early in the mornin'
To hear his hammah ring,
To hear his hammah ring.

John Henry went to the section boss,
Says the section boss what kin you do?
Says I can line a track, I kin **histe** a jack,
I can pick and shovel, too,
I can pick and shovel, too.

John Henry went to the tunnel
And they put him in lead to drive,
The rock was so tall and John Henry so small
That he laid down his hammah and he cried,
That he laid down his hammah and he cried.

The steam drill was on the right han' side,
John Henry was on the left,
Says before I let this steam drill beat
    me down,
I'll hammah myself to death,
I'll hammah myself to death.

Oh the cap'n said to John Henry,
I believe this mountain's sinkin' in.
John Henry said to the cap'n, Oh my!
Tain't nothin' but my hammah suckin' wind,
Tain't nothin' but my hammah suckin' wind.

John Henry had a pretty liddle wife,
She come all dressed in blue.
And the last words she said to him,
John Henry I been true to you,
John Henry I been true to you.

John Henry was on the mountain,
The mountain was so high,
He called to his pretty liddle wife,
Said Ah kin almos' touch the sky,
Said Ah kin almos' touch the sky.

histe—hoist, lift

Who gonna shoe yoh pretty liddle feet,
Who gonna glove yoh han',
Who gonna kiss yoh rosy cheeks,
An' who gonna be yoh man,
An' who gonna be yoh man?

Papa gonna shoe my pretty liddle feet,
Mama gonna glove my han',
Sistah gonna kiss my rosy cheeks,
An' I ain't gonna have no man,
An' I ain't gonna have no man.

Then John Henry he did hammah,
He did make his hammah soun',
Says now one more lick fore quittin'
    time,
An' I'll beat this steam drill down,
An' I'll beat this steam drill down.

The hammah that John Henry swung,
It weighed over nine poun',
He broke a rib in his left han' side,
And his **intrels** fell on the groun',
And his intrels fell on the groun'.

intrels—entrails,
innards

All the women in the West
That heard of John Henry's death
Stood in the rain, flagged the east
    bound train,
Goin' where John Henry dropped dead,
Goin' where John Henry dropped dead.

They took John Henry to the White
    House,
And buried him in the san'.
And every locomotive come roarin' by
Says there lays that steel drivin' man,
Says there lays that steel drivin' man. ❖

ON THE JOB
MINING TECHNICIAN

Mining technicians assist professional engineers, geologists, and geophysicists in the technical aspects of coal and ore mining. They perform a variety of tasks, including gathering information, performing chemical and physical tests, identifying samples of rock, observing mining operations, and surveying and drafting. Courses in math, chemistry, geology, and physics provide a helpful background for a two-year college or technical program in mining technology.

John Henry

Zora Neale Hurston

John Henry driving on the right hand side,
Steam drill driving on the left,
Says, 'fore I'll let your steam drill beat me down
I'll hammer my fool self to death,
Hammer my fool self to death.

John Henry told his Captain,
When you go to town
Please bring me back a nine pound hammer
And I'll drive your steel on down,
And I'll drive your steel on down.

John Henry told his Captain,
Man ain't nothing but a man,
And 'fore I'll let that steam drill beat me down
I'll die with this hammer in my hand,
Die with this hammer in my hand.

Captain ast John Henry,
What is that storm I hear?
He says Cap'n that ain't no storm,
'Tain't nothing but my hammer in the air,
Nothing but my hammer in the air.

John Henry told his Captain.
Bury me under the sills of the floor.
So when they get to playing good old **Georgy skin**
Bet 'em fifty to a dollar more.
Fifty to a dollar more.

John Henry had a little woman,
The dress she wore was red.
Says I'm going down the track.
And she never looked back.
I'm going where John Henry fell dead,
Going where John Henry fell dead.

Who's going to shoe your pretty lil feet?
And who's going to glove your hand?
Who's going to kiss your dimpled cheek?
And who's going to be your man?
Who's going to be your man?

About the Author

Eatonville, Florida, the hometown of Zora Neale Hurston (1891–1960), was the first American town founded by African Americans. Hurston grew up listening to stories ("big old lies"), sayings, songs, sermons, and tall tales. Years later, after studying anthropology, Hurston returned to her hometown to gather material for her two books of African-American folklore, *Mules and Men* and *Tell My Horse.* Hurston was educated at Howard, Barnard, and Columbia Universities.

Georgy skin—gambling game played by railroad workers

Zora Neale Hurston (pictured at left in 1938) collected *cultural history*—the stories, sayings, songs, sermons, tall tales, and home remedies of African Americans in her hometown of Eatonville, Florida. Gather information for a cultural history of your family, neighborhood, or community. Then put together a book of the folklore, crediting each person for the information he or she provided, along with any history about the story, song, saying, and so on.

My father's going to shoe my pretty lil feet;
My brother's going to glove my hand;
My sister's going to kiss my dimpled cheek;
John Henry's going to be my man,
John Henry's going to be my man.

Where did you get your pretty lil dress?
The shoes you wear so fine?
I got my shoes from a railroad man,
My dress from a man in the mine,
My dress from a man in the mine. ❖

Strange Legacies

Sterling A. Brown

One thing you left with us, **Jack Johnson.**
One thing before they got you

You used to stand there like a man,
Taking punishment
With a golden, spacious grin;
Confident.
Inviting big Jim Jeffries, who was boring in:
"Heah ah is, big boy; yuh sees whah Ise at.
Come on in . . . ."

Thanks, Jack, for that.

John Henry, with your hammer;
John Henry, with your steel driver's pride,
You taught us that a man could go down like a man,
Sticking to your hammer till you died.
Sticking to your hammer till you died.

Brother,
When, beneath the burning sun
The sweat poured down and the breath came thick,
And the loaded hammer swung like a ton
And the heart grew sick;
You had what we need now, John Henry.
Help us get it.

So if we go down
Have to go down
We go like you, brother,
Nachal' *men. . . .*

About the Author

A poet and teacher, Sterling A. Brown (1901–1989) was a pioneer in African-American studies. In 1931, Brown wrote the landmark essay "Negro Characters as Seen by White Authors." The next year, he published his first volume of poetry, *Southern Road,* which was praised for its replacement of dialect with the vernacular, or everyday, speech of African Americans. Born in Washington, D.C., Brown was educated at Williams College and Harvard University. For 40 years, Brown taught at Howard University.

Jack Johnson—
John Arthur Johnson (1878–1946), the first African-American boxer to hold the heavyweight title. He knocked out Jim Jeffries in a 15-round bout in 1910.

Nachal'—natural

Old nameless couple in **Red River Bottom,**
Who have seen floods gutting out your best **loam,**
And the **boll weevil** chase you
Out of your hard-earned home,
Have seen the drought parch your green fields,
And the **cholera** stretch your **porkers** out dead;
Have seen year after year
The **commissary** always a little in the lead;

Even you said
That which we need
Now in our time of fear,—
Routed your own deep misery and dread,
Muttering, beneath an unfriendly sky,
"Guess we'll give it one mo' try.
Guess we'll give it one mo' try." ❖

Red River
Bottom—The
Red River forms
the boundary
between
Oklahoma and
Texas, and then
flows into
Louisiana. The
reference is to
tenant farmers
who barely
made a living for
themselves,
especially when
floods destroyed
their crops.

loam—soil

boll weevil—a
type of beetle
that feeds on
and can do
severe damage
to cotton plants
and to the
cotton "bolls,"
the pods of ripe
cotton

cholera—a
disease that
affects the
intestines, in this
case of pigs
(porkers)

commissary—A
store that sells
food and sup-
plies, often on
credit, to be
paid for when
customers'
crops are
harvested.
Being "in the
lead" means
that the cus-
tomer always
owes the store
money.

UNDERSTANDING

1.  How are women portrayed in the poems in this lesson? In groups, compare the view of women presented in the poems with the condition of women today.

   Still working in your group, list things women do today that they did not do 50 years ago. Consider, for instance, jobs, activities, attire, and conduct.

2. Ballads use refrains and repetition to move emotions. Find examples of refrains and repetition in the poems by Hurston and Brown.

   John Henry's death, were it to occur while working for a company today, would result in a police investigation. Imagine yourself as an eyewitness at John Henry's death. Write an incident report following the format used by police. *Workshop 10*

3. How would you describe the attitudes toward work held by John Henry, Jack Johnson, and the nameless couple? Refer to the text to support your conclusions.

   If you were hiring someone, or choosing someone to become your partner in a part-time enterprise such as child care or lawn mowing, what interview questions would you raise in order to learn about this person's attitude toward work? List five questions. *Workshop 6*

A LAST WORD

What kind of legacy would you value most? How might courage and determination be the greatest legacies someone could pass on to you?

CONNECTING

1.  Brown refers to the adversity experienced by the "old nameless couple in Red River Bottom." What did it mean to be a sharecropper or tenant farmer in the South during the Depression? In what respects are conditions different today? Collaborate with several classmates to research this question. Create a multimedia presentation that contrasts the situation of blacks in the South in the 1930s with that today. *Workshops 15 and 23*

2. The steam drill replaced men using hammers. When technology replaces workers today, the workers are often able to learn new skills that equip them for new careers. Working in a small group, gather information about training and educational opportunities available in your region. Share the research tasks. Obtain pamphlets and brochures describing career training at community colleges. Write to the directors of personnel or human resources at large corporations to ask if they have apprenticeship programs. Present this information in an attractive display. *Workshop 18*

Contents of the Dead Man's Pockets

EXPLORING

Some people work hard now, putting off fun, in order to achieve long-term goals. They reject the pleasure of the moment because they know that sacrifices now will enrich their lives later on. Describe a time when you worked very hard, either physically or mentally. How did it feel to work so hard? Was there a "reward"? Discuss the pros and cons of postponing pleasure to concentrate on work.

THEME CONNECTION...
MISPLACED DETERMINATION

Tom Benecke reveals extraordinary determination when he climbs out on a ledge 11 stories above the ground to retrieve a yellow piece of paper. He risks his life to reclaim research notes he needs for a project. Tom's experience makes it clear that determination and courage should be used intelligently for causes that really matter.

TIME & PLACE

Tom Benecke lives on the 11th floor of a high-rise apartment building on Lexington Avenue, which runs the length of Manhattan in New York City. It is evening. Tom's wife, Clare, goes to the movies and will be gone about four hours. As was common in the 1950s, moviegoers went to see two features in one sitting. The playing of a newsreel between features was also common. Most households did not yet have television sets and newsreels presented major national and world events.

THE WRITER'S CRAFT

SUSPENSE

Finney is a master of suspense. The very title *Contents of the Dead Man's Pockets* makes readers wonder whether Tom Benecke will survive or crash to his death. Suspense occurs at several critical moments. For example, will he go out on the high window ledge? Suspense is the element in fiction that keeps readers in a state of uncertainty and forces them to keep reading to find out what will happen next.

Contents of the Dead Man's Pockets

Jack Finney

About the Author

Jack Finney (b. 1911) is well aware of the pressures of the advertising business; he worked for a time in an advertising agency in New York City before devoting himself to writing. The strange and bizarre are common elements in Finney's short stories and more than a dozen novels. His novels include *Time and Again, Marion's Wall, From Time to Time,* and *The Night People.* Finney was born in Milwaukee, Wisconsin. After working in New York City, he later moved to Mill Valley, California, where he still lives.

At the little living-room desk Tom Benecke rolled two sheets of **flimsy** and a heavier top sheet, carbon paper sandwiched between them, into his portable. *Interoffice Memo,* the top sheet was headed, and he typed tomorrow's date just below this; then he glanced at a creased yellow sheet, covered with his own handwriting, beside the typewriter. "Hot in here," he muttered to himself. Then, from the short hallway at his back, he heard the muffled clang of wire coat hangers in the bedroom closet, and at this reminder of what his wife was doing he thought: Hot, no—guilty conscience.

He got up, shoving his hands into the back pockets of his gray wash slacks, stepped to the living-room window beside the desk, and stood breathing on the glass, watching the expanding circlet of mist, staring down through the autumn night at Lexington Avenue, eleven stories below. He was a tall, lean, dark-haired young man in a pullover sweater, who looked as though he had played not football, probably, but basketball in college. Now he placed the heels of his hands against the top edge of the lower window frame and shoved upward. But as usual the window didn't budge, and he had to lower his hands and then shoot them hard upward to jolt the window open a few inches. He dusted his hands, muttering.

But still he didn't begin his work. He crossed the room to the hallway entrance and, leaning against the doorjamb, hands shoved into his back pockets again, he called, "Clare?" When his wife answered, he said, "Sure you don't mind going alone?"

"No." Her voice was muffled, and he knew her head and shoulders were in the bedroom closet. Then the tap of her high heels sounded on the wood floor and she appeared at the end of the little hallway, wearing a slip, both hands raised to one ear, clipping on an earring. She smiled at him—a slender, very pretty girl with light brown, almost blonde, hair—her prettiness emphasized by the pleasant nature that showed in her face. "It's just that I hate you to miss this movie; you wanted to see it too."

"Yeah, I know." He ran his fingers through his hair. "Got to get this done though."

She nodded, accepting this. Then, glancing at the desk across the living room, she said, "You work too much, though, Tom—and too hard."

He smiled. "You won't mind though, will you, when the money comes rolling in and I'm known as the Boy Wizard of Wholesale Groceries?"

"I guess not." She smiled and turned back toward the bedroom.

flimsy—thin paper used for typing carbon copies

At his desk again, Tom lighted a cigarette; then a few moments later as Clare appeared, dressed and ready to leave, he set it on the rim of the ashtray. "Just after seven," she said. "I can make the beginning of the first feature."

He walked to the front-door closet to help her on with her coat. He kissed her then and, for an instant, holding her close, smelling the perfume she had used, he was tempted to go with her; it was not actually true that he had to work tonight, though he very much wanted to. This was his own project, unannounced as yet in his office, and it could be postponed. But then they won't see it till Monday, he thought once again, and if I give it to the boss tomorrow he might read it over the weekend . . . . "Have a good time," he said aloud. He gave his wife a little swat and opened the door for her, feeling the air from the building hallway, smelling faintly of floor wax, stream past his face.

He watched her walk down the hall, flicked a hand in response as she waved, and then he started to close the door, but it resisted for a moment. As the door opening narrowed, the current of warm air from the hallway, channeled through this smaller opening now, suddenly rushed past him with accelerated force. Behind him he heard the slap of the window curtains against the wall and the sound of paper fluttering from his desk, and he had to push to close the door.

Turning, he saw a sheet of white paper drifting to the floor in a series of arcs, and another sheet, yellow, moving toward the window, caught in the dying current flowing through the narrow opening. As he watched, the paper struck the bottom edge of the window and hung there for an instant, plastered against the glass and wood. Then as the moving air stilled completely, the curtains swinging back from the wall to hang free again, he saw the yellow sheet drop to the window ledge and slide over out of sight.

He ran across the room, grasped the bottom edge of the window, and tugged, staring through the glass. He saw the yellow sheet, dimly now in the darkness outside, lying on the ornamental ledge a yard below the window. Even as he watched, it was moving, scraping slowly along the ledge, pushed by the breeze that pressed steadily against the building wall. He heaved on the window with all his strength and it shot open with a bang, the window weight rattling in the casing. But the paper was past his reach and, leaning out into the night, he watched it scud steadily along the ledge to the south, half-plastered against the building wall. Above the muffled sound of the street traffic far below, he could hear the dry scrape of its movement, like a leaf on the pavement.

The living room of the next apartment to the south projected a yard or more farther out toward the street than this one; because of this the Beneckes paid seven and a half dollars less rent than their neighbors. And now the yellow sheet, sliding along the stone ledge, nearly invisible in the night, was stopped by the projecting blank wall of the next apartment. It lay motionless, then, in the corner formed by the two walls—a good five yards away, pressed firmly against the ornate corner ornament of the ledge by the breeze that moved past Tom Benecke's face.

convoluted—
intricate,
involved

sidling—moving
sideways

He knelt at the window and stared at the yellow paper for a full minute or more, waiting for it to move, to slide off the ledge and fall, hoping he could follow its course to the street, and then hurry down in the elevator and retrieve it. But it didn't move, and then he saw that the paper was caught firmly between a projection of the **convoluted** corner ornament and the ledge. He thought about the poker from the fireplace, then the broom, then the mop—discarding each thought as it occurred to him. There was nothing in the apartment long enough to reach that paper.

It was hard for him to understand that he actually had to abandon it—it was ridiculous—and he began to curse. Of all the papers on his desk, why did it have to be this one in particular! On four long Saturday afternoons he had stood in supermarkets counting the people who passed certain displays, and the results were scribbled on that yellow sheet. From stacks of trade publications, gone over page by page in snatched half-hours at work and during evenings at home, he had copied facts, quotations, and figures onto that sheet. And he had carried it with him to the Public Library on Fifth Avenue, where he'd spent a dozen lunch hours and early evenings adding more. All were needed to support and lend authority to his idea for a new grocery-store display method; without them his idea was a mere opinion. And there they all lay in his own improvised shorthand—countless hours of work—out there on the ledge.

● ● ● ● ● ● ●

"For many seconds he believed he was going to abandon the yellow sheet."

● ● ● ● ● ● ●

For many seconds he believed he was going to abandon the yellow sheet, that there was nothing else to do. The work could be duplicated. But it would take two months, and the time to present this idea was *now,* for use in the spring displays. He struck his fist on the window ledge. Then he shrugged. Even though his plan were adopted, he told himself, it wouldn't bring him a raise in pay—not immediately, anyway, or as a direct result. It won't bring me a promotion either, he argued—not of itself.

But just the same, and he couldn't escape the thought, this and other independent projects, some already done and others planned for the future, would gradually mark him out from the score of other young men in his company. They were the way to change from a name on the payroll to a name in the minds of the company officials. They were the beginning of the long, long climb to where he was determined to be, at the very top. And he knew he was going out there in the darkness, after the yellow sheet fifteen feet beyond his reach.

By a kind of instinct, he instantly began making his intention acceptable to himself by laughing at it. The mental picture of himself **sidling** along the ledge outside was absurd—it was actually comical—and he smiled. He imagined himself describing it; it would make a good story at the office and, it occurred to him, would add a special interest and importance to his memorandum, which would do it no harm at all.

To simply go out and get his paper was an easy task—he could be back here with it in less than two minutes—and he knew he wasn't deceiving himself. The ledge, he saw, measuring it with his eye, was about as wide as the length of his shoe, and perfectly flat. And every fifth row of brick in the face of the building, he remembered—leaning out, he verified this—was indented half an inch, enough for the tips of his fingers, enough to maintain balance easily. It occurred to him that if this ledge and wall were only a yard above ground—as he knelt at the window staring out, this thought was the final confirmation of his intention—he could move along the ledge indefinitely.

On a sudden impulse, he got to his feet, walked to the front closet, and took out an old tweed jacket; it would be cold outside. He put it on and buttoned it as he crossed the room rapidly toward the open window. In the back of his mind he knew he'd better hurry and get this over with before he thought too much, and at the window he didn't allow himself to hesitate.

He swung a leg over the sill, then felt for and found the ledge a yard below the window with his foot. Gripping the bottom of the window frame very tightly and carefully, he slowly ducked his head under it, feeling on his face the sudden change from the warm air of the room to the chill outside. With infinite care he brought out his other leg, his mind concentrating on what he was doing. Then he slowly stood erect. Most of the putty, dried out and brittle, had dropped off the bottom edging of the window frame, he found, and the flat wooden edging provided a good gripping surface, a half-

inch or more deep, for the tips of his fingers.

Now, balanced easily and firmly, he stood on the ledge outside in the slight, chill breeze, eleven stories above the street, staring into his own lighted apartment, odd and different-seeming now.

First his right hand, then his left, he carefully shifted his fingertip grip from the puttyless window edging to an indented row of bricks directly to his right. It was hard to take the first shuffling sideways step then—to make himself move—and the fear stirred in his stomach, but he did it, again by not allowing himself time to think. And now—with his chest, stomach, and the left side of his face pressed against the rough cold brick—his lighted apartment was suddenly gone, and it was much darker out here than he had thought.

Without pause he continued—right foot, left foot, right foot, left—his shoe soles shuffling and scraping along the rough stone, never lifting from it, fingers sliding along the exposed edging of brick. He moved on the balls of his feet, heels lifted slightly; the ledge was not quite as wide as he'd expected. But leaning slightly inward toward the face of the building and pressed against it, he could feel his balance firm and secure, and moving along the ledge was quite as easy as he had thought it would be. He could hear the buttons of his jacket scraping steadily along the rough bricks and feel them catch momentarily, tugging a little, at each mortared crack. He simply did not permit himself to look down, though the compulsion to do so never left him; nor did he allow himself actually to think. Mechanically—right

FOCUS ON...
ART

While standing out on the ledge, Tom Benecke had a frightening view of Lexington Avenue from 11 stories up. Create that view in a drawing, painting, or print, using color and perspective to convey the vivid visual images of the scene. In the classroom, set up a gallery display of everyone's work.

◆ ◆ ◆ ◆ ◆ ◆ ◆ ◆ ◆ ◆ ◆ ◆ ◆ ◆ ◆

foot, left foot, over and again—he shuffled along crabwise, watching the projecting wall ahead loom steadily closer . . . .

Then he reached it and, at the corner—he'd decided how he was going to pick up the paper—he lifted his right foot and placed it carefully on the ledge that ran along the projecting wall at a right angle to the ledge on which his other foot rested. And now, facing the building, he stood in the corner formed by the two walls, one foot on the ledging of each, a hand on the shoulder-high indentation of each wall. His forehead was pressed directly into the corner against the cold bricks, and now he carefully lowered first one hand, then the other, perhaps a foot farther down, to the next indentation in the rows of bricks.

Very slowly, sliding his forehead down the trough of the brick corner and bending his knees, he lowered his body toward the paper lying between his outstretched feet. Again he lowered his fingerholds another foot and bent his knees still more, thigh muscles taut, his forehead sliding and bumping down the brick V. Half squatting now, he dropped

his left hand to the next indentation and then slowly reached with his right hand toward the paper between his feet.

He couldn't quite touch it, and his knees now were pressed against the wall; he could bend them no farther. But by ducking his head another inch lower, the top of his head now pressed against the bricks, he lowered his right shoulder and his fingers had the paper by a corner, pulling it loose. At the same instant he saw, between his legs and far below, Lexington Avenue stretched out for miles ahead.

He saw, in that instant, the Loew's theater sign, blocks ahead past Fiftieth Street; the miles of traffic signals, all green now; the lights of cars and street lamps; countless neon signs; and the moving black dots of people. And a violent instantaneous explosion of absolute terror roared through him. For a motionless instant he saw himself externally—bent practically double, balanced on this narrow ledge, nearly half his body projecting out above the street far below—and he began to tremble violently, panic flaring through his mind and muscles, and he felt the blood rush from the surface of his skin.

In the fractional moment before horror paralyzed him, as he stared between his legs at that terrible length of street far beneath him, a fragment of his mind raised his body in a **spasmodic** jerk to an upright position again, but so violently that his head scraped hard against the wall, bouncing off it, and his body swayed outward to the knife edge of balance, and he very nearly plunged backward and fell. Then he was leaning far into the corner again, squeezing and pushing into it, not only his face but his chest and stomach, his back arching; and his fingertips clung with all the pressure of his pulling arms to the shoulder-high half-inch indentation in the bricks.

He was more than trembling now; his whole body was racked with a violent shuddering beyond control, his eyes squeezed so tightly shut it was painful, though he was past awareness of that. His teeth were exposed in a frozen grimace, the strength draining like water from his knees and calves. It was extremely likely, he knew, that he would faint, slump down along the wall, his face scraping, and then drop backward, a limp weight, out into nothing. And to save his life he concentrated on holding on to consciousness, drawing deliberate deep breaths of cold air into his lungs, fighting to keep his senses aware.

Then he knew that he would not faint, but he could not stop shaking nor open his eyes. He stood where he was, breathing deeply, trying to hold back the terror of the glimpse he had had of what lay below him; and he knew he had made a mistake in not making himself stare

down at the street, getting used to it and accepting it, when he had first stepped out onto the ledge.

It was impossible to walk back. He simply could not do it. He couldn't bring himself to make the slightest movement. The strength was gone from his legs; his shivering hands—numb, cold, and desperately rigid—had lost all **deftness;** his easy ability to move and balance was gone. Within a step or two, if he tried to move, he knew that he would stumble and fall.

Seconds passed, with the chill faint wind pressing the side of his face, and he could hear the toned-down volume of the street traffic far beneath him. Again and again it slowed and then stopped, almost to silence; then presently, even this high, he would hear the click of the traffic signals and the subdued roar of the cars starting up again. During a lull in the street sounds, he called out. Then he was shouting *"Help!"* so loudly it **rasped** his throat. But he felt the steady pressure of the wind, moving between his face and the blank wall, snatch up his cries as he uttered them, and he knew they must sound directionless and distant. And he remembered how habitually, here in New York, he himself heard and ignored shouts in the night. If anyone heard him, there was no sign of it, and presently Tom Benecke knew he had to try moving; there was nothing else he could do.

Eyes squeezed shut, he watched scenes in his mind like scraps of motion-picture film—he could not stop them. He saw himself stumbling suddenly sideways as he crept along the ledge and saw his upper body arc outward, arms flailing. He saw a dangling shoestring caught

spasmodic—characterized by a sudden, involuntary muscle contraction

deftness—skill, ease

rasped—produced a grating sound in

between the ledge and the sole of his other shoe, saw a foot start to move, to be stopped with a jerk, and felt his balance leaving him. He saw himself falling with a terrible speed as his body revolved in the air, knees clutched tight to his chest, eyes squeezed shut, moaning softly.

Out of utter necessity, knowing that any of these thoughts might be reality in the very next seconds, he was slowly able to shut his mind against every thought but what he now began to do. With fear-soaked slowness, he slid his left foot an inch or two toward his own impossibly distant window. Then he slid the fingers of his shivering left hand a corresponding distance. For a moment he could not bring himself to lift his right foot from one ledge to the other; then he did it, and became aware of the harsh exhalation of air from his throat and realized that he was panting. As his right hand, then, began to slide along the brick edging, he was astonished to feel the yellow paper pressed to the bricks underneath his stiff fingers, and he uttered a terrible, abrupt bark that might have been a laugh or a moan. He opened his mouth and took the paper in his teeth, pulling it out from under his fingers.

By a kind of trick—by concentrating his entire mind on first his left foot, then his left hand, then the other foot, then the other hand—he was able to move, almost imperceptibly, trembling steadily, very nearly without thought. But he could feel the terrible strength of the

● ● ● ● ● ● ●

"It was extremely likely, he knew, that he would faint."

● ● ● ● ● ● ●

pent-up horror on just the other side of the flimsy barrier he had erected in his mind; and he knew that if it broke through he would lose this thin artificial control of his body.

During one slow step he tried keeping his eyes closed; it made him feel safer, shutting him off a little from the fearful reality of where he was. Then a sudden rush of giddiness swept over him and he had to open his eyes wide, staring side-ways at the cold rough brick and angled lines of mortar, his cheek tight against the building. He kept his eyes open then, knowing that if he once let them flick outward, to stare for an instant at the lighted windows across the street, he would be past help.

He didn't know how many dozens of tiny sidling steps he had taken, his chest, belly, and face pressed to the wall; but he knew the slender hold he was keeping on his mind and body was going to break. He had a sudden mental picture of his apart-ment on just the other side of this wall—warm, cheer-ful, incredibly spacious. And he saw himself striding through it, lying down on the floor on his back, arms spread wide, reveling in its unbelievable secu-rity. The impossible remoteness of this utter safety, the contrast between it and where he now stood, was more than he could bear. And the barrier broke then, and the fear of the awful height he stood on coursed through his nerves and muscles.

A fraction of his mind knew he was going to fall, and he began taking rapid blind steps with no feeling of what he was doing, sidling with a clumsy desperate swiftness, fingers scrabbling along the brick, almost hopelessly resigned to the sudden backward pull and swift motion outward and down. Then his moving left hand slid onto not brick but sheer emptiness, an impossible gap in the face of the wall, and he stumbled.

His right foot smashed into his left anklebone; he staggered sideways, began falling, and the claw of his hand cracked against glass and wood, slid down it, and his fingertips were pressed hard on the puttyless edging of his window. His right hand smacked gropingly beside it as he fell to his knees; and, under the full weight and direct downward pull of his sagging body, the open window dropped shudderingly in its frame till it closed and his wrists struck the sill and were jarred off.

For a single moment he knelt, knee bones against stone on the very edge of the ledge, body swaying and touching nowhere else, fighting for balance. Then he lost it, his shoulders plunging backward, and he flung his arms forward, his hands smashing against the window casing on either side; and—his body moving backward—his fingers clutched the narrow wood stripping of the upper pane.

For an instant he hung suspended between balance and falling, his fingertips pressed onto the quarter-inch wood strips. Then, with utmost delicacy, with a focused concentration of all his senses, he increased even further the strain on his fingertips hooked to these slim edgings of wood. Elbows slowly bending, he began to draw the full weight of his upper body forward, knowing that the instant his fingers slipped off these quarter-inch strips he'd plunge backward and be falling. Elbows imperceptibly bending, body shaking with the strain, the sweat starting from his forehead in great sudden drops, he pulled, his entire being and thought concentrated in his fingertips. Then suddenly, the strain slackened and ended, his chest touching the windowsill, and he was kneeling on the ledge, his forehead pressed to the glass of the closed window.

Dropping his palms to the sill, he stared into his living room—at the red-brown davenport across the room, and a magazine he had left there; at the pictures on the walls and the gray rug, the entrance to the hallway; and at his papers, typewriter, and desk, not two feet from his nose. A movement from his desk caught his eye and he saw that it was a thin curl of blue smoke; his cigarette, the ash long, was still burning in the ashtray where he'd left it—this was past all belief—only a few minutes before.

His head moved, and in faint reflection from the glass before him he saw the yellow paper clenched in his front teeth. Lifting a hand from the sill he took it from his mouth; the moistened corner parted from the paper, and he spat it out.

For a moment, in the light from the living room, he stared wonderingly at the yellow sheet in his hand and then crushed it into the side pocket of his jacket.

He couldn't open the window. It had been pulled not completely closed, but its lower edge was below the level of the outside sill; there was no room to get his fingers underneath it. Between the upper sash and the lower was a gap not wide enough—reaching up, he tried—to get his fingers into; he couldn't push it open. The upper window panel, he knew from long experience, was impossible to move, frozen tight with dried paint.

Very carefully observing his balance, the fingertips of his left hand again hooked to the narrow stripping of the window casing, he drew back his right hand, palm facing the glass, and then struck the glass with the heel of his hand.

His arm rebounded from the pane, his body tottering. He knew he didn't dare strike a harder blow.

But in the security and relief of his new position, he simply smiled; with only a sheet of glass between him and the room just before him, it was not possible that there wasn't a way past it. Eyes narrowing, he thought for a few moments about what to do. Then his eyes widened, for nothing occurred to him. But still he felt calm: the trembling, he realized, had stopped. At the back of his mind there still lay the thought that once he was again in his home, he could give release to his feelings. He actually would lie on the floor, rolling, clenching tufts of the rug in his hands. He would literally run across the room, free to move as he liked, jumping on the floor, testing and reveling in its absolute security, letting the relief flood through him, draining the fear from his mind and body. His yearning for this was astonishingly intense, and somehow he understood that he had better keep this feeling at bay.

He took a half-dollar from his pocket and struck it against the pane, but without any hope that the glass would break and with very little disappointment when it did not. After a few moments of thought he drew his leg onto the ledge and picked loose the knot of his shoelace. He slipped off the shoe and, holding it across the instep, drew back his arm as far as he dared and struck the leather heel against the glass. The pane rattled, but he knew he'd been a long way from breaking it. His foot was cold and he slipped the shoe back on. He shouted again, experimentally, and then once more, but there was no answer.

The realization suddenly struck him that he might have to wait here till Clare came home, and for a moment the thought was funny. He could see Clare opening the front door, withdrawing her key from the lock, closing the door behind her, and then glancing up to see him crouched on the other side of the window. He could see her rush across the room, face astounded and frightened, and hear himself shouting instructions: "Never mind how I got here! Just open the wind—" She couldn't open it, he remembered, she'd never been able to; she'd always had to call him. She'd have to get the building superintendent or a neighbor, and he pictured himself smiling, and answering their questions as he climbed in. "I just wanted to get a breath of fresh air, so—"

He couldn't possibly wait here till Clare came home. It was the second feature she'd wanted to see, and she'd left in time to see the first. She'd be another three hours or—He glanced at his watch; Clare had been gone eight minutes. It wasn't possible, but only eight minutes ago he had kissed his wife good-bye. She wasn't even at the theater yet!

SPOTLIGHT ON...
MANAGING TIME

In the story, Tom Benecke chooses to work ahead on an independent project rather than enjoy an evening out with his wife Clare. Based on Clare's resigned response to Tom's decision, it is clear that this is a choice Tom often makes. In any job and in all households, it is necessary to manage time, balancing the needs of work with those of home and family life. To work effectively at your job, school, or home, consider the following:

- Make a chart of everyday tasks.
- Determine the amount of time needed to perform each task.
- Make a list of tasks, short-term projects, physical activities, and family activities you would like to do when you have free time. Post this list in an easily visible place, such as a kitchen bulletin board.
- Use unexpected free time to choose and do one of the projects or activities you've listed

It would be four hours before she could possibly be home, and he tried to picture himself kneeling out here, fingertips hooked to these narrow strippings, while first one movie, preceded by a slow listing of credits, began, developed, reached its climax, and then finally ended. There'd be a newsreel next, maybe, and then an animated cartoon, and then **interminable** scenes from coming pictures. And then, once more, the beginning of a full-length picture—while all the time he hung out here in the night.

He might possibly get to his feet, but he was afraid to try. Already his legs were cramped, his thigh muscles tired; his knees hurt, his feet felt numb, and his hands were stiff. He couldn't possibly stay out here for four hours, or anywhere near it. Long before that his legs and arms would give out; he would be forced to try changing his position often—stiffly, clumsily, his coordination and strength gone—and he would fall. Quite realistically, he knew that he would fall; no one could stay out here on this ledge for four hours.

A dozen windows in the apartment building across the street were lighted. Looking over his shoulder, he could see the top of a man's head behind the newspaper he was reading; in another window he saw the blue-gray flicker of a television screen. No more than twenty-odd yards from his back were scores of people, and if just one of them would walk idly to his window and glance out . . . . For some moments he stared over his shoulder at the lighted rectangles,

interminable—
having or
seeming to have
no end

waiting. But no one appeared. The man reading his paper turned a page and then continued his reading. A figure passed another of the windows and was immediately gone.

In the inside pocket of his jacket he found a little sheaf of papers, and he pulled one out and looked at it in the light from the living room. It was an old letter, an advertisement of some sort; his name and address, in purple ink, were on a label pasted to the envelope. Gripping one end of the envelope in his teeth, he twisted it into a tight curl. From his shirt pocket he brought out a book of matches. He didn't dare let go the casing with both hands but, with the twist of paper in his teeth, he opened the matchbook with his free hand; then he bent one of the matches in two without tearing it from the folder, its red-tipped end now touching the striking surface. With his thumb, he rubbed the red tip across the striking area.

He did it again, then again, and still again, pressing harder each time, and the match suddenly flared, burning his thumb. But he kept it alight, cupping the matchbook in his hand and shielding it with his body. He held the flame to the paper in his mouth till it caught. Then he snuffed out the match flame with his thumb and forefinger, careless of the burn, and replaced the book in his pocket. Taking the paper twist in his hand, he held it flame down, watching the flame crawl up the paper, till it flared bright. Then he held it behind him over the street, moving it from side to side, watching it over his shoulder, the flame flickering and guttering in the wind.

There were three letters in his pocket and he lighted each of them, holding each till the flame touched his hand and then dropping it to the street below. At one point, watching over his shoulder while the last of the letters burned, he saw the man across the street put down his paper and stand—even seeming to glance toward Tom's window. But when he moved, it was only to walk across the room and disappear from sight.

There were a dozen coins in Tom Benecke's pocket and he dropped them, three or four at a time. But if they struck anyone, or if anyone noticed their falling, no one connected them with their source.

His arms had begun to tremble from the steady strain of clinging to this narrow perch, and he did not know what to do now and was terribly frightened. Clinging to the window stripping with one hand, he again searched his pockets. But now—he had left his wallet on the dresser when he'd changed clothes— there was nothing left but the yellow sheet. It occurred to him irrelevantly that his death on the sidewalk below would be an eternal mystery; the window closed—why, how, and from where could he have fallen? No one would be able to identify his body for a time, either—the thought was somehow unbearable and increased his fear. All they'd find in his pockets would be the yellow sheet. *Contents of the dead man's pockets,* he thought, *one sheet of paper bearing penciled notations—incomprehensible.*

He understood fully that he might actually be going to die; his arms, maintaining his balance on the ledge, were trembling steadily now. And it occurred to him then with all the force of a revelation that, if he fell, all he was ever going to have out of life he would then, abruptly, have had. Nothing, then, could ever be changed; and nothing more—no least experience or pleasure—could ever be added to his life. He wished, then, that he had not allowed his wife to go off by herself tonight—and on similar nights. He thought of all the evenings he had spent away from her, working; and he regretted them. He thought wonderingly of his fierce ambition and of the direction his life had taken; he thought of the hours he'd spent by himself, filling the yellow sheet that had brought him out here. *Contents of the dead man's pockets,* he thought with sudden fierce anger, *a wasted life.*

He was simply not going to cling here till he slipped and fell; he told himself that now. There was one last thing he could try; he had been aware of it for some moments, refusing to think about it, but now he faced it. Kneeling here on the ledge, the fingertips of one hand pressed to the narrow strip of wood, he could, he knew, draw his other hand back a yard perhaps, fist clenched tight, doing it very slowly till he sensed the outer limit of balance, then, as hard as he was able from the distance, he could drive his fist forward against the glass. If it broke, his fist smashing through, he was safe; he might cut himself badly, and probably would, but with his arm inside the room, he would be secure. But if the glass did not break, the rebound, flinging his arm

back, would topple him off the ledge. He was certain of that.

He tested his plan. The fingers of his left hand clawlike on the little stripping, he drew back his other fist until his body began teetering backward. But he had no leverage now—he could feel that there would be no force to his swing—and he moved his fist slowly forward till he rocked forward on his knees again and could sense that this swing would carry its greatest force. Glancing down, however, measuring the distance from his fist to the glass, he saw it was less than two feet.

It occurred to him that he could raise his arm over his head, to bring it down against the glass. But, experimenting in slow motion, he knew it would be an awkward blow without the force of a driving punch, and not nearly enough to break the glass.

Facing the window, he had to drive a blow from the shoulder, he knew now, at a distance of less than two feet; and he did not know whether it would break through the heavy glass. It might; he could picture it happening, he could feel it in the nerves of his arm. And it might not; he could feel that too—feel his fist striking this glass and being instantaneously flung back by the unbreaking pane, feel the fingers of his other hand breaking loose, nails scraping along the casing as he fell.

He waited, arm drawn back, fist balled, but in no hurry to strike; this pause, he knew, might be an extension of his life. And to live even a few seconds longer, he

"His death on the sidewalk below would be an eternal mystery."

felt, even out here on this ledge in the night, was infinitely better than to die a moment earlier than he had to. His arm grew tired, and he brought it down.

Then he knew that it was time to make the attempt. He could not kneel here hesitating indefinitely till he lost all courage to act, waiting till he slipped off the ledge. Again he drew back his arm, knowing this time that he would not bring it down till he struck. His elbow protruding over Lexington Avenue far below, the fingers of his other hand pressed down bloodlessly tight against the narrow stripping, he waited, feeling the sick tenseness and terrible excitement building. It grew and swelled toward the moment of action, his nerves tautening. He thought of Clare—just a wordless, yearning thought—and then drew his arm back just a bit more, fist so tight his

ON THE JOB
· · · · · · · · · · · · · · · ·
ADVERTISING ACCOUNT EXECUTIVE
· · · · · · · · · · · · · · · ·

Working for advertising agencies, account executives work closely with a client's advertising manager to create an advertising campaign. When developing a campaign, account executives must know their client's market, needs, and goals and tailor the campaign accordingly. Successful account executives are creative and have excellent speaking, listening, and information-gathering skills. Useful preparation for work in this field includes courses in marketing, advertising, business administration, and graphic design.

fingers pained him, and knowing he was going to do it. Then with full power, with every last scrap of strength he could bring to bear, he shot his arm forward toward the glass, and he said, *"Clare."*

He heard the sound, felt the blow, felt himself falling forward, and his hand closed on the living-room curtains, the shards and fragments of glass showering onto the floor. And then, kneeling there on the ledge, an arm thrust into the room up to the shoulder, he began picking away the protruding slivers and great wedges of glass from the window frame, tossing them in onto the rug. And, as he grasped the edges of the empty window frame and climbed into his home, he was grinning in triumph.

He did not lie down on the floor or run through the apartment, as he had promised himself; even in the first few moments it seemed to him natural and normal that he should be where he was. He simply turned to his desk, pulled the crumpled yellow sheet from his pocket, and laid it down where it had been, smoothing it out; then he absently laid a pencil across it to weight it down. He shook his head wonderingly, and turned to walk toward the closet.

There he got out his topcoat and hat and, without waiting to put them on, opened the front door and stepped out, to go find his wife. He turned to pull the door closed and the warm air from the hall rushed through the narrow opening again. As he saw the yellow paper, the pencil flying, scooped off the desk and, unimpeded by the glassless window, sail out into the night and out of his life, Tom Benecke burst into laughter and then closed the door behind him. ❖

UNDERSTANDING

1. Find passages that indicate Tom's motive for going after the yellow piece of paper. Discuss with several classmates times when you or someone you know took a risk. Perhaps you risked failure, embarrassment, missing a ride, losing something, or being injured.

   In a persuasive essay, explain when risks are justified and when they are not. ***Workshop 13***

2. Tom took stock of himself when he was under pressure. What had been his priorities in life and how did he come to regard them as a result of his frightening experience?

   Now take stock of your own priorities. Where is your life going? List the following headings on a sheet of paper, leaving space between the headings: Experience, Education, Career Interests, Skills. Under each heading, describe yourself. Then write a paragraph summarizing the directions your responses indicate you might take.

3. Jack Finney chooses words carefully to describe Tom's adventure. Find words you think work especially well to express Tom's feelings of terror. Compare your list of words with those of others in the class.

   In a small group, write a short story that portrays terror. Use Finney's words and any others that help you convey this feeling. Your goal is to be absolutely clear. Read your story to the class. ***Workshops 1 and 7***

CONNECTING

1. Many businesses exist that invite customers to take risks. Hang gliding, skydiving, scuba diving, bungee jumping, windsurfing, rock climbing, and whitewater rafting are examples of potentially dangerous activities that are advertised as exciting. Have each member of your group research a different activity-as-business that has a high element of risk. What, exactly, protects participants from the risks of the activity? Can risk be eliminated entirely? Would you recommend this activity? Present the results of this research to parents and classmates.

2. Research newspaper and magazine articles about people who have faced appalling challenges and survived. From these, derive a definition of heroic behavior. Prepare a visual display that identifies heroic traits and presents the experiences of a person in real life who displayed these qualities.

A LAST WORD

Unfortunately, many people need to have a drastic or life-threatening experience before they will make needed changes in their lives. What changes could you make to create a more balanced life for yourself? What changes could your family make to create more time to be together?

Contents of the Dead Man's Pockets

Lather and Nothing Else

EXPLORING

Imagine that after a terrible disagreement with an old friend, the two of you have become bitter enemies. With your group, imagine different situations when you might unexpectedly run into this former friend. How would you behave? For instance, what if the enemy's reserved seat at a concert turns out to be next to yours? Or how would you act if this person did not ask for, but clearly could benefit from, your help?

THEME CONNECTION...
A COURAGEOUS DECISION

From the moment the story opens as the enemy leader, Captain Torres, enters the barbershop, the barber struggles courageously to decide whether to use his razor to shave off Torres's beard or to do him harm. With determination, he squarely faces the question, resolved to make the right choice.

TIME & PLACE

This story takes place in a barbershop in a small South American village. Téllez was a Colombian, so very likely he has in mind a Colombian village. The time is probably the late 1950s, though government troops and rebels clashed in Central America during the 1960s, 1970s, and the 1980s, as well. The setting and time of events are less important in this story than the thoughts that occur in the barber's head. The conflict occurs inside the barber's mind as he considers what to do.

THE WRITER'S CRAFT

THEME

Writers tell stories because they want to convey one main idea—the theme—and usually some incidental ideas, too. To find the main theme in a story, look for repeated phrases, actions, or ideas. This central theme is referred to more than any other idea, and you can usually find direct or indirect references to the theme throughout a story. The title "Lather and Nothing Else" echoes the barber's phrase, for instance, "Just lather, and nothing else." He wants only lather on his hands, not blood.

Lather and Nothing Else

Hernando Téllez

e came in without a word. I was **stropping** my best razor. And when I recognized him, I started to shake. But he did not notice. To cover my nervousness, I went on **honing** the razor. I tried the edge with the tip of my thumb and took another look at it against the light.

Meanwhile he was taking off his cartridge-studded belt with the pistol holster suspended from it. He put it on a hook in the **wardrobe** and hung his cap above it. Then he turned full around toward me and, loosening his tie, remarked, "It's hot as the devil, I want a shave." With that he took his seat.

I estimated he had a four-days' growth of beard, the four days he had been gone on the last **foray** after our men. His face looked burnt, tanned by the sun.

I started to work carefully on the shaving soap. I scraped some slices from the cake, dropped them into the mug, then added a little lukewarm water, and stirred with the brush. The lather soon began to rise.

"The fellows in the troop must have just about as much beard as I." I went on stirring up lather. "But we did very well, you know. We caught the leaders. Some of them we brought back dead; others are still alive. But they'll all be dead soon."

"How many did you take?" I asked.

"Fourteen. We had to go pretty far in to find them. But now they're paying for it. And not one will escape; not a single one."

He leaned back in the chair when he saw the brush in my hand, full of lather. I had not yet put the sheet on him. I was certainly flustered. Taking a sheet from the drawer, I tied it around my customer's neck.

He went on talking. He evidently took it for granted that I was on the side of the existing **regime.**

"The people must have gotten a scare with what happened the other day," he said.

"Yes," I replied, as I finished tying the knot against his nape, which smelt of sweat.

"Good show, wasn't it?"

"Very good," I answered, turning my attention now to the brush. The man closed his eyes wearily and awaited the cool caress of the lather.

I had never had him so close before. The day he ordered the people to file through the schoolyard to look upon the four rebels hanging there, my path had crossed his briefly. But the sight of those mutilated bodies kept me from paying attention to the face of the man who had been directing it all and whom I now had in my hands.

It was not a disagreeable face, certainly. And the beard, which aged him a bit, was not unbecoming. His name was Torres. Captain Torres.

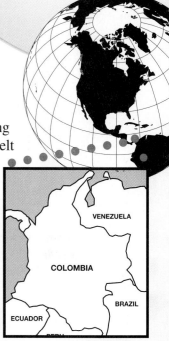

stropping—
sharpening by running back and forth on a thick piece of leather, the strop

honing—
sharpening

wardrobe—a
large piece of
furniture that
served as a
closet or coat
rack

foray—excur-
sion or raid

regime—
government in
power

whorls—circled
clusters of hair

ventured—
dared; took a
risk (by doing
something)

minutely—to a
very small
degree

I started to lay on the first coat of lather. He kept his eyes closed.

"I would love to catch a nap," he said, "but there's a lot to be done this evening."

I lifted the brush and asked, with pretended indifference: "A firing party?"

"Something of the sort," he replied, "but slower."

"All of them?"

"No, just a few."

I went on lathering his face. My hands began to tremble again. The man could not be aware of this, which was lucky for me. But I wished he had not come in. Probably many of our men had seen him enter the shop. And with the enemy in my house I felt a certain responsibility.

I would have to shave his beard just like any other, carefully, neatly, just as though he were a good customer, taking heed that not a single pore should emit a drop of blood. Seeing to it that the blade did not slip in the small **whorls.** Taking care that the skin was left clean, soft, shining, so that when I passed the back of my hand over it not a single hair should be felt. Yes. I was secretly a revolutionary, but at the same time I was a conscientious barber, proud of the way I did my job. And that four-day beard presented a challenge.

I took up the razor, opened the handle wide, releasing the blade, and started to work, downward from one sideburn. The blade responded to perfection. The hair was tough and hard; not very long, but thick. Little by little the skin began to show through. The razor gave its usual sound as it gathered up layers of soap mixed with bits of hair. I paused to wipe it clean, and taking up the strop once

more went about improving its edge, for I am a painstaking barber.

The man, who had kept his eyes closed, now opened them, put a hand out from under the sheet, felt of the part of his face that was emerging from the lather, and said to me, "Come at six o'clock this evening to the school."

"Will it be like the other day?" I asked, stiff with horror.

"It may be even better," he replied.

"What are you planning to do?"

"I'm not sure yet. But we'll have a good time."

Once more he leaned back and shut his eyes. I came closer, the razor on high.

"Are you going to punish all of them?" I timidly **ventured.**

"Yes, all of them."

The lather was drying on his face. I must hurry. Through the mirror, I took a look at the street. It appeared about as usual; there was the grocery shop with two or three customers. Then I glanced at the clock, two-thirty.

The razor kept descending. Now from the other sideburn downward. It was a blue beard, a thick one. He should let it grow like some poets, or some priests. It would suit him well. Many people would not recognize him. And that would be a good thing for him, I thought, as I went gently over all the throat line. At this point you really had to handle your blade skillfully, because the hair, while scantier, tended to fall into small whorls. It was a curly beard. The pores might open, **minutely,** in this area and let out a tiny drop of blood. A good barber like myself stakes his reputation on not permitting that to happen to any of his customers.

FOCUS ON...
HISTORY

Since the early 1800s, conservative and liberal forces have battled back and forth for control of Colombia's central government. Find out about Simón Bolívar, Rafael Nuñez, and Belisario Betancur Cuartas, a few of the leading figures in Colombia's power struggle. What key actions did each of these men take while in power? What effects did their actions have on the state of Colombia's people and government?

◆ ◆ ◆ ◆ ◆ ◆ ◆ ◆ ◆ ◆ ◆ ◆ ◆ ◆ ◆ ◆ ◆ ◆

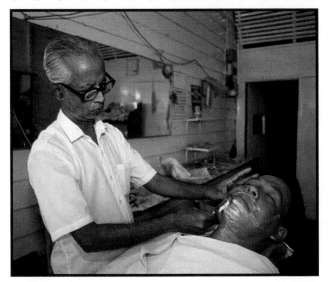

And this was indeed a special customer. How many of ours had he sent to their death? How many had he mutilated? It was best not to think about it. Torres did not know I was his enemy. Neither he nor the others knew it. It was a secret shared by very few, just because that made it possible for me to inform the revolutionaries about Torres's activities in the town and what he planned to do every time he went on one of his raids to hunt down rebels. So it was going to be very difficult to explain how it was that I had him in my hands and then let him go in peace, alive, clean-shaven.

His beard had now almost entirely disappeared. He looked younger, several years younger than when he had come in. I suppose that always happens to men who enter and leave barbershops. Under the strokes of my razor Torres was **rejuvenated;** yes, because I am a good barber, the best in this town, and I say this in all modesty.

A little more lather here under the chin, on the Adam's apple, right near the great vein. How hot it is! Torres must be sweating just as I am. But he is not afraid. He is a **tranquil** man, who is not even giving thought to what he will do to his prisoners this evening. I, on the other hand, polishing his skin with this razor but avoiding the drawing of blood, careful with every stroke—I cannot keep my thoughts in order.

Confound the hour he entered my shop! I am a revolutionary but not a murderer. And it would be so easy to kill him. He deserves it. Or does he? No! No one deserves the sacrifice others make in becoming assassins. What is to be gained by it? Nothing. Others and still others keep coming, and the first kill the second, and then these kill the next, and so on until everything becomes a sea of blood. I could cut his throat, so, swish, swish! He would not even have time to moan, and with his eyes shut he would not even see the shine of the razor or the gleam in my eye.

But I'm shaking like a regular murderer. From his throat a stream of blood

rejuvenated—made young again

tranquil—calm, relaxed

would flow on the sheet, over the chair, down on my hands, onto the floor. I would have to close the door. But the blood would go flowing along the floor, warm, indelible, not to be **staunched,** until it reached the street like a small scarlet river.

I'm sure that with a good strong blow, a deep cut, he would feel no pain. He would not suffer at all. And what would I do then with the body? Where would I hide it? I would have to flee, leave all this behind, take shelter far away, very far away. But they would follow until they caught up with me. "The murderer of Captain Torres. He slit his throat while he was shaving him. What a cowardly thing to do!"

And others would say, "The avenger of our people. A name to remember." ———— my name here. "He was the town barber. No one knew he was fighting for our cause."

And so, which will it be? Murderer or hero? My fate hangs on the edge of this razor blade.

I can turn my wrist slightly, put a bit more pressure on the blade, let it sink in. The skin will yield like silk, like rubber, like the strop. There is nothing more tender than a man's skin, and the blood is always there, ready to burst forth. A razor like this cannot fail. It is the best one I have.

But I don't want to be a murderer. No, sir. You came in to be shaved. And I do my work honorably. I don't want to stain my hands with blood. Just with lather, and nothing else. You are an executioner; I am only a barber. Each one to his job. That's it. Each one to his job.

The chin was now clean, polished, soft. The man got up and looked at himself in the glass. He ran his hand over the skin and felt its freshness, its newness.

"Thanks," he said. He walked to the wardrobe for his belt, his pistol, and his cap. I must have been very pale, and I felt my shirt soaked with sweat. Torres finished adjusting his belt buckle, straightened his gun in its holster, and smoothing his hair mechanically, put on his cap. From his trousers pocket he took some coins to pay for the shave. And he started toward the door. On the threshold he stopped for a moment, and turning toward me, he said:

"They told me you would kill me. I came to find out if it was true. But it's not easy to kill. I know what I'm talking about." ❖

ON THE JOB
COSMETOLOGIST

Cosmetologists—also called beauty operators, hairdressers, beauticians, or stylists—care for people's hair, skin, and nails. Most cosmetologists work in beauty salons. The most successful have a loyal following of clients. Helpful high school courses include health, psychology, and marketing. All states require cosmetologists to be graduates of an approved cosmetology school and to be licensed.

UNDERSTANDING

1. Create a three-column table with the headings "For Killing Captain Torres," "Against Killing Captain Torres," and "My Opinion." Locate in the story the barber's reasons for and against killing Captain Torres. In the third column, explain why you agree or disagree with each reason.

   Write an essay describing an important decision you once had to make. Explain why the decision was hard, what factors you had to consider, and why you chose as you did. ***Workshop 8***

2. Captain Torres says to the barber, "They told me you would kill me." What effect does his remark have on your interpretation of the barber's thoughts? With a partner, identify the barber's thoughts that seem less reliable once you have heard Captain Torres's parting comment. What do you think the barber would have done had he realized from the start that Captain Torres viewed him as a rebel? With your partner, write and act out a dramatic scene between the barber and Captain Torres illustrating your idea of what might have happened. ***Workshop 4***

3. Analyze the words the barber actually says to Captain Torres. Does he speak often? What does he say?

   Almost all employees must be good listeners. In a memo of complaint addressed to a supervisor, describe the behavior of a worker who did not listen well when you were his or her customer. ***Workshop 19***

CONNECTING

1. The barber mistakenly assumed that only very few people knew he was a revolutionary. In groups, discuss times when you thought you knew what was going on, only to find you were mistaken. Recall the reasons that hid the true situation.

   With your group, identify and research obstacles to clear communication at home, at school, and in the workplace. Create a series of posters that illustrate these obstacles.

2. The barber takes great pride in his work. He sets high standards for himself. He says, for example, "I am a painstaking barber . . . . A good barber like myself stakes his reputation on not permitting" even a drop of blood to be drawn by the razor. With a partner, interview students and adults to find out what performance standards they set for themselves at school or work. Create a chart to present your discoveries. ***Workshop 24***

A LAST WORD

Is violence or the threat of violence ever a viable solution to a problem? Would you consider the barber a cowardly or courageous man? Why?

The Scholarship Jacket

EXPLORING

How important is a promise? If you are promised a diploma when you earn enough credits, or a raise after six months if you do good work at a job, shouldn't you get them? And yet sometimes circumstances change. If a company's business drops off, can management still provide the promised raise? Sadly, many promises are no longer considered sacred. Marriages break up, bills aren't paid, deadlines aren't kept. Should people refrain from making promises so they don't have to break them later? Or should they only promise what they believe they can deliver? Describe a time when you were involved in a broken promise.

THEME CONNECTION...
PROMISES TAKE DETERMINATION

Promises and determination go hand in hand. Promise keepers use determination to keep their word. Whether it's a promise to yourself or a promise to others, the level of your determination will make it or break it.

TIME & PLACE

The story takes place in a small town in Texas, perhaps not far from the Mexican border. The narrator's father, a farm laborer, and her grandfather, also a farmer, just manage to make ends meet. Farm laborers or migrant workers of Mexican origin are common in Texas and other southwestern and western states where seasonal crops require temporary workers. This story probably takes place in the 1960s. Discrimination against migrant workers, however, still exists today.

THE WRITER'S CRAFT
SIMPLE VOCABULARY

Sometimes the most powerful stories are delivered in the simplest language. Many people mistakenly believe that the more difficult the vocabulary, the better the story. The best communicators do not necessarily choose the biggest words. Salinas's story is told in simple direct language.

The Scholarship Jacket

Marta Salinas

The small Texas school that I attended carried out a tradition every year during the eighth grade graduation; a beautiful gold and green jacket, the school colors, was awarded to the class valedictorian, the student who had maintained the highest grades for eight years. The scholarship jacket had a big gold S on the left front side and the winner's name was written in gold letters on the pocket.

My oldest sister Rosie had won the jacket a few years back and I fully expected to win also. I was fourteen and in the eighth grade. I had been a straight A student since the first grade, and the last year I had looked forward to owning that jacket. My father was a farm laborer who couldn't earn enough money to feed eight children, so when I was six I was given to my grandparents to raise. We couldn't participate in sports at school because there were registration fees, uniform costs, and trips out of town; so even though we were quite agile and athletic, there would never be a sports school jacket for us. This one, the scholarship jacket, was our only chance.

In May, close to graduation, spring fever struck, and no one paid any attention in class; instead we stared out the windows and at each other, wanting to speed up the last few weeks of school. I despaired every time I looked in the mirror. Pencil thin, not a curve anywhere, I was called "Beanpole" and "String Bean" and I knew that's what I looked like. A flat chest, no hips, and a brain, that's what I had. That really isn't much for a fourteen-year-old to work with, I thought, as I absentmindedly wandered from my history class to the gym. Another hour of sweating in basketball and displaying my toothpick legs was coming up. Then I remembered my P.E. shorts were still in a bag under my desk where I'd forgotten them. I had to walk all the way back and get them. Coach Thompson was a real bear if anyone wasn't dressed for P.E. She had said I was a good forward and once she even tried to talk Grandma into letting me join the team. Grandma, of course, said no.

I was almost back at my classroom's door when I heard angry voices and arguing. I stopped. I didn't mean to eavesdrop; I just hesitated, not knowing what to do. I needed those shorts and I was going to be late, but I didn't want to interrupt an argument between my teachers. I recognized the voices: Mr. Schmidt, my history teacher, and Mr. Boone, my math teacher. They seemed to be arguing about me. I couldn't believe it. I still remember the shock that rooted me flat against the wall as if I were trying to blend in with the graffiti written there.

"I refuse to do it! I don't care who her father is, her grades don't even begin to compare to Martha's. I won't lie or

About the Author

Marta Salinas is the author of numerous short stories, some of which have been published in the *Los Angeles Herald Examiner* and in *California Living* magazine. Her short story "The Scholarship Jacket" first appeared in *Cuentos Chicanos: A Short Story Anthology*.

falsify records. Martha has a straight A plus average and you know it." That was Mr. Schmidt and he sounded very angry. Mr. Boone's voice sounded calm and quiet.

"Look, Joann's father is not only on the Board, he owns the only store in town; we could say it was a close tie and—"

The pounding in my ears drowned out the rest of the words, only a word here and there filtered through. ". . . Martha is Mexican . . . resign . . . won't do it . . ." Mr. Schmidt came rushing out, and luckily for me went down the opposite way toward the auditorium, so he didn't see me. Shaking, I waited a few minutes and then went in and grabbed my bag and fled from the room. Mr. Boone looked up when I came in but didn't say anything. To this day I don't remember if I got in trouble in P.E. for being late or how I made it through the rest of the afternoon. I went home very sad and cried into my pillow that night so Grandmother wouldn't hear me. It seemed a cruel coincidence that I had overheard that conversation.

The next day when the principal called me into his office, I knew what it would be about. He looked uncomfortable and unhappy. I decided I wasn't going to make it any easier for him so I looked him straight in the eye. He looked away and fidgeted with the papers on his desk.

"Martha," he said, "there's been a change in policy this year regarding the scholarship jacket. As you know, it has always been free." He cleared his throat and continued. "This year the Board

decided to charge fifteen dollars—which still won't cover the complete cost of the jacket."

I stared at him in shock and a small sound of dismay escaped my throat. I hadn't expected this. He still avoided looking in my eyes.

"So if you are unable to pay the fifteen dollars for the jacket, it will be given to the next one in line."

Standing with all the dignity I could muster, I said, "I'll speak to my grandfather about it, sir, and let you know tomorrow." I cried on the walk home from the bus stop. The dirt road was a quarter of a mile from the highway, so by the time I got home, my eyes were red and puffy.

"Where's Grandpa?" I asked Grandma, looking down at the floor so she wouldn't ask me why I'd been crying. She was sewing on a quilt and didn't look up.

"I think he's out back working in the bean field."

I went outside and looked out at the fields. There he was. I could see him walking between the rows, his body bent over the little plants, hoe in hand. I walked slowly out to him, trying to think how I could best ask him for the money. There was a cool breeze blowing and a sweet smell of mesquite in the air, but I didn't appreciate it. I kicked at a dirt clod. I wanted that jacket so much. It was more than just being a valedictorian and giving a little thank-you speech for the jacket on graduation night. It represented eight years of hard work and expectation. I knew I had to be honest

● ● ● ● ● ● ●
"It represented eight years of hard work and expectation."
● ● ● ● ● ● ●

SPOTLIGHT ON...
MAKING
INFERENCES

In "The Scholarship Jacket," the author does not tell the reader exactly why there is a "change in policy" regarding the scholarship jacket. Rather, she lets the reader infer, or conclude, the cause behind the policy change based on context clues, such as the overheard argument, and supporting details, such as the fact that Joann's father is on the school board. You can infer meaning by using the following context clues:
1. Definition or restatement
2. Comparison/contrast
3. Example
4. Cause and effect
5. Supporting details
6. Sentence structure

with Grandpa; it was my only chance. He saw me and looked up.

He waited for me to speak. I cleared my throat nervously and clasped my hands behind my back so he wouldn't see them shaking. "Grandpa, I have a big favor to ask you," I said in Spanish, the only language he knew. He still waited silently. I tried again. "Grandpa, this year the principal said the scholarship jacket is not going to be free. It's going to cost fifteen dollars and I have to take the money in tomorrow, otherwise it'll be given to someone else." The last words came out in an eager rush. Grandpa straightened up tiredly and leaned his chin on the hoe handle. He looked out over the field that was filled with the tiny green bean plants. I waited, desperately hoping he'd say I could have the money.

He turned to me and asked quietly, "What does a scholarship jacket mean?"

I answered quickly; maybe there was a chance. "It means you've earned it by having the highest grades for eight years and that's why they're giving it to you." Too late I realized the significance of my words. Grandpa knew that I understood it was not a matter of money. It wasn't that. He went back to hoeing the weeds that sprang up between the delicate little bean plants. It was a time-consuming job; sometimes the small shoots were right next to each other. Finally he spoke again.

"Then if you pay for it, Marta, it's not a scholarship jacket, is it? Tell your principal I will not pay the fifteen dollars."

I walked back to the house and locked myself in the bathroom for a long time. I was angry with Grandfather even though I knew he was right, and I was angry with the Board, whoever they were. Why

The Scholarship Jacket

349

did they have to change the rules just when it was my turn to win the jacket?

It was a very sad and withdrawn girl who dragged into the principal's office the next day. This time he did look me in the eyes.

"What did your grandfather say?"

I sat very straight in my chair.

"He said to tell you he won't pay the fifteen dollars."

The principal muttered something I couldn't understand under his breath, and walked over to the window. He stood looking out at something outside. He looked bigger than usual when he stood up; he was a tall gaunt man with gray hair, and I watched the back of his head while I waited for him to speak.

"Why?" he finally asked. "Your grandfather has the money. Doesn't he own a small bean farm?"

I looked at him, forcing my eyes to stay dry. "He said if I had to pay for it, then it wouldn't be a scholarship jacket," I said and stood up to leave. "I guess you'll just have to give it to Joann." I hadn't meant to say that; it had just slipped out. I was almost to the door when he stopped me.

"Martha—wait."

I turned and looked at him, waiting. What did he want now? I could feel my heart pounding. Something bitter and vile tasting was coming up in my mouth; I was afraid I was going to be sick. I didn't need any sympathy speeches. He sighed loudly and went back to his big desk. He looked at me, biting his lip, as if thinking.

"Okay. We'll make an exception in your case. I'll tell the Board, you'll get your jacket."

I could hardly believe it. I spoke in a trembling rush. "Oh, thank you, sir!"

Suddenly I felt great. I didn't know about adrenaline in those days, but I knew something was pumping through me, making me feel as tall as the sky. I wanted to yell, jump, run the mile, do something. I ran out so I could cry in the hall where there was no one to see me. At the end of the day, Mr. Schmidt winked at me and said, "I hear you're getting a scholarship jacket this year."

His face looked as happy and innocent as a baby's, but I knew better. Without answering I gave him a quick hug and ran to the bus. I cried on the walk home again, but this time because I was so happy. I couldn't wait to tell Grandpa and ran straight to the field. I joined him in the row where he was working and without saying anything I crouched down and started pulling up the weeds with my hands. Grandpa worked alongside me for a few minutes, but he didn't ask what had happened. After I had a little pile of weeds between the rows, I stood up and faced him.

"The principal said he's making an exception for me, Grandpa, and I'm getting the jacket after all. That's after I told him what you said."

Grandpa didn't say anything, he just gave me a pat on the shoulder and a smile. He pulled out the crumpled red handkerchief that he always carried in his back pocket and wiped the sweat off his forehead.

"Better go see if your grandmother needs any help with supper."

I gave him a big grin. He didn't fool me. I skipped and ran back to the house whistling some silly tune. ❖

UNDERSTANDING

1. Why was the principal thinking about breaking the promise to Marta after her eight years of hard work?

   Assume you are Mr. Schmidt, angered by the principal's decision to make Marta pay for her jacket. You are submitting your letter of resignation. Write this letter, clearly stating your reasons for leaving. *Workshop 18*

2. Marta's grandfather was interested in the principle of the matter. What did he mean when he said, "Then if you pay for it, Marta, it's not a scholarship jacket"?

   By refusing to pay for the jacket, Marta's grandfather was living up to his principles. What is a principle? What are yours? Write down at least three principles you believe in and are willing to live up to. Discuss them in a small group. Post them where they can serve as a daily reminder. *Workshop 6*

3. What clues in the story might lead the reader to believe that discrimination was involved in the principal's decision?

   It is against the law to discriminate against a student because of his or her race. Discuss with your group how your school guards against racial discrimination. Write a persuasive essay intended to eliminate racism in your school. *Workshop 13*

CONNECTING

1. Eighth grade graduation is no longer a big event in many communities, mainly because of the rise of middle schools and junior highs. Working with a group, interview school administrators and faculty for their views on the best way to organize schools for students in K–9th grade. Write the result of your interviews in an article for the school paper. *Workshop 17*

2. Studies show that people will work harder when they are promised a reward. Recognition also is a highly regarded method of motivation. Working in a group, think of some way to reward a student in your school for an outstanding achievement: community service, school spirit, dedication to a project or cause. Establish criteria for awarding this honor, which may be no more than a certificate and recognition in the local media. Publicize your intent and encourage nominations from the student body. Finalize your plan, get approval from your school administrator, who should sign your certificate to make it official, and make your selection.

Pride

EXPLORING

Constant exposure to the elements of nature can wear down even rocks, concrete, and steel. Seemingly tough, unaffected, and resilient, in time they begin to show wear. Sometimes they break open in ugly holes. Are people the same way? Does everyone and everything have a limit—a "breaking point"?

THEME CONNECTION... COURAGE UNDER PRESSURE

To undergo strong pressure and keep from breaking takes courage and determination. To hold oneself together when everything else is falling apart is an act of extreme determination. The poet expresses her belief that even the proudest or strongest have a breaking point.

TIME & PLACE

Israel, the country where this poem was written, has mild, moist winters and hot, dry summers. Israel lies on the east end of the Mediterranean Sea, perhaps the area the poet describes. With a population made up of Jewish people from all over the world and a large number of Arabs, this country has been in continuous conflict with its Arab neighbors.

THE WRITER'S CRAFT
ONOMATOPOEIA

Using words whose sounds seem to express or reinforce their meanings is called *onomatopoeia.* For example, *splash, boom, whistle,* and *gurgle* sound like the noises they name. Some examples of onomatopoeia in the poem "Pride" include "crack" and "whips."

Pride

Dahlia Ravikovitch

I tell you, even rocks crack,
and not because of age.
For years they lie on their backs
in the heat and the cold,
so many years,
it almost seems peaceful.
They don't move, so the cracks stay hidden.
A kind of pride.
Years pass over them, waiting there.
Whoever is going to shatter them
hasn't come yet.
And so the moss flourishes, the seaweed
whips around,
the sea pushes through and rolls back—
the rocks seem motionless.
Till a little seal comes to rub against them,
comes and goes away.
And suddenly the rock has an open wound.
I told you, when rocks break, it happens by surprise.
And people, too. ❖

About the Author

Dahlia Ravikovitch (b. 1936) is Israel's leading woman poet. Born in Israel, she used to teach high school there as well. She writes short stories and poems and has two books published in English: *Dress of Fire* (1976) and *The Window: New and Selected Poems* (1989).

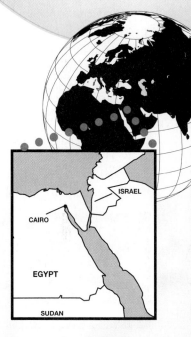

UNDERSTANDING

1. This poem does not rhyme, yet when read aloud it has a pleasing rhythm unaccentuated by rhyme. What elements of the poem make it sound pleasing when read aloud?

   Onomatopoeia is fun to work with. Brainstorm in a group words that sound like their meanings. Write a poem using some of these words. Share it with your group. *Workshop 2*

2. The writer hints in several places that she will attach this idea to human beings. What words and phrases give clues that lead up to the final line of the poem?

   Write a description of any object or person but don't give its name until the last line. Use figurative language (simile, metaphor, and personification) to convey ideas. Read your paper to the class or a small group. Can they guess the object or person before the last line? *Workshop 10*

3. The word *pride* has both negative and positive connotations. Which way is it used in the poem, as a positive quality or a negative one?

   Write a definition paper on the word *pride*. Provide the dictionary definition and then expand on it, explaining how the word is used and understood. *Workshop 8*

4. The poet says rocks break open suddenly, "by surprise." Do you agree with her about people? Do people break open suddenly, "by surprise"?

   Think back to moments when you have snapped in anger or frustration. Was it sudden and surprising, or did you feel it coming on? Write a personal essay or journal entry explaining the situation.

A LAST WORD

Why do some people use pride as a way to protect themselves? From what are they protecting themselves? What does such determination keep them from experiencing?

CONNECTING

1. Invite a psychiatrist or psychologist to speak to the class on how and why people break down. Is it sudden or predictable? How do professionals help people like this? *Workshops 18 and 24*

2. Many books provide strategies for living a happy, peaceful life without breakdowns or crack-ups. A life free of such things is possible. As a group, read as many "self-help" books as you can within a week's time, noting specific recommendations authors make for being physically and mentally healthy. Compare your notes with those of other groups. Develop a new list of recommendations based on everyone's input. Distribute the list to friends and family or get permission to post it in the library or in public places in your community.

Universal Soldier

EXPLORING

Nearly every generation of Americans has had to fight and/or support a war. What causes war? Who initiates it, maintains it, declares victory or accepts defeat? No one would admit to loving war, yet why does it persist? Is war a necessary evil or can it be avoided? Is it necessary for the country to maintain a strong army and sophisticated weapons, or might the money be spent better elsewhere?

THEME CONNECTION...
COURAGE AND WAR

Men and women receive awards for courage exhibited during war—the Medal of Honor, the Distinguished Service Cross. It also takes courage to refuse war, to stand up and announce that you don't believe in it and walk away. No awards exist for that action. The lyrics of "Universal Soldier" describe the poet's view on how to maintain peace and end war.

TIME & PLACE

In 1963 when this song was written, United States troops were not actively involved in the civil war in Vietnam, but our government had sent 6,000 military advisers in 1961 and 1962 and $400 million in military aid. There was great controversy as to whether the United States should send troops as well as advisers. In 1964, President Lyndon Johnson ordered air raids in Vietnam in retaliation for attacks on American military ships. From that time on, U.S. involvement increased. By 1965, more than 50,000 American troops were stationed in Vietnam; by early 1968, there were more than 500,000. More than 58,000 American soldiers lost their lives in Vietnam, and more than 153,000 were wounded.

THE WRITER'S CRAFT
PROTEST POETRY

Because poetry has amazing power to touch our souls, it is often used to present a cause. Almost every movement has had its songs and poems to propel it. This one belongs to the 1960s, a period in United States history noted for protest.

Universal Soldier

Buffy Sainte-Marie

He's five foot two and he's six feet four,
   he fights with missiles and with spears,
He's all of thirty-one and he's only seventeen,
   he's been a soldier for a thousand years.

He's a Catholic, a Hindu, an Atheist, a **Jain,**
   a Buddhist and a Baptist and a Jew,
  And he knows he shouldn't kill and he knows he always will
     kill you for me, my friend, and me for you;

And he's fighting for Canada, he's fighting for France,
    he's fighting for the U.S.A.,
  And he's fighting for the Russians and he's fighting for Japan,
   and he thinks we'll put an end to war that way.

And he's fighting for democracy, he's fighting for the Reds,
   he says it's for the peace of all,
He's the one who must decide who's to live and who's to die,
   and he never sees the writing on the wall.

But without him how would Hitler have condemned them at Dachau,
   without him Caesar would have stood alone.
He's the one who gives his body as a weapon of the war,
   and without him all this killing can't go on.

He's the Universal Soldier and he really is to blame,
   his orders come from far away no more,
They come from him and you and me, and, brothers can't you see,
   This is not the way we put an end to war. ❖

About the Author

Buffy Sainte-Marie (b. 1941) was born in Canada but grew up in New England. She is both a composer and vocal performer. Her best-known song is the one presented here, "Universal Soldier." In 1963 when this song was published, she was ill and recovering from drug abuse. The song was made a hit by Donovan, and for a long time many people thought that he had written it. Glen Campbell and the Highwaymen also recorded versions that were popular.

Jain—a follower of Jainism, a religion of India dating from the sixth century B.C.

UNDERSTANDING

1. Who is the Universal Soldier? What purpose does the author accomplish by making the soldier universal?

   The object or idea to which the term *universal* is applied is relevant any time, any place. In groups, brainstorm as many universal things or ideas as you can. Discuss the list, discarding those items that do not fit the definition.

2. Sainte-Marie blames the Universal Soldier for war. In fact, what would happen if all soldiers simply resigned? Would all wars stop?

   A strike, a group refusal to work, is often very effective in bringing about change. Research a significant strike that occurred in the United States. What were the causes and the results? Write a documented report on this topic.
   Workshop 21

3. This poem was written as a song and has a definite rhythm. How has the poet created this rhythm?

   These song lyrics make an excellent poem. Take the words to your favorite song and write them as a poem. Are they effective standing alone without the music? Share the words of your song and your opinion in a small group.
   Workshop 2

A LAST WORD

Human beings have been at war with one another since early civilization. Must we accept that there will always be war? What will it take to bring an end to war forever?

CONNECTING

1. History is filled with wars. As John Lennon said in his song "Imagine," imagine the world without war, "with nothing to live or die for." Is such a thing possible? Working with a group, conduct a survey of at least 20 people, as many different types of people as possible. Ask, "Is world peace possible?" and record both the answer and the reason for the answer. Your survey sheet might have three columns: Yes, No, and Reason. Allow plenty of room for the reason. Write and circulate a summary of your survey. *Workshop 16*

2. The United States now has a volunteer military, which means no one is forced to join. How then is the military able to maintain itself? Why do people join the military? Talk to recruiters for the army, navy, air force, and marines. What benefits do they offer that make the armed forces attractive to recruits? Prepare an oral presentation to report your findings. *Workshops 23 and 24*

WRAP IT UP

UNIT 7

1. A number of the selections in this unit explore the topics of personal conscience and political power: the excerpt from *Julius Caesar;* the short stories "Lather and Nothing Else" and "The Scholarship Jacket," and the song lyrics "Universal Soldier." Compare and contrast each selection's point of view on these topics.

2. "John Henry" and "Strange Legacies" celebrate the courage and determination of ordinary people who face enormous odds or overwhelming pressures. What makes each character, from John Henry to the "nameless old couple," a legend?

What qualities do they exhibit that are heroic? What makes their drive to survive so extraordinary? Why do you think people hand down from generation to generation stories or legends about the accomplishments and struggles of others? Use details from the selections to support your opinions.

WORKSHOPS

WORKSHOP 1
Elements of Fiction

WHAT IS FICTION?

Fiction is writing about imagined, or made up, characters and events. Some events or characters described in a work of fiction may be based on real-life experiences, but the story itself comes from the imagination of the writer. A writer's main purpose in writing fiction is to entertain while exploring events, themes, and human behavior.

POINTERS: FICTION WRITING

Two major types of fiction are novels and short stories. Although a novel is a long, complex work of fiction and a short story a brief work of fiction, they have in common certain elements.

1. **Character** A *character* is a person in a novel or short story. The character's actions, words, and thoughts reveal his or her qualities. The most important characters are the *protagonist* and the *antagonist*. The protagonist is the central figure, and the antagonist opposes the protagonist.

2. **Setting** The *setting* is the time and place the story happens. The setting consists of such things as the writer's descriptions of landscape, buildings, weather, and seasons.

3. **Mood** Mood refers to the emotion a story creates in the reader. A story's mood may convey, for instance, joy, sorrow, or anxiety. Writers use careful word choice to create mood.

4. **Conflict** Every story has a *conflict* around which events revolve. In a conflict, things struggle against each other. Usually, the main character is involved in the conflict, struggling against another character, nature, society, or himself or herself in order to reach a specific goal or desire.

5. **Plot** A *plot* is the series of events that occur in a story. Usually, a plot is made up of several parts. A story's *exposition* is the opening, which provides background information. The *inciting incident* introduces conflict. During the *rising action* of a story, a series of events happens in which the characters' actions and feelings intensify as problems become more complicated. The *climax* is the point of highest suspense or intensity. A story's *falling action* follows the climax and describes the results of the earlier events. The *resolution,* or ending of the story, occurs when the conflict is resolved. After the resolution, the writer may still need to tie up loose ends of the story. This final part of the plot is called the *dénouement.* The diagram below is often used to show the elements of plot.

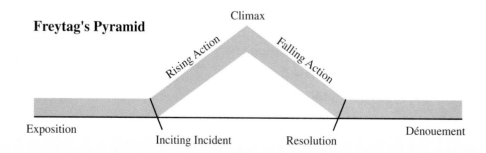

6. **Theme** The *theme* is a story's main idea.

Fiction Writing Sample

The following fiction excerpt is taken from the beginning of the short story "By Any Other Name," written by Santha Rama Rau.

The story's setting is established.

The opening, or exposition, of the story provides important background information.

At the Anglo-Indian day school in Zorinabad to which my sister and I were sent when she was eight and I was five and a half, they changed our names. On the first day of school, a hot, windless morning of a north Indian September, we stood in the headmistress's study and she said, "Now you're the *new* girls. What are your names?"

My sister answered for us. "I am Premila, and she"—nodding in my direction—"is Santha."

The narrator, one of the main characters in this story, is introduced.

The introduction of the conflict makes the reader want to know what will happen next.

The headmistress had been in India, I suppose, fifteen years or so, but she still smiled her helpless inability to cope with Indian names. Her rimless half-glasses glittered, and the precarious bun on the top of her head trembled as she shook her head. "Oh, my dears, those are much too hard for me. Suppose we give you pretty English names. Wouldn't that be more jolly? Let's see, now—Pamela for you, I think." She shrugged in a baffled way at my sister. "That's as close as I can get. And for *you*," she said to me, "how about Cynthia? Isn't that nice?"

My sister was always less easily intimidated than I was, and while she kept a stubborn silence, I said, "Thank you," in a very tiny voice.

PRACTICE

Use one of the following assignments to help you practice your fiction writing skills:

1. Write a character sketch describing a main character you would like to include in a story. In the sketch, give background information about the character.

2. Use Freytag's Pyramid to outline the plot of a short story you would like to write. For each of the plot elements in the pyramid, write a paragraph describing what will happen in your story.

3. Write a short story based on a conflict you experienced in your childhood. Use the traditional elements of plot illustrated in Freytag's Pyramid in your story.

WORKSHOP 2
Elements of Poetry

WHAT IS POETRY?

How would you describe or define poetry? What effect does poetry have on you when you read it? The poet Samuel Taylor Coleridge said, "prose = words in their best order; poetry = the best words in their best order." Poets use words with great control, arranging them to express emotions, experiences, and ideas. Poems capture the essence of an event or character.

POINTERS: WRITING POETRY

Poets use imagery, lines, stanzas, rhyme, rhythm, and sounds of letters to communicate images, emotions, ideas, sounds, and even stories. Read poetry aloud to hear its sounds.

1. **Imagery** An *image* is a word or phrase that describes how something looks, sounds, feels, tastes, or smells. A group of these sensory images is called *imagery.*

2. **Figurative language** refers to special combinations of words that poets use to make images. Similes, metaphors, personification, and hyperbole are examples of figurative language.

3. **Stanzas** Poems are often written in lines that are grouped together according to rules in stanzas. Poets don't always use stanzas, however. Sometimes they use *free verse,* when lines follow no stanza rules or patterns.

4. **Rhyme** The repetition of sounds at the ends of words, such as "moon" and "balloon," is called *rhyme.* Rhyming words that appear within lines of poetry are called *internal rhyme.*

5. **Rhythm** *Rhythm* is the beat of poetry created by combinations of stressed and unstressed syllables. The rhythmical pattern of a poem is called its *meter.* Poetry that is not written in a regular rhythmical pattern is known as *free verse.*

6. **Sound** The sound of a word is important in poetry. Sounds of words create feeling and music in a poem. *Alliteration* is the repetition of consonant sounds at the beginnings of words. *Assonance* is the repetition of vowel sounds within words. *Consonance* is the repetition of consonants at the ends of words. *Onomatopoeia* is the use of words that sound like the things to which they refer, such as "pop" and "creak."

7. **Speaker** The *speaker* of a poem is the character who speaks, but the speaker and the poet are not necessarily the same person. The speaker may be a person living in another time or place, an object, or an animal or insect. The speaker brings his or her viewpoint to the poem and the ideas expressed in it.

8. **Theme** The *theme* of a poem is its central, or main, idea. Through theme, the author presents a point of view or focuses on a particular idea.

Poetry Sample

Look at the use of rhyme and rhythm in this excerpt from "If I were loved, as I desire to be," written by Alfred, Lord Tennyson.

Rhymed end words *be* and *thee* and *earth* and *birth*

Pattern of accented and unaccented syllables to create a steady, regular rhythm

Speaker expresses feelings of desire.

> If I were loved, as I desire to be
> What is there in the great sphere of the earth,
> And range of evil between death and birth,
> That I should fear,—if I were loved by thee?

Poetry Sample

In the first two stanzas from William Stafford's poem "Fifteen," the poet uses stanza form, free verse rhythm, repetition, and figurative language to tell a story.

Lines of the poem are grouped into stanzas.

Free verse recreates the patterns of everyday speech.

Imagery helps readers see the motorcycle as the narrator saw it.

The phrase *I was fifteen* is repeated to emphasize the importance of the moment.

> South of the Bridge on Seventeenth
> I found back of the willows one summer
> day a motorcycle with engine running
> as it lay on its side, ticking over
> slowly in the high grass. I was fifteen.
>
> I admired all that pulsing gleam, the
> shiny flanks, the demure headlights
> fringed where it lay; I led it gently
> to the road and stood with that
> companion, ready and friendly. I was fifteen.

PRACTICE

Here are some ways you can practice using different elements of poetry in your poetry writing:

1. Write a poem telling about an important moment in the life of the narrator. In your poem, use the following elements: stanza form, free verse, imagery, and figurative language.

2. Write a poem that reveals the narrator's feelings about a topic such as love. In your poem, use any three or more elements of poetry. Identify the elements used and explain in a brief paragraph why you chose them.

3. Write a poem titled "Fifteen." Use at least three different elements of poetry. In a brief paragraph explain why you chose these elements when writing your poem.

WORKSHOP 3

Elements of Nonfiction

WHAT IS NONFICTION?

Nonfiction is a type of writing that presents facts, ideas, or opinions about real people, actual places, and true events. Autobiographies, biographies, essays, and articles are four of the types of nonfiction.

POINTERS: NONFICTION WRITING

Keep the following pointers in mind when writing nonfiction:

1. **Know your purpose.** Decide whether you are writing to inform, to express an opinion, to persuade, or to entertain. You may have more than one purpose in mind.

2. **Know your audience.** What do your readers already know about the topic? What information do you need to explain? Will they be receptive to your topic? Tailor your writing to their experience.

3. **Begin with a clear thesis statement.** This statement identifies the topic, your main idea, and your viewpoint on the topic. Your choice of words will reveal your *tone,* or attitude, toward the subject.

4. **Choose a method of organization.** Your purpose(s) for writing will help you decide how to organize your work such as chronologically or around main ideas.

5. **Use transitional words and phrases to clarify the order and relationship of ideas, events, and details.** Examples of transitional words and phrases are *first, mainly, as a result,* and *for example.*

6. **Conclude your nonfiction work with a summary of the main points, events, or ideas.** Explain the connection between the summary of main points or ideas and your beginning thesis statement.

Nonfiction Writing Sample

The following excerpt is taken from Maya Angelou's autobiographical account "Getting a Job," which appears in her autobiography *I Know Why the Caged Bird Sings.*

Thesis statement introduces the main idea, purpose, and tone.	Once I had settled on getting a job, all that remained was to decide which kind of job I was most fitted for. My intellectual pride had kept me from selecting typing, shorthand, or filing as subjects in school, so office work was ruled out. War plants and shipyards demanded birth certificates, and mine would reveal me to be fifteen, and ineligible for work. So the well-paying defense jobs were also out. Women had replaced men on the streetcars as conductors and motormen, and the thought of sailing up and down the hills of San Francisco in a dark-blue uniform, with a money changer at my belt, caught my fancy.
First-person point of view	
Chronological method of organization	

PRACTICE

Complete one of the following assignments to practice your nonfiction writing skills:

1. Write a brief autobiographical account describing your first job.

2. Write an essay on a subject about which you have strong feelings. In your essay, persuade your audience to take specific action.

WORKSHOP 4

Elements of Drama

WHAT IS DRAMA?

A *drama* is a play, a story performed by actors in front of an audience. Drama can take many forms, including theater plays, radio plays, television programs, and movies.

POINTERS: UNDERSTANDING DRAMA

All forms of drama have certain elements in common.

1. **Playwright** The *playwright* is the author of the play.

2. **Script** A *script* is the written form of the play, created from the imagination of the playwright.

3. **Stage directions** *Stage directions* describe how something in the play should look, sound, or be performed. They may also describe elements related to the acting of the play, such as entrances and exits, tone of voice, or gestures and movements.

4. **Cast** The *cast* is the list of characters appearing in the play usually listed in order of appearance.

5. **Dialogue** *Dialogue* is the speech recited by the actors in a play. Dialogue reveals the character's personalities and moves the story or plot forward.

6. **Act and Scene** An *act* is a major section of a play. A *scene* is a short part of an act and happens in one place and time. When the setting of a play changes, a new scene begins.

Script Sample

The following portion of script appears in Shakespeare's play *The Tragedy of Julius Caesar.*

Drama is divided into acts and scenes.	Act III, scene ii
	*(**Scene:** The Forum)*
Stage directions establish the setting and describe entrances of characters.	*[Enter* BRUTUS *and goes into the pulpit, and* CASSIUS, *and the citizens.]*
	CITIZENS. We will be satisfied! Let us be satisfied!
	BRUTUS. Then follow me and give me audience, friends.
Stage directions and characters are set in distinctive type.	Cassius, go you into the other street
	And part the numbers.
	Those that will hear me speak, let 'em stay here;
	Those that will follow Cassius, go with him;
Dialogue shows characters' personalities and mood of the play and moves the plot.	And public reasons shall he rendered
	Of Caesar's death.
	FIRST CITIZEN. I will hear Brutus speak.
	SECOND CITIZEN. I will hear Cassius, and compare their reasons . . .

PRACTICE

Use one of the following assignments to help you practice your drama writing skills:

1. Write a dialogue between two characters who have different reasons for taking the same action.

2. Write a scene in which a character attempts to persuade a crowd to his or her point of view.

WORKSHOP 5

Strategies for Reading

WHAT ARE STRATEGIES FOR READING?

When you read, you often do so for a reason: to learn information, to study, to take notes, to review, or to summarize. Learning to read more actively will help you get more out of the materials you read.

POINTERS: READING STRATEGIES

Here are a few strategies to help you read more actively:

1. **Question** When you read a word, phrase, or statement that is unclear or confusing, question it. You may be able to make sense of the word by its context in a sentence or paragraph.

2. **Connect** Relate what you are reading to people, places, and things you already know.

3. **Predict** Try to figure out what will happen next.

4. **Clarify** Return to questions you had earlier, and try to answer them.

5. **Evaluate** Draw your own conclusions about the characters, actions, and events in the story.

Applying Reading Strategies

Read the following excerpt from "The Circuit," a short story written by Francisco Jiménez. The call-outs show how one reader applied the strategies for reading actively.

Connect: I know what it's like to move from place to place.

Predict: This story might be about what it's like to be a migrant worker.

Question: Why does the narrator specifically dread moving to Fresno?

Question: What does the word *Carcanchita* mean?

Clarify: *Carcanchita* must mean "little jalopy."

Everything we owned was neatly packed in cardboard boxes. Suddenly I felt even more the weight of hours, days, weeks, and months of work. I sat down on a box. The thought of having to move to Fresno and knowing what was in store for me there brought tears to my eyes.

That night I could not sleep. I lay in bed thinking about how much I hated this move.

A little before five o'clock in the morning, Papá woke everyone up. . . .

While we packed the breakfast dishes, Papá went outside to start the "Carcanchita." That was the name Papá gave his old '38 black Plymouth. He bought it in a used-car lot in Santa Rosa in the winter of 1949. Papá was very proud of his little jalopy.

PRACTICE

1. Select an essay or a short story from your textbook that you have not yet read. As you read the story, write notes for each of the strategies: question, connect, predict, clarify, and evaluate.

2. Apply the strategies for reading to a story in the textbook that you have read. Write a brief essay evaluating the story, explaining the conclusions you have drawn about the characters and events.

WORKSHOP 6
Critical Thinking

WHAT IS CRITICAL THINKING?
Critical thinking is thinking about your thought processes. It means examining the way you think. Critical thinking involves several elements. Among these are your point of view, the question at issue, the purpose of a conversation, assumptions you are making, abstract terms you are using, the quality of the information you are depending upon, and the implications of your conclusions.

POINTERS: CRITICAL THINKING
Critical thinking skills will help you understand problems. These skills will also help you understand the opinions of others. Here are some guidelines to help you develop your critical thinking skills.

1. **Describe the real issue or problem.** Make sure you understand a problem before you begin to examine it. Rather than restate a fact, describe the conflict or issue raised by that fact.

2. **Raise relevant questions.** Reading "Harrison Bergeron" might cause you to question what it really means for all people to be equal.

3. **Recognize your own biases and those of others.** Try to put aside your differences. For example, even if you have difficulty getting along with a co-worker, you can still try to consider the co-worker's ideas. You should also look for bias that other people may have in their opinions.

4. **Question assumptions.** Allow yourself to question the assumptions made by an author, a co-worker, or a supervisor. In your mind, consider alternate interpretations of the problem or situation.

5. **Keep your mind open to new ideas and other points of view.** Listen with an open mind to others' opinions. Try not to feel threatened or attacked by someone who views an issue differently than you do.

6. **Evaluate new information.** Carefully consider information—and its sources—before accepting it as true. Realize that sometimes you might get new information that will cause you to think differently about an issue or even to reach a new conclusion.

7. **Consider implications and possibilities.** At first, a reader might think of "Stopping by Woods on a Snowy Evening" as a simple poem about nature. A critical thinker, however, considers what mood or point of view Frost may want to convey through simple images from nature.

8. **Support your opinions with evidence.** Your opinions will carry more weight with others if you can back them up with evidence. Be prepared to explain logical reasons for your conclusions.

PRACTICE
Answer one of the following questions to practice using your critical thinking skills.

1. How are the few details the reader receives about the niece and Mr. Nuttel in "The Open Window" important to the story's suspense and climax?

2. What personal biases might affect your reading of "There Will Come Soft Rains?" What biases might the author have?

3. How would you handle a situation in which your supervisor asks you to settle a difference of opinion you have with a co-worker?

WORKSHOP 7

The Writing Process

WHAT IS THE WRITING PROCESS?

Think of a piece of writing you recently completed. What steps did you take? No two writers approach writing the same way, but there are several steps in the *writing process* that are common.

POINTERS: DEVELOPING YOUR WRITING PROCESS

Every writer has a different work style, but all writers work through the same five steps of the writing process. As you write, you may move back and forth among the following steps:

1. **Prewriting** Prewriting is everything you do before you begin to write your memo, essay, article, or report. Prewriting occurs when you plan, ask questions, make notes, and narrow your topic. When you explore ideas about your topic, gather information, and organize your ideas, you are prewriting.

    During this stage you should identify your purpose and audience. Before you write, determine what your readers know, what they need to know, and why they need to know it. Knowing your audience will influence your purpose, tone, and presentation.

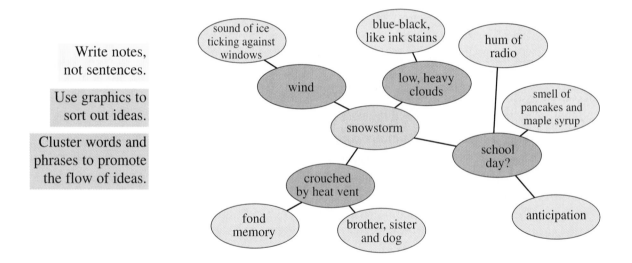

2. **Drafting** Getting your ideas down in rough sentences and paragraphs with a beginning, middle, and an end is the drafting stage of the writing process. If your prewriting plan is detailed and well organized, your rough draft may be fairly complete. If your prewriting notes are loosely organized, your draft may be somewhat unstructured. The important thing to remember when writing a draft is to get your ideas down in an understandable form, with a beginning, a middle, and a conclusion.

Rough Draft Sample

Writer begins with a solid topic sentence.

Writer gets the ideas down without worrying about spelling, grammar, and mechanics.

    I think of winter and the first snowfall when I see the blue-black clouds hang low and heavy in the sky. The anticipation slowly builds. Icy flakes tick against the glass windows. Still dressed in my pajamas, I crouch next to the heat vent, joining my brother and sister and our dog. Warm waves of air wash over us as we look out the window. Flakes swirled and settled against the front porch railing. Smells of pancakes and maple syrup drift toward us from the kitchen. Regularily we hear the sound of the spatula against the cast iron skillett. The ground is now covered with snow. We hear the low hum of the radio. My sister and I exchange glances. Was it too early to dare think of it—a snow day?

3. **Revising** The revising stage involves evaluating and improving your draft. In revising, focus on the organization of your ideas. Use clear sentences with strong supporting details and active verbs.

4. **Editing** In this stage, review your sentences and paragraphs for clear, correct construction and smooth transitions. Proofread word-by-word for errors in grammar, usage, and mechanics. Then set aside your writing for a day or two before carefully reading it again. You may evaluate your own draft, or you may choose to ask a peer reviewer to read it and make constructive comments.

Revised and Edited Draft

Writer has refined phrasing of topic sentence.

Writer has added detail and improved some phrasing.

Errors in mechanics and spelling have been corrected.

Error in verb tense have been corrected.

    When blue-black clouds, the color of smudged ink stains, hang low and heavy in the sky, my thoughts turn toward winter and the first snowfall. The anticipation slowly builds. Icy flakes, at first one or two, then dozens, tick against the glass windows. Still dressed in my green-striped flannel pajamas, I crouch next to the heat vent, joining my brother and sister and our dog Captain. Warm waves of air wash over us as we look out the window. Flakes swirl and settle against the front porch railing. Smells of pancakes and maple syrup drift toward us from the kitchen. Regularly we hear the scrape-and-flip of the spatula against the cast iron skillet. The ground is now covered with snow. We hear the low hum of the radio. My sister and I exchange glances. Is it too early to dare think of it—a snow day?

5. **Presenting/Publishing** How you present or publish your work depends on your audience and purpose for writing. For example, you may present or publish in the form of a class report, a news article, a letter to the editor, or a computer bulletin board memo.

PRACTICE

Complete one of the following assignments using the five steps of the writing process.

1. In a narrative essay describe a particularly memorable event from your childhood.

2. Write an article for your school newspaper that explores the advantages and disadvantages of living in your hometown.

3. Write a memo to your supervisor explaining why an upcoming seminar would be beneficial to you and your co-workers.

WORKSHOP 8
Writing a Composition

WHAT IS A COMPOSITION?

A *composition* has a clear point of view and uses strong details or examples to support its main idea. You might write a composition as a response to a story you read, for an in-class writing assignment, or for a variety of other writing situations that require brief but thoughtful responses.

POINTERS: WRITING A COMPOSITION

A good composition has strong, clear organization. Think of the parts of a composition as the beginning, the middle, and the end. When each of these parts relates to the main idea of the composition, the composition has unity. Refer to the following suggestions as you practice writing compositions:

1. **Determine your point of view.** Make sure you identify the topic and your point of view.

2. **Outline your ideas.** Sketch your ideas into three parts: a beginning, a middle, and an end.

3. **Begin with a thesis statement.** Introduce your main idea in a thesis statement, or a topic sentence. This statement may be at the beginning or end of the first paragraph.

4. **Place your supporting details in the middle.** The middle part of the composition is where you develop your main idea. Include details that clearly support your main idea.

5. **End with a strong statement.** The ending of your composition should tie together your ideas. In this paragraph, you might summarize the facts supporting your main idea or restate your thesis statement.

Sample Composition

First paragraph ends with a thesis statement that introduces main idea.

    Moving from the city to a small farm in the countryside marked a big change in my life. Before my family moved, I was certain that I would be miserable. However, through the move, I learned many lessons about myself and grew in ways I'd never thought possible.

Middle paragraph gives supporting details.

    The move was the beginning of many positive changes in my life and my relationships. I was able to spend more time with my father, who had quit his office job to start his own business at home. Because we had fewer friends, my brother and I began to rely on each other and see each other as friends rather than competitors. Most important, I discovered my love and interest in nature. When I was working in the yard or hiking through the woods, I felt a peace and joy that I'd never felt before.

End paragraph restates the composition's main idea.

    Although I sometimes miss the city and the friends I left behind, I realize that I'm happier now than I've ever been. I learned that if I open myself up to change, I can discover new and wonderful things.

PRACTICE

Complete one of the following assignments to practice writing a composition.

1. State your opinion about a book you've read, a movie you've seen, or a concert you've attended.

2. Describe a favorite holiday and its importance to you and your family.

WORKSHOP 9

Narrative Writing

WHAT IS NARRATIVE WRITING?

Narrative writing is writing that tells what happened. Knowing the elements of narrative writing will help you understand what you read and write.

POINTERS: NARRATIVE WRITING

Narrative writing describes an event or a series of events (in real life or as depicted in fiction), and is usually presented with specific details about time, place, people, and feelings or impressions.

1. **Sketch out a timeline to identify the key events about which you want to write.** Make certain that your narrative has a beginning (introduction), a middle (body), and an end (conclusion).

2. **Choose a method of organizing the details and the events.** In narrative writing, events are often organized in the order they happened. (See *Workshop 10* for more methods of organization.)

3. **Start with a thesis statement.** Identify your subject, main idea, and viewpoint.

4. **Introduce the problem or conflict.** Describe and expand the problem with specific details.

5. **Use transition words to show order.** Transition words such as *first, next,* and *afterwards* will clarify the order of events and details.

6. **End your narrative with a solution to the problem or a summary of events.**

Narrative Writing Sample

A thesis statement identifies the central idea.

The problem is introduced and developed.

Transitions help establish chronological organization.

Concluding sentences tell how the conflict was solved and relate the solution to the thesis statement.

Until recently, I'd never given much thought to the saying "It's a small world." However, a surprising encounter made me think differently. Last spring, my brother and I were traveling through New Zealand. Late one afternoon, our car broke down on a deserted stretch of road. Suddenly, we heard a truck coming down the road. The driver, a man who looked about my age, offered to help us. As he looked at the engine, he asked, "What brings you to New Zealand? Where are you from?" When we told him we were from Minnesota, he looked up and said, "Really? I spent some time in Minnesota as a kid. What part?" When we told him the name of our small hometown, the man looked startled and exclaimed, "No kidding! That's where my aunt and uncle live. I spent a year with them when I was ten." I stared at the man and asked slowly, "Is your name Don?" to which he replied, "Jim, is that you?" As it turned out, the man who stopped to help us on a deserted road in a country half way around the world was my childhood friend. I learned firsthand that it really is a small world after all.

PRACTICE

Complete one of the following assignments to practice your narrative writing skills.

1. Write a narrative about a recent social event in your community or at your school. Use chronological order to organize the events and details.

2. Write an account of a surprising or unexpected event in your life.

WORKSHOP 10
Descriptive Writing

WHAT IS DESCRIPTIVE WRITING?

Descriptive writing uses precise, vivid details to create a picture of a character, scene, or event. Sensory details that appeal to readers' senses of sight, hearing, smell, taste, and touch are often used. In a description, elements are organized in an appropriate way to achieve unity and logic, and transition words and phrases help establish the relationship between details.

POINTERS: DESCRIPTIVE WRITING

In all effective writing, ideas are connected to one another. In descriptive writing, the details must be arranged for the best effect. Methods of organization may be combined. For example, a writer may combine chronological order, spatial order, and order of impression to create a particular mood, such as suspense. When choosing a method of organization, refer to the following suggestions:

1. **Chronological order** Chronological order presents details and events in the order in which they happen. This method of organization is often used to describe a process or tell about a series of events. To show time relationships, use transitional words and phrases, such as *first, next, after, during, second, finally,* and *last.*

2. **Order of importance** Another way to organize your writing is to arrange details in order of importance, either from most important to least important, or from least to most.

3. **Spatial order** Spatial order arranges details by their physical location. When describing a place or object, spatial order may be particularly effective. To show the location of objects and their relationship to each other, use prepositional words and prepositional phrases, such as *above, below, behind, next to, on the left,* and *on the right.*

4. **Order of impression** In this method, details are placed in the order a character notices or perceives them. Sometimes, a writer arranges details simply in the order of the impression he or she is trying to convey to the reader.

Sample Descriptive Writing

Spatial order provides a logical description of the location of details.

Transition words and phrases clarify the spatial relationships.

Chris had told me that the car he bought needed "a little work." When he pulled the car up to the curb, I couldn't believe my eyes. My first view was of the front. The bumper was missing, the grill was rusted and dented, and the left headlight was broken. On the right side of the car, both door handles were gone. On the left side, large patches of rust showed through the cracked paint on the passenger side door. To the left of the side view mirror, a contorted coat hanger stood in for an antenna. From the back, the car looked like a reject from a demolition derby. The rear bumper, tied in place with rope, sagged dangerously low. Above the bumper, a gaping hole indicated where the trunk lock used to be.

PRACTICE

Complete one of the following activities to practice different methods of organization in your descriptive writing.

1. Describe a recent sports event at your school, using chronological order.
2. Describe a a place you enjoy visiting, using spatial order.
3. Describe an object that has special meaning to you, using order of impression.

POINTERS: INCIDENT REPORT

An incident report describes an incident, or event, in detail. Usually, the details in an incident report are organized in chronological order. To write an incident report, use the following guidelines:

1. **State the vital statistics.** Begin by identifying all of the vital elements of the incident, such as the time, location, people involved, conditions related to the cause of the incident, and so on.
2. **Describe what happened.** Describe the events in the order they happened.
3. **Use clear, precise language.** Choose words and phrases that describe exactly what you mean.
4. **Use transition words to organize details logically.** To show chronological order, use transition words such as *first, next, then, last,* and so on. To show cause-and-effect relationships among details, use transition words and phrases such as *because, as a result, then,* and *therefore.*
5. **List results.** Conclude your report by describing the results of the incident and the present status of the case or investigation.

Sample Incident Report

Date: January 4, 199–
Time: 8:25 a.m.

Vital statistics are identified in specific detail.

Location: front entrance ramp of Super Shopper Grocery, 7700 W. 80th Street
Parties involved: Katherine Gunner, 903 E. 63rd Street, Apt. #2
Related conditions: drizzling rain, icy patches on sidewalks leading to store and on entrance ramp

Events are described in chronological order.

Incident description: Gunner walked from the parking lot to the entrance ramp and slipped on an ice patch 2 feet in front of the door. The ice patch measured 3 feet $\times$ 4 feet. According to the store manager, John Wright, one application of deicing compound had been applied to the sidewalks and ramp at 7:00 a.m. Emergency medical technicians wrapped Gunner's ankle and transported her to St. Luke's Hospital.

Report concludes with results or status of case.

Status: According to Dr. Janet Walker, who treated Gunner at St. Luke's Hospital emergency room, Gunner sustained a sprained ankle. The case is pending a follow-up examination, set for January 11.

PRACTICE

Complete one of the following assignments to practice using descriptive writing in an incident report.

1. Use chronological order to describe a non-injury accident between two bicyclists.
2. Describe a series of follow-up examinations of Katherine Gunner's sprained ankle.

WORKSHOP 11

Résumé

WHAT IS A RÉSUMÉ?

A *résumé* is a written summary of your job experience and educational background.

POINTERS: WRITING A RÉSUMÉ

Information in your résumé should be divided into easy-to-read sections. Keep the following pointers in mind as you write your résumé:

1. **List your personal information.** Write your name, address, and telephone number at the top of your résumé. If appropriate, list your e-mail address.

2. **State your job objective.** State a specific type of job as a job objective.

3. **Describe your work experience.** Give important details about jobs you have held to date. List the dates you worked at each job, the name and address of the employer, and your main duties.

4. **Give your educational background to date.**

5. **Limit your résumé to one page.** The information on your résumé should be brief and easy to read.

6. **Use phrases rather than complete sentences.** Describe your experience in short, clear phrases that can be easily skimmed by the reader. Use action verbs.

7. **List any related skills, awards, or activities.** Mention accomplishments that relate to job skills.

Sample Résumé

Name, address, and telephone number are centered at top.

Paul Riccelli
920 Dean Street
Madison, WI 50005
415-555-5209

OBJECTIVE: To become a summer camp counselor

WORK EXPERIENCE:

Work experience shows writer's responsibility as well as qualifications.

June 1996–Present. Part-time stock person, The Green Grocer
Stocking shelves, taking inventory
September 1995–Present. Volunteer tutor,
Riverside Middle School
Assisting middle-school students in math and science

EDUCATION: Kennedy High School, Madison, 1996–Present
Sophomore, Honor Roll, G.P.A. 3.4

Award relates to skills a camp counselor might need.

AWARDS: Third-place in state swimming championships, 1996

PRACTICE

Prepare a résumé for a specific job that you would like to have. Include an objective and any special details that would relate to the job you choose.

WORKSHOP 12

Process Explanation

WHAT IS A PROCESS EXPLANATION?

If you had to explain a task to someone else, you would need to *explain a process,* or clearly relate the exact steps involved in a task.

POINTERS: EXPLAINING A PROCESS

When you explain a process in writing, you need to describe a sequence of events or steps to instruct or inform the reader. Refer to the following guidelines as you write a process explanation:

1. **Know your audience.** What do your readers already know about the process?

2. **Know your purpose.** How will your readers use the information you give them?

3. **Start with a thesis statement.** Clearly state for your readers what process you are explaining.

4. **Define unfamiliar terms.** Remember that your topic may be new to your readers. You should avoid using technical jargon for a nontechnical audience.

5. **Divide the process into manageable pieces.** Describe the steps in short, clear sentences.

6. **Arrange the steps in your process in chronological order.** Use transition words and phrases to help your readers follow the process. Use words such as *first, second, next, after,* and *last.*

7. **Check the steps in the process for accuracy.** You should be very familiar with the process you describe, either from reading, observing, or experiencing it firsthand.

8. **Use diagrams, charts, and other visual aids.** A combination of visuals and text can help the reader better understand a process. Use appropriate visuals when necessary.

Sample Process Explanation

Thesis statement identifies the process.

Transition words make the chronological order clear.

Writer avoids technical jargon.

What does it take to become an employee of our company? We'd like to explain the hiring process to you. First, all prospective employees must fill out an application at the personnel office. Next, the manager will call applicants to set up interviews. Each interview will take place at the personnel office and should last about thirty minutes.

After the interview, the manager will review his or her notes from each interview. During this stage, which lasts from one to two weeks, applicants should not call to find out if a decision has been made. At the end of the decision-making stage, the manager will make phone calls to inform each applicant of his or her status. At this time, the manager will make job offers to applicants who have been approved.

PRACTICE

Complete one of the following exercises to practice explaining a process.

1. Explain a technical process, such as how a fax machine transmits information.

2. Explain how school sports teams are selected for and advanced through a statewide championship.

WORKSHOP 13

Persuasive Writing

WHAT IS PERSUASIVE WRITING?

You probably have strong opinions on many subjects. But how can you convince others of your point of view? Mastering the art of *persuasive writing* is one way to get others to see things your way.

POINTERS: WRITING A PERSUASIVE ESSAY

In a persuasive essay, you want to convince your reader to share your beliefs or take certain actions. Persuasive essays can focus on many different topics. Refer to the following guidelines:

1. **Select an appropriate topic.** Any topic you choose should have at least two distinct "sides." Also, it should grab your readers' attention.

2. **State your position.** Clearly state the main idea of your essay in a thesis statement.

3. **Support your opinion with evidence.** Use facts, statistics, examples, opinions from experts, or observations that back up your opinion and make your argument stronger.

4. **Know your audience.** Think about what your audience already believes or knows about the topic. Develop arguments that will persuade them to share your opinion.

5. **Address possible opposing arguments.** Think about how your audience might argue against your opinion. Then use clear and precise language to defend your position.

6. **Avoid errors in logic.** Do not use stereotypes or oversimplifications, such as either/or statements that only present an issue in two ways. Be careful not to generalize your view of the topic.

7. **Organize your information.** Arrange your paragraphs in a logical order. You might present your most important points first. Perhaps you will address opposing arguments at the beginning, or you may put these arguments at the end. In any case, include a strong introduction and conclusion.

Sample Persuasive Essay

Thesis statement

Supporting opinion

Supporting arguments

You must see this summer's "Shakespeare in the Park" series. This year marks the tenth anniversary of the Shakespeare Players production, and this season promises to be the best yet. Carla Watson, theater critic for the local newspaper, raves that the performances are engaging, exciting, and relevant to our times. The company boasts a new costume designer, whose previous credits include work in London and New York. Bring blankets and food to picnic on the lawn before performances. Most important to students, all shows are free and open to the public. So mark the dates on your calendar now!

PRACTICE

Build your persuasive skills by completing one of the following assignments.

1. Write a persuasive essay to convince your school cafeteria to offer a specific menu item.

2. Write a persuasive essay asking your classmates to support a human rights issue you believe in.

3. Write a persuasive essay to persuade a friend to read a book you recently read and enjoyed.

376   Workshop 13

WORKSHOP 14
Analysis

WHAT IS AN ANALYSIS?
When you write an *analysis,* you examine a problem, question, or issue. The writer clearly states a subject, then proposes a solution. Opinions presented must be supported by outside sources.

POINTERS: ANALYSIS
Follow these guidelines when you prepare your analysis:

1. **Know your subject.** Before you begin writing, conduct research on your issue or subject. Make sure you have a complete understanding of all sides of the issue.

2. **Identify your assumptions.** How do you see the issue? Do you have any biases, or viewpoints that might keep you from seeing other sides of the issue? Try to remain objective.

3. **Gather information.** You can find information in a variety of sources. Books, journals, the Internet, CD-ROMs, or interviews are just some of the information resources available.

4. **Collect and organize evidence.** Gather evidence that supports the position you take on the issue. For each point you make, list at least one source or reference that supports that point.

5. **Draft and revise your analysis.** Use your outline and supporting points to write your analysis. Proofread carefully and revise the draft as needed.

Sample Analysis

Question is stated.	At last month's meeting, the neighborhood association proposed an ordinance preventing people from parking cars on the street. Is this ordinance necessary? The issue has been raised because of recent incidents of children running from behind parked cars and into the street.
Examples support the writer's opinions.	No one has been injured, but parents are concerned. I understand that having cars parked in driveways or garages will keep streets clear so drivers will be able to see children more easily. But consider this alternative: A recent safety study has shown that reducing the speed limit from 25 to 15 miles per hour in residential areas makes neighborhoods safer for children. Also, children need to practice street safety. I believe
Conclusion is stated.	that we can find ways to resolve this safety issue without passing the proposed ordinance.

PRACTICE
Complete one of these assignments to practice writing an analysis.

1. Study a character or author from one of the literature selections. Write a short analysis explaining why this person took a certain action. For example, you might analyze why Brutus killed Caesar.

2. Research a school issue such as whether to add or eliminate a sport or course offering. Analyze the reasons for and against the action. Then suggest what you believe should be done.

WORKSHOP 15

Comparison and Contrast

WHAT IS COMPARISON AND CONTRAST?

When you *compare and contrast* items, you explain how they are alike and different. School and work assignments will ask you to compare and contrast information, ideas, events, and people.

POINTERS: COMPARISON AND CONTRAST ORGANIZATION

1. **Select the items to compare and contrast and gather information about their similarities and differences.** In a Venn diagram (two overlapping circles) list what the two items have in common in the space where the circles overlap. List the differences in the outer parts of the circles.

2. **Write your topic sentence or thesis statement.** State your purpose and general subject.

3. **Decide how to organize the information.** The *whole-to-whole pattern* compares one whole topic to another by describing all features of one entire topic before going to the next. The *feature-to-feature pattern* compares the individual features common to both topics.

4. **Write your first draft and make revisions.** If one pattern isn't working well, try the other pattern of organization. Close by drawing a conclusion about the similarities and differences of your topic.

5. **Use transitions to make connections between features or ideas.**

Sample Comparison-Contrast Essay

Thesis statement
> Christopher Darden, the author and narrator of *In Contempt,* and the speaker in "Dear Mrs. McKinney of the Sixth Grade:" are both influenced by the judgment of older, wiser women; one is a grandmother, the other is a sixth-grade teacher.

Organized on the whole-to-whole pattern
> Nanny is Christopher Darden's lifeline during his teenage years. As Darden explains, "I felt as if my parents and siblings didn't understand me at all, as if I spoke a different language than they did, a language only Nanny understood." From the pride that Nanny showed in him, Darden learned to show respect for himself and others.

Transition
> Mrs. McKinney was the speaker's "favorite teacher at Garfield elementary." Like Darden's Nanny, she insists on "the need for discipline and regard." However, unlike Nanny, Mrs. McKinney remains separate from the speaker's life outside the classroom.

Closing draws a conclusion about the similarities and differences.
> One woman is a grandmother, the other a teacher. Regardless of their relationship to their young charges, both women insisted that the young men not fail themselves.

PRACTICE

1. In an essay, compare and contrast the speaker's attitude toward nature in the poems "Stopping by Woods on a Snowy Evening" and "Witness."

2. Write an essay comparing and contrasting what it means to be fifteen years old, as described in Bob Greene's article "Fifteen" and William Stafford's poem "Fifteen."

378

WORKSHOP 16
Summary

WHAT IS A SUMMARY?

A *summary* is a shortened version of text that presents the main ideas in the original order.

POINTERS: WRITING A SUMMARY

A summary of a literary work should be brief and clear. Keep the following guidelines in mind:

1. **Read the original work carefully.** Make sure you understand the original text.

2. **List the main ideas.** Use phrases to list the text's main ideas in order.

3. **Write your first draft.** Refer to your list of main ideas when you write the summary. When you come across difficult words, try to define them using words that are easier to understand.

4. **Reread the original and your draft.** Compare them to make sure you included the important ideas in a logical order. Place the same emphasis on ideas as the author of the original text did.

5. **Revise your summary.** Explain or delete words or concepts that readers might not understand.

6. **Edit your summary.** Include transition words and phrases so that each sentence leads smoothly to the next. Check your grammar, spelling, punctuation, and usage.

Original Passage from *When Heaven and Earth Changed Places*

He was very easygoing about everything and seldom in a hurry. Seldom, too, did he say no to a request—from his children to his neighbors. Although he took everything in stride, he was a hard and diligent worker. Even on holidays, he was always mending things or tending to our house and animals. He would not wait to be asked for help if he saw someone in trouble. Similarly, he always said what he thought, although he knew, like most honest men, when to keep silent. Because of his honesty, his empathy, and his openness to people, he understood life deeply.

Unimportant words and phrases have been deleted.

Ideas are presented in the same order as the original.

Difficult words are replaced with simpler ones.

Summary

An easygoing man, he rarely hurried or said no to a request. He was a hard and attentive worker, even on holidays. Whenever he saw someone in trouble, he helped. He was an honest man who knew when to speak and when to remain silent. His honesty, empathy, and openness to people led to his deep understanding of life.

PRACTICE

1. Summarize the advice F. Scott Fitzgerald gives to his daughter in a letter.

2. Summarize Mark Antony's speech in the excerpt from *The Tragedy of Julius Caesar.*

WORKSHOP 17

News and Feature Writing

WHAT ARE NEWS AND FEATURE WRITING?

Newspapers and magazines can include both *news writing* and *feature writing*. News writing, or reporting, gives readers up-to-date information. Feature writing provides readers with more human-interest information. News writers describe events and facts in an objective way; in other words, they do not show their personal opinions about the events or facts presented. Feature writers can focus on their readers' personal interests and emotions. A feature deals with facts but highlights the people and opinions surrounding the facts.

POINTERS: NEWS WRITING

Think of a news article as an upside-down pyramid. The first sentence, or lead, gives the most important information. Each of the next sentences offers less important details and facts.

1. **Answer the basic questions first.** Write the words *who, what, why, when, where,* and *how* on a piece of paper. Answer these questions in as few words as possible. (Omit any questions that are not important to your article.) Combine your answers into one or two sentences.

2. **Decide which other details to include.** Think about other details readers might want to know, such as how a certain news event might affect them. You may want to use quotations from people you interviewed. Then choose as many details as you have space to include in your article.

3. **Arrange the details in decreasing order of importance.** If the editor must shorten the article, details from the end of the article will be cut first.

4. **Make your first draft brief and objective.** Stick to the facts and important details. Do not reveal your feelings about the facts. Avoid opinion words such as *good,* and *unfortunately.*

5. **Revise and edit your article.** Make sure you have used terms readers will understand. Consider whether you have answered questions the readers might have. Use transitional words and phrases to make smooth connections. Check your grammar, spelling, and punctuation for correctness.

6. **Check your facts.** Make sure times, locations, dates, titles, and names are correct.

News Writing Sample

Lead sentence answers basic questions

Objective terms used

Quotation from interview included

Least important fact given last

A pre-dawn fire swept through the kitchen of the Little Mount High School cafeteria on Wednesday, October 23. No one was injured from the blaze, but smoke damage has forced the cafeteria to close indefinitely. Fire Marshall Linda Gregory stated that the fire apparently began around 5:00 in the morning. In a little less than an hour, the blaze had been contained. Although the official cause of the fire is still under investigation, Gregory says that "arson has been ruled out" as a possible cause. After viewing the damage, school principal Murray Peterson announced that a temporary cafeteria will be set up in the gym. Food will be prepared at nearby Marshall High School and transported to the high school.

PRACTICE

Complete one of the following assignments to practice your news writing skills.

1. Write a news article about a recent dramatic event in your community, such as a rescue or natural disaster. Remember to remain objective and report only the facts.

2. Write a news article about a recent political event that you were pleased to see happen. Make sure you keep your opinion out of the article so that readers will not guess your reaction to the event.

POINTERS: FEATURE WRITING

A feature article can include facts, but it is not written as an upside-down pyramid. Instead, its organization depends on the subject matter. Use the following pointers as you write your features:

1. **Select a topic that will interest your readers.** Look for the human-interest side of a news story. For example, you might write about how recent job layoffs have affected community members. You could conduct interviews with current and former students of this year's Teacher of the Year. You might write a historical feature explaining the history of a school or community event.

2. **Gather information.** This information may come from personal interviews, library research (especially if you are writing a historical feature), or computer databases and the Internet.

3. **Follow the rest of the writing process to complete your article.** Write your first draft, revise it, edit it. Begin your article with a personal story or fact that will grab the readers' attention. Also make sure that any other information you've included is correct.

Feature Writing Sample

Begins with a sentence that attracts readers' attention

Focuses on the human aspect of the story

For a healthy sixteen-year-old, Eric Quinn spends a lot of his time at the hospital. Eric is the founder of Sibling Support, a volunteer group at County Children's Hospital. Eric and nine other high school students volunteer their afternoons and weekends to spend time with the brothers and sisters of critically ill children.

"When I was eight, my older sister, Meg, was diagnosed with leukemia," Eric explains. "Over the next four years, until Meg got better, I spent a lot of time at the hospital. I think having someone to talk to and play with would have helped me during a tough time."

Through Sibling Support, children have an opportunity to play with other kids, get help on their homework, or just talk to someone. Eric says, "I really know what these kids are dealing with. It's a great feeling to know that I can help them."

PRACTICE

Complete one of these assignments to practice writing a feature story.

1. Scan recent newspapers for news stories. Then brainstorm human-interest angles on a few of the stories. Choose one and write a feature story about it. Gather any information you might need.

2. Interview someone in your school or community who has received an award. Focus on the human-interest side of the story, such as what the award means to the recipient. Then write a feature article for your school or local newspaper. Make sure to check carefully any facts you've included.

WORKSHOP 18

Business Letters

WHAT IS A BUSINESS LETTER?
A business letter is a piece of correspondence written to a workplace for a specific purpose.

POINTERS: **WRITING A BUSINESS LETTER**
Follow these guidelines when you write a business letter:

1. **Include the basic parts of a letter.** In the heading, give your address. Under the heading, write the complete date and the name, title, and mailing address of the recipient. In the body, write your message followed by a closing such as *Cordially* or *Sincerely yours* on a separate line. Place a comma after the closing, and sign the letter under the closing. Type your name under your signature.

2. **Type business letters in block form or modified block form.** To use block style, position each part of the letter flush left (aligned at the left margin). To use modified block style, place the heading, date, closing, and signature to the right of center. Keep the other parts of the letter flush left.

Letter of Inquiry or Request

A *letter of inquiry* asks for information. Make your request as polite and specific as possible. Explain what you would like to know, what you intend to do with the information, and where to send the information. Thank the recipient for taking the time to read and respond to your letter.

Heading, date, and address	290 Campbell Street Barrington, RI 02860 May 12, 199– Superintendent Grand Canyon National Park P.O. Box 129 Grand Canyon, AZ 86023
Salutation	Dear Superintendent:
Request for information	I plan to visit and camp at the Grand Canyon National Park this October. I would like information about obtaining a camping permit and about the park's hiking trails. Please send me an application for the permit as well as any brochures for the park's hiking trails.
Thanks	I look forward to exploring the Grand Canyon this fall. Thank you for sending the information.
Closing, sender's signature, and sender's typed name	Sincerely, *Michael Huang* Michael Huang

PRACTICE

Complete one of the following assignments to practice writing a letter of inquiry or request.

1. Write a letter to inquire about a fact or statistic you need to check for a research paper.

2. Write a letter of request to ask for an application, a photocopy of information, or some other document.

Letter of Application

In a *letter of application,* the sender indicates a personal interest in a specific position. You should limit a letter of application to one page and include information not found in your résumé, your availability for an interview, and how you can be contacted. After a job interview, you should send a follow-up letter expressing your thanks for the opportunity to interview and highlighting your strengths.

Follows business-letter format	39452 Corpus Christi Circle Houston, TX 77052
	Patricia Watson Watson's Books 8200 Federal Hill Road Houston, TX 77052
	Dear Ms. Watson:
Indicates position desired Lists applicant's qualifications, including those not found on résumé Stresses availability for an interview Tells how applicant can be contacted	I would like to apply for the position of part-time sales clerk. In addition to volunteering at my school library, I have a year of retail sales experience. I am familiar with the current bestseller lists. I also have specific knowledge and interest in computer-related books and materials. I would welcome the opportunity to discuss the possibility of using these skills at Watson's Books. I can be reached at 555-0194 after 4:00 p.m. weekdays. Thank you for your consideration. Sincerely, *Anita Consuelos* Anita Consuelos

PRACTICE

Complete one of the following assignments to practice writing a letter of application.

1. Write a letter to apply for a job at a business in your area.

2. Write a letter to apply for a volunteer position with a local charity. Remember to indicate your qualifications for the position.

WORKSHOP 19

E-mail/Memo

WHAT IS AN E-MAIL/MEMO?

A *memo* is a brief message usually written from one company employee to another for a specific purpose. *E-mail,* or electronic mail, is a memo sent rapidly through a computer network.

POINTERS: E-MAIL/ MEMO

To create an e-mail or memo, follow these guidelines:

1. **Begin with a heading.** Include who is receiving the memo, sender, date, and subject.

2. **State your main point.** State the main point or purpose of your memo as soon as possible.

3. **Be clear and concise.** Clearly explain what you want the recipient to know. Many memos announce a policy change or ask for action to be taken. Make clear what you want the recipient to do.

4. **Use an appropriate tone.** Remember that the recipient of your memo cannot see your face. He or she may be offended by a comment that you meant to be funny.

5. **Use upper- and lower-case letters.** Using all capitals in e-mail is difficult to read and is considered the equivalent of shouting—an undesirable mode of office communication.

6. **Find out your recipient's computer network address.** You can send e-mail messages only to others on the same network or a connecting network. You must use the person's exact address.

7. **Remember others may read e-mail.** Don't write anything that would be damaging if it were read by others. Fix errors, and always avoid offensive language.

Sample E-mail Memo

Heading	To: New_Hires@SuperCo.com From: Laura Els@SuperCo.com Date: October 2, 199- Subject: Employee Orientation
Main point	All new employees should attend next week's employee orientation meeting. The session will take place on Wednesday, October 7, from 9:00 a.m. to 11:00 a.m. in the employee lounge. Please remember to bring your employee information packet to the meeting.

PRACTICE

Complete one of the following assignments. Make up network addresses if necessary.

1. Write a memo requesting information from your supervisor for a progress report you are preparing. Clearly state the information you need and when you would like to have it.

2. Write an e-mail memo informing your co-workers of a change in your work schedule that will affect them. Give the specific information that you need to know. Also, indicate if any action needs to be taken on their part.

WORKSHOP 20
Brochure

WHAT IS A BROCHURE?

A *brochure* advertises products or services with colorful pictures and graphics and an attention-grabbing format. Its folded form makes it easy to hold or carry.

POINTERS: CREATING A BROCHURE

1. **Make an outline.** Decide what information you need to include and organize it in an outline. For example, if you are writing to advertise a baby-sitting service, you might include a list of your services, a description of your experience, and how customers can contact you.

2. **Write engaging copy.** Use vivid verbs and inviting adjectives to describe your product or service. Emphasize what you have to offer your customers.

3. **Arrange information to get your readers' attention.** Use small paragraphs, numbered or bulleted items, and short direct sentences to make your brochure easy to read.

4. **Add visuals.** Eye-catching photographs and simple charts emphasize the written information.

5. **Choose an attractive design.** Select the best quality paper available to you, add color where possible, and use lettering that stands out and is easy to read.

Sample Brochure

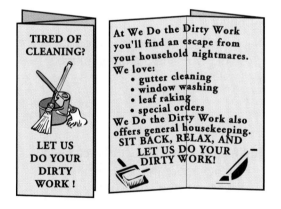

PRACTICE

Complete one of the following assignments to create a brochure.

1. Create a brochure that describes a product or service that you are offering to your classmates. Explain what you are offering and why students should buy your product or use your service.

2. Create a brochure that advertises a service offered in your community. Use appealing language and graphics to draw readers to your brochure.

WORKSHOP 21

Research Paper

WHAT IS A RESEARCH PAPER?
When you write a *research paper,* you choose a topic, research it in several information sources, and compile your findings in written form.

POINTERS: **TAKING NOTES**
In a research paper, you combine your ideas about your topic with ideas and writings from various sources. Therefore, it is important to avoid *plagiarism* in your paper. When you plagiarize, you take someone else's words or ideas and present them as your own. Plagiarism is a serious offense. Take care to document any ideas you draw from outside sources.

1. **Make source cards.** For each source you use, list the author, title, and publication information. Assign a number for each source, and write the number in the upper right-hand corner of the corresponding source card. These numbers will be easy references as you take notes from the sources.

2. **Write source information on note cards.** For each piece of information, make a separate note on a 3×5 note card. Write the number of the source in the upper-right hand corner. At the end of the note, write the page or pages where you found the information.

3. **Summarize general ideas.** If you want to note the main point of a source in few words, write a summary. For example, you might summarize two paragraphs in one or two sentences.

4. **Paraphrase key points.** When you paraphrase, you repeat an idea from a source in your own words. Make sure that your rewording is different from the original source.

5. **Copy direct quotations carefully.** If you want to use the exact words from a source, copy them exactly as they appear, including the exact punctuation. Enclose the words in quotation marks.

Sample Note Cards

4	4
Davis, Natalie Zemon and Arlette Farge, eds. <u>A History of Women in the West, Vol. III.</u> Cambridge, Massachusetts: The Belknap Press, 1993.	In Shakespeare's time, girls received a much more limited education than boys. (pp. 101–102)

Source number	Publication information	Number from source card	Writer summarizes in one sentence.

PRACTICE
Create source cards for two different sources, such as a book and a magazine article. Then take notes from each source. Create at least one of each type of note card: summary, paraphrase, and quotation.

POINTERS: CREATING A BIBLIOGRAPHY

A *bibliography* is an alphabetical list of the sources you used in your research paper. These sources might include books, magazine or encyclopedia articles, television programs, or personal interviews. Here are some general rules for arranging information in bibliography entries:

1. **List author information first.** The name of a book's author or editor appears at the beginning of an entry, last name then first name. If there is more than one author or editor, only the first person's name is reversed. For sources with no author or editor, start with the title.

2. **List title information.** After author information, give the source titles. If the same author has written different kinds of works, list articles or essays first, then the titles of books. Place titles of articles and essays in quotation marks. Underline or italicize titles of books and periodicals.

3. **List publication information.** After title information, list the place where the source was published, the publisher's name, the date of publication, and, if necessary, page numbers.

4. **Alphabetize your sources.** Arrange your sources in alphabetical order. Use the first word in the entry, whether it is a person's name or a title.

5. **Indent any lines that follow the first line of each entry.**

Sample Bibliography Forms

Book with one author	Coe, Michael D. *Breaking the Maya Code.* New York: Thames and Hudson, 1992.
Book with two or more editors	Foner, Eric and John A. Garrarty, eds. "Supreme Court." In *The Reader's Companion to American History.* Boston: Houghton Mifflin, 1991, pp. 1050–1055.
Magazine article	Lapham, Lewis H. "Lights, Camera, Democracy!" *The Atlantic Monthly,* August 1996, 33–38.
Encyclopedia article	"International Business Machines Corporation (IBM)." *The New Encyclopedia Britannica.* 1989 ed.
CD-ROM	*The 1995 Grolier Multimedia Encyclopedia,* Vers. 7.0.2. On CD-ROM. Macintosh. Chicago: Grolier Incorporated, 1995.
Web site	Human Space Flight [web site]. National Aeronautics and Space Administration; available from http://www.nasa.gov/NASA_homepage.html; INTERNET.

PRACTICE

Complete one of the following activities to practice creating a bibliography:

1. Use five different sources in your school library to create a bibliography. Remember to check your alphabetization and punctuation carefully.

2. Create a bibliography for a research paper about comets. Cite five sources and use at least three different kinds of sources of information.

WORKSHOP 22
Reading Charts and Graphs

WHAT ARE CHARTS AND GRAPHS?

Present facts or statistics in *charts and graphs,* which use pictures to present information. Newspapers, magazines, reference books, and business reports often use charts and graphs to show statistics. Knowing how to read and create graphic aids can help you understand and share information.

POINTERS: READING A LINE GRAPH

A *line graph* shows change over time. You might find a line graph in a history book or in a newspaper.

1. **Read the title.** The title names what information is being charted. It includes information about the period of time presented in the graph.

2. **Look at the axis labels.** A line graph is divided into a vertical axis and a horizontal axis. Read the labels on each axis to find out what data is being compared and the periods of time that the data cover.

3. **Find intersecting points.** Lines from the horizontal and vertical axes intersect at different points on the graph. Use the labels on each axis to interpret the information at each intersecting point.

4. **Analyze the graph.** Compare different points on the line graph to find highs and lows, patterns of increases or decreases, and other data.

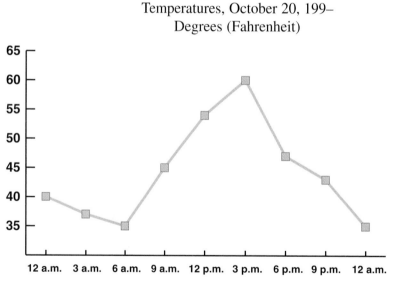

Sample Line Graph
Temperatures, October 20, 199–
Degrees (Fahrenheit)

PRACTICE

Practice reading a line graph by answering the following questions about the line graph on this page.

1. At what time did the temperature reach 54 degrees?

2. What was the warmest time of the day? How warm was it?

3. In which three-hour period did the temperature change the most? How much did it change?

POINTERS: READING A BAR GRAPH

A *bar graph* shows how things compare and contrast or how they change over time. As in a line graph, information in a bar graph is organized on a horizontal axis and a vertical axis. One axis displays numbers. The other axis shows bars that stand for the subjects being compared. Here are some tips for reading and understanding a bar graph:

1. **Read the graph title.** The title tells what information is being compared and contrasted.

2. **Look at the height or length of each bar.** To find out the amount that each bar represents, line up the end of a bar with a number on the opposite axis.

3. **Compare the bars.** To analyze the information in the bar graph, compare and contrast the lengths or heights of bars.

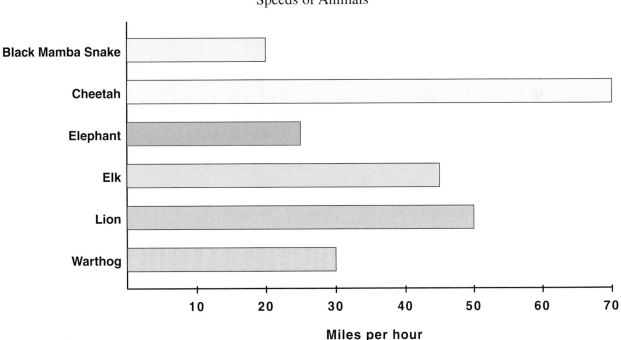

Sample Bar Graph
Speeds of Animals

PRACTICE

Practice reading a bar graph by answering the following questions about the bar graph on this page:

1. Which is the fastest animal? How fast can it run?

2. In a race between a lion and an elephant, which animal would win? How much faster can the winner run?

3. Which animal can reach a speed of 30 miles per hour?

WORKSHOP 23

Speaking Skills/Oral Presentations

WHAT ARE SPEAKING SKILLS AND ORAL PRESENTATIONS?

Developing your *speaking skills* will help you in school and on the job. As a student, you might deliver an oral report in class or give an election speech to your fellow students. As an employee, you might give an *oral presentation,* in which you share information and visual aids with co-workers or customers.

POINTERS: PRESENTATION TECHNIQUES

Public speaking makes many people nervous. You can feel more relaxed and confident if you follow these techniques for delivering an oral presentation:

1. **Know your topic.** Do any necessary research to familiarize yourself with the subject. If possible, choose a topic that you know about and that will interest your audience.

2. **Identify your purpose.** What do you want to accomplish with your oral presentation? Decide whether you want to provide information, persuade your audience, or motivate them.

3. **Analyze your audience.** How much does the audience already know about your topic? What information will you need to explain or provide? If your purpose is to convince your audience, think about how you will respond to any opposing attitudes or beliefs.

4. **Organize your presentation.** Plan the order in which you will cover your points. Prepare an outline that includes all your major points and some brief details about each. If you plan to use notecards during your talk, arrange them according to your outline.

5. **Prepare visuals.** A few visual aids will make your presentation more interesting and easier to understand. Graphs, drawings, photographs, models, videotapes, or actual equipment are types of visuals you may want to use. Display the visuals so that all audience members can see them.

6. **Practice your delivery.** Ask someone to listen to your presentation and offer suggestions on how to improve it, or record your presentation on video- or audiotape and review it yourself. Make sure you are speaking clearly and loudly enough and maintaining eye contact with your audience. Listen to how fast you speak. Be careful not to sound as if you are reading rather than speaking your ideas. Avoid using interrupters such as "um" or clearing your throat frequently.

7. **Deliver your presentation.** Direct the audience's attention to your visual aids at the appropriate times. Refer to your notecards when necessary. Follow your outline and speak naturally.

PRACTICE

Choose one of the following situations, and complete the activity to practice your speaking skills.

1. You are an employee at a software design company. You have a new idea for a computer game. Prepare an oral presentation for your co-workers to share your ideas. Incorporate at least one visual aid in your presentation.

2. You are a spokesperson for a community group. Prepare an oral presentation for an upcoming meeting at which you hope to persuade community members to take a certain action. Clarify your purpose and topic before you prepare your presentation.

WORKSHOP 24

Preparing for an Interview

WHAT IS AN INTERVIEW?

In an *interview,* people share information orally. In an information interview, you ask people questions that you have prepared about a specific topic. In a job interview, an employer shares information about a job and asks you questions about your experience. Whether you are the interviewer or the subject of the interview, you can make the most of the experience by preparing for the interview.

POINTERS: INTERVIEWING

Consider the following guidelines as you prepare for information interviews and job interviews:

1. **Pick an interview subject.** For an information interview, choose a person you want to interview and decide what information you need to gather. Have a well-defined purpose for your interview, such as finding out a person's job responsibilities or understanding a process.

2. **Make an appointment.** If you are the interviewer, call or write the person you wish to interview. Briefly explain the purpose of your interview and request a time to meet. When an employer contacts you to set up an interview, make careful notes of the time and place you agree to meet.

3. **Do background research.** You may need to do some background research to be fully prepared for an information interview. Before a job interview, make sure you have a general understanding of the company or workplace where you will be interviewing.

4. **Prepare questions and answers.** For an information interview, write at least four or five questions. Keep the words *who, what, when, where, why,* and *how* in mind as you write your questions. Try to avoid questions that can be answered simply with *yes* or *no.* Although an employer will ask most of the questions during a job interview, you can show interest in the position by making mental notes of a few questions you'd like answered. Focus on issues such as job responsibilities, rather than salary or vacation time. Be prepared to answer questions about why you would like the job and why you believe you would be a good employee.

5. **Make a good impression.** When you meet for the interview, you should always be on time and dressed neatly. Be polite and courteous—shake hands, smile, and make eye contact with the interviewer or with the person you will be interviewing.

6. **Bring any necessary items.** For an information interview, remember to bring your written questions, a note pad, and a pen or pencil. You might want to bring a tape recorder to record the interview. When you go to a job interview, bring a clean copy of your résumé.

PRACTICE

Practice for an interview in one of the following situations:

1. After receiving your job application, the owner of a local bookstore has phoned you for an interview. Go through the steps of preparing for the interview.

2. You are interested in pursuing a career in the medical field. Choose a subject for an information interview. Then complete the steps to prepare for the interview.

WORKSHOP 25

Filling Out Forms/Applications

WHAT ARE FORMS AND APPLICATIONS?

An *application* asks for personal information, such as your address, phone number, age, and gender. It inquires about your work experience and educational background. You may also be asked to list personal references, meaning people who will support the information you provide.

POINTERS: FILLING OUT FORMS

1. **Scan the application first.** Make sure you understand the information it requests before filling it out.

2. **Fill it out completely.** Write an answer for each category listed on the form. If you are uncertain of an answer or if a category doesn't apply to you, indicate that in the appropriate area of the application.

3. **Write neatly and clearly.** Make a good first impression.

4. **Review your answers.** Make sure that the information you've provided is complete and correct.

Sample Job Application

Duties are described in short phrases.

Past job is listed after current job.

References provide an employer with information about applicant's character.

Name: *Gloria Rawlings* **Today's Date**: *5-10-97* **Address:** *22 Chesterton Street, Houston, TX 77030* **Phone:** *(713) 555-2745* **Birthdate:** *4-19-82* **Sex:** *Female*
Job History (List each job held, starting with the most recent job.) 1. Employer: *Houston Public Library* Phone: *555-1200* Dates of employment: *September 1996 to present* Position held: *Part-time assistant* Duties: *reshelving books, checking out books for patrons* 2. Employer: *Alice and José Morales* Phone: *555-3328* Dates of employment: *February 1995 to August 1996* Position held: *babysitter* Duties: *care for six-year-old boy every other Saturday evening*
Education (List the most recent level of education completed.) *Sophomore, Lane Technical High School*
Personal References 1. Name: *Michael Patterson* Phone: *555-0285* Relationship: *Former teacher* 2. Name: *Alice Morales* Phone: *555-3328* Relationship: *Friend and former employer*

PRACTICE

In a group, brainstorm a list of forms and applications. Have each group member find an example and make photocopies for the group. Then distribute the copies and fill them out.

GRAMMAR WORKSHOP

Parts of Speech Overview

THE PARTS OF SPEECH

Knowledge of the parts of speech helps you to communicate your thoughts and ideas to others.

1. **Noun** A *noun* is a word that names a person, place, thing, or idea.

    Examples:　Martina, Texas, photograph, virtue

    Sentence:　The *photograph* of *Martina* was taken in *Texas.*

2. **Pronoun** A *pronoun* is a word that may be used in place of a noun or another pronoun.

    Examples:　I, me, we, us, you, she, her, he, him, they, them, it

    Sentence:　After Jack and Carla edited each other's report, *they* revised *their* work.

3. **Verb** A *verb* is a word that expresses an action or a state of being.

    Examples:　write, wink, crumple, is, felt

    Sentence:　Whenever Jessica *feels* uncertain of her writing, she *crumples* many pieces of paper.

4. **Adjective** An *adjective* is a word that modifies a noun or a pronoun.

    Examples:　smooth, round, brown, fuzzy

    Sentence:　*Smooth* and *fuzzy,* the *round* kiwi fruit fit into the palm of her hand.

5. **Adverb** An *adverb* is a word that modifies a verb, an adjective, or another adverb.

    Examples:　happily, slowly, hungrily, very, really, hardly

    Sentence:　The visitor *slowly* lifted the food to his mouth, then he *hungrily* reached for more.

6. **Preposition** A *preposition* relates a noun or pronoun to another word in the sentence.

    Examples:　above, along, among, behind, between, in place of, inside, outside, within

    Sentence:　The employees looked *behind* desks and *between* file cabinets, for the missing report.

7. **Conjunction** A *conjunction* is a word that connects two or more words or groups of words.

    Examples:　and, but, yet, or, nor, as soon as, in order that, therefore, unless

    Sentence:　Josie *and* Paulo usually eat dinner before 6:00 p.m., *unless* Paulo has basketball practice.

8. **Interjection** An *interjection* is a word, or group of words, that expresses feeling or emotion.

    Examples:　hello, help, hey, ouch, oh, yes, no

    Sentence:　*Hello!* I haven't heard from you in ages!

PRACTICE

Identify the part of speech for each italicized word in each sentence:

1. Heavy gray *clouds loomed* above as we walked along the *wooded* path.

2. *Watch out!* That long branch *blocking* the path is actually a *snake!*

3. Jumping *merrily* into muddy puddles, the *children* didn't hear *their* mother call *or* whistle.

4. *Throughout* the park, campers *and* hikers enjoyed the brisk *autumn* weather.

GRAMMAR WORKSHOP

Pronouns

POINTERS

1. A pronoun must agree with its antecedent, which is the noun or pronoun to which the pronoun refers, in number and gender.

> **Jamal** created **his** chart on the computer.

The antecedent *Jamal,* is singular and masculine, so the pronoun *his* is used. Sometimes, however, the gender of the antecedent is not provided.

> An **account manager** understands her clients' needs.

Since the account manager could be female or male, you have three possible options. You can include both gender pronouns.

> An **account manager** understands **her** or **his** clients' needs.

You can reword the sentence so that the antecedent is plural.

> **Account managers** understand **their** clients' needs.

You can reword the sentence so that the pronoun is unnecessary.

> An **account manager** understands clients' needs.

2. A singular indefinite pronoun antecedent takes a singular pronoun. Common singular indefinite pronouns include *anyone, each, either, everybody, everything, neither,* and *someone.* A common error is to choose a pronoun that agrees with a noun in the sentence instead of the indefinite pronoun antecedent.

> Incorrect: **Everyone** is responsible for **their** behavior.
> Correct: **Everyone** is responsible for **his** or **her** behavior.
> Incorrect: **Each** of the girls brought **their** bat and glove.
> Correct: **Each** of the girls brought **her** bat and glove.

3. *You* and *they* are always definite pronouns. Another common pronoun error is the indefinite use of *you* and *they.* If one of these words is used without referring to anyone in particular, replace it with a noun.

> Incorrect: To enter before the deadline, **you** must hurry.
> Correct: To enter before the deadline, **contestants** must hurry.
> Incorrect: **They** have a sale at the computer store today.
> Correct: **The computer store** is having a sale today.

PRACTICE

Find and correct the pronoun error in each sentence.

1. A doctor must be able to communicate with his patients.

2. At the local library, they depend on tax dollars for operation costs.

3. Derek showed their teacher the revised essay.

4. Neither of the men could finish eating their double cheeseburger.

GRAMMAR WORKSHOP

Adjectives and Adverbs

POINTERS

1. **Adjectives modify nouns and pronouns.** Adjectives tell *what kind, which one,* and *how many* about the nouns and pronouns they modify.

   > Theo writes his notes in a **three-ring blue** binder. (*Three-ring* and *blue* describe the noun *binder.*)

   > The **difficult** test took **three** hours to complete. (*Difficult* describes *test; three* tells how many *hours.*)

2. **Adverbs modify verbs, adjectives, and other adverbs.** Adverbs tell *when, where, how* or *to what extent* about the words they describe. Adverbs often end in *-ly.*

   > Aunt Isabella arrived **early.** (*Early* tells when Aunt Isabella arrived.)

   > Place the groceries **here.** (*Here* tells where to put the groceries.)

   > **Tomorrow** we need to finish the report. (*Tomorrow* tells when the report needs to be finished.)

   > The suitcases were **slightly** damaged. (*Slightly* tells to what extent the suitcases were damaged.)

3. **Avoid confusion with the modifiers *good, bad, well,* and *badly.*** *Good* and *bad* are adjectives; *well* and *badly* are adverbs. *Well* can be an adjective, but only when referring to someone's health.

   > Jeremy did a **good** job on his science project. (*Good* is an adjective describing *job.*)

   > Unfortunately, the new suit fit **badly.** (*Badly* is an adverb describing how the suit fit.)

   > Ms. Jones didn't feel **well** enough to present the award. (*Well* is an adjective describing Ms. Jones.)

4. **Comparative and superlative forms are sometimes misused.** The comparative of an adjective or adverb compares two things and is formed by adding *-er* to the end of the word or by using the word *more.*

   > Tonight's rehearsal was **shorter** than last week's.
   > His second novel is **more complex** than the first.

   When comparing three or more things, use the superlative form. The superlative is formed by adding *-est* to the end of the word or by using the word *most.*

   > This is the **briefest** conversation we have ever had.
   > Of the three sweaters, this one is the **most expensive.**

5. **Some adjectives and adverbs have irregular comparison forms.** Practice using these forms to help you remember what they are. When doubt, consult a dictionary.

   > good, better, best, bad, worse, worst, little, less, least

PRACTICE

Find and correct the adjective or adverb error in each sentence.

1. Which is the longest, the Mississippi River or the Nile River?

2. The new valve is functioning good.

3. Among Karen, Jessie, and Anita, Jessie is the faster sprinter.

4. Total disappointed, I pulled the burned cookies from the oven.

GRAMMAR WORKSHOP

Prepositions

POINTERS

1. **A preposition connects a noun, a pronoun, or a group of words acting as a noun to another word in the sentence. A preposition often shows the location of something.** The word being connected is called the object of the preposition. A preposition combined with the object of the preposition forms a prepositional phrase.

   Jason waited **outside the classroom.**

   Outside is a preposition. *Classroom* is the object of the preposition. *Outside the classroom* is the complete prepositional phrase, showing the location of Jason.

2. **Learn which words are prepositions.** Following is a list of common prepositions. Study this list so that you can recognize prepositions easily.

aboard	at	by	inside	outside	toward
about	before	concerning	into	over	under
above	behind	despite	like	past	underneath
across	below	down	near	pending	until
after	beneath	during	of	regarding	unto
against	beside	except	off	respecting	up
along	besides	excepting	on	since	upon
among	between	for	onto	through	with
around	beyond	from	opposite	throughout	within
as	but	in	out	to	without

3. **The placement of a preposition is important.** Sometimes a preposition comes after its object. This is especially true in spoken English. For formal writing, it is best to avoid this construction.

   Informal: Which story should I write **about?**
   Formal: **About** which story should I write?

   Sometimes a prepositional phrase is misplaced. Do not position a prepositional phrase too far from the word or words it modifies.

   Incorrect: The clerk filed the complaint **in the red jacket.**
   Correct: The clerk **in the red jacket** filed the complaint.

PRACTICE

Write a sentence for each prepositional phrase below, using the example as a guide.

   Example: behind the door
   Sentence: A surprise party waited for him behind the door.

1. around the corner
2. by tomorrow
3. before the interview
4. with Rosa and Mary
5. inside the coat pocket
6. during the storm

GRAMMAR WORKSHOP

Subject-Verb Agreement

POINTERS
A verb must agree in number with its subject.

1. **Make sure the verb agrees with the subject and not the object of a preposition.**

   Incorrect: The **number** of seats available for tonight's presentation **are** limited.
   Correct: The **number** of seats available for tonight's presentation **is** limited.

2. **A sentence may contain a noun or pronoun that follows a linking verb and describes the subject. The verb still agrees with the subject.**

   Incorrect: The **holidays is** a hectic time of year at work and at home.
   Correct: The **holidays are** a hectic time of year at work and at home.

3. **Watch for sentences in which the subject comes after the verb. The verb still should agree with the subject.**

   Incorrect: Behind the door **lurks** two large **cats.**
   Correct: Behind the door **lurk** two large **cats.**

4. **When a compound subject is joined by *or* or *nor*, the verb agrees with the subject that is closer to it.**

   Incorrect: Neither the coach nor the **players expects** to lose the Homecoming game.
   Correct: Neither the coach nor the **players expect** to lose the Homecoming game.

5. **Watch for intervening phrases or expressions.** Phrases such as *in addition to, as well as,* or *together with* do not change the number of the subject.

   Incorrect: **Flora and Jasmine,** as well as their friend Jake, **is tutoring** adult learners in reading.
   Correct: **Flora and Jasmine,** as well as their friend Jake, **are tutoring** adult learners in reading.

6. **Indefinite pronouns may be singular or plural.** Some indefinite pronouns, such as *anyone, every-thing,* and *each,* are always singular. Others, such as *few, both,* and *many,* are always plural. A few (*some, all, most,* and *none*) can be singular or plural. Determine the number of the indefinite pronoun. Then make the verb agree with it.

   Incorrect: **Everything** in the store **are reduced** 25%.
   Correct: **Everything** in the store **is reduced** 25%.

PRACTICE
Correct the agreement error in each sentence.

1. Deep inside his coat pocket was two crumpled dollar bills.

2. Most of the best seats in the theater is taken.

3. The students in this class works as volunteers for the Literacy Council.

4. Either Max or Muffin chew on my shoes.

5. Stretching exercises is a helpful warm-up before jogging.

GRAMMAR WORKSHOP

Capitalization

POINTERS

Here are a few guidelines to follow when deciding what to capitalize.

1. **Capitalize the first word of a quotation if the quotation is a complete sentence.** In a divided quotation, capitalize the first word of the second part, only when that word begins a new sentence.

> Our supervisor asked, "Who would like to demonstrate the new safety procedures?"
> "Do you know," Samuel asked, "when Career Day is this year?"
> "Ms. Martinez called," Gloria said. "She'd like for you to introduce the speaker at tonight's meeting."

2. **Capitalize proper nouns. A proper noun names a specific person, place, thing, or idea.**

> The **C**hang family just returned from a trip to **C**hina and **S**ingapore.
> Layed-off workers are being called back to **C**hrysler **C**orporation.
> While in **C**hicago, they watched the **C**ubs play at **W**rigley **F**ield.

3. **Capitalize titles that are used before a proper name or in direct address.** Titles that follow a proper name or are used alone are not capitalized.

> Did you know that **U**ncle John fought in the Vietnam War?
> While at the movie theater with my aunt and uncle, I saw **M**ayor Angela seated two rows ahead of us.

4. **Capitalize proper adjectives.** A proper adjective is formed from a proper noun. Do not capitalize the noun it modifies unless the noun would be capitalized when used alone.

> The **V**enetian canals are crowded with gondolas.
> Tomatillos and cilantro are staples of **M**exican cooking.

5. **Capitalize the main words in titles of works such as books, magazines, songs, and stories.** The article preceding a title is capitalized only when it is actually part of the title.

> Have you read Maxine Hong Kingston's novel *Woman Warrior?*
> The library carries back issues of *Time* magazine.
> Many of the Beatles' songs are being reissued, including "**T**he **L**ong and **W**inding **R**oad."
> Catherine Lim's story "**P**aper" explores issues of work and wealth.

6. **Capitalize the days of the week, the months of the year, and names of holidays.**

> Will you be able to attend the Student Council meeting on **T**hursday, **M**arch 12?
> We'll celebrate **T**hanksgiving with my grandparents.

PRACTICE

Find and correct the capitalization errors in these sentences. State the rule that should be followed.

1. What is your opinion of the character brutus in *julius caesar*?
2. Who is the new white house spokesperson?
3. The new thai market overflows with fruits, vegetables, and spices.
4. After christmas, Jacqueline starts working part-time for jameson and schlemmer, inc.
5. The class responded strongly to richard wright's essay "the library card."

GRAMMAR WORKSHOP

Commas

POINTERS

1. **Use a comma after an introductory participle or participial phrase (a verb or verb phrase that functions as a adjective).**

   Introductory Participle: Smiling, Sam tucked his report card into his pocket.

   Introductory Participial Phrase: Tasting the chili, Irma decided it needed a dash of Tabasco sauce.

2. **An introductory prepositional phrase requires a comma only if it is particularly long or would be misunderstood without one. If a sentence begins with more than one prepositional phrase, a comma should be used.**

   Until yesterday we had not heard the news.

   Into the late hours of the night, Peter continued harvesting row after row of corn.

3. **Use a comma after an introductory adverb clause.**

   After practicing her speech three times, Shawna felt prepared for the presentation.

   Use a pair of commas to set off an internal adverb clause that interrupts the flow of a sentence.

   The pasta salad, though left over from dinner, should be fine for lunch tomorrow.

4. **Use commas with nonessential elements.** Nonessential participial phrases, infinitive phrases, and adjective clauses all need to be set off with commas. A phrase or clause is nonessential if it is not necessary to understand the meaning of the sentence.

   The personnel director, who is in charge of hiring, posted an opening in the marketing department.

   Ms. Franks, to waste not a moment of time, started the meeting immediately.

   Anita and Teddy, whispering back and forth, caused a disruption.

5. **Use commas to separate three or more words, phrases, or clauses in a series.**

   Tonight's dinner menu includes chicken burritos, fruit salad, and brownies for dessert.

   Over the weekend Sally hopes to rake the leaves, write a few letters, and bathe the dogs.

   When our family cans tomatoes, Dad cleans the tomatoes, I chop them, and Mom simmers them.

6. **Use commas when writing dates and addresses.**

   The letter was dated May 21, 1988, but arrived only yesterday.

   The record store located at 300 South Wabash, Chicago, Illinois, is having a sale this week.

PRACTICE

Add commas to each sentence where needed.

1. Ship this package to 7234 Palm Drive Tampa Florida.

2. Petrifying Springs Park which is located in the middle of town has a natural mineral spring.

3. Shaking her head Jeanette couldn't believe what she saw.

4. For the party we'll need soda cookies chips and dip.

5. Behind the sack of seed in the tool shed the lucky chipmunk found refuge.

GRAMMAR WORKSHOP

Apostrophes

POINTERS

1. Use an apostrophe to form the possessive of a noun. For a singular noun, use an apostrophe followed by *s*, even if the word ends in *s*.

the **computer's** monitor	**Chopin's** nocturnes	the **fish's** gills
James's book	**Tomás's** turtle	the **glass's** contents

Exception: Some words that have three close *s* sounds use only the apostrophe.

Achilles' heel	for **goodness'** sake	**Odysseus'** journey

For a plural noun, put an apostrophe at the end of the word.

boys' jackets	**cooks'** secrets	**doctors'** responsibility

A plural noun that does not end in *s* forms its possessive the same way a singular noun does.

teeth's cavities	**women's** club	**children's** nursery

2. Use an apostrophe to form contractions. Contractions shorten two words into one. An apostrophe replaces the missing letter or letters.

she is = **she's**	he will = **he'll**	do + not = **don't**
will + not = **won't**	are not = **aren't**	they had = **they'd**

Spelling tip: Remember that the apostrophe replaces a missing *letter*, not a missing space.
Incorrect: Are'nt
Correct: Are**n't**

3. Apostrophes note the omission of one or more digits in a number.

the winter of **'96**   the class of **'03**

4. Apostrophes sometimes form past participles of verbs derived from nouns.

Tyson K.O.'d him in the second round.
I think I'm *Star Trek*'d out.

PRACTICE

1. Use an apostrophe to create the possessive form. Follow the example given.

Example: the ring of the bell	the bell's ring
the death of Caesar	the plot of a story
the hammer of John Henry	the howls of Charley
the wisdom of the Delaney sisters	the purpose of the poet

2. Form contractions for the following words.

you would	we will
they have	will not

GRAMMAR WORKSHOP

Quotation Marks

POINTERS
Use quotation marks in the following situations:

1. **To set off direct speech in dialogue.** Direct speech is enclosed in quotation marks.

   "Do you believe it?" Leah asked. "The meteorologist predicts a snow shower today. It's only October!"

   Note that the end punctuation goes inside the quotation marks.

2. **To set off quoted material in text.** Short quotations (less than five lines) should be placed within quotation marks.

   Maya Angelou claims we live in a time "when virtue is no longer considered a virtue."

   In his essay "The Library Card," Richard Wright describes how reading renewed his impulse to dream: "Now it surged up again and I hungered for books, new ways of looking and seeing. It was not a matter of believing or disbelieving what I read, but of feeling something new, of being affected by something that made the look of the world different."

3. **To distinguish certain titles.** The titles of essays, poems, articles, stories, and chapters should be enclosed in quotation marks.

   Marilyn Chin's poem "A Break in the Rain," was my favorite selection.
   Alison Dickie's article "Guarding the Rain Forest," made me think about conserving the environment.
   The short story "The Circuit," is by Francisco Jiménez.

4. **To set off definitions.** Writers sometimes define words in text. The word itself is in italics, with the definition enclosed in quotation marks.

   One definition of *pride* is "a sense of one's own dignity or value." Another definition is "conceit" or "arrogance."

5. **To provide special emphasis.** Quotation marks call special attention to the words they enclose.

   The term "World Wide Web" was unheard of five years ago.

PRACTICE
Correct each error in the use of quotation marks.

1. The term canopy refers to the highest branches of foliage that cover the rain forest.

2. After reading Richard Wright's essay The Library Card, she no longer took her library or reading privileges for granted.

3. The alarming rate of deforestation may prove true the poet's prediction that in order to describe the forests he "will have to speak/in a forgotten language.

4. In the short story The Teenage Bedroom, the teenage boy claims that when his mother enters his room, she yells, This room looks like a tornado hit it!

5. After we read Dream Variations, we talked about the Harlem Renaissance.

GRAMMAR WORKSHOP

Spelling

POINTERS

1. **Spelling counts.** Misspelled words may give your reader the impression that you are careless or unprepared for the writing task involved. Misspelled words can also make it difficult for a reader to understand your message. Spelling errors on a résumé or job application could cause a potential employer to consider your work sloppy and hire someone else.

2. **When revising a piece of writing, proofread it once solely to look for spelling errors.** Computer spelling checks can alert you to certain errors, but not to all possible errors. For example, if you spelled the word *deer* when you meant to spell *dear,* a computer spelling check would not alert you to this fact. Be sure to double-check the spelling of the names of people and places.

3. **Learn specific spelling rules.** Learning spelling rules will help you improve the accuracy of your spelling. You probably know the saying "Write *i* before *e* except after *c* or when sounded like *a* as in n*ei*ghbor and w*ei*gh."

believe	grief	eighth	sleigh	ceiling	deceive
niece	sieve	freight	weight	receipt	conceit

4. **Make a list of words you are likely to misspell.** Certain words give most of us spelling trouble. Keep track of the words that you find difficult to spell or that you repeatedly misspell. Use these words in your writing, and learn to spell them correctly so that you can cross them off your list.

5. **Do not be confused by homonyms or similar-sounding words.** Two words can sound the same, or nearly the same, but have two different meanings and two different spellings. Be careful not to write one word when you meant to use another. For example, an *effect* is a result; *affect* means to influence or to have an effect upon.

    Example 1: The **effect** of the lighting was dazzling.
    Example 2: Deforestation of the rain forests will **affect** everyone.

It's is the contraction for *it is; its* is the possessive form of *it.*

    Example 3: *It's* an unusually wet spring.
    Example 4: This sheep has had *its* fleece shorn.

Who's is a contraction of *who is; whose* shows the possessive form of *who.*

    Example 5: *Who's* cooking dinner tonight?
    Example 6: *Whose* beautiful scarf is this?

PRACTICE

Correct the spelling or word-choice errors in each sentence.

1. We flew across the snow in there sliegh.

2. I believe it's purpose was to decieve.

3. Whose visiting you're neice tomorrow?

4. Will their be a frieght charge?

GRAMMAR WORKSHOP

Writing Effective Sentences

What Is an Effective Sentence?

A complete sentence consists of a subject and a verb. An *effective sentence* is a complete sentence that says exactly what you mean.

POINTERS

1. **Effective sentences contain information that is clear and complete.** Make sure that your sentences express complete thoughts and say exactly what you mean.

    Less effective: A computer virus spread to every computer.
    More effective: An undetected computer virus spread rapidly to every computer.

2. **Effective sentences are concise.** Make your point in as few words as possible, choosing only those words that best convey your ideas.

    Less effective: As a result of an unexpected and violent storm that downed power lines and created winds of more than 40 miles an hour, commuters experienced frustrating delays during the morning rush hour.
    More effective: This morning's violent windstorm downed power lines and caused frustrating delays for rush-hour commuters.

3. **Effective sentences emphasize a main idea or key point.** In a longer sentence, you might choose to emphasize a detail by putting it last.

    Less effective: The triathlete completed her first competition by overcoming a physical disability and mental obstacles.
    More effective: The triathlete overcame a physical disability and mental obstacles to complete her first competition.

    Another option for emphasis is putting a key detail first.

    Less effective: The novel, which is a best-seller, has been nominated for a Pulitzer Prize.
    More effective: The best-selling novel has been nominated for a Pulitzer Prize.

PRACTICE

Rewrite the following sentences to make them more effective:

1. The innkeeper served a delicious late afternoon feast of breads, fruits, and cheeses to his guests who had spent the afternoon hiking among the autumn leaves.

2. The company president, who just joined the firm, announced a raise for all employees.

3. The football team, with only one minute of play remaining, recovered a fumble and scored the winning play.

LOSSARY OF LITERARY TERMS AND SKILLS

act   a major section of a work of drama

alliteration   the intentional repetition of the same beginning consonant sound in words that are close together

analogy   a comparison through simile or metaphor that explains something by illustrating its likeness to something else

analysis   a thorough examination of a problem, question, or issue in which the writer's opinion is clearly stated and other sources are presented to support that opinion

anecdote   a brief narrative about an incident or event that illustrates a specific point a writer or speaker wants to make; generally anecdotes are amusing and often biographical

antagonist   the character or force that works against the protagonist (central character) in a story

argument   the expressing and supporting of one's beliefs, in the attempt to convince others

assonance   the intentional repetition of vowel sounds within words

atmosphere   the general feeling that a piece of writing conveys

autobiography   the story of a person's life, told in the words of that person

ballad   a song-like poem that tells a story

bias   a personal belief, attitude, or judgment (either positive or negative) that prevents a person from being objective

biography   a form of nonfiction; the story of a person's life, written by someone else

blank verse   poetry that follows a regular rhythm but contains no rhyme

brochure   a folded document that advertises products or services (also known as a flyer or pamphlet) attracting readers with colorful pictures and graphics

cast   a list of characters appearing in a play, usually listed in order of appearance with a brief description

cause-and-effect relationship   a sequence in which one event (a cause) makes another event (an effect) happen

characterization   process through which an author reveals the qualities of a character, through the character's own words and actions, physical descriptions of the character, and the reactions of other characters

characters   the people portrayed in a novel, short story, or drama that take part in its events

chorus   a group of actors or a dancing company in a drama that speak together, commenting on the action of the play and often foreshadowing events to come

chronological order   the organization and presentation of details and events according to the order in which they occur

climax   the crisis, or most exciting point in a plot where emotion peaks and the conflict is at its worst point

comedy   drama that is intended to amuse through its light-hearted approach and happy ending

compare   to examine and explain how two or more things are similar

conclusion   a final observation or decision made after a reasonable number of facts are known

conflict   a clash of ideas, attitudes, or forces; a problem or struggle around which the story events revolve. Characters can have internal conflicts, in which they struggle with issues within themselves, and external conflicts, in which they have a problem with other characters or outside forces.

connotation   the images or feelings associated with certain words and phrases

consonance   the intentional repetition of consonant sounds at the ends of words

contrast   to examine and explain how two or more things differ

crisis   the climax, or most exciting point in a plot

definition   structured and objective words and phrases that explain or describe the characteristics or qualities of a subject

dénouement   the stage in plot development in which the conflict is resolved; all events that occur during the falling action

description   concrete and vivid words and phrases that appeal to the senses and enable the reader to re-create a scene, person, or image in the mind's eye

dialect   a special version of any language spoken in particular regions of a country; used to show a reader a specific culture or region

dialogue   a conversation between two or more characters in a work of fiction or drama

diction   word choice

drafting   the stage of the writing process in which a writer creates an unstructured draft of a work in rough sentences and paragraphs

drama   a story told only through action and dialogue, intended to be performed in front of an audience in a series of acts with several scenes each. Each scene typically depicts a secific place and time. Drama can take many forms including radio plays, television programs, and movies.

dramatic irony   when an audience knows more about what is happening in a play than do the characters involved in the events

editing   the stage of the writing process in which a writer reviews sentences and paragraphs for clear, correct construction and smooth transitions and proofreads word-by-word for errors in grammar, usage, and mechanics.

epic poetry long narrative poetry that tells a story of great adventure, usually of the glorious deeds of a nation's heroes, and often handed down orally. *Beowulf* and *The Odyssey* are examples.

essay a brief, structured nonfiction discussion of a single topic, in which the writer introduces a thesis, or main point, presents supporting evidence with examples and details in subsequent paragraphs, and draws a conclusion

evaluation an important reading strategy in which a reader makes judgments about the quality or value of something

fable a short tale told in poetry or prose to teach a moral lesson. When the main characters are animals that behave like humans to make a point about human behavior, these tales are called *beast fables.*

fact something that can be proven to be true beyond a reasonable doubt

falling action events in a plot that resolve the crisis

fantasy a form of fiction that involves fashioning an entirely original world of imaginary times and places tht are filled with magic and the supernatural. Familiar and realistic details are also included to help the reader willingly accept the world of fantasy.

farce a comedy that contains humorous characterizations and improbable plots

feature writing nonfiction writing presented in magazines and newspapers that focuses on information of general interest and attempts to involve readers emotionally through creative presentation of real people and events. It should include statements from witnesses and/or authorities and not introduce the writer's opinion.

fiction writing that is imagined, or made up, by a writer to communicate something about life to the reader. It may be based on real life experiences, but the story itself comes from the imagination of the writer.

figurative language imaginative words and phrases that often compare or describe two unlike things in a manner that is not meant to be taken literally; phrases that create a vivid image

first-person the perspective of a narrator who speaks from his or her own point of view

flashback an interruption in a natural time sequence used to describe earlier events. This technique allows an author to present the beginning of a story in a dramatic way.

folk tale a traditional story handed down through the generations, usually by word of mouth, that preserves a culture's ideas, customs, and wisdom gathered over time

foreshadowing a technique in which a writer gives clues or hints about a story's outcome

frame story a story within a larger story

free verse poetry that contains little or no regular rhyme or rhythm, freeing the poet from stanza patterns and measured lines

genre a category of literature characterized by a particular style, form, or content. Generally, literature is divided into three genres: *poetry, prose* (fiction and nonfiction) and *drama*

haiku a special form of poetry developed by the Japanese that captures a brief moment in nature. Consisting of three lines, it follows a strict syllable pattern; five syllables in the first line, seven in the next, and five in the last.

humor quality in writing that evokes laughter and relieves tension

imagery a mental picture created for the reader by the writer's skillful choice of words and details that appeal to the senses

inciting incident the stage in plot development where the story's main conflict is introduced

internal conflict a disturbance (often spiritual or moral) that occurs within an individual

interpretation the process of determining the meaning or importance of writing, speech, art, music, or actions

interview A source of information consisting of a conversation in which one person asks another prepared, open-ended questions that move the conversation toward revealing the knowledge desired

irony a tone in a piece of writing when there is a surprising difference between what is expected to happen and what actually occurs

jargon technical terminology that relates to only one area of interest (such as computers or medicine)

journal a personal diary or notebook in which a writer records his or her activities, experiences, thoughts, and feelings

legend a popular story that comes from past generations. Many legends offer explanations of how things came to be, but usually contain no historical information that can be verified.

letter a piece of correspondence directed to a particular audience and designed to achieve a specific purpose

limited omniscient point of view the third person point of view from which the narrator can enter one character's mind to let the reader know his or her motives, emotions, and thoughts

loaded language words that have strong emotional, and often negative, associations; used in media as a form of bias

main idea the most important point that a writer wants to communicate

memo a brief piece of business correspondence directed to a particular audience in the workplace; used to inform, request, instruct, or persuade

metaphor a direct comparison in which two things are described as if they were one and the same, that is, without the use of the words *like* or *as*

meter the number and pattern of syllables and stresses in a line of poetry

Glossary of Literary Terms and Skills

monologue   an emotional, and revealing speech by one character with another character listening

mood   the general feeling or atmosphere that a piece of writing conveys

moral   an instructive lesson about right and wrong taught in a fable, parable, short story, or poem; sometimes a moral is clearly stated; sometimes it must be implied from the actions and words of the characters

motivation   the reason or force that drives a character to behave in a certain way

myth   a fictional tale that explains the actions of gods or heroes or the origins of elements of nature

narrative   fiction, nonfiction, or poetry that details an event or series of events that have taken place

narrator   the person or character who is telling a story. A skillful narrator moves the action along, helping readers untangle details of time and place.

news writing   nonfiction writing presented in newspapers and magazines that presents readers with the most timely and accurate information about a current event using only objective and concise reporting of facts. It must answer the questions who, what, when, where, and why, in a brief manner.

nonfiction   writing that informs, concerning real people, places, and events. Examples of nonfiction are biography, autobiography, essays, speeches, letters, manuals, and narratives.

nonstandard English   words and phrases that do not meet the grammar and spelling conventions of written or spoken English; used by a writer to express a precise thought or create a special mood

novel   a book-length work of fiction

objectivity   the ability to present information without being influenced by emotion or personal opinions

omniscient point of view   the third person point of view from which the narrator is all-knowing and can freely enter character's minds to let the reader know their motives, emotions, and thoughts

onomatopoeia   the use of words whose sounds seem to express or reinforce their meanings. Examples are *splash* and *boom*

opinion   a belief that cannot be proven absolutely but that can be supported

oral tradition   the handing down of stories, folktales, parables, ballads, legends, and myths by word of mouth from generation to generation

parable   a short story written to point out a moral truth, in which a main character is often required to take a journey or to complete a task with several opportunities to make mistakes and learn the intended lesson

paraphrase   a summary of a work that presents the main ideas and helps clarify the difficult vocabluary and concepts in the original work

personification   figure of speech in which something that is not alive or not human is given human characteristics

persuasion   language a writer uses to convince a reader to think or act in a certain manner; a writer must state a clear position, support it with evidence, and address possible opposing arguments

play   a work of drama

playwright   the author of a work of drama

plot   the sequence of events in a story, consisting of an *introduction* or *exposition,* in which background information is provided for the reader; *inciting incident,* in which the story's main conflict is introduced; *rising action,* in which events become complicated and rise to a crisis; *climax,* where the crisis is at its worst and the story is at its highest point of suspense, *falling action,* which describes the results of the major events, and *resolution* and *dénouement* where the conflict is resolved and all loose ends are tied up

poem   concentrated, relatively brief work of literature, generally intense and emotional, that often uses figurative language to make an observation

point of view   the perspective of the narrator, such as third-person (a narrator who is an outside observer), first-person (a narrator who speaks from his or her own point of view), or second-person (a narrator who directly addresses the reader)

prediction   a reading strategy in which a reader constantly guesses about what is going to happen next

prewriting   the first stage of the writing process in which a writer plans, asks questions, makes notes, and narrows a topic before writing

propaganda   ideas, facts, or allegations used intentionally and improperly for the purpose of swaying an audience

proposal   a report that uses persuasion to convince a reader (usually an employer) to act on information provided

prose   the literary genre that is the ordinary form of written language including fiction and nonfiction forms

protagonist   the central character of a short story or novel

publishing   the final stage of the writing process in which a writer formats and presents a final work

quatrain   a four-line stanza where the final sounds of the first and third lines and the final sounds of the second and fourth lines are rhymed and each line stresses three syllables. Many of Emily Dickinson's poems are in quatrains.

realism   fiction that is believable, but not actually true, taking place in today's world, involving characters who act like real people and deal with life's actual problems, and containing no miracles or supernatural figures

repetition   the use of a word or phrase over and over again to emphasize specific meaning; used often in poetry and speeches

resolution   the stage in plot development in which the conflict is resolved

review an evaluation in the form of a commentary about an artistic work

revising the stage of the writing process in which a writer evalutes and improves a draft by focusing on the organization of the ideas presented and the clarity of the language

rhyme repetition of sounds at the ends of words in the lines of a poem

rhyme scheme a pattern of rhyming words that gives structure to a poem

rhythm the pattern of sounds and beats, stressed and unstressed syllables, formed by words in the lines of a poem

rising action events in a plot leading up to the crisis

romance exaggerated, unbelievable stories about incidents remote from ordinary life. Among the earliest romances were medieval stories about knights, kings, ladies in distress, enchantments, and adventures

satire a story that ridicules personal behavior or political institutions, often through the use of humor, irony, clever language, and absurd situations

scene a smaller section of a work of drama; a section within an act that happens in one place and time

science fiction the term given to short stories and novels that draw upon real science and technology and actual social institutions and problems to protray an imaginary future

script the written form of a play

sensory language words and phrases that engage a reader by appealing to the reader's senses

setting the time and place where the action of a story, novel, or drama occurs

short story fiction writing with clear setting, characters, plot, and theme, that presents a specific event in a compact time frame, generally focusing on one major conflict and how it is resolved

simile a figure of speech in which two things are compared through the use of the words *like* or *as*

soliloquy a long, emotional, and revealing speech by one character alone on stage

stage directions set of instructions or notes written by the playwright. These directions may describe scenery, props, lighting, costumes, music, or sound effects. They may also describe elements related to the acting of the play, such as entrances and exits, tone of voice, or gestures and movements.

stanza two or more lines of poetry that are grouped together to divide a poem into its form

subjective based on personal judgments, reactions, and emotions rather than on objective facts

summary a shortened version of an original work in which only the most important facts (main ideas) are presented in the order in which they originally appeared

supporting detail/evidence fact that provides more information about a main idea

surprise ending an interesting twist to the ending of a story that cleverly untangles the plot; used to trick or amuse the reader and show the strange behaviors of human beings

suspense the element in fiction or nonfiction that keeps a reader in a state of uncertainty and forces the reader to keep reading to find out what will happen next

symbol something that exists in and of itself and at the same time is used to represent something else

symbolism figurative language in which an object, person, or event represents something else; used to give deeper meaning to a poem or piece of fiction and to help readers understand events, characters, and themes.

theme the broad, general statement or belief about life or human nature presented in a piece of writing; a story's main idea.

third-person the perspective of a narrator who speaks as an outside observer

tone the attitude or feeling that a piece of writing conveys

topic sentence the sentence that states a paragraph's main idea, usualy at the beginning of the paragraph

tragedy a drama that ends in great misfortune or ruin for a major character, especially when a moral issue is involved

verbal irony when a speaker means the opposite of, or far more than, he or she actually says

visuals charts, graphs, diagrams, tables, and maps that can convey data with greater impact than words alone. Newspapers, journals, manuals, and business publications, and presentations use visuals extensively.

word choice a writer's choice of words, phrases, and techniques used to express thoughts and feelings and create clear characters, images, and events

GLOSSARY OF VOCABULARY TERMS

A

abstained (v.) stopped, resisted

abstracted (adj.) preoccupied, absent-minded

advocating (v.) supporting

agave (n.) a tropical plant with spiny leaves and tall spreading flowers

amalgam (n.) a mixture of a number of things, ideas, and so on

amethysts (n.) bluish-purple, semi-precious gemstones

amnesiac (adj.) pertaining to the memory gap caused by loss of consciousness

apertures (n.) openings

aphorisms (n.) short expressions of principles or wisdom

apocalypse (n.) the end of the world

arduous (adj.) needing great effort

assignation (n.) an agreed-upon meeting

atrophied (v.) wasted away

austere (adj.) serious

azure (adj.) sky-blue

B

becalmed (v.) made motionless

bludgeon (n.) a short stick used as a weapon

boll weevil (n.) a type of beetle that feeds on and can do sever damage to cotton plants and to the "bolls," the pods of ripe cotton

borax (n.) a white crystalline compound that occurs as a mineral; used for an antiseptic and cleansing agent, among other things

bulked (v.) loomed darkly, as the hull of a boat looks to a swimmer from below

butte (n.) a high, flat-topped area

C

cacophony (n.) harsh, jumbled sounds

calcified (v.) hardened, became inflexible

carrion (n.) birds who do not kill their prey but feed on already dead animals

castigate (v.) punish

champion (v.) fight for

cholera (n.) a disease that affects the intestines

chough (n.) a bird related to crows that has red legs and glossy black feathers

cleave (v.) cut open

commiserate (v.) sympathize with

conciliatory (adj.) trying to please or gain goodwill

conferred (v.) gave, bestowed

consummated (v.) completed

contiguous (adj.) touching; in direct connection

convoluted (adj.) intricate, involved

copse (n.) a stand of trees at the edge of a field or plain

cordovan (n.) fine-grained leather, usually colored burgundy

coveted (v.) wanted

curry (n.) a dish made with a curry powder, which is a combination of strong ground spices

D

deference (n.) respect or consideration

deftness (n.) skill, ease

degeneracy (n.) corruption

deluge (n.) flood

delusion (n.) a false belief

demure (adj.) modest

denunciation (n.) public condemnation

depraved (adj.) corrupt

disconcertingly (adv.) throwing into confusion

dividends (n.) revenues; income

doffed (v.) took off

dolorous (adj.) miserable

dorsal (adj.) located on the back

E

elongate (v.) stretch

endorphins (n.) proteins in the brain that naturally cause insensitivity to pain

escarpment (n.) steep slope

extolling (v.) praising

F

fast (v.) to abstain from food

fidelity (n.) loyalty

flash point (n.) temperature at which a volatile substance ignites with a flash

flay (v.) to strip meat of the skin

fleet (adj.) swift

floes (n.) large sheets of ice floating on the surface of a body of water

foray (n.) excursion or raid

ford (n.) a place to cross a river

G

gamboled (v.) skipped or leaped about, as if in play

genial (adj.) happy, friendly

H

homily (n.) a lecture on conduct

honing (v.) sharpening

hostelry (n.) inn

hypocrisy (n.) a situation in which one pretends to be something that he or she is not

I

ignominiously   (adv.) shamefully
impertinent   (adj.) somewhat rude or improper
imponderable   (adj.) incapable of being evaluated
impregnable   (adj.) incapable of being broken into
incendiary   (adj.) tending to inflame; relating to burning
incomprehensible   (adj.) completely unable to be understood
incurred   (v.) brought down upon oneself
indelibly   (adv.) in a way not able to be erased
insular   (adj.) "like an island," narrow-minded
interminable   (adj.) having or seeming to have no end
interred   (v.) placed in the grave or tomb
intimated   (v.) hinted at

J

jaded   (adj.) dulled
jalopy   (n.) a run-down automobile
joyances   (n.) delightful things

L

laissez-faire   (adj.) giving no direction or interference
lenient   (adj.) mild and tolerant
lollop   (n.) a bounding motion, such as the motion with which a hare moves through snow
lunar   (adj.) of or relating to the moon

M

malevolent   (adj.) bearing or doing evil
manifested   (v.) appeared
mantle   (n.) cloak
marred   (adj.) mutilated, destroyed, blemished
mechanistic   (adj.) attempt to explain human behavior in terms of physical and chemical influences
mesa   (n.) an isolated, relatively flat natural elevation
minutely   (adv.) to a very small degree
miscreant   (n.) evildoer
mitigating   (adj.) causing to become less harsh
moor   (n.) open, rolling land often containing boggy or swampy areas
moraine   (n.) an accumulation of dirt and stones deposited by a glacier

N

necromancer   (n.) magician
nondescript   (adj.) not easily described due to being plain or ordinary

O

okapi   (n.) an African animal closely related to the giraffe but with a shorter neck
opiate   (n.) a substance containing opium, causing dullness and inactivity

orthopedic

orthopedic   (adj.) intended to correct defects in the skeletal system
orthotics   (n.) supports or braces for weak joints or muscles

P

palpable   (adj.) noticeable, easily detected
palpitating   (v.) beating quickly
pariah   (adj.) wild
parole   (n.) a promise in exchange for partial or complete freedom
patently   (adv.) evidently
pathology   (n.) abnormal condition
pectoral   (adj.) located at the breast area
peevishness   (n.) irritability, grumpiness
petulantly   (adv.) rudely, with ill humor
pique   (n.) irritation
precarious   (adj.) unstable
prodigious   (adj.) plentiful
prostrated   (v.) overcome; mentally and/or physically exhausted
prowess   (n.) strength and agility
psychosomatic   (adj.) when physical symptoms are caused by emotional or mental issues

Q

querulous   (adj.) complaining, whining

R

rarefied   (adj.) relating to select group
rasped   (v.) produced a grating sound
recoiled   (v.) to shrink or spring back from fear
recompense   (n.) payment, exchange
rectory   (n.) house in which a member of the clergy lives
refinement   (n.) elegance of language, manners, and so on
regard   (n.) respect
regime   (n.) government in power
rejuvenated   (v.) made young again
repugnant   (adj.) distasteful
resin   (n.) referring to the sticky substance that oozes from fir and pine trees

S

sanctity   (n.) the quality or state of being holy or sacred
sari   (n.) a garment worn by Hindu consisting of yards of cloth that are draped to form a skirt and a shoulder covering
scree   (n.) stones or rocks lying at the base of a hill or cliff
scrutiny   (n.) close inspection
sedately   (adv.) quietly and calmly
seneschal   (n.) administrator
shuttlecock   (n.) official name of a badminton "birdie"
sidling   (v.) moving sideways
sinuous   (adj.) strong and lithe
slain   (v.) murdered
snipe   (n.) any of several game birds that dwell in marshy areas

spasmodic (adj.) characterized by a sudden, involuntary muscle contraction

staunched (v.) stopped

stealthily (adv.) slowly and secretly

steppes (n.) vast, flat, treeless areas

stropping (v.) sharpening by running back and forth on a thick piece of leather; the strop

subordinate (v.) make less important

supercilious (adj.) full of pride; haughty

surreal (adj.) unnatural; dreamlike

T

tacit (adj.) silent

tantamount (adj.) equivalent

taut (adj.) tense

temperance (n.) moderation

tepid (adj.) medium warm

titanic (adj.) huge; colossal

tranquil (adj.) calm, relaxed

V

ventured (v.) dared; took a risk (by doing something)

vesture (n.) garment

vindicate (v.) defend

W

wardrobe (n.) a large piece of furniture that served as a closet or a coat rack

warrens (n.) small passageways

whorls (n.) circled clusters of hair

wizened (adj.) dried, wrinkled

wrack (n.) the remains of something destroyed

Y

yew (n.) a type of evergreen tree

AUTHOR/TITLE INDEX

GENERAL INDEX

ACKNOWLEDGMENTS

Continued from copyright page

Excerpt from "An American Childhood" by Annie Dillard. Copyright © 1987 by Annie Dillard. Reprinted by permission of HarperCollins Publishers, Inc.

"Arthur Becomes King" by T. H. White. Reprinted by permission of The Putnam Publishing Group from *The Once and Future King* by T. H. White. Copyright © 1939, 1940. by T. H. White. Copyright © 1958 by T. H. White Proprietor.

"Beware: Do Not Read This Poem" by Ishmael Reed. Copyright © 1966 by Ishmael Reed from *New & Collected Poems.* (Atheneum) Reprinted by permission.

"A Break in the Rain" by Marilyn Chin. Originally published in *The Phoenix Gone, The Terrace Empty* by Marilyn Chin (Milkweed, 1994). Copyright © 1994 by Marilyn Chin. Reprinted with permission from Milkweed Editions.

"By Any Other Name" from *Gifts of Passage* by Santha Rama Rau. Copyright 1951 by Vasanthi Rau Bowers. Copyright renewed. Reprinted by permission of HarperCollins Publishers, Inc. First appeared in *The New Yorker.*

"Charley in Yellowstone" from *Travels with Charley* by John Steinbeck. Copyright © 1961, 1962 by The Curtis Publishing Co., © 1962 by John Steinbeck, renewed © 1990 by Elaine Steinbeck, Thom Steinbeck, and John Steinbeck, IV. Used by permission of Viking Penguin, a division of Penguin Books USA Inc.

"The Choice" by Dorothy Parker. Copyright 1926, copyright renewed 1954 by Dorothy Parker, from *The Portable Dorothy Parker* by Dorothy Parker, Introduction by Brendan Gill. Used by permission of Viking Penguin, a division of Penguin Books USA, Inc.

"The Circuit" by Francisco Jimenez. First appeared in the *Arizona Quarterly* (Autumn 1973). Copyright by Francisco Jimenez. Reprinted by permission of the author.

"Contents of the Dead Man's Pockets' by Jack Finney. Reprinted by permission of Don Congdon Associates, Inc. Copyright © 1956 by the Crowell-Collier Pub. Co., renewed 1984 by Jack Finney.

"Cooking a Mexican Sacrament" by Juana Vazquez Gomez. *The Oregonian,* Foodday, January 23, 1996.

"Dear Mrs. McKinney of the Sixth Grade" from *I Remember Root River* by David Kherdian. Copyright © 1978 by David Kherdian. Published by The Overlook Press, Woodstock, NY 12498. Used by permission.

"Deer Hunter and White Corn Maiden" from *American Indian Myths and Legends* by Richard Erdoes and Alfonso Ortiz, editors. Copyright © 1984 by Richard Erdoes and Alfonso Ortiz. Reprinted by permission of Pantheon Books, a division of Random House, Inc.

"The Dolphin and The Shark" by Carsten Stroud. Copyright by Carsten Stroud. Reprinted by permission of Carsten Stroud.

"Dream Variations" from Selected Poems by Langston Hughes. Copyright 1926 by Alfred A. Knopf, Inc. and renewed 1954 by Langston Hushes. Reprinted by permission of the publisher.

"The Falling Flowers" by Moritake. From *Haiku.* HarperCollins Publishers, 1974

"Fifteen" by Bob Greene. Reprinted by permission of Scribner, a Division of Simon & Schuster from *American Beat* by Bob Greene. Copyright © 1983 by John Deadline Enterprises.

"Fifteen" by William Stafford. Copyright © 1977 William Stafford from *Stories That Could Be True* (Harper & Row). Reprinted by permission of The Estate of William Stafford.

"Free and Equal" by Lalita Gandbhir. *The Massachusetts Review,* Volume 29, #4, Winter 1988-89. Reprinted by permission of The Massachusetts Review, Inc. Copyright © 1989 The Massachusetts Review, Inc.

"Future Tense" by Robert Lipsyte. Copyright © 1984 by Robert Lipsyte. From *Sixteen: Short Stories* by Donald R. Gallo ed. Used by permission of Dell Books, a division of Bantam Doubleday Dell Publishing Group, Inc.

"Getting a Job" from *I Know Why the Caged Bird Sings* by Maya Angelou. Copyright © 1969 by Maya Angelou. Reprinted by permission of Random House, Inc.

"A Giant Step" by Henry Louis Gates, Jr. *New York Times,* December 9, 1990. Copyright © 1990 by The New York Times Co. Reprinted by permission.

"Guarding the Rain Forest" by Alison Dickie. Reprinted by permission of the author.

"The Hard Way" and "Don't Assume" from *The Delany Sisters' Book of Everyday Wisdom* by Sarah and A. Elizabeth Delany with Amy Hill Hearth. Published in 1994 by Kodansha America, Inc. © by Amy Hill Hearth, Sarah Louise Delany and Annie Elizabeth Delany. Reprinted by permission.

"Harrison Bergeron" by Kurt Vonnegut. From *Welcome to the Monkey House* by Kurt Vonnegut, Jr. Copyright 1961 by Kurt Vonnegut, Jr. Used by permission of Delacorte/Seymour Lawrence, a division of Bantam Doubleday Dell Publishing Group, Inc.

"The Hitch-Hiker" by Lucille Fletcher. From *Radio's Best Plays.* Reprinted by permission of the William Morris Agency, Inc. on behalf of the author. Copyright 1947 by Lucille Fletcher.

"I'm Making You Up" by Chrystos. Reprinted from *Not Vanishing* (Press Gang, Vancouver, B.C. 1988) with permission.

"It Happened in Montgomery" by Phil Petrie. Reprinted by permission of the author.

"Lather and Nothing Else" by Hernando Tellez. Reprinted by permission from *Americas,* a bimonthly magazine published by the General Secretariat of the Organization of American States in English and Spanish.

"Letter to His Daughter—Aug. 8, 1933" by F. Scott Fitzgerald. From *The Crack-Up.* Copyright © 1945 by New Directions Publishing Corp. Reprinted by permission of New Directions Publishing Corp.

PHOTO & ILLUSTRATION CREDITS

Illustrations on pages 4, 13, 28, 34, 66, 98, 126, 130, 142, 147, 158, 174, 182, 196, 240, 254, 289, 297, 317, 325, and 346 were created by South-Western Educational Publishing. All other illustrations are in the public domain.